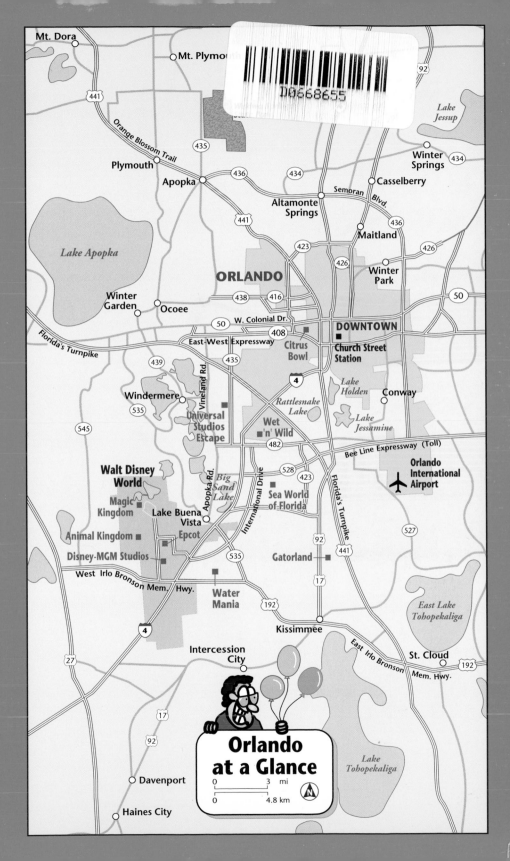

Orlando
at a Glance

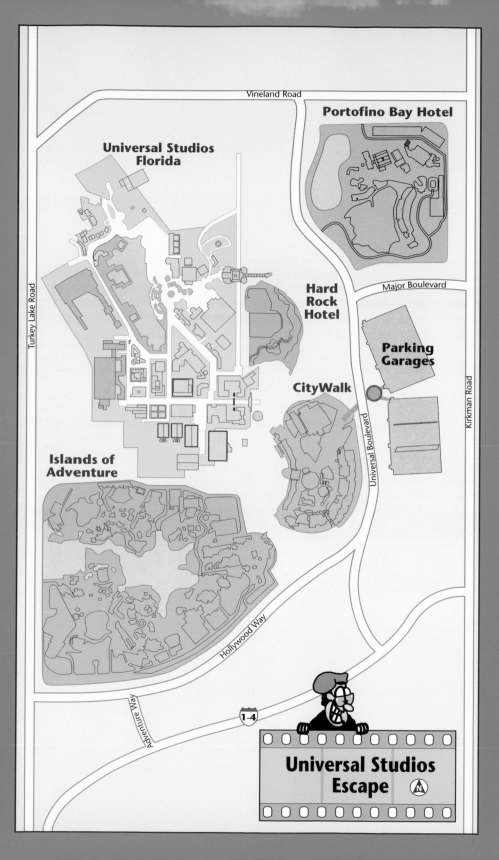

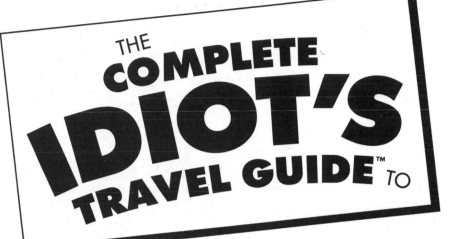

Walt Disney World & Orlando

by Jim and Cynthia Tunstall

Macmillan Travel USA   Alpha Books
Divisions of Macmillan Reference USA
A Pearson Education Macmillan Company
1633 Broadway, New York NY 10019-6785

ISBN 0-02-863093-9
ISSN 1096-7591

Editor: Naomi P. Kraus
Production Editors: Lori Cates and Carol Sheehan
Photo Editor: Richard Fox
Design by: designLab
Page Layout: Eric Brinkman and Sean Monkhouse
Proofreader: Bob LaRoche
Staff Cartographers: John Decamillis, Roberta Stockwell
Additional cartography: Peter Bogaty and Ortelius Design
Illustrations by Kevin Spear

Special Sales
Bulk purchases (10+ copies) of Frommer's and selected Macmillan travel guides are available to corporations, organizations, mail-order catalogs, institutions, and charities at special discounts, and can be customized to suit individual needs. For more information write to: Special Sales, Macmillan General Reference, 1633 Broadway, New York, NY 10019-6785.

Manufactured in the United States of America

5   4   3   2   1

Contents

Maps

About the Authors

Jim and **Cynthia Tunstall** are the idiots behind this guide.

Jim has been an editor and writer at the *Tampa Tribune* since 1978. Cynthia is a freelance writer and photographer. They have written hundreds of travel stories for publications such as *Better Homes & Gardens* and *Elegant Bride,* and they are the authors of two previous travel guides—*Adventure Guide to Northern Florida & the Panhandle* (Hunter Publishing, 1997), and *Adventure Guide to Orlando & Central Florida* (Hunter Publishing, 1998). They are native Floridians who live in Lecanto—a radar blip located 70 miles west of the Magic Mickey (and right around the corner from the *Twilight Zone*). They share their space with two horses, two dogs, two cats, a singular parrot, and a lot of cranky wildlife, including a gopher tortoise named Ike. Sometimes their rancho gets a little crowded.

An Invitation to the Reader

In researching this guide, we ran into more great places—hotels, restaurants, and shops—than ought to be allowed by federal law. We're sure you're going to find others. Please give us a holler if you do, so we can share them with another generation of travelers in upcoming editions. If you were disappointed with a recommendation, we'd love to hear about that, too. Please write to:

Jim and Cynthia Tunstall
The Complete Idiot's Travel Guide to
Walt Disney World & Orlando
Macmillan Travel
1633 Broadway
New York, NY 10019-6785

The editors will pass your mail on to us. They promise.

An Additional Note

Please be advised that travel information is subject to change at any time—and this is especially true of prices. We therefore suggest that you write or call ahead for confirmation when making your travel plans. The authors, editors, and publisher cannot be held responsible for the experiences of readers while traveling. Your safety is important to us, however, so we encourage you to stay alert and be aware of your surroundings. Keep a close eye on cameras, purses, and wallets, all favorite targets of thieves and pickpockets.

The following abbreviations are used for credit cards:

AE	American Express	EURO	Eurocard
CB	Carte Blanche	JCB	Japan Credit Bank
DC	Diners Club	MC	MasterCard
DISC	Discover	V	Visa
ER	enRoute		

Introduction

Bet you were worried we'd never get through all that warranty and warning stuff, huh? Well, it's over, and it's time to climb aboard the catapult or your favorite airline. You're headed for Orlando—arguably one of the most popular destinations in the entire world. Even those of us who live nearby and come regularly sometimes get lost on new streets that seem to sprout out of the orange groves overnight. Just like all folks who spend time in the "big city," our shorts get knotted over the traffic and the seemingly endless stream of new theme parks. So let's sort it out together.

You've made the first smart move by buying this book and starting from square one. You need to get into town, find the right place to stay, and cram as much fun and as many memories as possible into every waking moment. Heck, you can snooze on the boss's dime when you get back home.

We aren't called *The Complete Idiot's Travel Guide* for nothing—our plan is to lead you by the hand so that you don't get lost. That's important because it's easy to feel lost, or at a loss, when faced with a choice of more than 90,000 hotel rooms, six (soon to be seven) major theme parks, six water parks, 4,000 restaurants, and enough attractions to fill an encyclopedia. Mickey's Empire, also known as Walt Disney World, covers 47 square miles (30,000 acres) and that's just a fraction of Orlando's total picture.

It may seem a little overwhelming at first, but you and your family can get more dazzle for your vacation dollar in Orlando than in any other place on the planet. All you need is a little insider savvy, which is why we're here.

Step by step, we'll help you plan your trip to Orlando, get around the city, master the transportation monster, and wring the most out of every minute and every buck you devote to theme parks, restaurant meals, hotels, excursions, admissions, and entertainment.

That's why we're going to narrow the choices to the very best—not necessarily the most expensive or luxurious, but those that offer the most convenience, fun, or value, whatever your budget and your interests. If it's romance you're seeking, we'll tell you how to get married in a Cinderella setting, complete with a horse-drawn carriage. If you're bringing tots, we'll tell you about petting zoos and playgrounds. Older children? Orlando has one of the best, most hands-on science museums in the nation. Teens? Seniors? We have advice to offer even the most diverse of families.

Part 1 answers all those nagging questions you've been asking yourself, such as when to go, how to get there, whether to buy a package, and how much it's going to cost. It also gives you addresses, phone numbers, and Web sites where you can get more information.

Part 2 is about hotels. We discuss the various places you can stay around Orlando and Walt Disney World, and we pose questions to help you decide what kind of accommodations you want and what your needs are. Indexes are a special feature of this book. By using them, you don't have to read a hundred hotel reviews—just the ones in your preferred neighborhood and price range.

Part 3 is about geography—where things are and how to get around. The various areas of Orlando are described in terms of their convenience to the attractions.

Part 4 is about food, from hot-dog and burger stands in the theme parks to sit-down dinners in fine dining rooms where the napkins aren't made of one-ply paper. Once again, indexes will help you narrow your choices.

Part 5 describes the attractions of Orlando. There's a separate chapter on each of the biggest parks, and information about non-theme-park things to see and do while you're here. To help you hit all your must-see spots without getting worn out, we provide some sample itineraries for each park, and then lead you through the process of planning an itinerary of your own.

Part 6 belongs to the night. It's all about what there is to see and do when the sun goes down. We steer you to the hottest bars, clubs, and theaters, as well as some of Orlando's prime cultural attractions.

Extras

This book has several special features that you won't find in other guide-books. They will help you make better use of the information provided and do it faster.

As mentioned above, **indexes** cross-reference the information in ways that let you see at a glance what your options are in a particular subcategory—Italian restaurants, downtown hotels, hotels for people with disabilities, and so on.

We've also sectioned off little tidbits of useful information in **sidebars,** which come in several types:

Beating the Lines

These tips will help you spend more of your vacation on the rides and in the shows and less of it waiting in line. And believe us—lines are a fact of life in Orlando.

Time-Savers

Here you'll find ways to cut down on downtime, avoid lines and hassles, and streamline the business of traveling.

Tourist Traps

These boxes steer you away from rip-offs, activities that aren't worth it, shady dealings, and pitfalls.

Dollars & Sense

This pit stop helps you find tips on saving money and cutting corners to make your enjoyable trip affordable.

Extra! Extra!

Check these boxes for handy facts, hints, and insider advice.

Bet You Didn't Know

Here are your keys to interesting historical facts and trivia about the city.

 **Jake Ratings**

You will find these near the end of many of the ride and smaller attraction descriptions. Who better to evaluate the things that are supposed to appeal to the kid in all of us than a child? Jake, our grandson, was 7 when we researched this edition. He eagerly spent many days pounding the park pavement with us, though he wasn't real eager about some of the rides. Anyway, the soon-to-be intergalactically accepted Jake Rating is one 7-year-old's gut-honest evaluation of things, and since we consider him normal for his age, we offer his as a normal 7-year-old's reaction.

Sometimes the best way to fix something in your mind is to write it down, and with that in mind we've provided **worksheets** to help you put your thoughts in black and white, before making a decision. (Underlining or highlighting as you read along isn't a bad idea, either. In your school days, you probably ruined some perfectly good textbooks this way.)

A **kid-friendly icon** is used throughout the book to identify those activities, attractions, and establishments that are especially suited to people traveling with children.

The **Appendixes** at the back of the book list important numbers and addresses covering every aspect of your trip, from reservations to emergencies.

Part 1

Lock & Load: What You Need to Do Before You Leave for Orlando

Go on, daydream a little. Think about beautiful, sunny days when your greatest worry is whether you're going to ride the monorail before or after lunch.

Anticipation is half the fun, but there's a lot more waiting when you arrive. There are also a lot of choices to make. Making them doesn't involve rocket science, but planning now, before the landing gear drops, will help you get the most out of your vacation, which, no matter how rich or flexible you are, is probably limited by time, money, or both. Our best advice is to start front-end loading as early as possible—months in advance if you can. The sooner you take care of the details, the sooner you can relax and count the days till you meet Mickey.

There are countless Web sites and toll-free telephone numbers to help you plan your trip and, like a kid in a candy store, you may feel overwhelmed by the bushels of information available to you. It's our goal to help you pare those bushels to bouquets, and then to neat little nosegays.

Chapter 1

How to Get Started

In This Chapter

➤ Where to get information before you leave home

➤ How to prepare for the weather

➤ When to go

➤ Tips for travelers with special needs

Devil-may-care types may just blunder into town and take what comes, but most of you are more organized. You'd rather use your time and money wisely. So start early and look for good airfares, hotel rates, car-rental deals, and—most important—packages that combine all of the above while giving you some kind of savings.

If you're an organizational freak, you probably ought to pick a spare bookshelf, countertop, or drawer, and make it your battle headquarters for attacking Orlando. Then arm yourself with a notebook, highlighters, Post-its, and a shoe box or folder to hold loose materials such as maps and brochures as they arrive. (Don't forget to create an Internet folder for all the stuff you find in Surf City.) If you're a little less retentive, just stick everything inside the covers of this book (we already have nearly all the maps, hotel and restaurant reviews, and travel advice you could possibly want), and leave it someplace conspicuous as a constant reminder of the fun you're going to have.

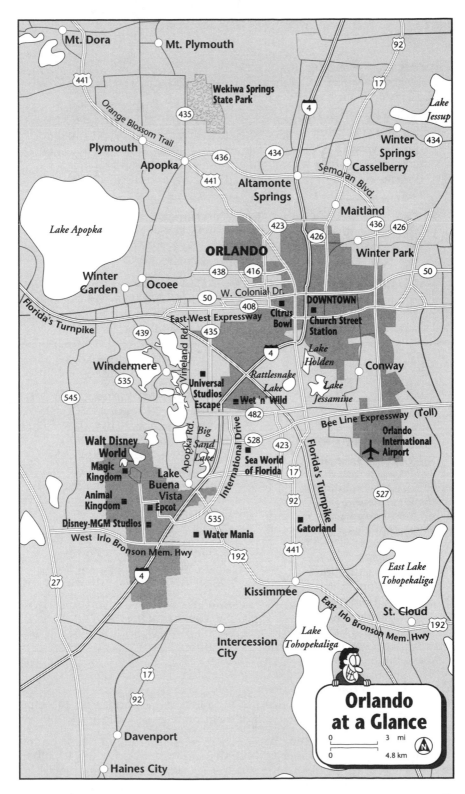

Orlando
at a Glance

0   3 mi

0   4.8 km

3

Envelope, Please

Several visitors' bureaus are eager to provide information on the Orlando area. Here are the best ones to contact:

➤ **FLA USA/Visit Florida,** 661 E. Jefferson St., Tallahassee, FL 32301 (☎ **888/735-2872** or 850/488-5607; www.flausa.com). This public-private venture is Florida's state tourism office. Make sure to ask for a copy of the *Florida Vacation Guide.* You also can ask for special brochures on golf, fishing, camping, biking, and the Black Heritage Trail.

➤ **Central Florida Convention & Visitors Bureau,** P.O. Box 61, Cypress Gardens, FL 33884 (☎ **800/828-7655** or 941/298-7565; www.cfdc.org/tourism). Ask these folks for vacation options along the Interstate 4 corridor between Tampa and Orlando.

➤ **Orlando/Orange County Convention & Visitors Bureau,** 6700 Forum Dr., Suite 100, Orlando, FL 32821 (☎ **800/551-0181** or 407/363-5871; www.goflorida.com/orlando). Folks at the bureau can send you brochures, visitors' guides, maps, and a special discount booklet—the "Magicard"—that's good for discounts on tourist attractions, meals, car rentals, and rooms.

Bet You Didn't Know

The ***Orlando Sentinel,*** the region's major daily newspaper, can be accessed on the Web at **www. orlandosentinel.com**. It's an excellent source of information about upcoming special events and shows.

➤ **Kissimmee–St. Cloud Convention & Visitors Bureau,** 1925 E. Irlo Bronson Memorial Hwy. (U.S. 192), Kissimmee, FL 34744 (☎ **800/ 327-9159** or 407/847-5000; www. floridakiss.com). This is the place to get information about tourist areas south of Disney.

➤ **Walt Disney World Co.,** P.O. Box 10000, Lake Buena Vista, FL 32830-1000 (☎ **407/934-7639;** www. disneyworld.com). Request the *Walt Disney World Vacations* brochure.

➤ **Winter Park Chamber of Commerce,** 150 E. New York Ave. (P.O. Box 280), Winter Park, FL 32790 (☎ **407/644-8281**). Shop here for information on the trendy, historic Winter Park area, which is 5 miles north of Orlando.

Weather Wise

There's no need for paranoia, but knowing a little about Florida's fits of temper can reduce the chance of one or all of them ruining your vacation.

Hurricanes   The last time one leveled Orlando was 10 million B.C., about the same time the peninsula emerged from the sea. Truth is, this part of the state is guarded from either coast by 35 miles of real estate. There's not much worry about a tidal surge, but a Category 5 (winds of 155 mph or worse) might tussle your hair and soak the way to Space Mountain. While Orlando isn't a common hurricane target, turn on your favorite weather channel if you're headed this way during hurricane season, June 1 to November 30, and consider trip insurance. Also, if you know a big blow blew through recently, call a third (i.e., nontourism) party. A good choice is the **Orange County Emergency Management Office (☎ 407/836-9140)**. Folks who work there will give you an impartial answer if you pose the most important posthurricane question: "Is Mickey still standing?"

Tornadoes   They're reasonably uncommon, but visit much more often than hurricanes, particularly during summer thunderstorms. You're more likely to run into one of these puppies at Universal Studios' "Twister" attraction, but don't take chances. Go indoors and stay clear of windows during thunderstorms, particularly if they come with tornado warnings.

Lightning   This is a nasty little sucker. At 50,000° it's five times hotter than the sun. It can reach out and zap you from 10 miles away. And it travels from 0 to 60 mph in—well, a speed gun has clocked it at 186,000 miles per second. You have to be pretty unlucky to be standing in the wrong place (under an oak, wading in water, or trying to hit a golf ball while wearing metal cleats and holding a metal club) at the wrong time (anytime a thunderstorm is heading your way). But some folks have that kind of luck, and most lightning victims don't live long enough for déjà vu.

Sun   Floridians are as proud of that big orange thing in the sky as Bubba is of his prize blue-trick hound. We even nicknamed our home the Sunshine State. The sun certainly is a friend of Florida tourism, but it isn't always a friend of tourists, especially the ones who arrive unprepared for its sucker punches. One of them, sunburn, is a bad hombre, but its evil twin—sun poisoning—can ruin your vacation. Most burns can be eased with over-the-counter creams like Solarcaine, or the natural soothing powers of an aloe shoot. But sun poisoning—a sunburn to the fourth or fifth degree—is far more dangerous. It can result in fever, chills, headaches, dizziness, nausea, and in worst cases, sunstroke. The burns run so deep in sun poisoning that the skin turns an angry purple, and if you press a finger against the offending area it remains dented for several seconds.

Prevention is simple. Lather your skin with a sunblock that has a 25 or higher rating. (*Do not* use a tanning oil. They're like slathering your sensitive skin with bacon grease and sticking it in a deep fryer.) And don't feel the ultimate souvenir to take back home is a Florida tan. It's not everything it's cracked up to be. Ask any native about the skin cancer scare.

Some of you, of course, won't listen. You'll skip the prevention advice and go straight to the I'm-on-fire-and-I-feel-a-bit-woozy phase. If that happens, don't waste time. Get help fast. Helping hands include the people at **Poison Control** (☎ 800/282-3171), **Ask-A-Nurse** (☎ 407/897-1700), **Florida Hospital** (☎ 407/897-1950), and the **Orlando Regional Medical Center** (☎ 407/237-6330).

Beating the Lines: When Should I Go?

Many savvy parents take their kids out of school a few days before or after holidays and vacations so they can visit the Orlando area before or after the most crowded times. Some schools allow it, especially if your trip will include a visit to an educational attraction on which the child can write a report, such as the Orlando Science Center or Sea World. This is also your best chance to beat some of the peak prices.

Orlando can also fill to the brim at less predictable times. Big conventions and sporting events (some as far away as the Daytona 500) can make hotel rooms scarce and expensive. Sometimes going a week earlier or later can make all the difference in the price you pay and your choice of rooms. Ask a hotel for rates on different dates, and be flexible if you can.

Slack times (well, relatively speaking) at the theme parks include the period just after Thanksgiving until mid-December, when the parks glitter with holiday activities and decorations. You'll have all the hoopla of the holidays without the crowds. The parks are also less crowded during the 6 weeks before and after spring breaks. Monday tends to be more crowded than later days in the week because most people on package tours arrive then.

Central Florida Average Temperatures

		Jan	Feb	Mar	Apr	May	June	July	Aug	Sept	Oct	Nov	Dec
High	°F	71.7	72.9	78.3	83.6	88.3	90.6	91.7	91.6	89.7	84.4	78.2	73.1
	°C	22.0	22.7	25.7	28.7	31.3	32.5	33.2	33.1	32.0	29.1	25.7	22.8
Low	°F	49.3	50.0	55.3	60.3	66.2	71.2	73.0	73.4	72.5	65.4	56.8	50.9
	°C	9.6	10.0	12.5	15.7	19.0	21.8	22.7	23.0	22.5	18.6	13.8	10.5

Tourist Traps

Stock up on featherweight rain ponchos or folding umbrellas at a discount store, and carry them with you at all times. If you have to buy one during a downpour at a tourist attraction, you'll get soaked on the price ($4–$5 for a plastic poncho that's so thin it tears on imaginary objects).

From the middle of June to the middle of September, weather forecasts vary hardly at all. Highs in the 90s are sometimes accompanied by suffocating humidity and afternoon thundershowers that leave the theme parks washed and sparkly. After sundown, it's usually comfortable, unless the rains come too early and the sun comes out again before evening, creating a steam bath.

Spring and fall are better, with long dry spells and infrequent rains. Winter weather in Orlando (mid-December through mid-March) is about as mild as the East gets. Most days are shirtsleeve-warm, except during cold fronts, which usually give several days' notice before plunging the mercury into the 20s or 30s. It isn't long before warm, dry sunshine is back again, but that's not much comfort if your vacation happens to coincide with a cold snap. Annual rainfall is 51 inches, and it rains on an average of 116 days each year.

Orlando Calendar of Events

Believe it or not, this is only a sampling—there are even more special events and festivals all year long. But these are the ones you may want to attend, or the times to avoid the crowds.

January

➤ **Zora Neale Hurston Festival of Arts & Humanities.** Here's a chance to learn about the life and works of some of America's most celebrated interpreters of Southern and African-American culture. The festival includes art, theatrical, and educational exhibits. It's held at Kennedy Boulevard and College Avenue in Eatonville, a small community near Maitland. Call ☎ **407/647-3307** for details.

➤ **CompUSA Florida Citrus Bowl.** This college bowl game is held annually in downtown Orlando. Tickets are sold beginning in late October or early November. Call ☎ **407/423-2476** for more information; call ☎ **407/839-3900** for tickets.

February

➤ **Bach Festival.** Take time to celebrate the devotion hundreds of singers and musicians have for the famed composer. The festival is at Knowles Memorial Chapel on the Rollins College campus in Winter Park. Held for more than 6 decades, this is one of the area's most anticipated events. Call ☎ **407/646-2182.**

➤ **Silver Spurs Rodeo.** Check out real cowboys as they compete in bull and bronco riding, calf roping, barrel racing, and more. This event offers a glimpse of the area's personality, pre-Disney. It's held at the Silver Spurs Arena, 1875 E. Irlo Bronson Memorial Hwy. (U.S. 192) in Kissimmee, on the third weekend in February. Call ☎ **407/847-5000** for details.

March

➤ **Kissimmee Bluegrass Festival.** Major bluegrass and gospel entertainers from all over the country perform at this 4-day event, beginning the first weekend of March at the Silver Spurs Arena, 1875 E. Irlo Bronson Memorial Hwy. Tickets are $12 to $20; multiday packages are available. More details are available by calling ☎ **800/473-7773.**

Bet You Didn't Know

Shamu, the killer whale at Sea World, eats more than 65,000 pounds of fish per year.

➤ **Central Florida Fair.** During 11 days in early March (some years beginning in late February), the fair features rides, entertainers, 4-H and livestock exhibits, a petting zoo, and food booths. The fair is held at the Central Florida Fairgrounds, 4603 W. Colonial Dr. Call ☎ **407/ 295-3247** for details.

➤ **Bay Hill Invitational.** Hosted by Arnold Palmer, this PGA Tour event is held in mid-March at the Bay Hill Club, 9000 Bay Hill Blvd. Call ☎ **407/876-2888** to fill in any blanks.

➤ **Spring Flower Festival.** From March to May at Cypress Gardens, there are stunning displays of colorful plants, flowers, and imaginative topiaries. You have to pay admission to the park to get into the festival. Call ☎ **941/324-2111** for details.

April

➤ **Fringe Festival.** More than 100 diverse acts from around the world participate in this eclectic event, held for 10 days at various stages in downtown Orlando. Call ☎ **407/648-1333** to get an event schedule.

➤ **Africana Fest.** Join African-Americans from near and far as they take part in a heritage celebration at Rollins College in Winter Park. For more information, call ☎ **407/646-1586.**

➤ **Mardi Gras at Universal Studios.** Okay, it's not the Big Easy—it's not even the Big Mobile. But entertainers, float-filled parades, food, and bellying up to the bar at Finnegan's Irish Pub can make this one of the best Mardi Gras festivals south of the Okefenokee. It's a huge street party held on Universal's back-lot streets. Call ☎ **407/363-8000** for details.

➤ **Church Street Station's St. Patrick's Day Party.** Traditional green beer and a not so traditional pot o' gold giveaway (emerald rings, airfare, and other stuff) help keep spirits high. Call ☎ **407/422-2434, ext. 405,** for information.

➤ **Annual Winter Park Sidewalk Arts Festival.** Held at Central Park, this is one of the Southeast's premier art fests. The 3-day event includes music, food, and kids' activities. For details, call ☎ **407/ 672-6390.**

May

➤ **Epcot International Flower and Garden Festival.** A month-long event with theme gardens, topiary characters, special floral displays, speakers, and seminars.

➤ **West Indian–American Carnival Celebration (Mardi Gras).** Central Florida Fairgrounds, Orlando. Get more information by calling ☎ **407/298-0612** or 407/298-2717.

June

➤ **Gay Weekend.** The first weekend in June draws tens of thousands of gay and lesbian travelers to Central Florida. In 1997, Universal City Travel offered a weekend package including tickets to Universal Studios, Sea World, and Church Street Station. This has all grown out of Gay Day, which has been held at Walt Disney World for about 5 years, drawing upward of 40,000 folks. Special events throughout the weekend cater to gay and lesbian travelers throughout Central Florida. Universal City Travel offers special packages (☎ **800/224-3838** for information). Also, get information on the Web at **www.gayday.com**.

➤ **Walt Disney World All-American College Orchestra and College Band.** The best collegiate musical talent in the country performs at Epcot and the Magic Kingdom throughout the summer. Call ☎ **407/824-4321** for details.

July

➤ **Independence Day.** Walt Disney World's Star-Spangled Spectacular brings bands, singers, dancers, and unbelievable fireworks displays to all the Disney parks, which stay open late. Call ☎ **407/824-4321** for details. Sea World also features a dazzling laser/fireworks spectacular; call ☎ **407/351-3600**.

➤ **Silver Spurs Rodeo.** This event returns to Kissimmee every year over the July 4th weekend (see "February," above, for more information).

September

➤ **Night of Joy.** Each September, the Magic Kingdom hosts a weekend Christian music festival featuring top artists. This is a very popular event; obtain tickets early. Admission to the concert is about $25 to $30 per night. Exclusive use of Magic Kingdom attractions is included. Call ☎ **407/824-4321** for details about the concert.

October

➤ **Halloween Horror Nights.** Universal Studios Florida transforms its studios and attractions for several weeks before Halloween—with haunted attractions, live bands, a psychopath's maze, special shows, and hundreds of ghouls and goblins roaming the studio streets. The studio essentially closes at dusk, reopening in a new macabre form an hour later. Special admission is charged. Call ☎ **407/363-8000** for details.

➤ **Walt Disney World Oldsmobile Golf Classic.** Top PGA tour players compete for a $1 million purse at WDW golf courses; daily ticket prices range from $8 to $15. The event is preceded by the world's largest golf tournament, the admission-free Oldsmobile Scramble. Call ☎ **407/824-4321** for details.

➤ **Epcot International Food & Wine Festival.** Enjoy food and beverages in an event that gives visitors a chance to sample the cuisine of 30 ethnic cultures. For information, call ☎ **407/824-4321.**

November

➤ **Mum Festival.** November's month-long flower festival at Cypress Gardens features millions of colorful blooming mums. Call ☎ **941/324-2111** for details.

➤ **Walt Disney World Festival of the Masters.** One of the largest art shows in the South takes place at Disney's Village Marketplace for 3 days, including the second weekend in November. The exhibition features top artists, photographers, and craftspeople. Free admission. Call ☎ **407/824-4321** for details.

➤ **Walt Disney World Doll and Teddy Bear Convention.** Top doll and teddy-bear designers from around the world travel to WDW for this major November event. Call ☎ **407/824-4321** for details.

➤ **Jolly Holidays Dinner Shows.** From late November to mid-December, these all-you-can-eat events are offered at the Contemporary Resort's Fantasia Ballroom. A cast of more than 100 Disney characters, singers, and dancers performs in an old-fashioned Christmas extravaganza. Call ☎ **407/W-DISNEY** for details and ticket prices.

➤ **Poinsettia Festival.** A spectacular floral showcase of more than 40,000 red, white, and pink poinsettia blooms (including topiary reindeer) highlights this flower festival from late November to mid-January at Cypress Gardens. Call ☎ **941/324-2111** for details.

Bet You Didn't Know

Since Walt Disney World opened in 1971, the total miles logged by monorail trains in the area is equal to about 25 trips to the moon.

➤ **Downtown Disney Holidays.** You can finish your holiday shopping (careful, it's a bit pricey, but the offerings are also a bit unusual) while watching a nightly tree lighting and being greeted by St. Nick. Call ☎ **407/824-4321** for further information.

December

➤ **Christmas at Walt Disney World.** During the Walt Disney World Christmas Festivities, Main Street is lavishly decked out with lights and holly, and visitors are greeted by carolers. An 80-foot tree is illuminated by thousands of colored lights. Epcot and MGM Studios also offer special embellishments and entertainment throughout the holiday season, as do all Disney resorts. Some holiday highlights include **Mickey's Very Merry Christmas Party,** an after-dark event with an admission of about $25. This takes place weekends at the Magic Kingdom along with a traditional Christmas parade and a breathtaking fireworks display; the admission price includes free cookies and cocoa, and a souvenir photo. The best part? Short lines for the rides. The **Candlelight Procession** at Epcot features hundreds of candle-holding carolers, a celebrity narrator telling the Christmas story, and a 450-voice choir. Call ☎ **407/824-4321** for details about all of the above, and ☎ **407/W-DISNEY** to inquire about hotel/events packages. The **Osborne Family Christmas Lights** at Disney–MGM is a dazzling display of millions of twinkling lights.

➤ **Christmas at Sea World.** Sea World features a special Shamu show and a luau show called Christmas in Hawaii. The 400-foot sky tower is lit like a Christmas tree nightly. Call ☎ **407/351-3600** for details.

➤ **Walt Disney World New Year's Eve Celebration.** For 1 night, the Magic Kingdom is open until 2am for a massive fireworks exhibition. Other New Year's festivities in the WDW parks include a big bash at Pleasure Island featuring music headliners, a special Hoop-Dee-Doo Musical Revue show, and guest performances by well-known musical groups at Disney–MGM Studios and Epcot. Call ☎ **407/824-4321** for details.

➤ The **Citrus Bowl Parade.** On an annually selected date in late December, the nationally televised parade features lavish floats and high-school bands. Reserved seats in the bleachers are $12. Call ☎ **407/423-2476** for details.

➤ **CompUSA Florida Citrus Bowl New Year's.** The official New Year's Eve celebration of the CompUSA Florida Citrus Bowl takes place at Sea World. Events include headliner concerts, a laser and fireworks spectacular, a countdown to midnight, and special shows throughout the park. Admission is charged. Call ☎ **407/423-2476** for details.

We Are Family: Traveling with Your Kids

Orlando loves children and makes every effort to deliver a vacation that the kids will never forget (and hope some day to repeat). The children's programs at Orlando's hotels put those in other cities to shame, offering goody bags, children's activities, kiddy pools and playgrounds, and special room furnishings, including beds that look like rocket ships or bear caves. Even business hotels here are kid-savvy.

In many hotels, kids also sleep and/or eat free and can get tucked in at night by a costumed character. All the theme parks

Time Savers

Disney–MGM Studios and Universal Studios offer parent–swap programs in which parents take turns watching each other's kids while the other parents ride. Disney parks, Universal Studios, and Sea World all have play areas within the attractions for parents and kids to take a break.

11

and major malls have strollers for rent, and almost any hotel can find a reliable baby-sitter for you. Every restaurant has lower-priced kids' menus, and some will even let kids eat free.

Travel Tips for the Senior Set

Seniors 55 and older get additional savings through the Magic Kingdom's Gold Club Card. The first perk is the cost: $50 for a 2-year membership, which is $15 cheaper than what young whipper-snappers pay.

The card means ticket discounts at the Magic Kingdom, Animal Kingdom, Epcot, Disney–MGM Studios, Pleasure Island, River Country, Typhoon Lagoon, and out-of-this-World attractions like Disneyland in California, Disneyland Paris, and Tokyo Disneyland, in case you get off at the wrong airport on the way home.

Gold Club members get 10% or 20% discounts at Disney resort hotels, special package-vacation offers, 10% off meals in some theme-park restaurants, up to 30% savings at National Car Rental, a 10% discount on AAA basic membership, and 10% off the sticker prices in the Disney Store and the Disney Catalog. New members get a couple of trinkets and subscriptions to the *Disney Magazine* and the *Magic Key Newsletter,* which contain club news and events. Call ☎ **800/313-4763** to sign up.

According to 1997 figures (the latest available), empty nesters averaged $169.40 per person daily in spending during an Orlando vacation, compared to $140.80 per person daily for the family visitor. And *that's* after the senior discounts they receive at many hotels, restaurants, and attractions. It's obvious that Orlando's charms are not limited to the younger generation. So it helps to carry a photo ID to prove you're a senior.

In addition, most of the major domestic airlines, including American, United, Continental, US Airways, and TWA, offer discount programs for senior travelers—be sure to ask whenever you book your flight.

Dollars & Sense

Walt Disney World parks don't offer senior discounts (they seem to have no problem luring the young at heart at regular prices), but almost all the other attractions do. Age limits vary, with some starting as young as age 50. Savings are usually 10%, sometimes more. The most generous discount is at Cypress Gardens, which gives seniors $5 off the $29.50 admission (a 17% discount).

The **American Association of Retired Persons (AARP)** offers discounts for members and spouses of any age. Many hotels, car-rental agencies, and restaurants in the Orlando area offer AARP discounts. Always ask. To join, contact AARP, 601 E. St. NW, Washington, DC 20049 (☎ **202/434-AARP**).

Mature Outlook, P.O. Box 9390, Des Moines, IA 50306-9519 (☎ **800/ 336-6330;** fax 847/286-5024), offers discounts on car rentals and hotel stays at many Holiday Inns, Howard Johnsons, and Best Westerns. The $20 annual membership fee also gets you $100 in Sears coupons and a bimonthly magazine. Membership is open to all Sears customers 18 and over, but the organization's primary focus is on the 50-and-over market.

The *Mature Traveler,* a monthly 12-page newsletter on senior citizen travel, is available by subscription ($30 a year) from GEM Publishing Group, Box 50400, Reno, NV 89513-0400. GEM also publishes *The Book of Deals,* a collection of more than 1,000 senior discounts on airlines, lodging, tours, and attractions around the country; it's available for $9.95 by calling ☎ 800/460-6676. Another helpful publication is *101 Tips for the Mature Traveler,* available from Grand Circle Travel, 347 Congress St., Suite 3A, Boston, MA 02210 (☎ 800/221-2610 or 617/350-7500; fax 617/350-6206).

Grand Circle Travel is one of the literally hundreds of travel agencies specializing in vacations for seniors. But beware: Many of them are of the tour-bus variety, with free trips thrown in for those who organize groups of 20 or more. Seniors seeking more independent travel should probably consult a regular travel agent. **SAGA International Holidays,** 222 Berkeley St., Boston, MA 02116 (☎ 800/343-0273), offers inclusive tours and cruises for those 50 and older.

Access Orlando: Advice for Travelers with Disabilities

A disability shouldn't stop anybody from traveling to the Orlando area; today, there are more options and resources for disabled travelers than ever before. *A World of Options,* a 658-page book of resources for disabled travelers, covers everything from biking trips to scuba outfitters. It costs $45 and is available from **Mobility International USA,** P.O. Box 10767, Eugene, OR 97440 (☎ 541/343-1284, voice and TDD; www.miusa.org). For more personal assistance, call the **Travel Information Service** at ☎ 215/456-9603, or 215/456-9602 for TTY.

Extra! Extra!

Wheelchair Wagon Express, Box 700637, St. Cloud, FL 43770 (☎ 407/957-2044; fax 407/957-2043), provides transportation for people in wheelchairs.

Many of the major car-rental companies now offer hand-controlled cars for disabled drivers. Avis can provide such a vehicle at any of its locations in the United States with 48-hour advance notice; Hertz requires between 24 and 72 hours of advance reservation at most of its locations.

Barrier Free Vacations, Sunset Harbour, Suite 205, 236 N. Derby Ave., Ventnor, NJ 08406 (☎ 609/487-9805; www.barrier-free-vacations.com), has a Web site literally choking with wonderful information about Florida destinations including plenty on the WDW empire. It has virtually everything mobility-impaired travelers need to know before and during their adventures. The menu includes information about rental homes, hotels, and campgrounds (rates are included); transportation options (from lift-equipped taxis to cars with hand controls); and hot links to other destinations. Barrier Free Vacations crowns Disney the most accessible destination on the planet.

Many of the theme parks rent electric scooters and wheelchairs to guests while they're inside. **Walker Medical & Mobility Products of Longwood** leases to folks who need assistance outside the parks. The package includes delivery to your hotel room, bed-and-breakfast, or condominium and there's a heavy-duty model for guests weighing up to 375 pounds. Walker's products fit into Disney's transports and monorails as well as rental cars. For more information, look at **www.walkermobility.com** or call ☎ **888/726-6837.**

You can rent wheelchair vans by calling **Wheelers Inc.** (☎ 407/826-0616) or **Vantage Mini Vans** (☎ 407/521-8002). **Wheelchair Getaways** (☎ 800/873-4973; www.blvd.com/wg.htm) rents specialized vans with wheelchair lifts and other features for the disabled in more than 100 cities across the United States.

All public buses in Orlando are wheelchair accessible. The buses serve Universal Studios, Sea World, the shopping areas, and downtown Orlando. Disney offers special shuttle buses to and from their hotels that can accommodate wheelchairs.

Travelers with disabilities may also want to consider joining a tour that caters specifically to them. One of the best operators is **Flying Wheels Travel,** 143 W. Bridge (P.O. Box 382), Owatonna, MN 55060 (☎ 800/525-6790). This company offers various escorted tours and cruises, as well as private tours in minivans with lifts. Another good company is **FEDCAP Rehabilitation Services,** 211 W. 14th St., New York, NY 10011. Call ☎ 212/727-4200 or fax 212/721-4374 for information about membership and summer tours.

Under Florida law, every hotel and motel must have at least one wheelchair-accessible room, and a few, including **Best Western Buena Vista Suites** (☎ 407/239-8588), **Embassy Suites** (☎ 407/239-1144), and **Sleep Inn** (☎ 407/396-1600), have wheel-in showers. If you're looking for rock-bottom rates, **Hostelling International Orlando/Kissimmee Resort** is wheelchair accessible. It has a pool, a lake, air-conditioning, and en suite bathrooms. Rates are $14 per person. Contact **Hostelling International,** 733 15th St. NW #840, Washington, DC 20005 (☎ 202/783-6161; fax 202/ 783-6171; www.taponline.com). Make your special needs known when making reservations.

Accessibility at the Parks

Most attractions at the various theme parks, especially newer ones, are designed to be accessible to a wide variety of people. People with wheelchairs and their parties are often given preferential treatment so they can avoid long lines. (Of course, they also get the parking spaces closest to the entrance.)

Walt Disney World is extremely accommodating to disabled guests. Mickey even publishes a *Guidebook for Guests with Disabilities.* To obtain a copy, call ☎ **407/824-4321.** Some examples of Disney services:

➤ Almost all Disney resorts have rooms specifically designed for the disabled. Some of the older Disney hotels have rooms that are only wheelchair accessible—ask whether your room is truly disability-friendly when booking.

➤ Braille directories are located inside the Magic Kingdom in front of the Main Street train station and in a gazebo in front of the Crystal Palace restaurant.

➤ Complimentary guided-tour audiocassette tapes and recorders are available at Guest Services to assist visually impaired guests.

➤ Personal translator units are available to amplify the audio at selected Epcot attractions (inquire at Earth Station).

Universal Studios also publishes a *Disabled Guest Guidebook,* rents wheelchairs, and provides information about Telecommunications Devices for the Deaf (TDD). Universal provides audio descriptions on cassette for visually impaired guests and has sign-language guides and scripts for all its shows (advanced notice is required; call ☎ **407/363-8000** for details).

Most of the attractions at **Sea World** are easily accessible to those in wheelchairs. Sea World provides a Braille guide for the visually impaired. It also provides a very brief synopsis of shows for the hearing impaired. For information, call ☎ **407/351-2600.**

Out & About: Advice for Gay & Lesbian Travelers

Gay Weekend and Gay Day at Walt Disney World started several years ago. They have grown from small events to a 5-day weekend spread across several Orlando-area parks. The annual festival attracts an estimated 120,000 gay and lesbian visitors. Gay Day (it has its own Web site: **www.gayday.com**) is held the first Saturday of June with other events wrapped around the weekend. If you want more information, go to the Orlando area in the *Gay Guide to Florida* on the Internet (**http://gay-guide.com**).

The local gay newspaper is *The Triangle,* which you'll find on newsstands or by calling ☎ **407/425-4527** or 407/849-0099.

For additional information, contact **Gay & Lesbian Community Services,** 714 E. Colonial Dr., Orlando, FL 32084 (☎ **407/THE-GAYS**).

Accommodations that cater to gays and lesbians include **A Veranda Bed and Breakfast,** 115 N. Summerlin Ave. (☎ **800/420-6822** or 407/849-0321). This downtown cluster of cottages offers five units, each with its own entrance, cable TV, and telephone with answering machine.

Chapter 2

Money Matters

In This Chapter

➤ Money: how much and what kind?

➤ Budgeting your trip

➤ Pinching pennies

Want to see Disney for under $200? Sorry. The only way to do that is to choose the near-virtual tour—on video. We'd love to give you the magic formula for visiting Orlando on a wing and a prayer, but that idea is more of a fantasy than Mickey. The puppet meisters at the world's most-visited tourist Mecca are geniuses at separating you from the contents of your wallet, lining included. They recognize that this is the trip of a lifetime for a few of you, and for others, it's at least the year's big blowout. They appreciate the Pied-Piper grip that Mickey has on your kids, who will be begging for T-shirts, ears, and all sorts of doodads. They also know you and your spouse will be tempted to end your honeymoon, first or second, with that $110 fixed-price dinner at Victoria and Albert's. In other words, they've got you. Your lips are already around the hook.

So let's discuss portable funds, keeping them safe, and squeezing every nickel until the buffalo is worn to a calf.

Should I Carry Traveler's Checks or the Green Stuff?

Traveler's checks are a dinosaur from the days when people used to write personal checks all the time, instead of going to an ATM. In those days, travelers couldn't be sure of finding a place to cash checks. Since they could be replaced if lost or stolen, traveler's checks were a sound alternative to stuffing your wallet with cash at the beginning of a trip.

These days, traveler's checks are less necessary because most cities have 24-hour ATMs linked to a national network that most likely includes your bank at home. **Cirrus** (☎ **800/424-7787** or 800/4CIRRUS) and **Plus** (☎ **800/843-7587**) are the two most popular networks; check the back of your ATM card to see which network your bank belongs to. The 800-numbers provide specific ATM locations where you can withdraw money while on vacation. You should withdraw only as much cash as you need every couple of days so that you don't feel insecure carrying around a huge wad of cash.

Bet You Didn't Know

Orlando has more than 90,000 hotel rooms and is still growing. By the turn of the century, another 10,000 should be added.

Still, if you feel you need the security of traveler's checks and don't mind the hassle of showing identification every time you want to cash a check, you can get them at almost any bank and there's a reasonably good chance a hometown bank will do it free. **American Express** offers checks in denominations of $10, $20, $50, $100, $500, and $1,000. If your banker is a grinch, you'll pay a service charge ranging from 1% to 4%, though AAA members can obtain checks without a fee at most AAA offices. You can also order American Express traveler's checks over the phone by calling ☎ **800/221-7282;** American Express gold and platinum cardholders that call this number are exempt from the 1% fee.

Tourist Traps

Many banks have begun to impose a fee ranging from 50¢ to $3 every time you use an ATM in a different city. Your own bank may also charge you a fee for using ATMs from other banks. Also keep in mind that some cards have a *daily* withdrawal limit regardless of your balance. Don't let your cash reserves get too low.

Visa also offers traveler's checks, available at Citibank locations across the country and at several other banks. The service charge ranges between 1.5% and 2%; checks come in denominations of $20, $50, $100, $500, and $1,000. **MasterCard** also offers traveler's checks. Call ☎ **800/223-9920** for a location near you.

ATMs to the Left of Me, ATMs to the Right of Me

In Central Florida you're never far from an ATM machine. In fact, they have become about as common as corner phone booths used to be. You can find ATMs belonging to major networks at every major mall in greater Orlando, at banks, on Main Street and in Tomorrowland in the Magic Kingdom, in the

Disney Crossroads Shopping Center, at the WDW All-Star Sports Resort, at Disney–MGM Studios, at Epcot, at Pleasure Island, at Sea World, at Universal Studios, and at most of the area's Circle K and 7-11 convenience stores. There's a real bank, a **Sun Trust,** on Main Street in the Magic Kingdom and at 1675 Buena Vista Dr. across from Disney Village. Both branches are open weekdays 9am to 4pm, Thursday until 6pm. Maps given out at most of the major theme parks show where you can find an ATM. Some practically beckon in neon. After all, the object is to get you to *spend, spend, spend.*

Plastic

Credit cards are invaluable when traveling. They are a safe way to carry money and provide a convenient record of all your travel expenses when you arrive home.

Disney parks, resorts, shops, and restaurants (though not the fast-food outlets) accept American Express, MasterCard, and Visa.

Tourist Traps

Disney Dollars, currency imprinted with Disney characters instead of presidents, come in denominations of $1, $5, and $10. They are redeemable as cash anywhere throughout the Disney universe, but they're not worth any more than regular dollars and they're not worth the hassle. They just mean you'll be waiting in two more lines: one when you buy them and one when you cash them in. So what's the point? Well, some folks just get giddy with everything Mickey. Others find them one of the less costly souvenirs.

In addition, Disney hotel guests get a charge card that can be used to charge everything within Walt Disney World to their hotel room. There is also a Disney credit card, available through any Disney store. It can be used at any Disney store, catalog, restaurant, or vacation property.

You can also get **cash advances** off your credit cards at any bank (though you'll start paying interest on the advance the moment you receive the cash, and you won't receive frequent-flyer miles on an airline credit card). At most banks, you don't even need to go to a teller; you can get a cash advance at the ATM if you know your PIN number. If you've forgotten your PIN number or didn't even know you had one, call the phone number on the back of your credit card and ask the bank to send it to you. It usually takes 5 to 7 business days, though some banks will do it over the phone if you tell them your mother's maiden name, the number of freckles on your right shoulder, or pass some other kind of security clearance.

Stop, Thief! (What to Do If Your Money Gets Stolen)

Orlando's wholesome, friendly image persuades many travelers to let their guard down, often with disastrous results. Crimes against tourists are one of

Central Florida's biggest problems, so don't become a statistic. Take the same precautions you would take at home. For those of you who live on Walton's Mountain, that means using ATMs only in well-lighted areas, shielding your numbers from prying eyes, and never putting anything in the trash that has your account number or other personal information on it.

Almost every credit-card company has an emergency 800-number you can call if your wallet or purse is stolen. They may be able to wire you a cash advance off your credit card immediately, and in many places, they can get you an emergency credit card in a day or two. The issuing bank's 800-number is usually on the back of the credit card.

Bet You Didn't Know

Plenty of coins are dropped in Disney fountains as visitors stop to make a wish. To literally squeeze every dime out of its operations, Disney has devised an elaborate mechanical system to get that change out of the fountains and back into the tills of its restaurants and stores—dried, sorted, and rolled—sometimes by the end of the day. Incredible, huh?

What? Okay, time-out for a question from an idiot in Atlanta? Well, yeah, you're right—it *doesn't* help much if the card is stolen with your wallet or purse. But you can call **800/555-1212**—that's 800 directory assistance—to get the number. Also, though it is worth its weight in gold, they may not swipe this guidebook. **Citicorp Visa's** U.S. emergency number is ☎ **800/645-6556. American Express** cardholders and traveler's check holders should call ☎ **800/221-7282** for all money emergencies. **MasterCard** holders should call ☎ **800/307-7309.**

Dollars & Sense

Set a spending limit. Kids should know they have a set amount to spend on souvenirs and toys. So should Mom and Dad.

If you opt to carry traveler's checks, be sure to keep a record of their serial numbers so that you can handle just such an emergency.

Odds are that if your wallet is gone, you've seen the last of it, and the police aren't likely to recover it for you. However, after you realize that it's gone and you cancel your credit cards, it is still worth a call to inform the police. You may need the police report number for credit-card or insurance purposes later.

So, What's This Trip Gonna Cost?

That's a complicated question, but the answer is—probably more than you originally thought. The average family spends enough money in a day at Walt Disney World to rival the per capita income of a Third World nation.

Even if you stay at modestly priced hotels, skip the most expensive restaurants, drink nothing but water all day, and refrain from buying a life-size Shamu doll that has to be shipped home in a moving van, a trip to Orlando can add up quickly. Admission prices and parking at the theme parks alone can set you back close to $200 per day for a family of four.

Dollars & Sense

Entertainment Publications, Inc. offers a book of deep discounts for Orlando hotels, restaurants, airfares, and attractions. The book, which sells for $34.95, will pay for itself during your first few days in Florida. Call ☎ **800/374-4464** to order it.

But before you start to panic, remember, there are lots of ways to save money, and we're here to share them with you throughout this book. Take a good look at sidebars called "Dollars & Sense" for some smart consumer tips.

We can make some educated guesses about your final vacation bill, depending on the hotel you choose. So when you plan your vacation budget (see the worksheet at the end of this chapter), start with your hotel room. All the other pieces will fall into place much more easily.

Lodging

Your choice of hotel will determine many other costs, including:

➤ Whether you need a rental car always, sometimes, or not at all;

➤ Whether you must eat all meals in restaurants or can prepare simple breakfasts and lunches in your room;

➤ How much you pay in tips and taxes, which are charged as a percentage of the room rate;

➤ Whether you'll pay extra for children's activities.

Tips on Tipping

Generally tip 15% for restaurant service and cab rides; more if the service merits it. At the end of your stay, don't forget the unsung who may deserve a little something. The hotel housekeeper probably deserves $1 to $2 a day for multiple days of cleaning your messes, making your beds, and keeping you supplied with fresh towels. You may also leave more than that for those who made extra beds, supplied a crib, cleaned up after a pizza party, or vacuumed after Fido shed half of his coat on the shag carpet.

A dollar should do for a hotel staffer who delivers the extra pillows or hair dryer you requested—presuming the service is prompt and you didn't have to make a second or third call. If the doorman has been helpful, give him a few dollars when you leave, plus $1 when he hails a cab for you.

A dollar a bag is fair for luggage handlers, but if one person unloads your bag from the car and another carries it to your room, you don't need to tip both of them. Valet parking attendants get $1 to $2 for retrieving the car, though the hotel may also charge you a hefty valet parking fee. Theme-park employees, except for restaurant servers or private tour guides, are not tipped.

All this assumes that gratuities are not already part of your package. If you pay a service charge on your hotel bill, that's supposed to cover all other tips to the bell staff and housekeeping. Always check hotel and restaurant bills to see whether an automatic service charge has been added. If you really want to be ahead of the game, ask when you make reservations. There's no point in tipping twice.

Tourist Traps

Orlando, a former swamp, doesn't have mountains or oceans, so don't pay extra for a hotel room with a so-called view. Most hotels and all of WDW are so perfectly manicured that almost every room looks out on a beautiful scene.

Transportation

Obviously, getting there is going to cost you either airfare or gas money. Whether you're flying or driving, refer to chapter 3 for more details on how to save serious dough. Since Orlando is such a major destination, many airlines offer competitive rates and frequent sales.

Chapters 4 and 8 deal with rental cars, shuttle service, and other modes of transportation in Orlando. If you're renting a car, you can probably get a rate of $25 to $35 per day for a basic economy model. You don't need more unless your family is bigger than a basketball team.

But weigh the pros and cons of staying at a Disney resort before renting. They usually have higher rates, but if you're going to concentrate your time in the Disney theme parks, you may not need a rental car at all, since free transportation to the parks is included.

Tourist Traps

Check every bill every time to see whether a tip, which may be listed as a "service charge," has already been added. It's an increasingly common practice in Orlando. At the plush spas, including those at the Lake Buena Vista Palace and at Disney's Grand Floridian, the service charge is a whopping 18%. With charges like that, you sure don't want to tip twice.

What Things Cost in Orlando/Walt Disney World

Taxi from airport to WDW hotels, party of four	$43
Shuttle fare, airport to WDW, per adult for up to five adults	$45
Bus fare from the airport to downtown	75¢
Cheapest room, cheapest season, WDW Grand Floridian Beach Resort	$299
Double room at Doubletree Resort & Conference Center	$159
Cheapest room, cheapest season, WDW All-Star Resort	$74
Campsite with full hookup at Fort Wilderness Resort	$39
Bed-and-breakfast for two, Comfort Inn Maingate, low season	$45
Room that sleeps up to four, off-season, Days Inn Maingate East	$59
Toll I-75 to I-4 or the Bee Line	$2.50
Burger, fries, and soda at fast-food restaurants in theme parks	$5–$7.50
Burger, fries, and soda at fast-food restaurants outside theme parks	$2–$5
Chicken noodle soup at Race Rock Orlando	$4.50
Early-bird dinner, Kobé Japanese restaurants	$8.95
Popcorn in WDW parks	$2 single, $3.75 double, $4 triple
5-day Park-Hopper Pass to WDW	$189 adults; $151 ages 3–9
Family pass, whole family, whole year, Orlando Science Center	$60
Dinner, beverages, and a show at Arabian Knights Dinner Show	$36.95 adults; $23.95 ages 3–11
Evening admission, Pleasure Island	$18.95 (adults only)
Camp Holiday, Holiday Inn Main Gate East	$2/hour first child; $1/hour each additional child
Mouseketeer Club child care, WDW Contemporary Resort	$4/hour, 4-hour maximum
Evening child care center, WDW Polynesian Resort	$8/hour, 3-hour minimum

What If I'm Worried I Can't Afford It?

Stop worrying! You supply the common sense and we'll supply the insider tips that will help you shave the cost of your Orlando vacation. Here's a list of strategies to keep in mind:

➤ **Buy a package.** This doesn't mean an escorted tour, just a package of airfare and accommodations purchased together. When you're traveling to the Orlando area, packages are a must. You can book airfare, hotel, ground transportation, and even some sightseeing just by making one call to a travel agent or packager for a lot less than if you tried to put the trip together yourself. (If it's not a lot less, find another agent or packager.) See chapter 3 for details on the leading package-tour operators that will get you to Orlando.

➤ **Go in the off-season.** If you can travel at nonpeak times (September to November, or April to June, for example), you'll find hotel prices that are as much as half off the prices offered during peak months.

➤ **Travel on off-days of the week.** Airfares vary depending on the day of the week. Staying over on a Saturday night can cut your airfare by more than half. If you can travel on a Tuesday, Wednesday, or Thursday, you may find cheaper flights to your destination. When you inquire about airfares, ask whether you can obtain a cheaper rate by flying on a different day.

Dollars & Sense

The **Magic Kingdom Club Gold Card** program ($65 per person annually and free for many government employees) provides discounts on WDW lodgings and tickets. Call ☎ **714/ 490-3200** or write Magic Kingdom Club, P.O. Box 3850, Anaheim, CA 92803.

➤ **Always ask for corporate, weekend, or other discount rates.** Membership in AAA, frequent-flyer plans, trade unions, AARP, or other groups may qualify you for discounted rates on car rentals, plane tickets, hotel rooms, even meals. Ask about *everything;* you could be pleasantly surprised.

➤ **Ask whether your kids can stay in your room with you free.** A room with two double beds usually doesn't cost any more than one with a queen-size bed. And many hotels won't charge you the additional person rate if the additional person is pint-size and related to you. Even if you have to pay $10 or $15 for a rollaway bed, you'll save hundreds by taking only one room.

➤ **Reserve a hotel room with a kitchen and do your own cooking.** It's not much of a vacation for the family chef or dishwasher, but you'll save a lot of money if you don't eat in restaurants three times a day. Even if you only make breakfast and an occasional bag lunch in the kitchen, you'll still save in the long run. And you'll never be shocked by a hefty room-service bill.

➤ **Stock up on drinks yourself.** If your room doesn't have a refrigerator, buy a disposable foam cooler in a discount store and keep juices, milk, and sodas on ice in your room and car. A small orange juice at a hotel sells for about $3.50; a bedtime glass of milk from room service can cost $5 or more. Ice is free in most hotels.

➤ **Pace yourself so you're not tempted to splurge.** Your money goes fastest when you are too hungry, too thirsty, or too tired to care. Start the day with a big breakfast, which will cost less at a fast-food restaurant than at your hotel, and less at your hotel than inside a theme park. (Several restaurants have breakfast buffets going for around $3.99 or $4.99 a head.) Stop often at drinking fountains. Cold sodas at the attractions are sinfully overpriced, but if you must buy them consider the souvenir cups that come with free refills. If you're going to stick around all day in summer and have a heavy-duty thirst, they can be a bargain. Leave the parks before you're too exhausted to use free transportation, which requires waiting and standing in line. Taxi fares are outrageous.

➤ **Brown-bag it to the parks, the beach, and attractions that provide shady picnic areas.** Note, however, that the theme parks, ballparks, and some other attractions are wise to this scheme and won't let you bring in your own food or drinks.

Dollars & Sense

Sales tax is not charged on supermarket food, but a 6% to 7% tax is added to restaurant and take-out meals. So if you can prepare some of your meals in your suite or condo, you save twice.

➤ **Skip the fast food.** Deli sections in Orlando-area supermarkets sell ready-to-eat meals ranging from sandwiches and salads to full hot meals for much less than you'd pay at fast-food chains.

➤ **Try expensive restaurants at lunch, not dinner.** And don't forget to check out early-bird specials.

➤ **Pick up every free tourist magazine you see.** They all contain coupons for savings on restaurants and tickets.

➤ **You don't have to spend every day at a theme park.** Discover your hotel's pool, sundeck, playground, gardens, workout facilities, get-togethers, and other freebies.

➤ **Don't send clothes to the hotel laundry.** The bills will be astronomical. The hotel may have a coin-op machine for guest use.

➤ **Who needs souvenirs?** They're usually overpriced and you don't have room in your luggage anyway. If you're on a budget, here's a place to tighten up.

Budget Worksheet: You Can Afford This Trip

Expense	Amount
Airfare (× no. of people traveling)	
Car rental (if applicable)	
Lodging (× no. of nights)	
Parking (× no. of nights)	
Breakfast may be included in your room rate (× no. of nights)	
Lunch (× no. of nights)	
Dinner (× no. of nights)	
Baby-sitting and resort's kiddy programs	
Attractions (admission charges to museums, theme parks, tours, theaters, nightclubs, etc.)	
Transportation (cabs, theme-park shuttle, buses, etc.)	
Souvenirs (T-shirts, postcards, that antique you must have)	
Tips (think 15% of your meal total plus $1 a bag every time a bellhop moves your luggage)	
Don't forget the cost of getting to and from the airport in your hometown, plus long-term parking (× no. of nights)	
Grand Total	

Chapter 3

How Will I Get There?

In This Chapter

➤ How to make a travel agent work for you

➤ The pros and cons of package tours

➤ The plane truth

➤ How to fly smart

You know it. We know it. The airlines and highway departments know it. Getting there *isn't* half the fun. But your journey doesn't have to be a hassle, either.

Orlando is totally geared for tourists. Its services are designed to get you started on your vacation quickly and efficiently. The Orlando airport is clean, modern, and bright, and it's served by most major airlines. Airport exits connect to the interstate or turnpike that, in turn, connect to highways and the attractions. The moment your airplane burns a little landing-gear rubber, you're in the heart of the action—a mere 30 or 40 minutes from just about anywhere you want or need to be.

Travel Agent: Friend or Foe?

A good travel agent is like a good mechanic or a good plumber: hard to find, but invaluable once you've locked in on the right one. The best way to find a five-star motel is the same way you find a good plumber, mechanic, or even doctor—word of mouth.

Any travel agent can help you find a bargain airfare, hotel, or rental car. A good travel agent will stop you from ruining your vacation because you tried to save a few dollars on the wrong deal. The best travel agents can tell you how much time you should budget for a destination, find you a cheap flight that doesn't require you to change planes in Chicago, St. Louis, *and* Atlanta, get you a better hotel room for about the same price, arrange for a competitively priced rental car, and even give recommendations on restaurants.

Travel agents work on commission. The good news is that *you* don't pay the commission—the airlines, accommodations, and tour companies do. The bad news is that unscrupulous travel agents will try to persuade you to book vacations that snap them the most money in commissions, and at the same time, take up the least amount of their time.

Bet You Didn't Know
Hungry guests at Universal Studios consume more than 1.1 million burgers and 130 miles of hot dogs annually. Please pass the Maalox.

To make sure you get the most out of your travel agent, do a little homework. Read about your destination (you've already made a sound decision by buying this book) and pick out some accommodations and attractions you think you'd like. If you have access to the Internet, check prices on the Web in advance (see "Happy Landings: Winning the Airfare Wars," later in this chapter, for more information on how to do that) so you can do a little prodding.

Then take your guidebook and Web information to your travel agent and ask the agent to make the arrangements for you. Because travel agents have access to more resources than even the most complete travel Web site, they should be able to get you a better price than you could get yourself. And they can issue your tickets and vouchers right there. If they can't get you into the hotel of your choice, they can recommend an alternative, and you can look for an objective review in your guidebook right then and there. It's always more effective to be a well-informed consumer.

In the past 2 years, some airlines and resorts have begun limiting or eliminating travel-agent commissions altogether. The immediate result has been that travel agents don't bother booking these services unless the customer specifically requests

Dollars & Sense
Travel agents receive a commission from WDW, and they are a better source of information than WDW itself because (1) WDW doesn't have a toll-free number, and (2) WDW agents answer your questions but do not volunteer any money-saving tips. Shop around among airlines, too. Delta is the big player in WDW packages. Since some travel agents play favorites and, as we mentioned earlier, snub some carriers because they don't pay as much in commissions, doing your homework in advance can really pay dividends. As you'll discover in a few minutes, most major airlines have 800-numbers, so the only thing this costs you is your time.

them. But some travel-industry analysts predict that if other airlines and accommodations throughout the industry follow suit, travel agents may have to start charging customers for their services. When that day arrives, the best agents should prove even harder to find. But chin up: Reservation agents with most frequent-flier clubs will (or at least can) turn the trick. Just to be sure, call two or three times (most have toll-free numbers), get a 24-hour confirmation number for any rate that's different, and then go with the best and cancel the others.

After you've read all the information below on package tours, you can let your travel agent book the same airline package (at no added cost to you) plus add-ons such as airport transfers and side trips.

The Pros & Cons of Package Tours

Package tours are not the same thing as escorted tours. They're simply a way of buying your airfare and accommodations at the same time. And for popular destinations like Orlando, they really are the smart way to go, because they save you money. In some cases, a package that includes airfare, hotel, and transportation to and from the airport will cost you less than just the hotel alone if you booked it yourself.

That's because packages are sold in bulk to tour operators, who resell them to the public. It's kind of like buying your vacation at Sam's Club or another membership discount club, except that it's the tour operator who buys the 1,000-count box of garbage bags and resells them 10 at a time at a cost that undercuts what you'd pay at your average neighborhood supermarket.

Dollars & Sense

Do you belong to AAA or another auto club, AARP, or any organization that provides travel bookings? It's likely they can cut you a discount deal on an Orlando package.

Packages vary as much as garbage bags, too. Some packages offer a better class of hotels than others. Some offer the same hotels for lower prices. Some offer flights on scheduled airlines, whereas others book charters. In some packages, your choice of accommodations and travel days may be limited. Some packages let you choose between escorted vacations and independent vacations; others will allow you to add on excursions or escorted day trips (also at prices lower than if you booked them yourself). And it really pays to compare, because different packages may include accommodations at the same hotel for different prices.

Pick a Peck of Pickled Packagers

The best place to start looking for packages is the travel section of your local Sunday newspaper. Also check the ads in the back of national travel magazines like ***Travel & Leisure*** and ***Condé Nast Traveler,*** or those that have a travel arm, like ***Elegant Bride*** and other publications that appeal to honeymooners. **Liberty Travel** (many locations; call ☎ **888/271-1584** to find an agent near you) is one of the biggest packagers in the Northeast, and it usually boasts a fat ad in Sunday papers. You won't get much in the way of service, but you'll get a good deal. **American Express Vacations** (☎ **800/241-1700**) is another option, though these folks sometimes defer to a local travel agency affiliate.

Disney offers a dizzying array of package choices that can include airfare, accommodations on or off Disney property, theme-park passes, a rental car, meals, a Disney Cruise Line cruise, courses at the Disney Institute, and/or a stay at Disney's beach resorts in Vero Beach or Hilton Head. And unlike the main Disney number, the number to call for a **Disney vacation package** is free: ☎ **800/828-0228.** Some packages are tied into a season and others are themed to a special vacation such as golf, a honeymoon, or a spa makeover.

Bet You Didn't Know

Star of more than 120 cartoons and movies, Mickey Mouse made his film debut in 1928's *Steamboat Willie.* His significant other, Minnie (no relation), also appeared in the film. Mickey's dad almost named him Mortimer, but his mom (Mrs. Disney) persuaded her husband that Mortimer was too pompous a name for a mouse and suggested Mickey.

It's hard to beat a Disney Vacation Company package for an all-Disney vacation, especially if you get other discounts such as the Magic Kingdom Club or you are a Disney shareholder. For those who want to see more than Walt Disney World, and most people do, comparisons are definitely in order. A really motivated travel agent could put together a package of Disney and non-Disney accommodations and attractions for less than what Disney charges. Of course, given Mickey's knack for emptying wallets, that's a no brainer.

So should you book with Walt Disney World Vacation Company? In a nutshell:

➤ Nobody knows Walt Disney World's pleasures and treasures better.

➤ Your WDW vacation can be seamless, including a cruise or beach stay.

➤ Accommodations in almost all price ranges are available.

But:

➤ WDW resort guests all get the same perks, whether you buy Disney's package or somebody else's.

➤ You have to prod the agents for money-saving tips, such as going a day earlier or later than your stated dates.

➤ Some package features, such as a welcome cocktail, have little or no dollar value.

The best answer: Compare and trust your gut. If you find a travel agent who goes above and beyond for you, book your vacation that way. Otherwise, using the vacation company is likely your best option.

Another good resource (and a reason for shopping outside WDW) is the airlines, which often package their flights with accommodations. When you pick an airline, you can choose one that has frequent service to your hometown and the one on which you accumulate frequent-flyer miles. Among the airline packages, your options include **American Airlines FlyAway Vacations** (☎ 800/321-2121), **Delta Dream Vacations** (☎ 800/872-7786), and **US Airways Vacations** (☎ 800/455-0123).

Dollars & Sense

There are some fudge factors affecting package prices. The same package at the same hotel can differ in price if a different-class room is included, or if one package-tour operator buys in greater bulk from that particular hotel and gets a deeper discount. Package prices are also affected greatly by the days you fly. US Airways's rates are cheapest for departures Sunday through Wednesday, returning any day but a weekend.

The Orlando market is cutthroat-competitive, so don't overlook a package just because it has features you won't use. You may find you can fly from New York to Orlando, pick up a rental car, but discard the 4 hotel nights (to stay with relatives or friends), yet you will still pay less than if you had booked your airfare and car rental separately. Here are some sample prices we were quoted for mid-June 1999.

Delta Dream Vacations (☎ 800/872-7786), the big fish in the Orlando pond, quoted a 4-night WDW vacation for two adults and two children (ages 8 and 10) that includes accommodations in Disney's Dixie Landings, airfare from New York (La Guardia, because JFK had only a night departure), transfers, taxes, cancellation insurance, and a 4-day Park Hopper Pass for $2,804. That's based on a mid-June departure, as are the two samples that follow. You can get a better rate if you don't visit during the summer peak.

US Airways Vacations (☎ 800/455-0123) quoted $2,532 for a quad room at Disney's Dixie Landings for 4 nights, airfare from New York (JFK), airport transfers, cancellation insurance, and 5-day unlimited passes to all the WDW parks. That's for the same family of four. The fifth-day park pass may be a wash unless you arrive early enough on the first day and depart late enough on the fifth to use them, but there isn't a lesser rate for a shorter pass. The **Disney Institute** (☎ 800/4-WONDER) offered a 3-night package for $2,698 for the family including round-trip air from JFK, four of the institute's programs (Camp Disney programs for kids), an option menu that includes spa treatments, a dinner per person or a 1-day, 1-park pass, cancellation insurance, a $50 gift certificate, airport transfers, and a bungalow with two queen-size beds.

Happy Landings: Winning the Airfare Wars

The airfare game is capitalism at its finest. Passengers within the same cabin on an airplane rarely pay the same fare. Rather, they pay what they—the market—will bear. This translates into a roll of the dice unless you know how to shop.

Business travelers who need the flexibility to purchase their tickets at the last minute, to change their itinerary at a moment's notice, or who want to get home before the weekend pay the premium rate, known as the full fare. Passengers who can book their ticket long in advance, who don't mind staying over Saturday night, or who are willing to travel on a Tuesday, Wednesday, or Thursday, pay the least, usually a fraction of the full fare. The same price cuts apply to those of you who are flexible enough to take advantage of discounts offered if you can fly with a few days' notice. On most flights, even the shortest hops, the full fare is close to $1,000 or more, but a 7-day or 14-day advance-purchase ticket costs closer to $200 to $300. Obviously, it pays to plan ahead.

Bet You Didn't Know

Most airlines will put a no-strings "courtesy hold" on your reservations for 24 hours (some airlines will hold your reservation for up to 7 days). It locks in your rate while giving you time to shop around.

The airlines also periodically hold sales, during which they lower the prices on their most popular routes. These fares have advance-purchase requirements and date-of-travel restrictions, but you can't beat the price: usually no more than $400 for a cross-country flight. Keep your eyes open for these sales as you're planning your vacation, then pounce on them. The sales tend to take place in seasons of low travel volume. You'll almost never see a sale around the peak summer vacation months of July and August, or around Easter, spring break, Thanksgiving, or Christmas, when people have to fly, regardless of cost.

Consolidators, also known as bucket shops, are a good place to check for the lowest fares. Their prices are much better than the fares you can get yourself, and are often even lower than what your travel agent can get you. You'll see their ads in the small boxes at the bottom of the page in your Sunday travel section. Some of the most reliable consolidators include ☎ **800-FLY-4-LESS** and ☎ **800-FLY-CHEAP.** Another good choice, **Council Travel** (☎ **800/226-8624**), caters especially to young travelers, but their bargain-basement prices are available to people of all ages.

Dollars & Sense

Do you own stock in Walt Disney World? If so, special discounts are available to you. Call **Shareholder Relations** at ☎ **818/505-7040** during Pacific Time business hours.

Surfing the Net to Fly the Skies

Another way to find the cheapest fare is by using the Internet to search for you. After all, that's what computers do best—search through millions of pieces of data and return information in rank order. The number of virtual travel agents on the Internet has increased exponentially in recent years. Agencies now compete the way locksmiths do in the Yellow Pages for the first alphabetical listing, inventing names like AAAA-Aardvark Air & Sea Specialty Packagers or 00007 Travel Consultants.

There are now too many companies to mention, but a few of the more-respected ones are **Travelocity** (www.travelocity.com), **Microsoft Expedia** (www.expedia.com), and **Yahoo!'s Flifo Global** (http://travel.yahoo.com/travel/).

All of them provide variations of the same service, though some have special requirements. Just enter the dates you want to fly and the cities you want to visit, and the computer looks for the lowest fares that are available.

Bet You Didn't Know

Goofy first appeared, along with Mickey Mouse, in a 1932 cartoon called *Mickey's Revue.* Though his original name was Dippy Dawg, which later evolved into Dippy the Goof, and finally, Goofy, there has been, for years, an ongoing controversy as to exactly what kind of animal he is. The claim of Disney representatives that he is supposed to be a human being has never been substantiated. His original name may at least give a clue as to what his creator intended.

The Yahoo! site has a feature called "Fare Beater," which will check flights on other airlines or at different times or dates in hopes of finding an even cheaper fare. Expedia's site will e-mail you the best airfare deal once a week if you so choose. Travelocity uses the SABRE computer reservations system that most travel agents use, and it has a "Last Minute Deals" database that advertises really cheap fares for those who can get away at a moment's notice.

If you're a member of the get-up-and-go set, **Smarter Living** provides free consumer information on the Web. Specials from 19 airlines are sent your way via e-mail, customized to your preferred airport, each Wednesday. Included is a summary of discount fares for the following weekend, so you need to be footloose to use the service. Subscribers also get information on rental cars and hotels. In addition to being free, Smarter Living swears it won't sell your personal information to junk mailers, a.k.a. Spammers. If you want more information about Smarter Living, wax your board and surf on over to its Internet site at **www.smarterliving.com**.

Great last-minute deals are also available directly from the airlines through a free e-mail service called **E-savers.** Each week, the airline sends you a list of discounted flights, usually leaving the upcoming Friday or Saturday, and returning the following Monday or Tuesday. You can sign up for all the major airlines at once by logging on to:

Epicurious Travel   http://travel.epicurious.com/travel/

Mining Company   http://airtravelminingco.com/

Travel Zoo   www.travelzoo.com/menul.asp

You can also call the airlines or go to each individual airline's Web site:

Air Canada   ☎ 800/776-3000; www.aircanada.ca/home.html

American Airlines   ☎ 800/433-7300; www.americanair.com

America West Airlines   ☎ 800/235-9292; www.americawest.com/

Continental Airlines   ☎ 800/525-0208; www.flycontinental.com

Delta Airlines   ☎ 800/221-1212; www.delta-air.com/res/

Northwest Airlines   ☎ 800/225-2525; www.nwa.com

Southwest Airlines   ☎ 800/435-9792; www.southwest.com

TWA   ☎ 800/221-2000; www.twa.com

US Airways   ☎ 800/428-4322; www.usairways.com

Does It Matter Which Airport I Fly Into?
Orlando International Airport

(MCO) is the major player, but it's not the only game in town. Some large charter flights go into **Sanford Orlando International Airport,** which is 20 minutes north of downtown Orlando and about 35 minutes north of the attractions area, farther away from all things Disney than Orlando International. If you come in on one of the packages that uses this airport, ground transportation should be included, but ask anyway.

As long as you're price shopping, see whether you can get to **Tampa (TPA)** cheaper than to MCO. With today's see-saw prices, discounts, and deals, it's always possible. Tampa is less than 2 hours southwest of the attractions area and 30 minutes east of the Gulf beaches. A Tampa package that combines airfare, a rental car, and beach accommodations before or after your Orlando visit can be a bonanza as

Extra! Extra!

If you have special dietary needs, be sure to order a special meal. Most airlines offer vegetarian meals, macrobiotic meals, kosher meals, meals for the lactose intolerant, and several other meals in a large variety of categories. Ask when you make reservations whether the airline can accommodate your dietary restrictions. Some people without any special dietary needs order special meals anyway because they are made to order, unlike the mass-produced dinners served to the rest of the passengers. Alas, they still taste and digest like airline food.

can one we'll explore later—Universal Studios or Sea World "flex" tickets when you decide to include Tampa's Busch Gardens.

The Comfort Zone:
How to Make Your Flight More Pleasant

The seats in the front row of each airplane compartment, called the **bulk-head seats,** usually have the most legroom. But they have some drawbacks. Because there's no seat in front of you, there's no place to put your carry-on luggage, except in the overhead bin. Also, the front row may not be the best place to see the in-flight movie. And lately, airlines have started putting passengers with young children in the bulkhead row so the kids can sleep on the floor. This is terrific if you have kids.

Emergency-exit row seats also have extra legroom. They are assigned at the airport, usually on a first-come, first-serve basis. Ask when you check in whether you can be seated in one of these rows. In the unlikely event of an emergency, you'll be expected to open the emergency exit door and help direct traffic. This, of course, doesn't count in-air emergencies. It's usually better to keep the door closed for a spell if this happens.

Beating the Lines

Delta has stopped allowing families with children to board first on Orlando flights. Since more travelers have kids than have not, it's fairer to the other passengers, and really better for the kids because they aren't cooped up any longer than necessary.

Wear comfortable clothes. The days of getting dressed in a coat and tie to ride an airplane went out with granny dresses and Nehru jackets. It's smart to dress in layers, though; "climate-controlled" aircraft cabins are anything but predictable. You'll be glad to have a sweater or jacket that you can put on or take off as the onboard need dictates.

Bring some toiletries aboard on long flights. Cabins are notoriously dry places. If you don't want to land in Orlando with the complexion of a mummy, take a travel-size bottle of moisturizer or lotion to refresh your face and hands at the end of the flight. If you're taking an overnight flight (a.k.a. the red-eye), don't forget to pack a toothbrush to combat the feeling upon waking that you've been sucking on your seat cushion for 6 hours. Manicure maniacs should file this away—*never* bring an unsealed container of nail polish remover into an airline cabin. The cabin pressure will cause the remover to evaporate and will damage your luggage. The accompanying smell won't make you popular with your seatmates either. If you wear contact lenses, take them out before you board and wear glasses instead, or at least bring eyedrops. No sense spending some of your hard-earned cash having "soft" lenses surgically removed at an Orlando hospital.

Jet lag usually isn't a problem for flights within the United States, but some people are affected by the 3-hour time changes coming from California. The best advice is to get acclimated to local time as quickly as possible. Stay up as long as you can the first day, and then try to wake up at a normal time the second day. Drink plenty of water on both days, as well as on the plane, to avoid dehydration.

And **if you're flying with kids,** don't forget chewing gum for ear-pressure problems with swallowing (adults with sinus problems should chew as well), a deck of cards or favorite toys to keep them entertained, extra bottles or pacifiers, and diapers if needed.

Even if *you're* not flying with kids, keep in mind that many people on Orlando flights *are* bringing their little monsters. Inbound, they'll be swinging from the overheads, excited about the journey to see Mickey Mouse. Outbound, they'll fill all the luggage racks with souvenirs and stuffed toys before you can stow your briefcase.

Beating the Lines

Ask for a seat toward the front of the plane. The minute the captain turns off the "Fasten Seat Belts" sign after landing, people jump up out of their seats as though someone just shouted "fire drill!" They stand in the aisles and wait for 5 to 10 minutes while the ground crew puts the gangway in place. The closer to the front of the plane you are, the less hurry-up-and-wait you'll have to do. Why do you think they put first class in the front?

Worksheet: Fare Game—Choosing an Airline

Arranging and booking flights is a complicated business—that's why a whole industry has grown up to handle it for you. If you're hunting for a deal, though, it helps to leave a trail of breadcrumbs through the maze so you can easily find the way to your destination and back. You can use this worksheet to do just that.

There's a chance that you won't be able to get a direct flight, especially if you're looking to save money, so we've included space for you to map out any connections you'll have to make. If a connection is involved in the fares you're quoted, make sure to ask how much of a layover you'll have between flights, because no one likes hanging around the airport for 8 or 10 hours. That said, because airline overbooking is reaching epidemic proportions, any quoted layover is a "best-case" scenario. Takeoffs are frequently delayed while the airlines pack their planes to capacity—some flights are held an hour until another airplane lands, shuffling unscheduled passengers into empty seats. Even if that doesn't happen, most of today's flights are so overbooked (20% or higher) they are delayed until enough volunteers take their free tickets and fly later. (If you have the time to spare, getting "bumped," as it's called, is a great way to get free round-trip airfare for your next trip; you'll be delayed in most cases only until the next scheduled flight.) Getting back to the worksheet: As best as you can, allow for layover times in the appropriate places so you can compare them easily when you go back over everything to make your flight decision.

Just to make it all that much easier, we've included a sample worksheet at the end of the chapter to get you started. Check it out, then get down to business. Good luck.

Other Ways to Get There

Driving to Orlando is a good choice unless (1) the distance is so great that it eats up too much of your vacation, or (2) you don't have an air-conditioned car. Without A/C, you and your family will dread driving around the area.

The city lies just off the Florida Turnpike, which links with I-75 at Wildwood. (I-75 runs from the Midwest to southwest Florida.) The city is also on I-4, which runs between Daytona Beach and Tampa. At Daytona, it joins I-95, the north–south interstate that runs the length of the eastern seaboard.

Orlando can also be reached on **Amtrak,** which stops downtown at 1400 Sligh Ave. (between Columbia and Miller), and at 111 Dakin St. in Kissimmee. The downtown train station is 2 blocks from a LYNX bus station, where buses run once an hour to the International Drive area. From there, you'll still need a taxi to get to Walt Disney World hotels, a ride costing about $28. If you debark at the Kissimmee station, taxi fare to the hotels is also $28.

The **Auto-Train (☎ 800/USA-RAIL)** is a unique service that allows you to bring your car from Lorton, Virginia (2 hours from Philadelphia and 4 hours from New York), to Sanford, which is 23 miles northeast of Orlando. Ride in a passenger seat or a sleeping car for the overnight trip.

Central Florida

| 0 | | 20 mi |
| 0 | | 32 km |

37

1   Schedule & Flight Information Worksheets

Travel Agency: _____   **Phone #:** _____

Agent's Name: _____   **Quoted Fare:** _____

Departure Schedule & Flight Information

Airline: _____ Airport: _____

Flight #: _____ Date: _____ Time: _____am/pm

Arrives in _____ Time: _____am/pm

Connecting Flight (if any)

Amount of time between flights: _____ hours/mins.

Airline:_____ Flight #:_____ Time: _____am/pm

Arrives in _____ Time: _____am/pm

Return Trip Schedule & Flight Information

Airline:_____ Airport: _____

Flight #: _____ Date: _____ Time: _____am/pm

Arrives in _____ Time: _____am/pm

Connecting Flight (if any)

Amount of time between flights: _____ hours/mins.

Airline:_____ Flight #:_____ Time: _____am/pm

Arrives in _____ Time: _____am/pm

2   Schedule & Flight Information Worksheets

Travel Agency: _____ Phone #: _____

Agent's Name: _____ Quoted Fare: _____

Departure Schedule & Flight Information

Airline: _____ Airport: _____

Flight #: _____ Date: _____ Time: _____am/pm

Arrives in _____ Time: _____am/pm

Connecting Flight (if any)

Amount of time between flights: _____ hours/mins.

Airline:_____ Flight #:_____ Time: _____am/pm

Arrives in _____ Time: _____am/pm

Return Trip Schedule & Flight Information

Airline:_____ Airport: _____

Flight #: _____ Date: _____ Time: _____am/pm

Arrives in _____ Time: _____am/pm

Connecting Flight (if any)

Amount of time between flights: _____ hours/mins.

Airline:_____ Flight #:_____ Time: _____am/pm

Arrives in _____ Time: _____am/pm

3 Schedule & Flight Information Worksheets

Travel Agency: _____ **Phone #:** _____

Agent's Name: _____ **Quoted Fare:** _____

Departure Schedule & Flight Information

Airline: _____ Airport: _____

Flight #: _____ Date: _____ Time: _____am/pm

Arrives in _____ Time: _____am/pm

Connecting Flight (if any)

Amount of time between flights: _____ hours/mins.

Airline:_____ Flight #:_____ Time: _____am/pm

Arrives in _____ Time: _____am/pm

Return Trip Schedule & Flight Information

Airline:_____ Airport: _____

Flight #: _____ Date: _____ Time: _____am/pm

Arrives in _____ Time: _____am/pm

Connecting Flight (if any)

Amount of time between flights: _____ hours/mins.

Airline:_____ Flight #:_____ Time: _____am/pm

Arrives in _____ Time: _____am/pm

4 Schedule & Flight Information Worksheets

Travel Agency: _____ **Phone #:** _____

Agent's Name: _____ **Quoted Fare:** _____

Departure Schedule & Flight Information

Airline: _____ Airport: _____

Flight #: _____ Date: _____ Time: _____am/pm

Arrives in _____ Time: _____am/pm

Connecting Flight (if any)

Amount of time between flights: _____ hours/mins.

Airline:_____ Flight #:_____ Time: _____am/pm

Arrives in _____ Time: _____am/pm

Return Trip Schedule & Flight Information

Airline:_____ Airport: _____

Flight #: _____ Date: _____ Time: _____am/pm

Arrives in _____ Time: _____am/pm

Connecting Flight (if any)

Amount of time between flights: _____ hours/mins.

Airline:_____ Flight #:_____ Time: _____am/pm

Arrives in _____ Time: _____am/pm

Chapter 4

Tying Up the Loose Ends

In This Chapter

➤ The ins and outs of renting a car

➤ Travel insurance tips

➤ What to do in case of illness

➤ Bugsy and the Beasties

➤ Making reservations and getting tickets ahead of time

➤ (Groan) Packing

Okay, you're almost there. Now all you have to do is find a place to stay (we'll tackle that separately in chapters 5 and 6), plan your itinerary, make the reservations, put the dog in the kennel, stuff your bags with anything that's clean, water the geraniums, pay the mortgage, and perform 50 other last-minute feats of magic. Some of these "details" will save you from wasting precious vacation hours waiting in line, calling around town, and buying the dental floss you forgot to bring. In this chapter we'll help you make sure you remember everything, right down to bringing a comfortable pair of walking shoes. We'll also help you make some vital decisions like whether to rent a car and what to do if you get sick.

That said, put your seat in the upright position.

Here we go.

Do I Need to Rent a Car in Orlando?

Maybe you can't imagine being anywhere in America without a sedan or pickup truck. But before you charge that rental, think about it. Do you really need one? Before making your decision, remember that parking is an added expense at the mega-theme parks, the Bob Carr Performing Arts Centre, the convention center, sports events, and some hotels and restaurants.

If your trip overwhelmingly centers on Walt Disney World, you can survive very nicely without a car. Everything is there: the parks, restaurants, night-clubs, entertainment of all kinds, golf, tennis, boating, water parks, nature watching, and swimming pools galore. All transportation within WDW is free—the monorail, buses, and ferries—although it can sometimes take hours, and several transfers, to get where you need to go. That rental will be useful in getting you around faster, and it can also get you out of the high-priced World to find the moderately priced restaurants and shops in the real world. Still, your best bet is to skip the car if you're spending any time exclusively in WDW. If not, or if that WDW stay is followed by an outside visit, then a rental is usually a necessity. There are some exceptions—especially if you're staying on International Drive, where there are a lot of hotels, restaurants, and recreation options. Many of the hotels have shuttles to the parks; other shuttles run between International Drive's attractions and to down-town. You may spend about 30 minutes or so daily waiting on the shuttles, but they are much cheaper than a rental car.

If your vacation orbit includes trips to Tampa or Daytona, large shopping malls, and supermarkets to stock the kitchenette, then you have to have wheels. This isn't a city where you want to depend on the taxis, which are expensive, or the bus system, which is good, but serves routes more useful to local consumers than to tourists.

Be a Smart Shopper

If you decide to rent a car, remember that car-rental rates vary even more than air-line fares. The price depends on the size of the car, the length of time you keep it, where and when you pick it up and drop it off, where you take it, and a host of other factors including the phase of the Moon. Travelers under 25 years old will howl at the Young Renter's Fee assessed by all the major car-rental agencies—that is, if they rent to you at all. The fee can tack on an extra $25 per day to the price of a rental, so make sure to ask about extra fees when calling for a rate quote.

Asking a few key questions could poten-tially save you hundreds of dollars. For example, weekend rates may be lower

Time-Savers

There are Internet resources that can make comparison shopping easier. For exam-ple, Yahoo!'s partnership with Flifo Global travel agency allows you to look up rental prices for any size car at more than a dozen rental companies in hun-dreds of cities. Just enter the size of car you want, the rental and return dates, and the city where you want to rent, and the server returns a price. It will even make your reservation for you. It's no more complicated than aim-ing your browser at **http://travel.yahoo.com/travel/** and then clicking on "Reserve car" in the options listed.

Tourist Traps

Some car-rental companies offer refueling packages, in which you pay for an entire tank of gas up front. The price is usually fairly competitive with local gas prices, but you don't get credit for any gas remaining in the tank. If you reject this option, you pay only for the gas you use, but you have to return it with a full tank or face a charge of $3 to $4 a gallon for any shortfall. It's best to skip the gas-in-advance option and simply fill up on the return voyage. Make sure you allow time for that final petrol stop, and don't oversleep. It's tough to return home, and it's worse to miss your flight and have to face an airline hassle on top of it.

than weekday rates. Ask whether the rate is the same for a Friday morning pickup as it is for Thursday night. If you're keeping the car 5 or more days, a weekly rate may be cheaper than the daily rate. Some companies may assess a drop-off charge if you don't return the car to the same renting location; others don't have the charge. Ask whether the rate is cheaper if you pick up the car at the airport, or at a location in town.

If you see an advertised price in your local newspaper, be sure to ask for that specific rate; otherwise, you may be charged the standard (higher) rate. Don't forget to mention membership in AAA, AARP, frequent-flyer programs, and trade unions. These usually entitle you to discounts ranging from 5% to 30%. Ask your travel agent to check any and all of these rates.

On top of the standard rental prices, other optional charges apply to most car rentals. The Collision Damage Waiver (CDW), which requires you to pay for damage to the car in a collision, is illegal in some states, but is covered by many credit-card companies. Check with your credit-card company before you go to avoid paying this hefty fee (as much as $10 a day).

The car-rental companies also offer additional liability insurance (in case you harm others in an accident), personal accident insurance (in case you harm yourself or your passengers), and personal effects insurance (in case your luggage is stolen from your car). If you have insurance on your car at home, you are probably covered for most of these unlikelihoods. If your own insurance fails to cover you for rentals, or if you don't have automobile insurance, you should consider the additional coverage (the car-rental companies are liable for certain base amounts, depending on the state). But weigh the possibility of getting into an accident or losing your luggage against the cost of these types of coverage (as much as $20 a day combined), which can significantly add to the price of your rental.

You can find information on car-rental companies at or near Orlando International on the Internet (**www.bnm.com/orldo.htm**). Some of the major rental companies are:

Alamo ☎ **800/327-9633** or 800/354-2322; www.bnm.com/alamo.htm

Avis ☎ **800/331-1212;** www.bnm.com.avis.htm

Budget ☎ **800/537-0700**; www.drivebudget.com

Dollar ☎ **800/800-4000**; www.bnm.com.dollar.htm

Enterprise ☎ **800-551-3390**; www.pickenterprise.com

Hertz ☎ **800/654-3131**; www.bnm.com/hertz.htm

National ☎ **800/227-7368**; www.nationalcar.com

Thrifty ☎ **800/367-2277**; www.bnm.com/thriftyo.htm

Value ☎ **800/468-2583**; www.value-car-rental.com

If you don't feel like running with the big dogs for transportation, there are plenty of local or regional companies around. They include:

Americar ☎ **800/743-7483**; www.bnm.com/amero.htm

Carl's Rent A Van ☎ **800/565-5211**; www.bnm.com/cvans.htm

Global Rent A Car ☎ **877/851-2202**; www.bnm.com/global.htm

InterAmerican ☎ **800/327-1278**; www.bnm.com/ia.htm

Specialty Vans ☎ **888/871-2770**; www.bnm.com/specialo.htm

Car-Rental Comparison Worksheet			
Company	Type of Car	No. of Days	Rate
Alamo (☎ 800/327-9633)			
Avis (☎ 800/331-1212)			
Budget (☎ 800/527-0700)			
Dollar (☎ 800/800-8000)			
Enterprise (☎ 800/551-3390)			
Hertz (☎ 800/654-3131)			
National (☎ 800/227-7368)			
Thrifty (☎ 800/367-2277)			
Value (☎ 800/468-2583)			
Other			
Other			
Other			

What About Travel Insurance?

There are three kinds of travel insurance: trip-cancellation, medical, and lost luggage. Trip-cancellation insurance is a good idea if you have paid a large portion of your vacation expenses up front—say, if you bought a package— and would lose out if your trip were canceled. (You shouldn't buy this type of insurance from the packager.) It's also a savior if you or someone in your party gets sick or dies and you can't go.

Dollars & Sense

The airlines are responsible for reimbursing you $1,250 for lost luggage on domestic flights; if you plan to carry anything more valuable than that, keep it in your carry-on bag.

But the other two types of insurance don't make sense for most travelers. Your existing health insurance should cover you if you get sick while on vacation (but check to make sure that you are fully covered when away from home). And your homeowner's insurance should cover stolen luggage if you have off-premises theft. Check your existing policies before you buy any additional coverage and perhaps waste money.

Some credit cards (American Express and certain gold and platinum cards, for example, Visa and MasterCard) offer automatic flight insurance against death or dismemberment in case of an airplane crash.

If you still feel you need more insurance, try one of the companies listed below. But don't pay for more insurance than you need. For example, if you need only trip-cancellation insurance, don't purchase coverage for lost or stolen property. Trip-cancellation insurance costs approximately 6% to 8% of the total value of your vacation.

The reputable issuers of travel insurance include:

➤ **Access America,** 6600 W. Broad St., Richmond, VA 23230 (☎ **800/ 284-8300**)

➤ **Mutual of Omaha,** Mutual of Omaha Plaza, Omaha, NE 68175 (☎ **800/228-9792**)

➤ **Travel Guard International,** 1145 Clark St., Stevens Point, WI 54481 (☎ **800/826-1300**)

➤ **Travel Insured International, Inc.,** P.O. Box 280568, East Hartford, CT 06128 (☎ **800/243-3174**)

What If I Get Sick Away from Home?

Bring all your medications with you, as well as a prescription in case you need a refill. Orlando pharmacists can network with your home pharmacist by telephone, but a written Rx will save time and expense. If you have health insurance, carry your identification card in your wallet. Bring an extra pair of contact lenses in case you lose one. The same thing goes for eyeglasses if you can't see without them. And don't forget small supplies of over-the-counter medications for common travelers' ailments. Yes, you can buy them here in a convenience or drugstore, but if you forget and get a headache or nausea in a theme park, you're going to take a pounding at the counter as well as in the head or stomach.

If you suffer from a chronic illness, talk to your doctor before taking the trip. For such conditions as epilepsy, diabetes, or a heart condition, wear a **Medic Alert Identification Tag,** which will immediately alert any doctor to your condition and give him or her access to your medical records through Medic Alert's 24-hour hot line. Membership is $35, plus a $15 annual fee. Contact the Medic Alert Foundation, P.O. Box 1009, Turlock, CA 95381-1009 (☎ **800/825-3785;** www.medicalert.org).

If you worry about getting sick away from home, purchase medical insurance (see the section on travel insurance above). It will cover you more completely than your existing health insurance.

If you do get sick, ask the concierge or front desk at your hotel to recommend a local doctor—most hotels have a doctor and dentist on call—or steer you to the nearest emergency room or walk-in clinic.

Extra! Extra!

We hope you don't need any medical care on your trip, but just in case: For nonemergencies, try **Orlando Regional Walk-in Medical Care** (☎ 407/841-5111); **Housemed/ Mediclinic** (☎ 407/396-1195); **Mainstreet Physicians** (☎ 407/238-1009); or **Buena Vista Walk-In Center** (☎ 407/239-7777). The 24-hour **Walgreen's** at 534 Hunt Club Blvd. (☎ 407/869-5220) has a drive-through pharmacy. You can call in your prescription, then pick it up without having to leave your car.

If a child or pet swallows a Florida plant that you fear is unsafe, call **Poison Control** at ☎ **800/282-3171.** Among the more common poisonous flowers found in the Orlando area are oleander, lantana, and trumpet vine.

Mean Streets, Flying Teeth & Nasty Natives: Last-Minute Warnings

Roadkill   When it comes to mean streets, Orlando's are the worst—and not just for four-footed residents. This is the most dangerous city in the country for those who travel upright, according to the Surface Transportation Policy Project in Washington, D.C. In 1996, 177 pedestrians died or were seriously injured in vehicle run-ins. A formula using pedestrian fatalities, population, and the number of people who walk to work ranked the Tampa Bay area as second worst in the country, with Miami–Fort Lauderdale coming in third. Wide roads that are designed to move traffic quickly and a lack of sidewalks, streetlights, and crosswalks, are to blame for Florida's shameful ranking. Maybe it doesn't need to be said, but just in case: Be careful out there when you're traveling on foot.

A Word About Bugs Florida is the bug world's version of an all-you-can-eat buffet. Bloodsuckers, especially those of the winged persuasion, are in heaven every time a two- or four-legged critter comes within range. The worst times are an hour before dawn and dusk on still, dry days. Those of you foolish enough to wander outside touristville's controlled atmosphere (that's any-where not misted with Raid every 15 seconds) are at their mercy, although marshland and pastures are the worst, and few visitors get that sidetracked in Central Florida. Most of our bugs—such as worms, roaches, and all but two or three kinds of spiders—are pretty icky, but also pretty harmless. Some, such as fire ants and scorpions, pack a nasty wallop, but they don't have the range of the (drum roll, please) aerial armada.

Mosquitoes are number two on the hit list. They use a needlelike nose to drill through your skin and slurp a three- or four-course meal. Floridians quickly get accustomed to seeing and hearing mosquito-fogging trucks prowling the streets every evening. Their value is questionable. On an indi-vidual basis, if you must go outside, then arguably your best bets are store-bought repellents that have DEET as their active ingredient. Though it dates to 1954, the chemical remains the gold standard for discouraging mosquitoes.

Sand gnats are unquestionably Public Enemy No. 1. They're also called flying teeth, no-see-ums, punkies, and #@$%#s! They're practically invisible and, like mosquitoes, their radar hones in on carbon dioxide, the stuff exhaled by every mammal on the planet. They're crazy for water-buffalo breath; water buffaloes are like Häagen-Dazs to them. But they're somewhat scarce in Florida, so you become a pinch-hitter. The best remedy is to slather a thick layer of mineral oil on your skin. Political correctness aside, it drowns them. But most folks aren't inclined to spend their vacations dripping with oil, so the next best options are to (a) stay indoors in the hours around dawn and dusk, (b) steer clear of the swamps, coastal areas, and riverfronts that are their favorite neighborhoods (unfortunately they're the favorite of develop-ers, too), or (c) wear fine mesh clothes, keep a hat on your noggin, and coat bare skin areas with something like Deep Woods Off!, a DEET repellent. Though it's not as effective as it is against mosquitoes, applying it often enough will give you some peace.

Wild Things Many tourist seasons ago, most of Florida's roadside attractions peddled baby alligators. Gullible snowbirds took them north with bushels of oranges and lawn flamingos, giving the tiny-but-toothy reptiles happy homes until the novelty wore off—which usually happened a few weeks and several punctured fingers later. The two life forms often parted company with a rush and a flush. That's how the legendary monsters of New York's sewers came into being. Gators got a bum rap on that one. The same isn't true for snowbirds. They're still gullible. So are some residents.

For their sake, these words of warning:

> Don't pet the alligators.
>
> Don't feed them either.
>
> Don't even get close, especially in the wild.

You'll see plenty of them at a safe distance in some of the smaller tourist parks around Central Florida. But the wild ones turn up in some civilized places during their spring "dating" season. In the less-than-likely event that this happens to be the place where you're standing, calmly move your carcass, but don't block their escape route, the most direct path to the water. Most alligators are more than happy to leave you alone. Be smart and return the favor.

The same goes for Florida's vast range of snakes. While most are utterly harmless, there are a few (moccasins, coral snakes, and various members of the rattlesnake family) that can ruin your vacation—or worse. Don't take a chance.

Just let them be.

Two on the Aisle: Making Reservations & Getting Tickets Ahead of Time

Compared to New York and San Francisco, where restaurant tables at the best places are snapped up weeks in advance, Orlando is easy. In most instances, you can wait until you get to Florida to make dining reservations. Your hotel's concierge will be glad to help.

At Walt Disney World, a system called **Priority Seating** is used. With it, you make a reservation that ensures you'll get the next available table after your arrival at the restaurant. It's not like a traditional reservation, where an empty table is held for you, but it's far better than just showing up and waiting your turn. Still, waits of up to an hour or more sometimes happen. We explain exactly how the system works in chapter 9.

Evening shows can be booked as far in advance as you wish; **restaurants and character meals** can be booked up to 60 days in advance by calling ☎ **407/ WDW-DINE.** Note in our restaurant listings that a few restaurants in WDW and elsewhere require reservations at all times.

Ticketmaster is the key player in ticketing for most events in Orlando. If you know of a blockbuster event that will be playing while you're in town, check first with your hometown Ticketmaster outlets to see whether they sell tickets for it. If you live as close as Miami or Atlanta, they probably do. Otherwise, call the

Bet You Didn't Know

Universal Studios (☎ **407/224-7638**) offers free seating for special events that are being filmed or televised. Even locals sometimes get the word about these late in the game. Your best bet is to write well in advance, listing the dates you'll be in town. Ask what tickets are available. Write Universal Studios, 1000 Universal Studios Plaza, Orlando, FL 32819. **Walt Disney World,** including Pleasure Island and Downtown Disney, is constantly hosting film shoots, world-class sports events, and special shows (☎ **407/ 824-4321;** www. disneyworld.com).

Ticketmaster outlet here, ☎ **407/839-3900,** or go to its Web site (**www.ticketmaster.com**). Ticketmaster accepts American Express, MasterCard, and Visa, and takes calls from 9am to 9pm Monday to Friday and 9am to 7pm Saturday and Sunday.

Dozens of rock, rap, jazz, pop, country, blues, and folk stars are in town during any given week, and they are featured on a page called "New Tix" in the **Orlando Sentinel's Calendar section,** published every Friday. Pick it up while you're here, or find it online at **www.orlandosentinel.com**.

For tickets to events at the **Daytona International Speedway,** which is only a couple of hours from Orlando, call ☎ **904/253-7223.**

Silver Springs, an hour north of Orlando, has become the Nashville of Central Florida, with appearances by artists like the Gatlin Brothers, Johnny Cash, Tanya Tucker, and Randy Travis. Call ☎ **800/234-7458.** Seating is almost unlimited and is not reserved, but you can avoid standing in long lines by buying park admission tickets in advance. Concerts are included, so arrive early and spend the day seeing Florida's oldest tourist attraction.

Be advised that if you wait to make any of your reservations until you arrive, or try to make any local calls for that matter, you will encounter the city's latest quirk. Because of Orlando's rapid growth, as of June 1999, even if you make a **local** call within Orlando's 407 area code, you must still dial the area code before dialing a phone number. This is supposed to help deal with a shortage of phone numbers, although how this system will help is beyond us. Don't burden your brain with that puzzle, just dial the 10 digits.

Bet You Didn't Know

As a rule, you're allowed two pieces of carry-on luggage, both of which must fit into the overhead compartment or under the seat in front of you. Some airlines, however, are limiting this to one bag and others are strictly enforcing the two-bag limit—ask at the time you book your flight! Show your carry-ons when first checking in to avoid problems at the gate or on board. All airlines have become strict about not exceeding the size limit.

Heigh-Ho, Heigh-Ho, Let's Get This Show on the Road! Time to Pack!

Start your packing by taking everything you think you'll need and laying it out on the bed. Then get rid of half of it. Remember, suitcase straps can be particularly painful to sunburned shoulders.

Some essentials:

➤ Leave the snowshoes, ski masks, and thermal underwear at home. But it does get a tad brisk some winter mornings in Central Florida. There is usually a 3-day cycle: wet, windy, and cold; still colder and sometimes frosty; bright and beginning to warm.

The rest of the time it's hard to tell winter from late spring or early autumn. Bring clothes for layering (a sweater, a light jacket, and a couple of sweatshirts).

➤ "Shirt and Shoes Required." That's the most common sign welcoming diners to Florida restaurants. It summarizes our way of life: casual, but not gross. Please, no short-shorts, tank tops, outer-underwear, or see-throughs in the dining room. (You may not care, but the rest of us are trying to eat.) Beyond those, there aren't many rules. A few of the classier joints might insist on a coat, fewer yet a tie, but sports coats or, heaven forbid, suits, are pretty much a waste of time and luggage space unless you're planning something special. Slacks and a nice shirt or blouse are sufficient for most everywhere and nice shorts are a pretty universal sight, even at night. Most hosts know you've spent the day trapped in the theme parks and they're happy you saved some money to share with them.

➤ Sun cover-ups are essential. Even on cool, cloudy days, you can get a blistering burn. Bring a hat (preferably one with a brim) and sunglasses, too. Don't forget to bring sunscreen with a 25 rating or higher and preferably waterproof so it's less likely to get washed away by sweat or the pool. *Don't forget an umbrella or poncho, regardless of the season.* Florida is as wet as it is warm, and the umbrella and poncho prices in theme parks have been known to cause sticker shock.

➤ If you bring two bathing suits, you'll always have a dry one ready to slip into. Beach shoes are a plus if you'll be going to the Atlantic or the Gulf, where sands can have patches of shell rubble. In summer, they also can become as hot as a griddle. Shoes also help around the pool deck, which can grow all sorts of fungi.

➤ Bring at least two pairs of shoes and plenty of socks so you can start each day with fresh, dry footwear. That standby pair is even more valuable after a visit to one of the many theme parks that have water rides. Even if you stay off the flumes, waiting in line on hot days is tougher on the tootsies than marine boot camp. A lot of theme-park veterans carry extra shoes and socks with them, changing footwear around halftime. If you're visiting from early spring to late fall, bring a lot of lightweight shirts (T-shirts work very well) and shorts to stay cool. And for the sake of your fellow patrons, an extra swipe of deodorant doesn't hurt either.

Extra! Extra!

Loop a brightly colored snippet of cloth or a short scarf through the handle of your luggage. That will keep you from having to lift heavy pieces that look like yours off the baggage conveyor to check the identification tags for your name. Space permitting, it's also a smart idea to pack some toiletries and a clean shirt and undies in your carry-on in case you suffer lost-luggage syndrome.

When packing, start with the biggest, hardest items (usually shoes), then fit smaller items in and around them. Pack breakable items in between several layers of clothes, or keep them in your carry-on bag. Put things that could leak, like shampoos and suntan lotions, in Ziploc bags. Lock your suitcase with a small padlock (available at most luggage stores, if your bag doesn't already have one), and put an identification tag on the outside.

Pack a book in one of your carry-ons if you want to read something other than magazine and newspaper handouts on the plane. Space is tight in carry-ons, but other options, depending on your personal preferences, include breakable items, a personal headphone stereo, a snack to replace the airline handout, any vital documents you don't want to lose in your luggage (like your return tickets, passport, and wallet), and some empty space for the sweater or jacket you might need in flight or in the air-conditioned terminal.

Don't Forget Your Toothbrush! A Packing Checklist

- [ ] Socks (bring two pairs for each day during the hottest months)
- [ ] Underwear (we told you this was an Idiot's Guide)
- [ ] Shoes (don't forget a good pair of walking shoes for the parks)
- [ ] Pants and/or skirts
- [ ] Shirts or blouses
- [ ] Sweaters and/or jackets
- [ ] Umbrella and/or poncho (essential for Orlando's late-afternoon thunderstorms)
- [ ] A belt
- [ ] Shorts
- [ ] Bathing suits (and maybe a beach towel; better resorts provide them free)
- [ ] Workout clothes if you'll be using your hotel's gym
- [ ] Toiletries (don't forget a razor, toothbrush, comb, deodorant, makeup, contact lens solution, hair dryer, extra pair of glasses, sewing kit, sunscreen)
- [ ] Camera (don't forget the film; it can be very expensive when you're traveling)
- [ ] Medications (pack these in a carry-on so that you'll have them even if you lose your luggage)

Part 2

Finding the Hotel That's Right for You

First things first. You need a place to rest your bones. The place you pick will determine a lot of other things about your vacation: whether you need to rent a car, how your itineraries will line up, and how much you'll be spending.

Take one thing to the bank: You won't have a shortage of choices. At last count there were about a billion resorts, hotels, motels, condos, and bed-and-breakfasts in Central Florida. And all of them seem to have a gimmick. Where, you may ask, are you supposed to begin? How are you supposed to tell the tasteful from the tacky?

That's where we come in. In chapter 5, we'll start by giving you some strategies and money-saving tips. We'll also fill you in on the decisions you have to make when choosing a location. Then in chapter 6, you'll find the reviews of what we consider to be the very best options out there. We've even thrown in an easy-to-use worksheet so you can zero in on the one you want.

So clean your bifocals, sharpen your pencil, and take your phone off the hook. No distractions allowed.

Chapter 5

Pillow Talk: The Lowdown on Orlando's Hotel Scene

In This Chapter

➤ To Mickey or not to Mickey?

➤ How to choose a hotel

➤ A look at what it'll cost you—plus tips on how to save

➤ Hotel strategies for families traveling with kids

➤ Getting a great room

We're going to get this show on the road by letting you in on two things you can take for granted. Almost every hotel here has been built or renovated in the past 25 years, so the facilities should be reasonably modern (the lamps and refrigerators shouldn't shock you and the TVs work swell without rabbit ears). And they all try to make every kid feel like Mickey's personal guest.

So, your main choices boil down to location and price, and though you'll pay more for the best locations, you may find it worth the convenience. The closer your hotel is to the stuff you want to do and see, the less time you'll spend hemmed in by a traffic jam or walking the wastelands from Parking Area ZZZZZ to the theme-park entrance. Saving a few dollars by staying in the suburbs will be a mistake if the cost in aggravation is higher.

Location, Location, Location

Think you're going to save a pile of dough by checking into a room as far from WDW as possible? Sorry. People are flocking to Central Florida for a lot of reasons that have zip to do with theme parks: weddings, honeymoons, business and investing, conferences, spring break, conventions, visiting all of the grandmas and grandpas who have retired here, even fleeing to "high"

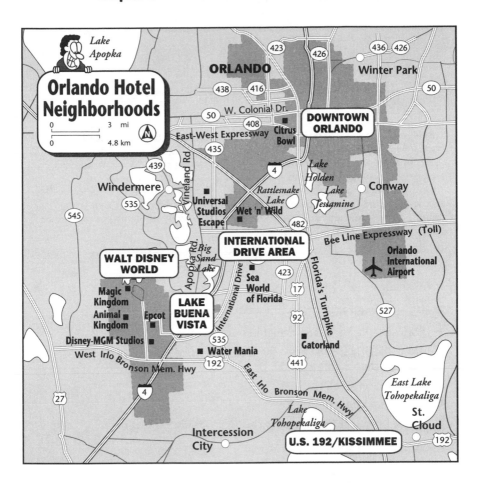

ground when a hurricane pounds the coast. As we've said before, if you're searching for a maximum Mickey experience, you may actually save money by staying within WDW because you won't have to rent a car. Take a gander at "Should I Bunk with Mickey?" later in this chapter to learn more.

Here are some pros and cons about each of the hotel neighborhoods in the Orlando area.

Walt Disney World

The hotels and resorts in this category are located smack dab at ground zero. If all you care about are daily trips to the Disney theme parks, this choice may be a no-brainer. They're also all on the Disney Transportation System, which means you can skip a car rental (unless you want to reach brave new worlds beyond Walt's) and, therefore, save money on that front.

But convenience doesn't come without a price. The cheapest hotels in WDW cost twice what you'd pay in nearby Kissimmee for the same accommodations. And without that rental, you're trapped in a World where everything from meals to spa services is equally inflated.

Tourist Traps

Minibars are the one-armed bandits of the innkeeping world. Most of you know what to expect: a canned soft drink for $2.50, a shot of liquor at $3.50, and $4 for a tiny box of crackers. The modern variation even has mysterious sensors that charge your room if a product is removed for 15 seconds. (So don't get the idea you can guzzle tonight and replace it with a cheaper bottle tomorrow from the liquor store down the street.) After you arrive in your room, make sure the kids know these treats are strictly off-limits, or make sure that such luxuries are in your budget.

In a nutshell:

➤ It's seamless magic from the service to the landscaping.

➤ Some WDW perks are available only to WDW hotel guests.

➤ Security is tops.

But:

➤ You pay a premium price.

➤ The immersion in pixie dust may get old after a few days.

➤ You won't see the "real" Florida.

Lake Buena Vista Area (Official WDW Hotels)

Think of this neighborhood, located close to Disney Crossroads and Pleasure Island, as a bedroom community for Walt Disney World. You'll get many of the same perks enjoyed by people staying inside WDW (some of these are official Disney hotels even though they're not owned by Disney or on Disney land), but you won't be constantly pounded by the Disney hoop-de-do. You'll still get free transportation to and from the parks (but not on the WDW transportation system).

In a nutshell:

➤ The area is so new and meticulously maintained that it fairly sparkles.

➤ There's a wider range of hotels and restaurants (read—some non-Disney options) in every price category.

➤ You're conveniently located close to WDW without being inside it 24 hours a day.

Tourist Traps

Don't make a telephone call from your room without understanding your hotel's policy; ask when you check in. Some offer free local and toll-free calls, but others charge $1 or more *each* time you pick up the telephone, even if you're using your calling card or charging the call to your home number.

Say you dial an 800-number to access your phone-card service. The party you're calling doesn't answer, or the line is busy. The fact that you didn't reach your party is irrelevant. The hotel charges you $1.75 each time the 800-number answers the call. It considers that a completed call.

Charging long-distance calls to your room is worse. Hotels charge top-dollar long-distance rates, fees, *and* surcharges. (In another line of work they would be busted for loan-sharking.)

Many pay phones in Central Florida now cost 35¢ or more for a local call, but they're still a bargain compared to local calls placed from your room at 50¢, 75¢, or more.

But:

➤ This is still a high-rent district.

➤ It's tougher to manage without a car.

U.S. 192/Kissimmee

This once-sleepy city is actually closer to Walt Disney World than Orlando is. The highway is lined shoulder to shoulder with hotels, attractions, and restaurants—many of them priced for us Joe Six-Packers. Yet the city also offers historic neighborhoods and nice folks who were born and grew up here.

In a nutshell:

➤ You can't beat the price for a room.

➤ Restaurants and other services are priced to match.

➤ Many hotels offer shuttle service to the theme parks.

But:

➤ You'll need a car.

➤ Your vacation clock ticks on while you're sitting in traffic.

➤ Fast-food joints and gas stations aren't a pretty sight.

International Drive Area

This is the nerve center of the greater Orlando attractions area. It's convenient to all of the theme parks including Sea World and Universal Studios. There's some schlock, but at these real-estate prices only the better restaurants, hotels, and attractions stick around very long.

In a nutshell:

➤ It's convenient to theme parks, shopping, the airport, and I-4.

➤ This classy area (at least the area that's south of Sand Lake Road) captures the upbeat theme-park mood without hitting you over the head with a sledgehammer.

➤ You don't need a car because there's a shuttle among the hotels and eateries and many hotels offer shuttles to theme parks.

But:

➤ Big events at the Convention Center congest the area.

➤ Crooks love this area because tourists let down their guard. Keep your wits about you if you stay or even visit there.

Downtown

Believe it or not, Orlando was a city before that mouse moved in. Downtown is an increasingly vibrant neighborhood, with countless bars, restaurants, coffeehouses, and a nighttime theme park for adults, Church Street Station.

In a nutshell:

➤ It's convenient to museums, sports events, and cultural performances.

➤ Downtown Orlando is very attractive due to pretty lakes, parks, and green spaces.

➤ There are more full-service hotels catering to business travelers and devoid of over-the-top themes.

But:

➤ Pockets of sleaze and crime are problems.

➤ It's difficult to manage without a car.

➤ Much of downtown doesn't have the look of shiny newness found in the attractions area.

➤ And it takes 40 minutes (more during the wicked traffic hours) to reach the parks.

The Price Is Right

The **rack rate** is the maximum rate that a hotel charges for a room. It's the rate you'd get if you walked in off the street and asked for a room for the night. It's also the rate on the card posted on the back of your hotel room door, unless some spring breakers took it home as a souvenir.

But *you don't have to pay it.* Hardly anyone does. Just ask whether there's a discounted or better rate. In most cases you'll get one.

Room rates usually depend on many factors, not the least of which is how you make your reservation. A travel agent may be able to negotiate a better price with certain hotels than you could get by yourself because the hotel gives the agent a special discount.

Reserving a room through the hotel's 800-number, rather than calling the hotel directly, may also result in a lower rate. On the other hand, the central reservations number may not know about discount rates at specific locations. For example, local franchises may offer a special group rate for a wedding or family reunion, but they may neglect to tell the central booking line. Your best bet is to call the local number *and* the 800-number and see which one gives you a better deal.

Dollars & Sense

Be sure to mention membership in AAA, AARP, frequent-flyer programs, and any other corporate rewards program when you make your reservation. You never know when it might be worth a few dollars off your room rate.

Room rates also change with the season, and as occupancy rates rise and fall. If a hotel is close to full, it is less likely to extend discount rates; if it's close to empty, it may be willing to negotiate. Some resorts offer midweek specials; some downtown hotels offer cheaper weekend rates.

Room prices are subject to change without notice, so even the rates quoted in this book may be different from the actual rate you receive when you make your reservation.

About Our Price Categories

Orlando is inexpensive when compared to New York or San Francisco. Sure, you can pay $1,500 a night for a suite in one of the better hotels, but there are tons of bargains begging for you to find them and you'll generally get good value for your money here.

We're going to use these breakdowns:

$$$$$	=	$250 and up
$$$$	=	$200 to $250
$$$	=	$100 to $200
$$	=	$50 to $100
$	=	under $50

What Do You Get for Your Money?

It starts with location. You pay a premium for staying in Walt Disney World, but you may save the difference because you don't have to rent a car and pay the daily parking fee in the theme parks. (See "Should I Bunk with Mickey?" later in this chapter.) Rooms with "water views" aren't worth the extra money. Actually, they're a joke by Florida standards. The ocean is miles away, and there is no pristine river running through Orlando, so rooms with "water views" mean you're overlooking (a) a small lake, (b) a retention pond, or (c) the hotel sprinkler system. In other words, don't waste the money. Rooms overlooking nightly fireworks at one of several theme parks may be worth a few extra dollars if it means you can watch them from the privacy of your own balcony.

Hotels without restaurants are cheaper, but they're inconvenient unless you have a car, or the hotel is within walking distance of affordable restaurants. It's also a plus if your hotel sits on a free shuttle or trolley line. You should inquire if it has an airport shuttle available. No sense paying if you don't have to.

Most hotels are priced for two people, so if you're a single or a family, extra homework is in order. Some hotel rates are the same for one to four people in a room, while other hotels charge extra per person for more than double occupancy, although young children may sleep free in their parents' room.

Dollars & Sense

A kitchenette may cost only a few dollars extra per day, but it can buy you big savings if you make your own breakfasts, lunches, and snacks.

Also, keep in mind that everything at the priciest hotels is expensive: restaurants, room service, telephone calls, children's programs, and even that glass of cold beer you order at the pool bar. This snowballs when you add a 15% tip and the sales tax. Don't pop for the most expensive hotel unless you have a champagne budget for everything else, too.

Finding Bargains

Just when you think you have high season and low season figured out, you find out that Orlando hotels are full because of some convention or event you never heard of. Generally, though, the area's hotel rates rise and fall according to school vacations, which in turn determine when most families are free to travel.

Heaviest times are summer, Easter and spring break, Christmas week, and holiday weekends. But there's a lot of wiggle room, because school holidays vary from state to state, and even country to country (don't forget that children from Europe, Asia, and South America are some of Mickey Mouse's biggest fans).

At most WDW hotels, there are three different rate seasons, which vary slightly from year to year. Roughly, they are as listed here:

Low season (a.k.a. Value Pricing)	January 1 to February 6 and August 24 to December 17
Regular rates	February 7 to March 20 and April 3 to August 23
High season (a.k.a. Holiday Pricing)	March 21 to April 2 and December 18 to 31

Note that at deluxe resorts like Disney's BoardWalk Inn, Disney's BoardWalk Villas, Disney's Old Key West, and the Villas at the Disney Institute, Value Pricing season begins 6 weeks earlier (roughly July 5).

Non-Disney hotels tend to mirror these rate seasons, but you never know when a downtown convention or a special event in a nearby city (like the Daytona 500) can play havoc with rates and availability.

If you're quoted what seems like a really high rate, be flexible and try another set of dates. You may be pleasantly shocked at the difference a few days can make.

Taxes & Service Charges

There is a state sales tax of 6% on all hotel rooms, restaurant meals, and bar drinks. In addition, Orange County (Orlando, Winter Park, Maitland) levies a 5% bed tax on hotel rooms, bringing the total tax to 11%. In Osceola County (Kissimmee–St. Cloud), the bed tax is 6%, thus doubling the tax on a hotel room.

What Kind of Place Is Right for You?

No matter where you stay in Orlando, especially in the attractions area, it's likely that whimsy and mouse ears will play a big role. Even the regal Peabody, one of the finest hotels in the South, has real ducks swimming in its lobby fountain just for the fun of it. Just as gaming motifs rule in places like Las Vegas and Atlantic City, Orlando's hotels never stray far from the magic.

But there's more variety here than you may have guessed. Orlando has a number of B&Bs, two hostels, campgrounds, cabins, fish camps, condos, time shares, and chain hotels and motels that don't cater to theme-park travelers. The sources we list in chapter 1 will be glad to supply lists of offbeat lodgings that are not covered here.

This book, however, assumes that you're coming for a typical Orlando vacation. The hotels we recommend are listed to give you the widest possible variety of price ranges and locations close to the attractions area.

Bet You Didn't Know

Disney employees appearing in costume as the Kingdom's most famous cartoon characters, such as Mickey and Minnie, are not allowed to speak as they meet park visitors. That's because your child would immediately know that the voice was wrong.

Should I Bunk with Mickey?

Inside Walt Disney World, there are 15 WDW-owned hotels and nine under private ownership that are designated as "official" hotels. They come in every price range (including a campground) and have significant benefits over staying outside the World. If Disney is high on your list of vacation priorities (or your kids' list of priorities), it might make sense to stay in the Mouse's house.

Here's why:

➤ You get unlimited free transportation (which would cost $6 to $12 per person per day at many hotels) to and from all Disney parks as well as to a variety of other Disney attractions.

➤ You're guaranteed admission to all the parks, even when all the parking lots are full.

➤ If you rent a car, you can park it free in any WDW lot.

➤ You can arrange for Disney characters to show up for meals with your kids at several hotel restaurants.

➤ You get preferred tee times at any of the Disney golf courses.

➤ At the higher-end resorts, villas, and campgrounds (except the Dolphin), you get charge privileges throughout the World.

➤ And here's a real biggie: They let you into all four major parks 90 minutes before everybody else on alternating days of the week. So if you can roll the family out of bed early, you can enjoy the facilities, and stay relatively free of crowds.

The best place to start looking for info on a Disney hotel is the **Central Reservations Operations,** P.O. Box 10000, Lake Buena Vista, FL 32830-1000 (☎ **407/W-DISNEY** [that's 934-7639]), which is open Monday through Friday 8am to 10pm, Saturday and Sunday 9am to 6pm. They can recommend a hotel that will fit your plans and budget.

Family Ties: Hotel Strategies for Families Traveling with Kids

Most Orlando hotels adore children and fall all over themselves to create a vacation that will keep the kids begging to come back. We've marked the most kid-friendly hotels with a special icon. Even so, you can expect almost any Orlando hotel to give your kids the red-carpet treatment.

The most common room configuration contains two double beds, which can be crowded for a family of four. "Kids sleep free in your room," means in existing bedding; a crib or roll-away bed may cost extra, so ask explicitly.

If you want more privacy, or separate beds for older children, think about getting a suite. At many of the all-suite hotels, for the price of a double room, you get a double (or queen or king) bedroom, one bath, a living room with sofa bed, and televisions and tele-phones in each room. However, in most one-bedroom suites, guests sleeping on the sofa bed can't get to the bathroom without walking through the bedroom. Ask when you reserve whether this is the case.

Usually, a two-bedroom villa or suite has a master bedroom with its own bathroom, and a second bathroom that is shared by the second bedroom and the people who are sleeping on the sofa bed in the living room.

Some other tips: Compare costs for super-vised children's play programs. Are they just day care, or do they offer evening hours so Mom and Dad can have a night out? Do kids eat free or at discounted rates? Is a special children's menu avail-able? Is the dining room child-friendly? Is room service available for those times

Bet You Didn't Know

Walt Disney built Disneyland in Anaheim, California, in 1955, and it quickly became one of the most popular tourist attractions in the country. However, though he conceived Disney World and initiated its plan, he didn't live to see his Florida parks open; the Magic Kingdom opened its gate in 1971, 6 years after Walt passed away.

when the kids are fussy and you just want a simple meal in privacy? Are there plenty of low-priced noshes available? (Show me the food court.) How about a refrigerator where you can keep juices, milk, and sodas so you're not spending a fortune just for drinks? Do rooms have microwaves? Is there a kiddy pool or a playground where the kids can burn off excess energy?

Older offspring aren't forgotten in Orlando, where hotels commonly offer VCRs, video rental, in-room video games or an on-site video arcade, bicycle rental, and other treats for hard-to-please teens and preteens.

Tourist Traps

It's likely that you'll be approached at a tourist attraction, park, or beach by a time-share huckster who offers an attractive premium (such as free tickets to a theme park) if you'll listen to a spiel. Decide what your time is worth, because they'll take a good chunk of it. Also, you'll see a lot of promotions around the area that say you can get cheap tickets—for example, two Disney tickets for $20 each when the going rate is more than $40 apiece. Beware: This, too, is a time-share tactic. Salesmen and women at these places range from aggressive to human, but even the latter steal 2 to 3 hours of your time before it's over.

What If I Didn't Plan Ahead?

If you arrive without a reservation during high season, well, good luck, but you're probably out of it. You might find something in the area with the help of the **Official Visitor Center,** 8723 International Dr., Suite 101, Orlando, FL 32819 (☎ **407/363-5872**), which is open 8am to 8pm every day except Christmas. It offers discount ticket sales, free brochures, information in many different languages, and free assistance in finding last-minute lodgings. From I-4, exit onto Sand Lake Road, go east to International Drive, turn right and go about half a mile, and look for the Official Visitor Center on your right.

Exceedingly helpful, too, is the **Kissimmee–St. Cloud Convention & Visitors Bureau** (☎ **800/333-KISS** or 407/847-5000). Call them from the airport if you need a room.

Extra! Extra!

Most of the areas in Orlando have grown too crowded for seven-digit dialing. As of December 1, 1999, callers in Orlando, Kissimmee St. Cloud, and other parts of Orlando, Osceola and Seminole counties, will have to dial 10 digits—407 + the seven-digit local number. You don't need a "1" before the area code unless you are making a long-distance call from *outside* this zone.

Getting the Best Room

Somebody has to get the best room in the house. It might as well be you.

Always ask for a corner room. They're usually larger, quieter, and closer to the elevator, which can be important if you're above the ground floor. They often have more windows and light than standard rooms, and they don't always cost more. So ask.

When you make your reservation, ask if the hotel is renovating. If it is, request a room away from the renovation work. Many hotels now offer nonsmoking rooms; by all means ask for one if you don't smoke or if smoke or its stale odor bothers you. Inquire, too, about the location of restaurants, bars, and discos in the hotel—these could all be a source of irritating noise. In any case, check out your room before you unpack. Then ask for another room if you don't like the one assigned to you. Most hotels are willing to accommodate you on this unless they're packed.

A Word About Smoking

Florida law permits smoking only in certain places. As a result, many public areas, including the airport, are now entirely smoke-free. Most hotels offer no-smoking rooms or floors; be sure to request your choice when you book.

Hotels A to Z

Okay, this is it—it's time to choose your place to snooze.

We're going to get things rolling with some lists that break down the best hotels by neighborhood and price. Then we'll review each of them, giving you all of the information you need to decide the place that's best for you.

If you're like most travelers, you really don't want to read about every hotel in Orlando. Get a life, right? Only travel writers and others missing several chromosomes would want to do something like that. You're normal; you want somebody else to wade through all of the minutiae, pick out the best ones, then arrange them according to location and price range. Well, that's where we come in—we're chromosomally challenged. We're also getting paid to do a mess of things normal folks don't give a flip about doing—like scouting hundreds of places to stay in Orlando. We've whittled them to the best—a few dozen—so you don't have to waste your time reading reviews of places we're not enthusiastic about.

The reviews are arranged alphabetically and each hotel's location appears under its name—check the locations against the maps to give yourself a solid idea of where the hotels are in relation to where you want to be and what you want to see.

As far as price goes, we've noted rack rates in the listings and also preceded each entry with a dollar-sign icon to make quick reference easier. The more dollar signs under the name, the more you pay. But note that these are general guidelines used primarily for comparison. In some seasons, packages, or discount deals, you can stay in **$$$$** hotels for **$$** rates. You also can find **$$$$** rooms and suites in some **$** and **$$** hotels. Rates are per room, based on double occupancy. It runs like this:

$$$$$	=	$250 and up
$$$$	=	$200 to $250
$$$	=	$100 to $200
$$	=	$50 to $100
$	=	under $50

Parking is free pretty much everywhere, so we haven't wasted your time by noting that over and over on every listing.

Kids We've also added a "kid-friendly" icon to those hotels that are especially good for families, though just about all of these places make a special effort to welcome young 'uns. We've also included special features throughout called "Extra! Extra!" that will direct you to the best hotels for those of you with special considerations in mind.

Hint: As you read through the reviews, keep track of the ones that appeal to you. We've included a chart at the end of this chapter where you can rank your preferences, but to make matters easier on yourself now, why don't you just put a little check mark next to the ones you like or dog-ear the page if you want? Remember how your teachers used to threaten you with boiling oil or some other hideous form of punishment if you wrote in your books or bent the page corners? Well, the heck with them. You own this puppy! Do it if it makes you feel warm and fuzzy.

Quick Picks: Orlando's Hotels at a Glance
Hotel Index by Location

Walt Disney World

Disney Institute $$$$$

Disney's All-Star Movie Resort $$

Disney's All-Star Music Resort $$

Disney's All-Star Sports Resort $$

Disney's Beach Club Resort $$$$$

Disney's BoardWalk Inn & Villas $$$$$

Disney's Caribbean Beach Resort $$$

Disney's Contemporary Resort $$$$

Disney's Coronado Springs Resort $$$

Disney's Dixie Landings Resort $$$

Disney's Fort Wilderness Resort and Campground $–$$$$

Disney's Grand Floridian Beach Resort $$$$$

Disney's Old Key West Resort
$$$$$

Disney's Polynesian Resort
$$$$$

Disney's Port Orleans Resort
$$$

Disney's Wilderness Lodge
$$$–$$$$

Disney's Yacht Club Resort
$$$$$

Walt Disney World Dolphin
$$$$$

Walt Disney World Swan
$$$$$

Lake Buena Vista (includes Official Disney Hotels)

Doubletree Guest Suites Resort
$$$

Grand Cypress Resort (Villas)
$$$$$

Grosvenor Resort $$$–$$$$

Hilton at Walt Disney World
Village $$$–$$$$$

Holiday Inn Sunspree Resort
$$–$$$

Hyatt Regency Grand Cypress
Resort $$$$–$$$$$

Perri House Bed & Breakfast
$$–$$$

Wyndham Palace Resort
$$$–$$$$

Wyndham Safari Resort $$$

U.S. 192/Kissimmee

Best Western Kissimmee $$

Comfort Inn Maingate $

Days Inn Eastgate $$

Econo Lodge Maingate
East $

Holiday Inn Hotel & Suites
Main Gate East $$–$$$

Holiday Inn Nikki Bird Resort
$$

Homewood Suites Maingate
$$$

Howard Johnson
Inn–Maingate East $$

Super Eight Motel $–$$

International Drive Area

Castle Doubletree Hotel $$$

Country Hearth Inn $$

Orlando Marriott $$$

Peabody Orlando $$$$$

Radisson Twin Towers $$$

Summerfield Suites $$$$

Wellesley Inn Orlando
$$–$$$

Downtown Orlando

Best Western Orlando West
$$

Harley of Orlando $$$

Radisson Plaza Hotel Orlando
$$$

Near Orlando International Airport

Renaissance Orlando
Hotel–Airport $$$

Campgrounds & RV Resorts in Kissimmee

Kissimmee/Orlando KOA $

Raccoon Lake Camp Resort $

Near North Orlando

Higgins House Bed and
Breakfast $$$

Meadow Marsh Bed and
Breakfast $$$

67

Hotel Index by Price Category

$$$$$ ($250 and up)

Disney Institute (Walt Disney World)

Disney's Beach Club Resort (Walt Disney World)

Disney's BoardWalk Inn & Villas (Walt Disney World)

Disney's Grand Floridian Beach Resort (Walt Disney World)

Disney's Old Key West Resort (Walt Disney World)

Disney's Polynesian Resort (Walt Disney World)

Disney's Yacht Club Resort (Walt Disney World)

Grand Cypress Resort (Lake Buena Vista)

Grosvenor Resort (Lake Buena Vista/Official Disney Hotel)

Hyatt Regency Grand Cypress Resort (Lake Buena Vista)

Peabody Orlando (International Drive Area)

Walt Disney World Dolphin (Walt Disney World)

Walt Disney World Swan (Walt Disney World)

$$$$ ($200 to $250)

Disney's Contemporary Resort (Walt Disney World)

Disney's Wilderness Lodge (Walt Disney World)

Grosvenor Resort (Lake Buena Vista/Official Disney Hotel)

Hilton at Walt Disney World Village (Lake Buena Vista/Official Disney Hotel)

Hyatt Regency Grand Cypress Resort (Lake Buena Vista)

Summerfield Suites (International Drive Area)

Wyndham Palace Resort (Lake Buena Vista/Official Disney Hotel)

$$$ ($100 to $200)

Buena Vista Palace Resort & Spa (Lake Buena Vista/Official Disney Hotel)

Castle Doubletree Hotel (International Drive Area)

Disney's Caribbean Beach Resort (Walt Disney World)

Disney's Coronado Springs Resort (Walt Disney World)

Disney's Dixie Landings Resort (Walt Disney World)

Disney's Port Orleans Resort (Walt Disney World)

Disney's Wilderness Lodge (Walt Disney World)

Doubletree Guest Suites Resort (Lake Buena Vista/Official Disney Hotel)

Grosvenor Resort (Lake Buena Vista/Official Disney Hotel)

Harley of Orlando (Downtown Orlando)

Higgins House Bed and Breakfast (near North Orlando)

Holiday Inn Hotel & Suites Main Gate East (U.S. 192/Kissimmee)

Holiday Inn Sunspree Resort (Lake Buena Vista)

Homewood Suites Maingate (U.S. 192/Kissimmee)

Meadow Marsh Bed and Breakfast (Near North Orlando)

Orlando Marriott (International Drive Area)

Perri House Bed and Breakfast (Lake Buena Vista)

Radisson Plaza Hotel Orlando (Downtown Orlando)

Radisson Twin Towers (International Drive Area)

Renaissance Orlando Hotel–Airport (Near Airport)

Wellesley Inn Orlando (International Drive Area)

Wyndham Safari Resort (Lake Buena Vista)

$$ ($50 to $100)

Best Western Kissimmee (U.S. 192/Kissimmee)

Best Western Orlando West (Downtown Orlando)

Comfort Inn Maingate (U.S. 192/ Kissimmee)

Country Hearth Inn (International Drive Area)

Days Inn Eastgate (U.S. 192/Kissimmee)

Disney's All-Star Movie Resort (Walt Disney World)

Disney's All-Star Music Resort (Walt Disney World)

Disney's All-Star Sports Resort (Walt Disney World)

Holiday Inn Hotel & Suites Main Gate East (U.S. 192/Kissimmee)

Holiday Inn Nikki Bird Resort (U.S. 192/Kissimmee)

Holiday Inn Sunspree Resort (Lake Buena Vista)

Howard Johnson Inn–Maingate East (U.S. 192/Kissimmee)

Perri House Bed and Breakfast (Lake Buena Vista)

Super Eight Motel (U.S. 192/Kissimmee)

Wellesley Inn Orlando (International Drive Area)

$ (under $50)

Comfort Inn Maingate (U.S. 192/Kissimmee)

Econo Lodge Maingate East (U.S. 192/Kissimmee)

Kissimmee/Orlando KOA (U.S. 192/Kissimmee)

Raccoon Lake Camp Resort (U.S. 192/Kissimmee)

Super Eight Motel (U.S. 192/Kissimmee)

$–$$$$

Disney's Fort Wilderness Resort and Campground (Walt Disney World). Campsites are in the $ category. For $$$$ you can get a "cabin" that sleeps up to six and has a full kitchen and bath.

Surfin' Safari

Don't you hate arriving at your long-awaited dream vacation only to find you've booked your family into Chateau Flea Bag? Your spouse is calling you Scrooge, the children are screaming for a pool, and you're so far from the Magic Kingdom you'd have to change time zones to get there. Well, there's a

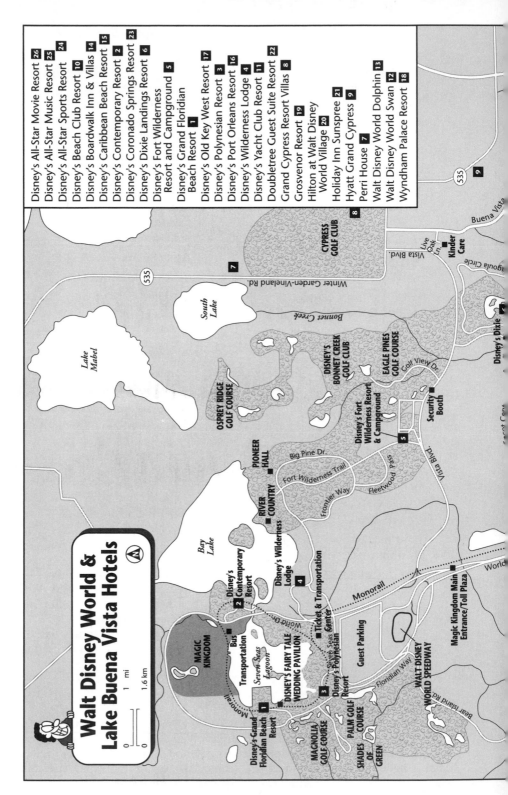

Walt Disney World & Lake Buena Vista Hotels

Disney's All-Star Movie Resort **26**
Disney's All-Star Music Resort **25**
Disney's All-Star Sports Resort **24**
Disney's Beach Club Resort **10**
Disney's Boardwalk Inn & Villas **14**
Disney's Caribbean Beach Resort **15**
Disney's Contemporary Resort **2**
Disney's Coronado Springs Resort **23**
Disney's Dixie Landings Resort **6**
Disney's Fort Wilderness Resort and Campground **5**
Disney's Grand Floridian Beach Resort **1**
Disney's Old Key West Resort **17**
Disney's Polynesian Resort **3**
Disney's Port Orleans Resort **16**
Disney's Wilderness Lodge **4**
Disney's Yacht Club Resort **11**
Doubletree Guest Suite Resort **22**
Grand Cypress Resort Villas **8**
Grosvenor Resort **19**
Hilton at Walt Disney World Village **20**
Holiday Inn Sunspree **21**
Hyatt Grand Cypress **9**
Perri House **7**
Walt Disney World Dolphin **13**
Walt Disney World Swan **12**
Wyndham Palace Resort **18**

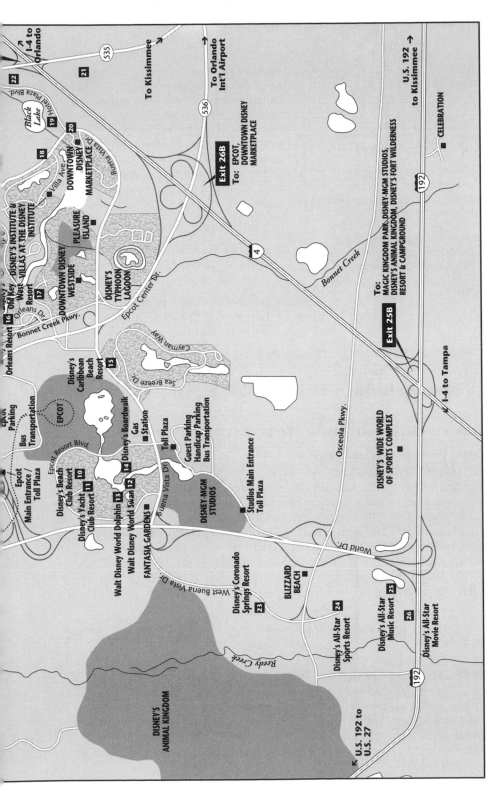

Extra! Extra!

Disney resort guests get an added benefit: The theme parks open 90 minutes early for resort guests on a rotating basis. Monday, Thursday, and Saturday it's the Magic Kingdom; Tuesday and Friday it's Epcot; Sunday and Wednesday it's Disney–MGM Studios.

way to take some of the risk out of the game of room roulette. If you can get on the Internet, you can get a glimpse of most of the hotels and campgrounds in this area. Many provide pictures of their lodging along with information on distances to area attractions, and the availability of amenities. Here are a few sites (and telephone numbers) to get you started.

➤ **Go Orlando**   www.go2orlando.com/

➤ **Florida Hotels and Discount Guide** ☎ **888/729-7705;** www.flhotels.com/orlando/caribe.html

➤ **Discount Lodging on the Internet** ☎ **877/766-6787;** www.discounthotelsamerica.com/

➤ **Resort Marketing** ☎ **800/204-5593** or 407/532-1544; www.rmitravel.com/

➤ **Discount Hotels**   www.smarterliving.com

Our Favorite Orlando Hotels from A to Z

Best Western Kissimmee
$$. U.S. 192/Kissimmee.
Location is the selling point for this full-service hotel, which is close to many of the major attractions. Specials include rooms for as low as $35 a night subject to availability. The trimmings include a nine-hole golf course, two pools, a tiki bar, Kicker's Pub, and breakfast and dinner buffets in a family-style restaurant where kids 10 and under eat free with one paying adult. Transportation to Walt Disney World, Animal Kingdom, MGM Studios, and EPCOT is available for a fee, as are van and limo service from Orlando International Airport.

2261 E. Irlo Bronson Memorial Hwy. (U.S. 192). ☎ *888/511-7081 or 407/ 846-2221. Fax 407/846-1095.* **Rack rates:** *$49.95–$59.95 standard double. AE, DISC, MC, V.*

Best Western Orlando West
$$. Downtown Orlando.
This two-story garden-style and family owned hotel is 8 miles from Universal and 2 miles from Church Street Station. For eats there's the Celebrity Deli, which offers huge deli-style sandwiches and daily lunch specials. Other amenities include a pool, guest laundry, and free cable television. Pets are accepted for a small deposit.

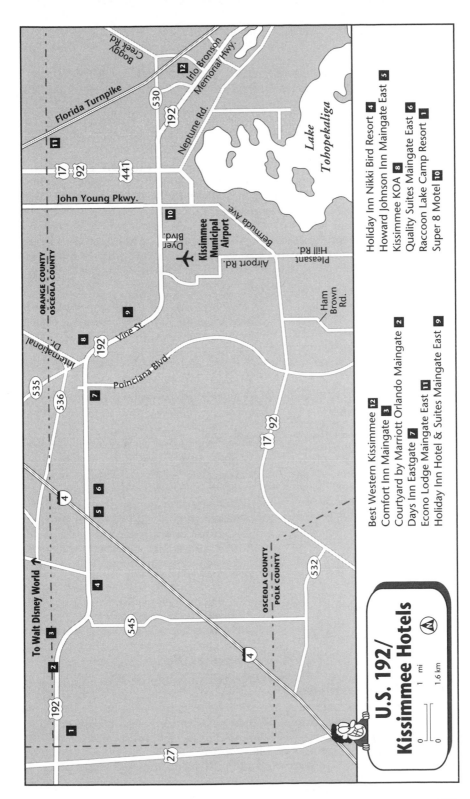

U.S. 192/
Kissimmee Hotels

1 mi
1.6 km

Best Western Kissimmee **12**
Comfort Inn Maingate **3**
Courtyard by Marriott Orlando Maingate **2**
Days Inn Eastgate **7**
Econo Lodge Maingate East **11**
Holiday Inn Hotel & Suites Maingate East **9**

Holiday Inn Nikki Bird Resort **4**
Howard Johnson Inn Maingate East **5**
Kissimmee KOA **8**
Quality Suites Maingate East **6**
Raccoon Lake Camp Resort **1**
Super 8 Motel **10**

2014 W. Colonial Dr. ☎ ***800/528-1234*** *or 407/841-8600. Fax 407/843-7080.*
Rack rates: *$59–$79 standard double. Discounts for AAA and seniors. AE, CB, DC, DISC, MC, V.*

Castle Doubletree Hotel

$$$. International Drive.

The Castle is a midsize hotel (216 rooms and suites) with architecture that resembles a storybook castle. The lobby boasts European art and mosaic tile murals. Piped-in sounds of chirping birds greet you at the entrance. Beware of the gargoyle beast that loves to greet guests as they enter the lobby. In-room features include a minibar, a large television with a Sony Play Station, a minirefrigerator, a coffeemaker, and three telephones. A courtyard surrounds a medium-size round pool with a fountain constructed of a trio of fish as the base. Café Tu Tu Tango and Austin's Steakhouse will satisfy almost any hunger.

8629 International Dr. ☎ ***407/345-1511.***
Rack rates: *$119–$210. Discounts for AAA, AARP, corporate, and military. AE, DC, DISC, MC, V.*

Extra! Extra!

Disney has added another to its list of All-Star Resorts. The newest is the All-Star Movie Resort that opened early in 1999. This newcomer raised the total number of All-Star rooms to 5,760. The resort features a Mickmongus Buzz Lightyear and other three-to four-story Disney characters including the Mighty Ducks, the Love Bug, and 101 Dalmatians. The resort has two pools, one with a Fantasia theme, and the other with a hockey theme.

Comfort Inn Maingate

$–$$. U.S. 192/Kissimmee.

Only a mile from the main entrance to the Magic Kingdom, you can have a clean, comfortable (though typically plain vanilla) motel room, with little extras, such as the coffeemaker and refrigerator, adding a touch of home. A Waffle House is across the street. Opt for a garden room overlooking the gazebo for a surprisingly pretty setting at rock-bottom rates. Discounted WDW tickets are available; round-trip transportation to the parks is $7.

7571 W. Irlo Bronson Memorial Hwy. (U.S. 192). ☎ ***800/221-2222*** *or 407/ 396-7500. Fax 407/396-7497.* ***Rack rates:*** *$45–$99 double. AE, CB, DC, DISC, JCB, MC, V.*

Country Hearth Inn

$$. International Drive.

I-Drive is the high-rent district, but here's an amazing deal. It's a homey, hospitable hotel in the heart of the attraction action, just across the street from the convention center. Combine country decor with a pool, room refrigerators, ceiling fans, and a private patio or balcony, and you've got a winner for skinflint travelers. Deluxe rooms have sofa beds, hair dryers, microwaves, and coffeemakers. The weekly wine-and-cheese parties, the free continental breakfast, and features such as room service and free HBO put this in the Best Buy category. Discounted WDW tickets are available; a shuttle to WDW parks is $10. The restaurant is modestly priced; the Front Porch lounge serves up happy-hour prices from 5:30 to 7pm.

9861 International Dr., between the Bee Line Expressway and Sand Lake Rd. ☎ ***800/447-1890*** *or 407/352-0008. Fax 407/352-5449.* **Rack rates:** *$89–$139 double. Extra person $10. Children under 18 stay free in parents' room. AE, CB, DC, DISC, MC, V.*

Extra! Extra!

If you're traveling with kids, you're in the right landing zone. Orlando is the most kid-friendly destination on the planet. We've singled out those hotels with the most exceptional children's programs, but it's hard to go wrong. Just about all the hotels and motels in the area go all out for families. The **hotels in Walt Disney World** are in a class by themselves. All of them are ideal for children. In addition to the Disney hotels, our top picks are the **Doubletree Guest Suites Resort** (Lake Buena Vista; $$$), the **Hilton at Walt Disney World Village** (Lake Buena Vista; $$$–$$$$$),the **Holiday Inn Hotel & Suites Main Gate East** (U.S. 192/Kissimmee; $$–$$$), the **Homewood Suites Maingate** (U.S. 192/Kissimmee; $$$), and the **Holiday Inn Sunspree Resort** (Lake Buena Vista; $$–$$$).

Days Inn Eastgate
$$. U.S. 192/Kissimmee.

You're in the heart of theme-park country here. Balconies overlook the swimming pool. A picnic area and a children's play area are on the grounds. A cafe is open for breakfast; other restaurants are a short drive away. Discount tickets to attractions are available; a shuttle to the WDW parks is $7 round-trip.

5245 W. Irlo Bronson Memorial Hwy. (U.S. 192), between Poinciana and Polynesian Isle blvds. ☎ ***800/423-3864*** *or 407/396-7700. Fax 407/396-0293.* **Rack rates:** *$59–$89 for up to 4 people. Higher rates during special events. AE, CB, DC, DISC, JCB, MC, V.*

Disney Institute
$$$$$. Walt Disney World.

The Disney Institute offers learning vacations and educational enrichment programs through a series of hands-on activities that run the spectrum from computer animation to rock climbing and photography. It also offers a full-service spa and expert fitness personnel in the gym. The accommodations range from bungalows to three-bedroom grand villas. All have kitchens or kitchenettes. The Institute's restaurant is called Seasons.

1960 Magnolia Way, Lake Buena Vista. ☎ **800/496-6337** *or 407/827-1100. Fax 407/827-4100.* **Rack rates:** *$204–$1,475 per room. AE, MC, V.*

Dollars & Sense

According to the latest available figures, hotel rates are highest in March, when they average about $85, and lowest in August, when they average about $70. Year-round, the average daily rate is just over $75.

 ### Disney's All-Star Movie Resort
$$. Walt Disney World.

Larger than life-sized Disney movie favorites decorate the exterior of the newest All-Star Resort. Two pools, a kids' area, an outdoor bar, a food court with movie marquees, a gift shop, and an arcade are among the features.

1901 W. Buena Vista Dr. ☎ **407/W-DIS-NEY** *or 407/939-7000. Fax 407/ 939-7111.* **Rack rates:** *$74–$104 double. Children under 18 stay free in parents' room. Extra charge for additional adults nightly. AE, MC, V.*

Disney's All-Star Music Resort
$$. Walt Disney World.

This is a good value if you want to stay on a WDW-owned property. In this thoroughly music-themed resort, you'll find lots of young people (including entire school bands), sardine-size rooms (about 260 square feet), and round-the-clock good times. The kids, including teenagers, will love the ambiance here. Who cares if you don't have 24-hour room service? Rooms, though small, are comfortable; rates are rock-bottom, and the swimming pools are supersize. Dine in the food court, play the video arcade, or walk to the near-by pinewoods. Even though children under 18 stay in your room free, we'd suggest getting two rooms unless you've shrunk the kids.

1801 W. Buena Vista Dr., at World Dr. and Osceola Pkwy. ☎ **407/W-DISNEY** *or 407/939-6000. Fax 407/354-1866. www.disneyworld.com.* **Rack rates:** *$74–$104 double. Children under 18 stay free in parents' room. Extra charge for additional adults nightly. AE, MC, V.*

Disney's All-Star Sports Resort
$$. Walt Disney World.

Substitute a sports theme and this place is practically a clone of the All-Star Music Resort. The sports motif is so captivating and complete that your little pitcher will love it. Again, two rooms are definitely better than one for a family of four or more, cutting into the price advantage. One of the big swimming pools has a baseball theme; the other has a surfer motif. Room

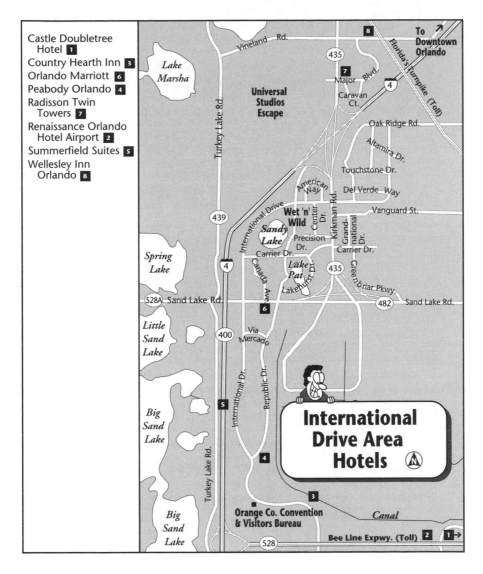

Castle Doubletree
  Hotel **1**
Country Hearth Inn **3**
Orlando Marriott **6**
Peabody Orlando **4**
Radisson Twin
  Towers **7**
Renaissance Orlando
  Hotel Airport **2**
Summerfield Suites **5**
Wellesley Inn
  Orlando **8**

Lake
Marsha

Universal
Studios
Escape

To
Downtown
Orlando

Vineland Rd.

Florida's Turnpike (Toll)

435

Major Blvd.

4

Caravan
Ct.

Oak Ridge Rd.

Altamira Dr.

Touchstone Dr.

Del Verde Way

Vanguard St.

American Way

Kirkman Rd.

Grand national Dr.

Turkey Lake Rd.

439

International Drive

Wet 'n'
Wild

Center Dr.

Sandy
Lake

Precision
Dr.

Carrier Dr.

Carrier Dr.

Greenbriar Pkwy.

Spring
Lake

4

Canada Ave.

Lake
Pat

435

Lakehurst Dr.

482

Sand Lake Rd.

528A Sand Lake Rd.

6

Little
Sand
Lake

400

Via
Mercado

Big
Sand
Lake

International Dr.

Republic Dr.

5

International
Drive Area
Hotels Ⓐ

4

3

Big
Sand
Lake

Orange Co. Convention
& Visitors Bureau

Canal

528

Bee Line Expwy. (Toll) **2** **1**→

service is available for pizza only, but there are lots of meal choices available
in the food court.

1701 W. Buena Vista Dr., at World Dr. and Osceola Pkwy. ☎ *407/W-DISNEY
or 407/939-5000. Fax 407/354-1866. www.disneyworld.com.* **Rack rates:**
*$74–$104 double. Children under 18 stay free in parents' room. Extra charge for
additional adults nightly. AE, MC, V.*

Disney's Beach Club Resort
Kids   *$$$$$. Walt Disney World.*
Picture yourself in a swank, turn-of-the-century New England resort next to
the local yacht club. The 25-acre lake, which serves as the pool, seems as big
as the Atlantic (sans sharks, of course); the gardens picture perfect. Spacious
rooms have two queen-size beds or a king and a double. You'll also have an

in-room safe, a ceiling fan, an extra telephone in the bath, and decor bright-ly done in blonde wood and pastels. Ask for a room with a balcony overlook-ing the water. You can order from 24-hour room service, have a clambake in the Cape May Café, or book a Disney-character breakfast.

1800 Epcot Resorts Blvd., off Buena Vista Dr. ☎ ***407/W-DISNEY** or 407/ 934-8000. www.disneyworld.com.* **Rack rates:** *$264–$350 double, depending on the view and the season. Children under 17 stay free in parents' room. AE, MC, V.*

Extra! Extra!

If you're looking for a romantic getaway or the perfect spot for a honeymoon, consider a spa package at the **Wyndham Palace Resort** (Lake Buena Vista; $$$–$$$$), where you can also have a romantic dinner at Arthur's 27. At **Disney's Grand Floridian Beach Resort** (Walt Disney World; $$$$$), you can book a king-size room, enjoy some decadent spa treatments, and have a candlelit dinner one night in the fabulously romantic (though wickedly expensive) Victoria and Albert's. The **Peabody Orlando** (International Drive; $$$$$) provides all the pampering a couple needs for a romantic recharge. Surprise your partner by ordering a VIP turndown. (It's not just mints on the pillow but something fabulous like chocolate-covered strawberries, milk and cookies, or two tiny bottles of a special liqueur.) For lovebirds on a more mod-est budget, the **Harley of Orlando** (Downtown; $$) provides a nostalgic flight to the 1940s. Ask about special weekend packages. At the **Grand Cypress Resort** (Lake Buena Vista; $$$$$), newlyweds will find a more inti-mate alternative in lodging. Hidden in natural surroundings with golf, tennis, and an equestrian center, the resort will customize individual packages.

 ## Disney's BoardWalk Inn & Villas
$$$$$. *Walt Disney World.*

Atlantic City in its heyday would never match this complex's "seaside" enter-tainment, plush accommodations, and real wooden boardwalk. Rich furnish-ings and roomy rooms, which sleep up to five, add up to homelike comforts in a nostalgic setting. The villas, which sleep up to 12, have kitchens and washer-dryers. Some have whirlpools. The ambiance may be homey, but the service and amenities are uptown all the way: concierge, 24-hour room ser-vice, free newspaper, boat transport to MGM and Epcot, swimming pools, tennis, whirlpool, croquet, jogging path, playground, supervised child care, and free valet parking. Rooms overlooking the boardwalk have the best views, but they can be noisy.

2101 N. Epcot Resorts Blvd., off Buena Vista Dr. ☎ ***407/W-DISNEY** or 407/ 939-5100. www.disneyworld.com.* **Rack rates: Inn** *$254–$329 standard double, depending on season, level, and view.* **Villas** *come in studios or one- or* *two-bedroom units and cost $254–$685. Three-bedroom grand villas cost $1,150–$1,540. Children under 18 stay free in parents' room. AE, MC, V.*

Disney's Caribbean Beach Resort
$$$. Walt Disney World.

Imagine you're in Jamaica, Martinique, or Aruba. Each of this resort's five two-story complexes forms an island "village," deliciously themed to a splashy, tropical setting. With 2,112 rooms, this is a hotel of Las Vegas proportions. The villages rim a lake where you can watch the ducks or jog the path that surrounds it. The swimming pool looks like an ancient fort. Rooms are bright and comfortably furnished in the pineapple theme that stands for "welcome" in the West Indies. Walk to Parrot Cay, where there are picnic tables and a nature trail. Dine at a choice of moderately priced stalls in the food court or on American favorites in the Captain's Tavern.

*900 Cayman Way, off Buena Vista Dr. ☎ **407/W-DISNEY** or 407/934-3400. Fax 407/354-1866. www.disneyworld.com. **Rack rates:** $119–$184 double. Extra adult $12. AE, MC, V.*

Disney's Contemporary Resort
$$$$. Walt Disney World.

An enormous pyramid large enough to swallow the monorail, this original WDW hotel still holds a lot of magic for loyal guests, even if it doesn't seem as contemporary as it once did. The pool area is a miniature water park. The decor is *moderne;* oversize rooms are adequate for a family of four or five, and contain two queen-size beds and a child's daybed. One of the best things about staying here is that you can hop on the monorail and come back to the hotel for lunch, a nap, or a swim, and still be back in the Magic Kingdom in time for the afternoon parade and additional fun. The 15th-floor California Grill has great food and great views, or you can dine in the Concourse Steakhouse or Contemporary Café. You can also book a character breakfast here for the kids.

*4600 N. World Dr. ☎ **407/W-DISNEY** or 407/824-1000. Fax 407/354-1866. www.disneyworld.com. **Rack rates:** $214–$460 double. Children under 17 stay free in parents' room. AE, MC, V.*

Disney's Coronado Springs Resort
$$$. Walt Disney World.

Terra-cotta tiles, earthen colors, and Spanish Colonial design give you a sense of stepping into northern Mexico or the southwestern United States. The main lobby has a lower profile (fewer stories); it's bright, colorful, and warm inside, like a marketplace, but not boisterous. The interior is adorned with Spanish lanterns, Mexican folk art, and doves that encircle the skylight. There is a 95,000-square-foot convention center and 1,967 moderately priced rooms, some overlooking the 15-acre Lago Dorado, or Golden Lake. The better the view, the higher the room price. Each guest area has its own pool, but the main pool offers a 46-foot Mayan pyramid with water rushing down its ceremonial stone steps, a water slide that winds its way past a jaguar, and a bridge to deposit you in the 120-by-90-foot swimming pool. Restaurants include the outdoor Pepper Market and the Maya Grill, open for breakfast and fine dinner dining.

1000 W. Buena Vista Dr. ☎ *407/934-7639. Fax 407/939-1001.* **Rack rates:** *$119–$139 standard room. Discounts for AAA, AARP, corporate, and military. Free transportation to Walt Disney World theme parks. Free self-parking; valet parking available. AE, MC, V.*

Disney's Dixie Landings Resort
$$$. Walt Disney World.

With two double beds in each room, these units offer ample space for a family of three or four, and the modest prices attract families by the boatload. It's a boisterous place, with a Cajun theme that calls for waterfalls, rustic furnishings, and a fishin' hole where you can angle for catfish. Dine on American or Cajun cuisine at various restaurants, or order pizza from room service. Swim in a choice of six pools, or shop in Fulton's General Store. Boats go to Pleasure Island, Port Orleans, and the Village Marketplace.

1251 Dixie Dr., off Bonnet Creek Pkwy. ☎ *407/W-DISNEY or 407/934-6000. Fax 407/934-5777. www.disneyworld.com.* **Rack rates:** *$119–$184 for up to 4 in a room. AE, MC, V.*

Disney's Fort Wilderness Resort and Campground
$–$$$$. Walt Disney World.

This may be one of the priciest campgrounds in the world, but you get a lot of bang for your buck. Even primitive tent campers have all the pools and playgrounds of a first-rate resort at their doorstep. Bring your camper or rent an on-site RV that sleeps six and has a full kitchen. After a day at the parks, come back to dine in Trails End or Crockett's Tavern, or fire the grill and do it yourself. If you want some time away from the Mickster, you can go horseback riding or swimming, meet your new neighbors, fish, and play baseball, tennis, or golf. Some campsites accept pets. From the beach, you can see the nightly water pageant in summer. The Hoop-Dee-Doo Musical Revue plays nightly in Pioneer Hall.

3520 Fort Wilderness Trail. ☎ *407/W-DISNEY or 407/824-3000. Fax 407/ 354-1866. www.disneyworld.com.* **Rack rates:** *$39–$74 campsite with full hookup; $179–$254 trailer, known in Disney-speak as Wilderness Homes; $204–$275 Wilderness Cabin. Add $2 per person for more than 2 adults in a campsite, and $5 per person for more than 2 adults in a Wilderness Home. AE, MC, V.*

Disney's Grand Floridian Beach Resort
$$$$$. Walt Disney World.

The grand summer mansions of Newport and Jekyll Island inspired the Victorian splendor that characterizes this opulent (and expensive) 40-acre resort on the shores of the Seven Seas Lagoon. The interior is filled with the elegance of yesteryear, and the spacious grounds are a photographer's paradise. Return to a more gracious past in a room richly furnished with chintz, mahogany, and a four-poster bed. Balconies overlook picture-book gardens and lakes. You can sail on a 200-acre lagoon, play croquet, or swim in the big pool with its poolside cabanas. Order from 24-hour room service, or dine in a half-dozen restaurants; don't miss afternoon tea in the Garden View Lounge. Take WDW transportation to the theme parks; a trolley takes you around the resort.

4401 Floridian Way. ☎ *407/W-DISNEY or 407/824-3000. Fax 407/354-1866. www.disneyworld.com.* **Rack rates:** *$299–$645 double, depending on the view and season. Extra adult $15. AE, MC, V.*

Kids Disney's Old Key West Resort
$$$$$. Walt Disney World.

Time-share isn't always a nice word in Orlando, but Disney does it right. When the owners of these units aren't in residence, the accommodations are available to guests. The homelike furnishings (big-screen TVs, VCRs, extra telephones, and much more) make this a good choice for longer stays. Unpack, stock the pantry, and make yourself at home in a studio or a villa with one, two, or three bedrooms. Enjoy the sandy playground, swimming pools, tennis courts, video arcade, whirlpool, health club, or boating. In the recreation center, two free Disney movies play nightly.

1510 N. Cove Rd., off Community Dr. ☎ *407/W-DISNEY or 407/827-7700. Fax 407/354-1866. www.disneyworld.com.* **Rack rates:** *from $229 for a studio in low season to $1,050 for a three-bedroom Grand Villa during the holidays. AE, MC, V.*

Extra! Extra!

If you want a kitchen so you can do some of your own cooking, check out the following:

➤ Disney's BoardWalk (Walt Disney World; $$$$$)

➤ Disney's Fort Wilderness Resort and Campground (Walt Disney World; $–$$$$)

➤ Doubletree Guest Suites Resort (Lake Buena Vista; $$$)

➤ Howard Johnson Inn–Maingate East (U.S. 192/Kissimmee; $$)

➤ Summerfield Suites (International Drive; $$$$)

➤ Super Eight Motel (U.S. 192/Kissimmee; $–$$)

 Disney's Polynesian Resort
$$$$$. Walt Disney World.

It wasn't easy to re-create the lushness of Hawaii in Central Florida, with its occasional droughts and freezes, but Disney magic did the trick, transporting guests to the South Pacific. This resort combines the convenience of monorail access to the parks with the privacy of spread-out accommodations that seem far more off the beaten track than they really are. Relax in a hammock on the white-sand beach, book a character breakfast, water-ski, jog the 1.5-mile trail, fish, or hop on the monorail or boat to the Magic Kingdom. A 24-hour ice-cream parlor is included among the restaurants and lounges. This is one of Disney's oldest resorts, but it hasn't lost its luster.

1600 Seven Seas Dr. ☎ *407/W-DISNEY or 407/824-4000. www.disneyworld. com.* **Rack rates:** *$274 standard double; $345–$530 garden or lagoon view; $595–$1,425 suite. AE, MC, V.*

Disney's Port Orleans Resort
$$$. Walt Disney World.

It's like visiting New Orleans in time for Mardi Gras, but missing the customary sleaze. The seven buildings that make up the resort have 1,008 guest rooms and old-fashioned New Orleans charm. A large pool, located in the recreation area, Doubloon Lagoon, has a slide in the shape of a sea serpent. Restaurants include a themed food court inside the building known as the Mint, where authentic Mardi Gras floats are part of the decor. The Bonfamilles Café serves steaks, seafood, and Creole dishes.

2201 Orleans Dr., off Bonnet Creek Pkwy. ☎ *407/W-DISNEY or 407/934-5000.* **Rack rates:** *$119–$154 standard double. Discounts for AAA, AARP, corporate, and military. Valet parking available. AE, MC, V.*

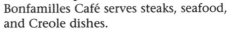

Extra! Extra!

If you're into nightlife, the closest hotels to the WDW after-dark hot spots, Pleasure Island and Downtown Disney, are the **Wyndham Palace Resort** (Lake Buena Vista; $$$–$$$$), **Disney's Dixie Landings Resort** (Walt Disney World; $$$), **Disney's Old Key West Resort** (Walt Disney World; $$$$$), **Disney's Port Orleans Resort** (Walt Disney World; $$$), and the **Grosvenor Resort** (Lake Buena Vista; $$$–$$$$).

Disney's Wilderness Lodge
$$$–$$$$. Walt Disney World.

Yippie-I-Aye-Yellowstone! This huge take-off on the Old Faithful Inn at the historic national park is a wonderful eyeful with a huge lobby and an open foyer that launches nine floors straight up. The rooms are located on three of those sides with landings on all four (the fourth has places to sit, sip, and stargaze, or to watch the inside world below). There's a mammoth fireplace soaring to the ceiling, with rocking chairs before it, and an interior thermostat set low enough that the fire can burn in the summer without causing the sweats. There's also an artificial spring that leads to some meandering rapids and a small waterfall that eventually ends at the pool. Geysers shoot water into the sky every hour on the hour, just like Old Faithful. Restaurants include Whispering Canyon Café, which serves three family-style meals a day; Roaring Forks, a light snackery; and Artist Point, where the fine dining comes with a Pacific Northwest flare.

901 Timberline Dr. ☎ ***407/824-3200.** **Rack rates:** $180–$390 standard double; $575–$825 suite. Discounts for AAA, AARP, corporate, and military. AE, MC, V.*

Extra! Extra!

If you want a gorgeous swimming pool, lots of places have what you're looking for, but not all pools are created equal. All the Disney hotels have gorgeous pools, but our favorites are at **Disney's Caribbean Beach Resort** (Walt Disney World; $$$), which re-creates a Caribbean fort with cannons and stone walls, and **Disney's Coronado Springs Resort** (Walt Disney World; $$$), where the main pool has a 46-foot Mayan pyramid with water rushing down its ceremonial stone steps. If you want beautiful and big, the **Hyatt Regency Grand Cypress** offers an 800,000-gallon, half-acre pool that has 12 waterfalls, with whirlpools underneath and a suspension bridge.

Disney's Yacht Club Resort
$$$$$. Walt Disney World.
Surround yourself with fellow commodores and imagine you're living the good life on Martha's Vineyard or Nantucket. The nautical theme is tastefully elegant; real yachties will love the hardwoods, shiny brasses, and the staff's 1880s swim costumes. The resort also boasts grassy lawns and an eye-popping swimming pool. There's a working fireplace in the lobby bar and several restaurants, including a pubby lounge, a cafe, and a plush steak house. Rooms are done in a nautical motif; French doors open onto the balcony. There's round-the-clock room service, and the resort has the same facilities as Disney's Beach Club Resort (above).

1700 Epcot Resorts Blvd. ☎ ***407/W-DISNEY** or 407/934-7000. Fax 407/ 354-1866. www.disneyworld.com.* **Rack rates:** *$264–$540 double; $445–$1,285 suite. Rates vary according to season and view. AE, MC, V.*

Kids Doubletree Guest Suites Resort
$$$. Lake Buena Vista/Official WDW Hotel.
Families appreciate the kid-glove treatment that pint-size guests receive here. Kids have their own check-in desk, pool, activities, theater, and menus. You get enough of a kitchen to whip up light meals, and you're in a central location

for theme parks and Orlando's best shopping. Luxury-seekers will be wowed by the seven-story atrium lobby and the many little extras, such as a TV in the bathroom. Suites have wet bars, refrigerators, coffeemakers, and microwave ovens, and provisions are sold on-site. Take the free shuttle to the theme parks, or stay "home" to enjoy the big pool, whirlpool, and kiddy pool with fountain. Play tennis or volleyball, use the fitness room, rent a boat, jog, or shop.

Extra! Extra!

If you want the best tennis and golf facilities, look no further than Disney's Contemporary Resort (Walt Disney World; $$$$) or Disney's Wilderness Lodge (Walt Disney World; $$$–$$$$).

2305 Hotel Plaza Blvd., just west of Apopka–Vineland Rd./FL 535. ☎ ***800/ 222-8733*** *or 407/934-1000. Fax 407/934-1101.* **Rack rates:** *$159–$199 for up to 6 in a one-bedroom suite; to $475 for a two-bedroom suite. Children under 18 stay free in parents' room. AE, CB, DC, DISC, MC, V.*

Econo Lodge Maingate East
$. U.S. 192/Kissimmee.

Those seeking quiet will appreciate this motel, a cluster of low-rise units secluded along Kissimmee's strip, and sitting well back from the roar of the busy highway. Breakfast and lunch are available; snacks are sold at the pool bar. Rooms have balconies, and there's a pool, a kiddy pool, volleyball, shuffleboard, picnic tables, barbecue grills, and coin-operated guest laundry facilities. Scheduled shuttles serve the theme parks and airport. When you're having breakfast under the oak trees around the pool, it's a country vacation; when you hop on the free shuttle to Walt Disney World, it's uptown all the way.

4311 W. Irlo Bronson Memorial Hwy. (U.S. 192), between Hoagland Blvd. and FL 535. ☎ ***800/ENJOY-FL*** *or 407/396-7100. Fax 407/239-2636.* **Rack rates:** *$29–$79 for up to 4 people. AE, CB, DC, DISC, MC, V.*

Grand Cypress Resort (villas)
$$$$$. Lake Buena Vista.

This is the sister site of the Hyatt Grand Cypress. The villas, a short drive from the larger hotel, offer privacy not found in most resorts, great views of the golf courses and canals, and resident ducks that wander up onto your patio when they hear the door open (so be prepared with crackers or bread crusts). You can play 45 holes of golf on Jack Nicklaus–designed courses or take lessons at the golf academy. The horse crowd will find a top-of-the-line equestrian center. Riding lessons and packages are available; a 1-hour lesson costs $80. The Villas of Grand Cypress offer 146 luxury rooms with patios or balconies, and Roman tubs. Dining is available in the elegant Black Swan Restaurant with a view of the ninth green.

1 N. Jacaranda. ☎ *800/835-7377 or 407/239-4700. Fax 407/239-7219.* **Rack rates:** *$275–$1,500. Free self-parking; free shuttle service to Hyatt Grand Cypress, equestrian center, clubhouse, and all the resort's recreational facilities. AE, CB, DC, DISC, MC, V.*

Grosvenor Resort
$$$–$$$$. Lake Buena Vista/Official WDW Hotel.

If you prefer traditional styling, plenty of stay-at-home entertainment (including a dinner theater and a VCR in your room), and a moderate price in a central location, look no further than the Grosvenor. A stately Colonial look and a forest of palms welcome guests to a homey resort that has a Sherlock Holmes museum, Disney characters, and a Saturday-night mystery theater. Each room has a coffeemaker, a safe, room service, a minibar (stocked on request), and a VCR. The resort offers tennis, swimming, a whirlpool, a playground, and lawn games. Dine in Baskerville's, Moriarty's Pub, or the 24-hour food court. Discount theme-park tickets and a complimentary shuttle are available.

1850 Hotel Plaza Blvd., just east of Buena Vista Dr. ☎ *800/624-4109 or 407/828-4444. Fax 407/828-8192. Free self-parking; valet parking $6 nightly.* **Rack rates:** *$99–$250 double. AE, CB, DC, DISC, MC, V.*

Harley of Orlando
$$$. Downtown Orlando.

If you want to be away from the theme parks, the mellow old Harley, in Orlando's recently revived downtown area, is for you. You can walk to downtown clubs and restaurants, or drive just a couple of minutes to the Centroplex for performances, games, and conventions. Ask for a room with a balcony overlooking Lake Eola Park, with its pretty fountains and vast greenways. Rooms are smallish and somber, but the trade-offs include a pool, a sundeck, free newspapers on weekdays, and a handy location. You can do your dining and drinking on-site or at Church Street Station, which is a short walk away. The free Lymmo, a downtown shuttle, also stops here.

151 E. Washington St. ☎ *800/321-2323 or 407/841-3220. Fax 407/849-1839.* **Rack rates:** *$109–$150 double. AE, MC, V.*

Higgins House Bed and Breakfast
$$$. Near North Orlando.

This 1894 Victorian inn is in Sanford, near Lake Monroe and the St. Johns River. Three rooms and Cochrane's Cottage are available for guests. The inn and grounds have a Victorian garden, decks, and hot tubs, and continental breakfast is served in a formal dining room.

420 S. Oak Ave. ☎ *800/584-0014 or 407/324-9238. Fax 407/324-5060.* **Rack rates:** *$95–$150. AE, DISC, MC, V.*

Hilton at Walt Disney World Village
$$$–$$$$$. Lake Buena Vista/Official WDW Hotel.

The Hilton promises a touch of posh pampering to help you recover from the relentless theme-park brouhaha. When you lose yourself in its 23 acres, which contain two big lakes, the World and your desire for Prozac seem miles away. Count on Hilton to provide everything the family or business traveler could ask for: telephones with voice mail and modem jack, coffeemaker, plenty of dining choices from simple to splurge, two swimming pools plus a kiddy pool, a health club with a sauna, tennis courts, rental boats, a beauty/barber shop, and a supervised child care center.

*1751 Hotel Plaza Blvd., just east of Buena Vista Dr. ☎ **800/782-4414** or 407/827-3890. Fax 407/827-3890. www.hilton.com. Free self-parking; valet parking available. **Rack rates:** $150–$320 double; $50 more for tower room. Children of any age stay free in parents' room. Ask about packages and weekend rates. AE, CB, DC, DISC, MC, V.*

Extra! Extra!

If you're disabled, we suggest you start by calling **Barrier Free Vacations** (☎ **800/749-5635;** www.barrier-freevacations.com). They can arrange a WDW vacation that includes accommodations with roll-in shower, WDW tickets, and airport transfers in a wheelchair-accessible vehicle. Note, too, that **all Walt Disney World hotels,** transportation, and entertainment are wheelchair accessible. (But guests in wheelchairs can't board the monorail at the Contemporary Resort. Stay at the Polynesian or Grand Floridian for monorail access, or elsewhere for access to buses.) In addition to the Disney hotels, we recommend the **Wyndham Palace Resort** (Lake Buena Vista; $$$–$$$$) and the **Holiday Inn Hotel & Suites Main Gate East** (U.S. 192/Kissimmee; $$–$$$).

Holiday Inn Hotel & Suites Main Gate East
$$–$$$. U.S. 192/Kissimmee.

There are several branches of the Holiday Inn chain around Orlando, but this is one of the best because of its sprawling grounds, kid- and pet-friendly rooms, and location (only 3 miles from the Magic Kingdom). We like the nice mix of mouse-themed merriment and no-nonsense hospitality. All the rooms are child-safe and feature refrigerators, microwaves, and VCRs. Specially designed Kidsuites™ have a playhouse that sleeps up to three. Suites have hair dryers, microwaves, refrigerators, VCRs, CD players, irons, and ironing boards. Some have whirlpool tubs. Shuttles to WDW are free. Transportation to other parks and attractions is available.

5678 E. Irlo Bronson Memorial Hwy. (U.S. 192). ☎ *800/FON-KIDS (800/ 366-5437) or 407/396-4488. Fax 407/396-1296. www.familyfunhotel.com.* **Rack rates:** *$49–$119 double; Kidsuites $30–$40 extra. AE, CB, DC, DISC, MC, V.*

Holiday Inn Nikki Bird Resort
$$. U.S. 192/Kissimmee.

The resident mascot, Nikki, wanders this resort where kids 12 and under eat free in Angel's Diner as long as they're accompanied by paying adults. Nightly entertainment includes songs, puppet shows, magic shows, and games. Rooms have a refrigerator, microwave, and safe. Free transportation is provided to WDW parks.

7300 W. Irlo Bronson Memorial Hwy. (U.S. 192). ☎ *800/206-2747 or 407/ 396-7300. Fax 407/396-7555.* **Rack rates:** *$89 standard double. Discounts for AAA, AARP, and corporate. AE, DC, DISC, MC, V.*

Holiday Inn Sunspree Resort
$$–$$$. Lake Buena Vista.

The large pink resort is located off Interstate 4 at State Road 535. Sunspree caters to families with children. On check-in kids get goodie bags, and the inn offers a castle-shaped movie theater, an activity program called Camp Holiday, a Cyber arcade, and kids age 12 and younger eat free if an adult is buying an entree. For a slight increase you can get rooms upgraded to include a "Kidsuite," a themed area inside the parents' room with its own bunk beds, CD player, Super Nintendo, television, and VCR. There are 231 Kidsuites incorporated within the regular rooms. All rooms have a coffeemaker, microwave, small dining table, and refrigerator.

Dollars & Sense

Call the special toll-free guest services number (☎ **800/TOUR-FLA** [800/868-7352]) to arrange tickets and all sorts of reservations so you can create your own custom Magic Mickey vacation package.

13351 State Rd. 535. ☎ *800/366-6299 or 407/239-4500. Fax 407/239-7713.* **Rack rates:** *$78–$131 standard double; $97–$168 Kidsuite. Free parking and scheduled shuttle service is provided to the Disney parks; transportation to other attractions is available for a fee. Attraction tickets can be purchased in the hotel lobby. AE, DC, DISC, MC, V.*

Homewood Suites Maingate
$$$. U.S. 192/Kissimmee.

These moderately priced family suites are located less than 5 miles from Walt Disney World. One-bedroom suites come with king-size or two double beds. Two-bedroom suites are available, some with fireplaces. Each suite is fully furnished with a kitchenette, ice maker, dishwasher, coffeemaker, microwave, stove, and cooking utensils. The bedroom has two double beds, cable television, VCR, and pullout sofa bed for extra guests. Free continental breakfast is served each morning, snacks and beverages in the afternoon, and there's an evening social hour with complimentary drinks. Laundry facilities are available. The hotel has a pool, whirlpool, gym, kiddy pool, picnic area with gas barbecue grills, and a sandpit where kids can dig with plastic shovels. There's also free scheduled transportation to Walt Disney World theme parks. Pets are accepted (but cats have to stay out of the sandpit).

3100 Parkway Blvd. ☎ ***800/225-5466*** *or 407/396-2229. Fax 407/396-4833.* **Rack rates:** *$139–$159. Discounts for AAA, AARP, military, and corporate. AE, MC, V.*

Howard Johnson Inn–Maingate East
$$. U.S. 192/Kissimmee.
Howard Johnson isn't known for its hoity-toity touches, but this particular branch works hard at keeping its rating as one of HJ's top motels. You'll be in the heart of Kissimmee's strip, just 3 miles from the Magic Kingdom. You'll find a swimming pool, whirlpool, kiddy pool, video arcade, and coin-operated laundry, as well as a free shuttle to the Disney parks. Family suites have full kitchens and living rooms with sofa beds. Efficiencies have a sink, refrigerator, and two-burner cooktop. A pool bar serves snacks. An IHOP and a huge water park are next door; lots of other places to eat are within a short drive.

2009 W. Vine St. (U.S. 192 at Thacker Ave.). ☎ ***800/288-4678*** *or 407/ 396-1748. Fax 407/649-8642. www.Hojo.com.* **Rack rates:** *$75–$95 for up to 4 people; $95–$115 family suite. Children under 19 stay free in parents' room. AE, CB, DC, DISC, MC, V.*

Extra! Extra!

If you want a spa vacation, the **Wyndham Palace Resort** (Lake Buena Vista; $$$–$$$$) has a European-style spa with a long menu of spa and salon services. In Walt Disney World, **Disney's Grand Floridian Beach Resort** (Walt Disney World; $$$$$) has the most lavish spa. The **Walt Disney World Swan** (Walt Disney World; $$$$$) has a full-service Body by Jake, aerobics, personal trainers, classes, and a full range of the latest machines.

⭐Kids Hyatt Regency Grand Cypress Resort
$$$$–$$$$$. Lake Buena Vista.
This resort is a step away from the crowds, located on 1,500 acres of lushly landscaped and natural Florida greenways. Inside, the lobby is a tropical paradise. Outside, an 800,000-gallon pool covers half an acre. Accommodations range from standard rooms to spacious suites within the 18-story structure. Guests can enjoy water sports on a 21-acre lake, hike, and play tennis or racquetball. The health club has sauna and steam rooms. The five restaurants include Hemingway's (seafood and steaks), La Coquina (New World cuisine), White Horse Saloon (barbecue, prime rib),

and the Cascades and Palm Cafe (casual fare). The resort has supervised children's activity programs.

1 Grand Cypress Blvd. ☎ ***800/233-1234*** *or 407/239-1234. Fax 407/239-1234.* ***Rack rates:*** *$235–$395. Free self-parking; valet parking available. AE, CB, DC, DISC, MC, V.*

Kissimmee/Orlando KOA
$. U.S. 192/Kissimmee.
This campground is 5 miles from Disney World, 8 miles from Sea World, and 11 miles from Universal. Free shuttle service runs daily to Disney attractions; twice a week shuttles go to Universal and Sea World. Open year-round, it has full hookups, paved pads, pull-through sites, tables, tent sites, air-conditioned cabins with front porches, a store, picnic shelters, a heated pool, and a recreation hall and clubhouse.

4771 W. Irlo Bronson Memorial Hwy. (U.S. 192). ☎ ***800/562-7791*** *or 407/ 396-2400. Fax 407/396-7577.* ***Rates:*** *$37.95–$39.95 site; $49.95–$53.95 cabin. AE, DISC, MC, V.*

Meadow Marsh Bed & Breakfast
$$$. Near North Orlando.
Located west of downtown Orlando on 12 acres, it has two suites and one cottage with double whirlpools, and two rooms with old-fashioned tubs or shower. A three-course breakfast is served each morning in a tearoom overlooking a vast meadow that is surrounded by century-old oak trees.

940 Tildenville School Rd. ☎ ***888/656-2064*** *or 407/656-2064. Fax 407/ 654-0656.* ***Rack rates:*** *$95–$199. MC, V.*

Orlando Marriott
$$$. International Drive.
If you need some time away from the theme parks, the Marriott is a relaxation station par excellence. You're minutes away from most of the attractions, yet the classy, parklike setting will make you feel that you're in a secluded resort. Roam 48 sunny acres (and be thankful you don't have to pay the accompanying I-Drive property taxes), swim in three pools, play tennis, or jog. Villa suites are available with full kitchens. Free trams offer 24-hour service around the grounds; you can ride round-trip to WDW for $8. Dine in the hotel's restaurants or in many other choices nearby. Discounted attractions tickets are available.

8001 International Dr., at Sand Lake Rd. ☎ ***800/421-8001*** *or 407/351-2420. Fax 407/345-5611.* ***Rack rates:*** *$124–$159 double; $175–$350 suite. AE, CB, DC, DISC, MC, V.*

Peabody Orlando
$$$$$. International Drive.
A favorite of business travelers and visiting celebrities, the Peabody is famous for the ducks in its lobby fountain. A prestigious business address, its proximity

to the theme parks, and a location within walking distance of the Convention Center make this a fine choice for those who want the best. Rooms have two phones, cable TV with a laser movie disc player, a small TV in the bathroom, and 24-hour room service. Unlimited shuttles to theme parks are $6 a day. There's also an Olympic-length swimming pool, a 7-mile jogging path, and a high-tech fitness center; guests also enjoy golf privileges nearby. Your dining options range from a formal restaurant to the B-Line Diner.

9801 International Dr., between the Bee Line Expressway and Sand Lake Rd. ☎ *800/PEABODY (800/732-2639) or 407/352-4000. Fax 407/351-0073.* **Rack rates:** *$300–$360 double; $495–$1,350 suite. Ask about packages and senior discounts. Free self-parking; valet parking available. AE, CB, DC, DISC, MC, V.*

Perri House Bed & Breakfast
$$–$$$. Lake Buena Vista.
Just 5 minutes from Walt Disney World, this rustic inn on 4 acres has a bird sanctuary. It has eight guest rooms with private baths. A continental breakfast buffet is served.

10417 Centurion Court. ☎ *800/780-4830 or 407/876-4830. Fax 407/876-0241.* **Rack rates:** *$89–$139. AE, DC, DISC, MC, V.*

Raccoon Lake Camp Resort
$. U.S. 192/Kissimmee.
Located on Lake Raccoon, and close to all major theme parks, this campground is open year-round. It has full hookups, pull-through sites, tables, tent sites, a boat ramp, water access, fishing, miniature golf, a playground, swimming pool, store, laundry, recreation hall, and clubhouse. One- and two-bedroom cabins, and cottages and trailers, are rented. Free WDW transportation is available.

8555 W. Irlo Bronson Memorial Hwy. (U.S. 192). ☎ *800/776-YOGI (800/ 776-9644) or 407/239-4148.* **Rates:** *$29–$32 RV; $15 tent; $29–$35 cabin. Extra adult $3. AE, DISC, MC, V.*

Radisson Plaza Hotel Orlando
$$$. Downtown Orlando.
The downtown Radisson offers 340 guest rooms and 27 suites with sitting rooms. Lando Sam's Restaurant and Lounge are good places to refuel and relax. Outdoor options include two tennis courts, a pool with Jacuzzi, and tanning decks. There's also a fully equipped weight room. The Radisson is 20 minutes from Disney World.

60 S. Ivanhoe Blvd. ☎ *800/333-3333 or 407/425-4455. Fax 407/843-0262.* **Rack rates:** *$164 double. AE, CB, DC, DISC, MC, V.*

Radisson Twin Towers
$$$. International Drive.
With 760 rooms, this hotel's no lightweight. The Palm Court Restaurant is backed up by the Citrus Shoppe Deli, which is open 24 hours a day. The Lobby Bar features piano music. There's also a pool bar and Trophy's Sports Bar and Grille, where you can eat hors d'oeuvres while enjoying live music or sports on the big-screen TV. Other trimmings include a whirlpool spa, heated Junior Olympic pool, children's pool and play area, exercise facility, hair salon, and shops. Transportation is provided to Universal Studios Florida, Sea World, and Wet 'N' Wild.

5780 Major Blvd. ☎ *800/327-2110 or 407/351-1000. Fax 407/206-1759.*
Rack rates: *$109–$169 double. AE, CB, DC, DISC, MC, V.*

Renaissance Orlando Hotel–Airport
$$$. Near Airport.
Here's the ideal place to stay if you have a limited amount of time and need to be close to the airport on the day you arrive and the day you leave. The hotel is designed for business travelers, with spacious rooms and a big bathroom with TV speaker, hair dryer, and telephone. But there's no reason families can't also enjoy all the amenities, including a whirlpool, a fitness center, a big pool, a sauna, and six golf courses within 10 miles. A shuttle to the theme parks is $26 per person, round-trip.

5445 Forbes Place, at the corner of State 436 and State 528, just east of the Turnpike. ☎ *800/HOTELS-1 (800/468-3571) or 407/240-1000. Fax 407/ 240-1005. www.renaissancehotels.com.* ***Rack rates:*** *$115–$175 double. Free self-parking; free long-term parking for guests. MC, V.*

Time-Savers

So you think you want to stay in a Disney hotel, but you're still confused about which one to choose? Call Disney's Central Reservations Office at ☎ 407/ W-DISNEY. These folks can take your reservations at any of the Disney hotels, resorts, villas, official hotels, or Fort Wilderness homes and campsites. They'll be happy to recommend specific accommodations to suit your needs, and they can set you up with a package that includes meals, tickets, and other features. Everyone is friendly at Disney, but don't forget to ask ('cause they won't tell you unless you do) about discounts and specials that are available. You might not get a discount for your entire stay, but every little bit helps. Most of the Disney properties offer military, AAA, AARP, corporate, group, and American Express Card discounts.

Dollars & Sense

So what's the best deal in town? We think you'll get the most bang for your buck at the following four Disney hotels: Dixie Landings, Port Orleans, the All-Star Music Resort, and the All-Star Sports Resort. Outside the Magic Kingdom you can stretch that dollar further at Days Inn Eastgate and Econo Lodge Maingate East.

Summerfield Suites
$$$$. International Drive.

These two-bedroom suites can sleep up to eight people (if they're really into togetherness). Balconies overlook a courtyard filled with rustling palms. Sun-seekers will feel immediately at home in a suite that's more than just a bedroom. Take time away from the theme parks to luxuriate in verdant grounds with the ambiance of a fine resort. Units have homey features such as iron and ironing board, full kitchen, TV in both the living room and the bedrooms, and multiple telephones. Continental breakfast is free; extra courses can be purchased. The hotel has a pool, kiddy pool, fitness center, coin-operated laundry, video arcade, and 24-hour sundries shop. The shuttle to WDW is $7.

8480 International Dr., between the Bee Line Expressway and Sand Lake Rd. ☎ *800/830-4964 or 407/352-2400. Fax 407/238-0778.* **Rack rates:** *$209–$319 suite. AE, CB, DC, DISC, MC, V.*

Super Eight Motel
$–$$. U.S. 192/Kissimmee.

When you can get this close to WDW for prices like these, and get extras like two junior Olympic-size pools and free continental breakfast, you've found a whale of a deal. Guest Services sells attraction tickets at a discount; the shuttle to the parks costs $12; airport transport is also available. Apartments have full eat-in kitchens, so they're a great choice for families. An IHOP is next door, but for fancier dining you'll need good walking shoes or a car.

1815 W. Vine St., on U.S. 192, between Bermuda and Thacker aves. ☎ *800/325-4348 or 407/8847-6121. Fax 407/847-0728.* **Rack rates:** *$34.95–$89.95 for up to 4 people in a standard room; $64.95–$119 for a two-bedroom apartment. AE, CB, DC, DISC, MC, V.*

 Walt Disney World Dolphin
$$$$$. Walt Disney World.

The 56-foot-high dolphins that sit atop this 1,509-room hotel can be seen for miles around, so your jaw will already have dropped by the time you enter the lobby of this wildly designed creation of trendy architect Michael Graves. The room size doesn't exactly fit the price, but the "entertainment" architecture is a hoot (those dolphins look more like gigantic Seussian fish). The grounds are lavishly landscaped, and amenities include 24-hour room service, a health club, floodlit tennis courts, boat rental, a 3-mile jogging trail, a sandy beach, and many restaurants. Camp Dolphin provides supervised kids' play. The resort shares facilities with the Walt Disney World Swan next door. You can walk to Epcot or use free WDW transportation.

1500 Epcot Resorts Blvd., off Buena Vista Dr. ☎ *800/227-1500 or 407/ 934-4000. Fax 407/934-4884. **Rack rates:** $285–$450 double. Free self-parking; valet parking $6 nightly. AE, CB, DC, DISC, MC, V.*

Walt Disney World Swan
$$$$$. Walt Disney World.

Like its dolphin-topped neighbor, this one is capped with 46-foot swans that can be seen from afar. (Some critics believe that's unfortunate.) Its fascinating design, whether you love it or hate it, is also the work of Michael Graves. Standard rooms with two doubles will be cramped for families; rooms with a king-size bed and sleeper sofa are a better choice. From here, you can walk to Epcot or take WDW transportation to the other parks. Choose from an array of restaurants here and in the Westin-operated Dolphin, or order from 24-hour room service. Swim the Olympic-size pool, work out in the fitness center, and let the business center take care of job worries if you're silly or unfortunate enough to have them along.

1200 Epcot Resorts Blvd., off Buena Vista Dr. ☎ *800/248-7926 or 407/ 228-3000. Fax 407/934-4499. **Rack rates:** $285–$450 double; $340–$370 concierge-level double; up to $1,750 suite. Children under 18 stay free in parents' room. Free self-parking; valet parking $8 nightly. AE, CB, DC, DISC, MC, V.*

Extra! Extra!

The "coming soon" signs are hanging at Universal Studios. Beginning in the fall of 1999, and ending in 2005, Universal is planning to open five on-site hotels that combined will have thousands of rooms. The **Portofino Bay Hotel,** a 750-room Loews property, will open first in September 1999. It's modeled after the Italian seaside village and, like the Disney resorts, comes with features including early theme-park admission, VIP access, character dining, priority restaurant seating, and free transportation. The hotel will have eight restaurants and bars, a world-class spa, and an activity center for kids. At press time, prices were not yet available, but you can get more information on booking a room, and on Universal vacation packages, by calling ☎ **877/U-ESCAPE.**

Wellesley Inn Orlando
$$–$$$. International Drive.

Located just minutes from area attractions, the new Wellesley Inn Orlando provides luxuriously appointed guest rooms, complimentary continental breakfast, a microwave, and a refrigerator in all rooms. Other amenities include an outdoor heated pool, guest laundry, and tickets to area attractions. A buffet breakfast is included, and weekend specials are sometimes available.

5635 Windhover Dr. ☎ *800/444-8888 or 407/345-0026. Fax 407/345-8809.*
Rack rates: *$50–$109 standard double; $79–$129 suite. Discounts for AAA, AARP, corporate, military, and Sam's Club. Free self-parking; valet parking available. AE, CB, DC, DISC, MC, V.*

Dollars & Sense

Internet users can grab an added advantage by surfing for special discounts at area hotels. (If you're not computer friendly, don't pout. We've included phone numbers just for you.) Florida Hotels and Discount Guide (**www. flhotels.com/orlando/caribe.html**) specializes in discount lodging (☎ **888/729-7705**). Discount Hotels America (**www.discounthotel samerica.com/**) provides similar services (☎ **877/766-6787**). Check out the folks at Resort Marketing (**www.rmitravel.com/**) for discounted rack rates and car rentals (☎ **800/204-5593** or 407/532-1544).

Wyndham Palace Resort
$$$–$$$$. Lake Buena Vista/Official WDW Hotel.

The lakefront setting and spacious grounds lend a resort atmosphere to what is also a first-class hotel for business travelers, honeymooners, and spa-seekers. It's great if you want to see the attractions but also want a place to get away from it all at day's end. On the edges of Walt Disney World, but not immersed in the Mickey merriment around the clock, this posh hotel has 1,014 rooms and offers restaurants (including the famous Arthur's 27), lounges, pools, gardens, and sundecks. Disney-character breakfasts are served in the cafe. The Kids Stuff program and The Spa are outstanding. Shuttles to the theme parks are free.

1900 Lake Buena Vista Dr., just north of Hotel Plaza Blvd. ☎ *800/327-2990 or 407/827-2727. Fax 407/827-6034. www.bvpalace.com.* **Rack rates:** *$149–$254 standard double; $224–$304 Crown Level; $259–$339 one-bedroom suite, $408–$568 two-bedroom suite. Packages available including spa service or WDW admissions. Free self-parking; valet parking $7 nightly. AE, CB, DC, DISC, MC, V.*

Wyndham Safari Resort
$$$ Lake Buena Vista.

Safari is the theme, from African symbols on the building exterior to shades of beige-and-black furniture upholstered in animal-skin patterns on the inside. The pool has a 79-foot slide designed to look like a python. There is also a kiddy pool, a whirlpool, and a deli where you can get sodas, burgers, ice cream, and snacks. Restaurants are within walking distance of the hotel.

12205 Apopka–Vineland Rd. ☎ ***800/423-3297*** *or 407/ 239-0444. Fax 407/ 239-2732.* ***Rack rates:*** *$109–$139 double. Seasonal rates slightly higher. Discounts for AAA and corporate. Free transportation to Walt Disney World theme parks. AE, DISC, MC, V.*

Magical Mickey Vacations

A lot of package deals have punch—sometimes, too much. But maybe that's part of the grand plan in Mickeyland. They want you to keep coming back. It's called Marketing 101.

Mickey's Magicians offer three seasonal packages annually:

➤ Sunshine Getaway, January 1–11

➤ Fall Fantasy, August 29–November 17

➤ Magical Holidays, November 27–December 25

You get breakfast at selected resorts, then a ticket to ride, run, or walk into the world of nonstop fun. The 4-night packages include an unlimited Magic Pass with Disney Flex Feature included. The Magic Pass means check-in to check-out admission to the Magic Kingdom, Epcot, Disney–MGM Studios, and Animal Kingdom, as well as Pleasure Island, River Country, Typhoon Lagoon, Blizzard Beach, Wide World of Sports, and Disney transportation. The Flex Feature gives each guest the choice of:

➤ One Character or Disney Resort Hotel breakfast

➤ Nine holes of golf at the Oak Trail Course

➤ One Mickey 'N' Y

➤ One Animal Kin

➤ One T-shirt from Bongos, McDona Virgin Megastore or Wolfgang Puc

Extra! Extra!

During the Christmas season, Disney pulls out all the stops with Mickey's Very Merry Christmas at the Magic Kingdom, Holidays Around the World at Epcot, and the Disney–MGM Studios Holiday Spectacular. Packages are available during this special time of year when all of the theme parks at the Magic Kingdom deck the halls for Christmas. Three-night stays are ̲̲̲̲̲̲̲̲̲ and if you book a ̲̲̲̲̲ ̲̲ay, it includes the ̲ Magic Pass and ̲̲lex Feature. To ̲ of these seasonal ̲̲, call Walt Disney ̲̲mpany at ☎ **800/** **̲96.**

➤ One theme-park tour

➤ Admission to DisneyQuest (see chapter 16) with 80 play units

➤ Lunch or dinner at the All-Star Café plus a souvenir gift

➤ One Fantasmic hat with three collector's pins at MGM Studios

➤ One Children's Fishing Excursion at the Grand Floridian Resort (ages 6–12)

➤ A 1^1/2-hour tennis clinic at the Grand Floridian or Contemporary Resort

Magical Packages

Resort Magic   Three or more nights at select Walt Disney resorts, including a Magic Pass and Disney's Flex Feature.

Dollars & Sense

This **Golf Getaway** is a good deal, if not a steal. Spend 2 days or more at a Disney resort on or off the fairways, and get 18 holes of golf per person for each night's stay. A round of golf at a Disney golf course costs $90 to $110 for 18 holes depending on the course. We checked prices for a 4-night stay at **Dixie Landings.** The per-couple package cost including tax is $1,630.60 for an upgraded room and $1,542.20 for a standard double. Depending on the season, rates at Dixie Landings are $139–$184, with an average of $161 per night. A 4-night stay would cost $644 per couple. One round of golf per person per day averages $100; four double rounds would cost $800. The total for room and golf only is $1,532.75 including 6% sales tax. Plus, the package gives you extras like greens fees, a golf cart, and a bucket of balls for the driving range. You also get to choose one of these options: dinner at a selected resort, a spa treatment, a 30-minute golf lesson, a tennis lesson, or an admission to Cirque du Soleil.

Deluxe Magic   Includes all of the features of Resort Magic plus three meals daily, including Disney Character dining and dinner shows. You also get unlimited use of the recreational facilities, and adult discovery program (16 or older) admission to Keys to the Kingdom at the Magic Kingdom, Inside Animation at Disney–MGM Studios, Gardens of the World at Epcot, and Hidden Treasures of the World Showcase at Epcot. Youth discovery programs (ages 7–15) at Camp Disney are also included, and the whole family can enjoy the Family Magic Experience at the Magic Kingdom, and Behind the Seeds at Epcot.

Sand 'N' Castle Magic   Spend some time on the beach at Disney's Vero Beach Resort soaking up the sun, then head back to the Magic Kingdom (it's a 2-hour drive one-way). The package includes 4 nights at a Disney resort, 3 nights at the beach, and the Magic Pass and Disney's Flex Feature.

The Grand Plan

This is the mother of all packages. Hang on to your wallet because Mickey wants the whole wheel of cheese!

To help you plan your assault on the Magic Kingdom, you need your own coordinator, because it's not a small world after all. Don't worry, one is assigned, and you'll be glad to have him or her help you navigate through more than 250 restaurants and the unlimited recreational activities. You also need a personal banker.

Bet You Didn't Know

Disney offers a dining plan. Before you arrive you can prepay for your meals during your stay. Adults (at this Disney cash register, that means anyone 10 and older) pay $55 per day; children (3–9) are $16. Disney adds a $5-per-day bonus credit for each adult and $2 per day for youngsters. For a 2-night stay, two adults with two kids would pay $504 and get $532 to spend.

The Grand Plan starts at $1,309 per adult, Juniors (10–17) are $803, and children 3–9 are $587 for 3 nights at Disney's Contemporary Resort. Other participating resorts are:

➤ Disney's Grand Floridian Beach Resort

➤ Disney's BoardWalk Inn Resort

➤ Disney's BoardWalk Villas Resort

➤ Disney's Beach Club Resort

➤ Disney's Yacht Club Resort

➤ Disney's Polynesian Resort

In a nutshell, the plan gives you:

➤ The Magic Pass with Disney Flex Feature

➤ Breakfast, lunch, and dinner including character dining and Disney shows

➤ Unlimited use of the resort recreation options including golf, fishing, and boating

➤ Adult discovery programs, including Keys to the Kingdom and Inside Animation, Gardens of the World, and Hidden Treasures of the World Showcase

➤ Camp Disney for the younger set

➤ Family discovery programs including Family Magic Experience and Behind the Seeds at Epcot

➤ Light snacks and refreshments

➤ A fireworks cruise

➤ Admission to Cirque du Soleil

➤ Private golf and tennis lessons (10 and older)

➤ One 50-minute spa treatment (10 and older)

➤ Disney Institute personal enrichment programs

➤ Exclusive Disney grand gift

➤ Child entertainment centers (4–12)

➤ Nightly turndown service

➤ Complimentary admission nightly to Atlantic Dance at Disney's BoardWalk

➤ Mickey 'N' You Photo

➤ Unlimited use of Disney's transportation system

For appointments and scheduling, call ☎ **407/934-7639,** or see your Grand Plan coordinator.

Matrimoniously Mickey—or, Ain't Love Grand?

Did you know (or do you care) that you can get hitched at Disney? Ceremonies range from the traditional to the real mind-stretchers. Disney does nuptials throughout the Magic Kingdom and at Disney's Wedding Pavilion, which overlooks the lake with Cinderella's Castle in the background. Theme weddings are a specialty here, including tying the knot in front of Cinderella's Castle while you're dressed as the prince and princess. On the other end of the spectrum, there are private affairs with just the two of you, a wedding gift, your hotel room, dinner for two, and admission to the theme parks.

If a reception is in your plans, the Disney folks are happy to oblige. Picture arriving at the reception in Cinderella's glass coach. As they like to say, "If you can dream it, we can do it."

After the ceremony, you can choose from several honeymoon options in WDW or take an island-hopping honeymoon aboard the Disney *Magic*, the flagship of the new Disney cruise line (see chapter 16).

Help, I'm So Confused!

For some of you, the decision is easy: You want to stay in the best hotel, closest to the Magic Kingdom, and price isn't an object. For everyone else, though, there are trade-offs to be made among price, location, and convenience.

That's where organization helps. Some folks charge a ton of money to get you organized, but we're throwing it in free, just because we like you.

Here, then, is a chart. You probably read through the reviews earlier in this chapter and said, at least a few times, "Hey, that one sounds good." You might have even followed our advice and put a little check next to those establishments, or even dog-eared the page. Well, you're ahead of the game. (If you didn't, we hope you have a good memory or made reservations already.) To save you the later pains of flipping through dozens of pages to compare and contrast, jot down the names and vital statistics now of the places you like. Use the chart below, get everything lined up and orderly, and then scan the line to see how they stack up against each other. As you rank them in your mind, rank them in the column on the right, too; that way you can have your preferences ready when making reservations, and if there's no room at the inn for choice number one, you can just move on to number two

Hotel Preferences Worksheet

Hotel	Location	Price per night

Advantages	Disadvantages	Your Ranking (1–10)

Part 3

Learning Your Way Around Walt Disney World & Orlando

You don't have to be a complete idiot to feel a bit overwhelmed by everything going on in Orlando. Navigating the various sections of Walt Disney World alone can raise your blood pressure 20 points—to say nothing of venturing into downtown Orlando and daring the highway traffic and staccato exit ramps.

Rest easy, though. It's not as complicated as it looks at first—especially if someone else is doing the driving. Even if you are the one behind the wheel, most of the attractions in this handy-dandy guide are confined to the area bounded by downtown Orlando to the north, the airport to the east, Walt Disney World to the west, and the Kissimmee–St. Cloud area to the south. Trust us, if you head the wrong way and cruise east from the airport, it'll only be about an hour before you hit the Atlantic Ocean and have to turn around. Ditto if you head too far west. Tampa Bay and the Gulf of Mexico will restore your senses.

If you're like a lot of visitors, you might not get to downtown Orlando; therefore, you'll do less driving and less navigating. Those of you who take public or guest transportation everywhere (this is a very real possibility if you're staying in one of the WDW hotels) will find the only maps you'll have to decipher are those for the theme parks.

Chapter 7

Getting Your Bearings

In This Chapter

➤ Getting from point A (the airport) to point B (your bed)

➤ Figuring out the lay of the land

➤ Getting more info once you've arrived

The flight is over and you're finally on the ground in the Land of Magic Mickey and the Munchkins. Now the fun begins, but only after you've maneuvered your way through the airport maze and survived a dose of Interstate 4, which, due to its frequent traffic jams, is also known as the World's Largest Parking Lot.

Let's take it from the top, by the numbers.

Your Flight Just Landed—Now What?

The signs in Orlando International Airport are said to be "clear and concise." That's tourist-czar hype. They may be concise, but clear is another story. There *may* be an airline information desk somewhere on your concourse, and it *may* be staffed, and it *may* not have a line that reaches to Jimmy Buffett's Margaritaville, but chances are you won't see anyone except other confused tourists, all rushing about. But you'll have to depend on those signs and your personal radar to navigate to vital areas like rest rooms, baggage claim, car-rental desks, and the exits. You can check out airport services before you fly at the Orlando airport's helpful Web site, **http://fcn.state.fl.us/goaa**.

When you land and get off the plane, you'll find yourself in what the airport calls an Airside Building. In other words, you're out *here* and need to go in *there*—the Main Terminal building. To get *there*, you ride the "AGT System," which is one of those CIA-like abbreviations for something no more complex than a shuttle. Look for the big sign that says SHUTTLE TO TERMINAL & BAG CLAIM. It's only a short hop to the terminal, and if you just miss the shuttle, don't despair. They arrive and depart every 2 or 3 minutes. (Since they're automatic, once the doors close, that's that.)

The terminal has two sides, A and B. You'll hear an announcement during your shuttle journey to the Main Terminal about where to go to get your bags.

So now you're safely inside the Main Terminal (you're on level 3, by the way). Baggage claim is downstairs on level 2. There are signs that say BAG CLAIM with arrows pointing the direction you should go. But don't worry about the arrows. Just follow all the people who just got off the shuttle with you. Everyone's looking for the same place.

You'll find pay phones just inside the doors between the baggage claim and the passenger pickup areas.

Dollars & Sense

Big savings can be found in the many free magazines and tabloid newspapers in every hotel lobby, restaurant, shop, rest stop, and gas station along the interstates. Take one of each. They're filled with coupons good for discounts and freebies. But don't take their advice about the best restaurants in town. Most recommend only the restaurants that advertise with them.

If you are arriving from another country like Britain, Canada, or California, you'll go through an Immigration Checkpoint, then to baggage claim, then Customs before you take the little shuttle to the Main Terminal. And then— here's the blue-light special—you get to put your bags onto a moving belt so you can grab them *again* in the Main Terminal. (If this seems like a cruel American joke, it's more like revenge. You do it to us when we visit your home.) Do you need to find a Currency Exchange? You'll discover booths on the arrival level, level 3, in the terminal. Their operating hours coincide with the arrival of international flights, so don't worry if you're arriving early or late.

Getting Mobile

All of the taxis and shuttle vans for hotels and such stop on the same level as baggage claim. That's level 2. If you already have a shuttle reservation, there's probably a space number on it, so just follow the signs to that space to get your ride. Level 2 is also the level where friends or relatives can pick you up. City buses and car rentals are on level 1. That's one level beneath baggage claim. You go there even if the car-rental agency is off-site and picking you up in a courtesy van.

The **city bus (Lynx)** stops at spaces 21–23 on level 1 on the A side of the terminal. Buses leave every 30 to 60 minutes daily, 6:30am to 8:30pm, with less frequent service Sunday and holidays. For 75¢ (exact change), you can ride to the main bus depot downtown on Pine Street, but these buses aren't set up to accommodate any more luggage than you can carry in your lap.

Taxis, which stop on level 2, are metered. The fare (for up to eight passengers) from the airport to Walt Disney World is a whopping $43. A trip to International Drive is about $26, to downtown $17, and to Lake Buena Vista $32. A taxi may be a good option if you don't need or want a rental car, and if there are three or more people in your party ($43 to Walt Disney World is still cheaper than the price of three people in a shuttle). You should, of course, make sure your hotel doesn't offer free airport pickup.

Dollars & Sense

If you have a family, it may be cheaper to rent a car than to take shuttles or taxis around Orlando. Car rentals in Florida are cheaper than almost any place on Earth, so even considering what it costs to park, and to fill the gas tank, you may still come out ahead. Besides, a car will give you the freedom to eat at cheaper, out-of-the-World places if you're staying at Mickey's.

A **shuttle** ride from the airport to Walt Disney World or Lake Buena Vista costs $25 round-trip for adults, $17 for kids 4 to 12 (kids 3 and under are free). Taking a shuttle to International Drive costs a couple of dollars less for the round-trip. It usually costs a little more than half the round-trip price for a one-way ride if you've decided you just can't ever leave Orlando (or if you are getting a ride back to the airport). Shuttle companies that serve Orlando and the attractions area are **Mears** (☎ **407/427-1694;** www.mears-net.com/index1.htm) and **Transtar** (☎ **407/856-7777;** www.thetravelguide.com/transtar/). You can reserve your shuttle ride in advance either by phone or on the company's Web site. While you're there, look for coupons. There's usually some kind of discount offered.

Car-rental companies with branches **at** the airport include **Avis** (☎ 800/831-2847), **Budget** (☎ 800/537-0700), **Dollar** (☎ 800/800-4000), and **National** (☎ 800/227-7368). Rental companies **near** the airport provide shuttle service to their facilities. These include **Alamo** (☎ 800/327-9633), **Enterprise** (☎ 800/551-3390), **Hertz** (☎ 800/654-3131), **Interamerican** (☎ 407/859-0414), **Thrifty** (☎ 800/367-2277), and **Value** (☎ 800/468-2583). See chapter 4 for consumer tips on how to save when you reserve your car in advance.

If you'll be getting a rental car, collect your bags on level 2 and follow the signs to level 1 or to the Rental Cars area. Here you'll find either a counter with personnel to check you in or, if the rental company is off-site, a bank of free telephones you can use to call for a pickup. The largest companies run continuous shuttles in the bus lane outside level 1. Your wait probably won't be longer than 20 minutes.

The car-rental folks will give you a map. Take time to look it over, and get specific directions from the rental agent. Make sure you understand exactly where you need to go as you leave the airport, because things happen fast after that. As they're giving you the directions, also ask if any signs or landmarks are hard to spot, especially the ones as you're leaving the airport. The last thing you want to do after a long flight is take multiple laps around the airport. There is no prize money in the Orlando 500.

Some Directions to Give You Direction

Here are some quick **directions for getting from the airport to Walt Disney World:** Leaving the airport, most people take FL 528 (the Bee Line Highway—it's a toll road) west for approximately 12 miles to its intersection with I-4. Go west on I-4 to exit 26, marked EPCOT/DISNEY VILLAGE, and follow the signs. An alternate route is to go southwest on the Central Florida Greenway (FL 417), another toll road. FL 417 will intersect with FL 536; keep left. FL 536 will cross over I-4 and become Epcot Drive. From there, follow the signs to your destination.

North, South, East, West: Getting Yourself Oriented

If you arrive at the airport, you will be almost due east of Walt Disney World, northeast of the Kissimmee–St. Cloud area, and southeast of downtown Orlando. Almost all vacationers to Orlando exit the airport via the **Bee Line Expressway** (also known as FL 528), which is the most direct route to International Drive, Florida's Turnpike, and I-4, the interstate road that links WDW to downtown Orlando.

Any idiot can see on the map that I-4 runs north and south, but the government sign painters think of it as an east–west road. (This is what makes America great—diverse thinking.) Anyway, from the Bee Line, go "east" (or north) if you're drawing a bead on downtown or Universal Studios and "west" (or south) to get to WDW and the U.S. 192/Kissimmee. Of course, you'll be confused. Everyone is, except the sign painters.

The best map is the **Walt Disney World Property Map,** which you can request before you leave home by calling ☎ **407/ 824-4321.**

Tourist Traps

You'll see signs that read TOURIST INFORMATION everywhere and most of them promise some kind of discount attraction tickets. But most of these are attached to T-shirt shops. They're operations hawking time-shares and other real-estate "bonanzas." Stick with the official information centers listed in this book.

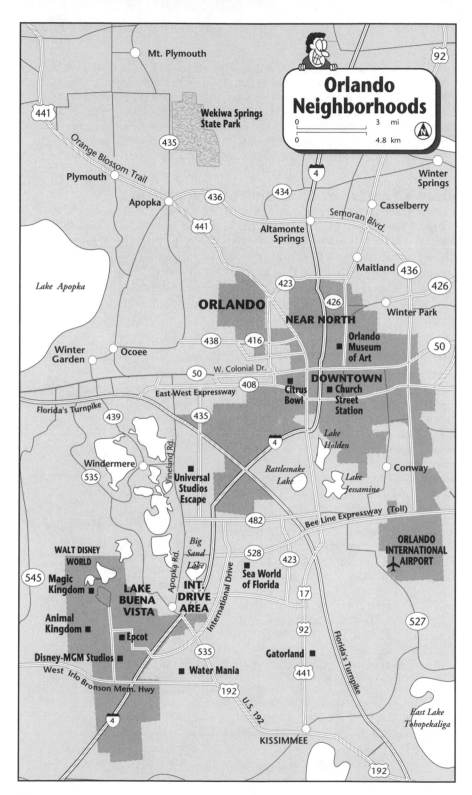

Orlando
Neighborhoods

Walt Disney World

This is the World you've probably come to visit. WDW is actually not located in Orlando; it's a few miles southwest of the city, and it's really a city unto itself. It contains **several** theme parks (oh, no, one is definitely not enough), plus splashy resorts and hotels of all price ranges, restaurants, and water parks. You want it? Well, they have it. Disney even has its own transportation system that links everything up into one nicely organized and convenient bundle.

But convenience has its price. The cheapest hotels here cost about twice what you'd pay in Kissimmee for the same accommodations. And if you don't rent a car, you're trapped in a World where everything from meals to spa services is equally high-priced.

Lake Buena Vista Area (Official WDW Hotels)

Lake Buena Vista is Disney's next-door neighbor, where you'll find "official" (though non–Disney-owned) hotels; it's close to the Disney Village, Downtown Disney, and Pleasure Island. Not a bad place, really, if you want to be close to but not quite drowning in all the hubbub, and you'll have free transportation to and from the WDW theme parks (though you're not on the WDW transportation system). There are plenty of places to stay and eat here.

Kissimmee/U.S. 192

This once-sleepy city is closer to Walt Disney World than Orlando is, which comes as a surprise to most people. You're just a short drive from Mickey and many of the smaller attractions if you stay here. First impressions count though, and most folks find this area a tad on the tacky side, with strings of modest motels and restaurants, including every fast-food joint known to Western civilization. The main plus? Convenience and bargains.

International Drive Area

This is a 7- to 10-mile stretch of road north of the Disney parks, between FL 535 and the Florida Turnpike. It's where you'll find Sea World and Universal Studios, plus plenty more attractions, not to mention dozens of hotels, motels, restaurants, and shopping centers. You'll probably hear people refer to this as **I-Drive.**

Downtown

Before Mickey moved into Orlando in 1971, parts of the city were dying, but this is an increasingly vibrant neighborhood with countless bars, restaurants, coffeehouses, and a night-time entertainment complex for adults called Church Street Station. It's near the Orlando Science Center, which opened in 1997. And there's Lymmo, a free shuttle-bus system, to get you around.

Near North

These are the suburbs north of downtown Orlando. You'll find many restaurants here that might be worth the drive if you are getting tired of theme parks, but it's a little too far out of the way to stay out here. Just north of "near North" is **Winter Park,** a lovely, unspoiled town with lots of beautiful old-money homes.

Street Smarts: Where to Get Information Once You're Here

It's worth stopping at the Orlando/Orange County Convention & Visitors Bureau's **Official Visitor Center** at 8723 International Dr., at the southeast corner of I-Drive and Austrian Row. Tickets to all attractions and many dinner shows are available at a discount here. You'll save only a few dollars on WDW tickets, but up to 10% to 20% on others. Tickets are sold daily 8am to 7pm except Christmas.

If you're driving down to the Orlando area from points north, stop on I-75 about 1¹/₂ hours north of Orlando at the **Disney/AAA Travel Center** at exit 68, S.R. 200 in Ocala (☎ **904/854-0770**). It's easy-on, easy-off the interstate, and it offers souvenirs, information, tickets, and hotel reservations at attractive discounts. It's open daily 9am to 6pm; in July and August until 7pm.

Local free publications come and go, and change their names often, so it's hard to know which one to recommend. *See Magazine* has been around the longest, and it's pretty good.

Chapter 8

Getting Around

In This Chapter

➤ Using your own two wheels

➤ The magic bus

➤ Hoofin' it

One of Orlando's tragedies is that the city's fathers grabbed greedily for the sudden windfall that came with Walt Disney World without planning for the infrastructure that would be required in a major city. That was well received by taxpayers in 1971, but today's—including visitors—are paying the price through limited public transportation, horrendous traffic jams, high tolls, increasing taxes on hotels and meals, and very few areas where you can get around on foot. Hundreds of acres of orange groves were bulldozed to make room for the subdivisions that were thrown together with little green space and no sidewalks. (See "Roadkill" under "Mean Streets, Flying Teeth & Nasty Natives: Last-Minute Warnings," chapter 4, as a reminder of the grim fringe benefits.)

Fortunately, tree-shaded pockets remain in downtown Orlando from before the growth explosion. And some of the newer areas, such as International Drive, were built with some thought for aesthetics, pedestrians, and sensible transportation systems. Walt Disney World is a model of accessibility, with a superb transportation network and massive neighborhoods, such as Celebration and The BoardWalk, made just for walking. Universal Studios Escape, which we'll visit in depth in chapter 17, will also be a complete world unto itself. As we enter the new millennium, it will have its own hotels with thousands of rooms.

Time-Savers

State Road 528, locally called the Bee Line or Bee Line Expressway, is a toll road. So are the Central Florida Green Way (FL 417) and the East–West Expressway (FL 408). Unmanned toll booths require exact change, so travel with a good supply of quarters. Don't try to avoid the tolls on the Bee Line by taking the city streets through Pine Hills between I-4 and Hiawassee. Locals have dubbed the area "Crime Hills." Pay the 75¢. Traffic, or the lack thereof, is another reason to take the toll roads.

Not since the Gold Rush has a North American city grown as quickly and haphazardly as Orlando. Anything we write today is subject to change. But once you get a general picture of the city, remember to avoid the rush hours, and learn a few shortcuts, you'll find that getting around Orlando is (almost) a breeze.

Note: Details on the Walt Disney World transportation system, which you can use if you choose a hotel in WDW, are in chapter 11.

By Car

Just over half of Central Florida's visitors drive here, and most of those who arrive by air rent a car, so it's safe to assume Orlando's roads and streets are filled with a lot of people who don't know exactly where they are, just like you. Here are some tips that will have you negotiating the highways like a native.

➤ Rush hour on I-4 is generally from 7 to 9am and 4 to 7pm. Other busy times include big games or events at the O'rena or Citrus Bowl, or big conventions at the Convention Center. Stay off I-4 if at all possible during these hours; driving any distance during these periods will take at least twice as long as you think.

Tourist Traps

If you buy discount tickets from roadside vendors, read the fine print to make sure they have no restrictions on dates or times. Fact is, it's best not to buy from them. Stolen tickets frequently burn visitors. Officials may know the tickets' serial numbers and confiscate them at the gate.

➤ Remember, I-4 runs north and south, but the sign painters think of it as an east–west road. From the Bee Line, you'll want to go "east" (or north) to go downtown or to Universal Studios, and "west" (or south) to get to WDW and U.S. 192/Kissimmee.

Time-Savers

As you approach Walt Disney World by car, watch for signs that tell you where to tune on your AM dial to get last-minute tourist information. When you're in other areas, stay tuned to a station such as AM 580, which has frequent traffic reports and advice on avoiding accident scenes and other delays. You can save hours if you know when to duck off the highway onto an alternate route. The better traffic reporters suggest some options.

➤ Under Florida law, you can turn right on red after coming to a full stop and making sure that the coast is clear (unless the signs say otherwise). Local drivers will get steamed if you clog the right-turn lane. If you're sitting at a red light with your blinker on and hear horns blaring behind you, chances are they're in your honor. Make sure it's clear, then *move it.*

➤ Traffic must stop when school buses are loading or unloading in either direction, except on a divided high-way that has either a barrier or a dividing space of 5 feet or more.

Dollars & Sense

Full-service gas stations charge 3¢ to 6¢ more per gallon than self-service stations. Some stations have two-tier pricing, charging a few cents more per gallon if you use a credit card. Ask or read the pump before using a credit card.

➤ International Drive is called I-Drive. Irlo Bronson Memorial Highway is U.S. 192, which everyone calls 192. Florida Route 528 is the Bee Line Expressway. State Road 50 is more commonly called Colonial Drive.

➤ A Florida handicap permit is required for parking in handicap parking places. Handicap permits from other states are honored, but a disabled parking plate alone won't do.

➤ Along a 12-mile stretch of U.S. 192 in Kissimmee, 25-foot-high markers start at Walt Disney World and extend nearly to Splendid China, brightly marking the many points of interest. The westernmost marker is Marker 4; the remaining pairs are numbered in sequence and in pairs, one on each side of the highway. If you phone for directions to a restaurant, hotel, or attraction, it's likely you'll be told it's "just past Marker" so-and-so.

➤ In an emergency, you can reach the Florida Highway Patrol on a cell phone by dialing ☎ [*]FHP.

A Few More Tips on the Local Lingo

Locals have their own vocabulary, and visitors can get lost unless they know that:

➤ OBT and "The Trail" are Orange Blossom Trail, which is also U.S. 441 and U.S. 17–92. Don't confuse it with Orange Avenue, which is also a north–south street, just east of OBT.

➤ OIA and MCO both refer to the airport.

Also, don't confuse Winter Park, Winter Garden, and Winter Haven. They're all towns in Central Florida.

By Bus

Orlando's **Lynx** city bus system is a work of art, with each bus brilliantly designed in a different motif. Bus stops are identified by a lynx paw print. The fare is 75¢ and exact change is required. For more information, call ☎ **407/841-8240.**

Buses run between the airport and downtown, but they aren't the best way for tourists to sightsee, shop, or get to and from hotels, restaurants, and points of interest.

Another bus system, **I-Ride,** operates every 10 to 15 minutes 7am until midnight every day on International Drive between Sea World and American Way, which is the site of a Howard Johnson's, a Comfort Inn, and a Denny's just west of Kirkman Road (Route 435). One-way fare is 85¢ for adults and 25¢ for seniors, with exact change required. Children under 12 ride free when accompanied by an adult. Trolleys are air-conditioned. When you get aboard, ask about daily and weekly passes.

Dollars & Sense

Run, don't walk, to the Orlando/Orange County Convention & Visitors Bureau's **Official Visitor Center** at 8723 International Dr., at the southeast corner of I-Drive and Austrian Row. Tickets to all attractions and many dinner shows are available at a discount. You'll save only a few dollars on WDW tickets, but 10% to 20% on others. Tickets are sold daily 8am to 7pm except Christmas.

Culture Quest, a tour bus of Orlando's top cultural attractions, makes a terrific shuttle system. You can ride the entire circuit to orient yourself before starting out on your own to visit points of interest, or you can get on and off as you please. The bus operates from five hubs:

➤ Westgate Towers, 7600 W. Hwy. 192, Kissimmee

➤ Florida Plaza, 5730 E. Hwy. 192, Kissimmee

➤ Lake Buena Vista Factory Stores, state roads 535 and 536

➤ The Mercado, 8445 International Dr.

➤ Mystery Fun House, 5767 Major Blvd. (North International Drive area)

Stops include Church Street Station, the Orlando Science Center, Civic Theaters, the Orange County Museum of Art, the Orange County Historical Museum, Leu Gardens, the Cornell Fine Arts Museum, the Winter Park Scenic Boat Tour, the Langford Resort Hotel, Albin Polasek Galleries, the Shoppes of Park Avenue, the Morse Museum of American Art, the Enzian Theater, the Maitland Art Center, the Center for Birds of Prey, the Zora Neale Hurston National Museum of Fine Arts, and the Orlando City Hall Terrace Galleries.

Shuttle tickets—which are available at welcome centers, your hotel's concierge desk, and the hubs—cost $12 for adults and $9 for children 4 to 17 for the loop tour; $18 for adults and $12 for children for full service from the hubs to cultural attractions; and $10 for adults and $8 for children for round-trip transportation from the hubs to Church Street Station. For more information, call ☎ **407/855-6434,** or visit the Web site at **www.coachlines.com**. Shuttles run continuously through the day; the route takes about 1¹/₂ hours.

Bet You Didn't Know

Downtown Orlando has romantic **horse-drawn carriage rides** from Church Street Station through the downtown area. They run daily 7:30pm to midnight for $25 per couple, or $30 for three or four people.

Lymmo is a free bus system that runs in its own lanes in downtown Orlando, stopping at 13 spots including the Orlando Arena, Church Street Station, and City Hall. It stops at an additional six points if passengers want to get off or on. Buses run Monday to Thursday 6am to 10pm, until midnight on Friday; Saturday 10am to midnight; and Sunday 10am to 10pm.

The **Mears Transportation Group** (☎ **407/423-5566**) is the leading operator of tours from Orlando to Cypress Gardens, Kennedy Space Center, Busch Gardens Tampa, and other Central Florida points of interest. Check with your hotel desk for tours offered by Mears and other operators.

Put One Foot in Front of the Other

Orlando isn't a walking city like San Francisco or New York, but the downtown grid around Church Street Station has many clubs and restaurants. Winter Park, just north of downtown, is also known for its downtown area of smart shops, restaurants, cafes, and galleries. For pub crawling, it's best to focus on Downtown Disney, Church Street Station, or the Mercado, where you can stroll from show to shop to bistro.

Need more walking? We doubt it. It'll be the last thing you want to do after spending a day at one of the theme parks.

Part 4

Orlando's Best Restaurants

At last! You're safely tucked into your hotel room and exhausted from a day or more of travel. But you're not quite ready to crash and burn because your internal fuel tank is running perilously low. Well, don't fret. You're in luck. Few cities offer as many dining options as this one, because few have so many visitors. There was a day when Orlando was two-dimensional. There were the basic fast-food huts and the basic steak houses. Period. But those days are long over. Yes, there are more pancake houses and burger barns than ought to be legal in the free world, but growth has elevated Orlando into the big leagues, if not the World Series. The area has a vast menu of exciting restaurants with innovative chefs, clever themes, and professional service. Because Central Florida attracts visitors from every corner of the planet, you are assured of finding literally any kind of cuisine that tickles your taste buds. That means if you want to go ethnic, consider yourself gone. Even though they probably won't be spicy or authentic enough for New Yorkers or San Franciscans, the ethnic restaurants should please Middle Americans, and perhaps even a few fickle palates, as quality and quantity continue to improve.

Several members of the local restaurant circuit also offer live entertainment or special, even unusual, experiences you can't get anywhere else. But that's enough of an appetizer for the moment. Load up your family, put the sedan in gear, and point the headlights toward restaurant row. The lines will only get longer.

Chapter 9

ALL-U-CAN EAT
SPAGHETTI
AND MEATBALLS

The Lowdown on the Orlando Dining Scene

In This Chapter

➤ Tips on Walt Disney World Priority Seating

➤ What's hot now

➤ Choosing where to eat and how much to spend

➤ Dressing the part

➤ Dining with Disney characters

➤ Fast food galore

Orlando's explosive growth since the early 1970s has brought with it an explosion of good kitchens that have lifted the city out of the humdrum life and into a new world of exciting opportunities. Top hotels brought in noted chefs to make such restaurants as Dux (in the Peabody Hotel) and Arthur's 27 (in the Buena Vista Palace) the darlings of the culinary circuit. Even beyond the core attractions area, neighborhoods such as Winter Park have become sophisticated settings for dining and strolling.

There are 64 sit-down restaurants on Disney property. That doesn't include the many food courts, the self-serve snack bars, or any of the restaurants at the official Disney hotels in Lake Buena Vista. In recent years, celebrity chefs (like Wolfgang Puck) and just plain celebrities (like Gloria Estefan) have opened restaurants, adding to the wealth of choices. If the mood strikes you, you can dine in a Victorian time warp at the elegant Victoria and Albert's, or you can feast at a Moroccan palace, a Japanese teahouse, or a loony bin filled with cackling cartoon characters.

And if you're here from late October to late November, save a day or night for the annual **Epcot International Food & Wine Festival,** where the food, wine, and entertainment of 30 nations invade this theme park's answer to the United Nations, the World Showcase.

The city's near-quixotic quest to keep visitors entertained every minute of every day has spawned dinner theaters galore; currently, about a dozen of them vie for the tourist dollar. You can eat with the Mob one night, in the opera the next night, with gladiators or knights in armor the third night, and beside Arabian horsemen and women another. While these are neither known for the best eats nor the best acting, they do offer a two-for-one night out at usually reasonable prices, and the fun in virtually every case is PG-rated.

Bet You Didn't Know

You can take I-4 to Sanford and embark on a moonlight dinner-and-dancing cruise aboard the *Rivership Romance* (☎ 800/ 423-7401 or 407/321-5091; www.rivershipromance.com). But you don't have to go under the moonlight. The line has an assortment of cruise options and prices available.

Table for Four Coming Right Up: A Word About WDW Priority Seating

"Reservations" is a word not uttered by most WDW restaurants. The Land of the Madcap Mouse offers "Priority Seating." It's Disney's way of ensuring that you get the first available table, *after you arrive.* Since a table isn't kept empty for you, you will probably have to wait a few minutes after you get to the restaurant.

The popularity of the Priority Seating system has made it far more difficult to get a table just by walking in. **We strongly recommend calling ahead.** You can stake a claim to a table at WDW restaurants by calling ☎ **407/WDW-DINE** (407/ 939-3463).

You can also make priority-seating reservations once you are inside the Disney parks. We suggest you do this quickly upon your arrival. At Epcot, you can do this at your restaurant of choice, the Germany Pavilion, Guest Relations, or the Worldkey Information Satellite on the main concourse to World Showcase. In the Magic Kingdom, reserve at the restaurants

Dollars & Sense

Check free tabloids and magazines, which are stacked everywhere in Orlando hotels, for coupons good for a second meal free, some kind of a discount, or a free dessert with a meal. Watch for ads for a kids–eat–free special. You also can find these coupon publications in tourist information centers, most of the convenience stores, and in newspaper racks, among other places.

119

themselves. Ditto for Disney–MGM Studios, where you can also make the request at the Hollywood Junction Station on Hollywood Boulevard. At Animal Kingdom, Guest Relations will take care of things for you.

What's Hot Now

The exciting thing about Orlando, even for those who live here, is that new restaurants are popping up faster than you can say "pesto and sun-dried tomatoes."

Everyone loves the dining-entertainment complexes that are sweeping the city. Park in one spot and you're at the doorsteps of dozens of restaurants, clubs, and shows, so you can stroll and browse around until you find the one that piques your interest. The most recent big splashes are Downtown Disney, Pointe Orlando, and CityWalk, the new Universal Studios Escape "in" spot that should be fully opened by the time you are reading this. While there is an ebb and flow among the trendiest places, even some established complexes like Old Town, Pleasure Island, Church Street Station, and the Mercado continue to draw swarms of humanoids. And Downtown Orlando, once almost a ghost town after dark, has become a hotbed of smart clubs and restaurants.

Time-Savers

The least expensive places to eat in the theme parks feature self-service, but these fast-food joints may also have long lines. You may be tempted to try to eat and run so that you can spend more time riding the rides, but we believe your feet will ultimately be happier if you allow the time and money for a sit-down place that takes reservations. You'll have more energy throughout the day and avoid that late-afternoon fade that infects most tourists. Besides, the standard wait for a 3- or 4-minute ride is 30 minutes, so taking a restaurant break costs you little more than line time.

For the kids, there are character breakfasts galore, in and out of the theme parks.

If you're a meat-and-potatoes type or prefer a classic chophouse, drive-thru fast food, a familiar chain restaurant, or deli take-out, Orlando can serve them up in spades. While Orlando's growth (read—clutter) makes some of them a little harder to find, even those without three-story arches can be spotted with a little planning.

Location, Location, Location

➤ The **World Showcase at Epcot** is the ultimate place to wander for a choice of ethnic restaurants, with stunning settings. Each pavilion has two or more venues—usually one for leisurely sit-down dining and another for quicker, less expensive food. There are also snack carts throughout the loop.

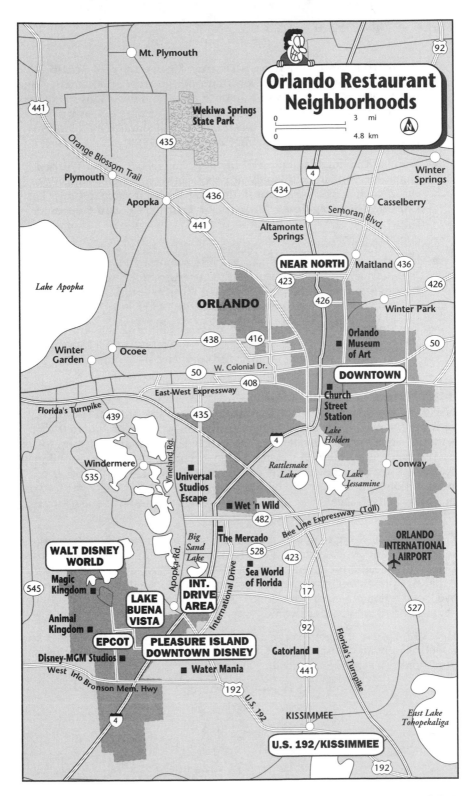

Orlando Restaurant Neighborhoods

➤ **Pleasure Island, Downtown Disney, Church Street Station,** and the **Mercado** are complexes that offer an array of restaurants, plus plenty of bars, shops, people-watching areas, and diversions to enjoy before and after dinner. They make for a full evening out, as will Universal's CityWalk, which, as we said earlier, should be fully operational and ready to fill your dance card by fall 1999.

➤ Many of the hotels and most of the larger malls have **food courts,** where everyone in your family or party can go in different directions to get their choice of food, then sit down at the same table to eat it. Try **Commander Ragtime's Midway of Fun, Food, and Games** at Church Street Exchange for a riot of food stalls, shops, and coin-gobbling games.

➤ If you're hankering for a romantic stroll, window shopping, sidewalk cafes, restaurants, or bars, walk **Fifth Avenue** in Winter Park, **Disney's BoardWalk,** or **Woodland Boulevard** (U.S. 17–92) in DeLand, a little college town an hour north of WDW off I-4.

➤ The **Universal Studios** area also offers good dining and strolling choices. You can get from Cape Cod to San Francisco in a New York minute, with a choice of dining, drinking, and shopping.

The Price Is Right

Naturally, the price of a meal will depend on what you order. If you pig out, or order the most expensive dishes on the menu, you'll spend more than if you order moderately. Chapter 10 gives you two kinds of price listings for each restaurant: a dollar ($) system that gives you an idea of what a full meal will cost and a price range for the entrees on the menu. The two pieces of information combined should help you choose the place that's right for you and your budget. One dollar sign means inexpensive and five dollar signs (the maximum) means extravagant.

One important thing to note is that all the listings are for good (often excellent) restaurants where you get a satisfying meal. We didn't list any crummy places just because they were cheap; neither did we list any outrageously expensive places where you pay an arm and a leg for well-arranged lettuce. We listed restaurants that serve good-quality food at a fair price, even though some of them aren't for everyone.

Here's how we've categorized restaurants according to price. If you order an appetizer, a main course, a dessert, and one drink, then add tax and tip, you'll probably spend, per person:

$$$$$	=	$60 and up
$$$$	=	$40 to $60
$$$	=	$25 to $40
$$	=	$15 to $25
$	=	$15 and under

Saving on Drinks

You've been around the block before. Drinks of any type, even sodas and bottled waters, can add substantially to the cost of a meal. A couple of kids sucking down sodas by the liter can double the price of an inexpensive burger meal, unless you're lucky enough to find a place that offers free refills. Don't be too shy to ask about the restaurant's policy on them. At some fast-food restaurants, self-serve drink refills are on the house. Many establishments refill coffee and iced tea free, but charge for refills on everything else.

A refillable mug at the various Disney resorts will run you about $8 to $9, and will net you free, or much cheaper refills. The mugs are supposedly good only at the resort at which you purchased them, but some (like the ones at Port Orleans and Dixie Landings, or the All-Star resorts) can be used at several of the Disney hotels' food courts without anyone making a fuss.

Orlando's clean tap water is a good idea for both your health and your wallet. In the hot Florida sun, you'll want to drink as much water as you can to keep your cool. Water is also cheerfully served in most restaurants (although you may have to ask for it in a few places). Only in the snootiest places would a waiter assume that you want high-priced bottled water. Don't give them the chance.

Dollars & Sense

Lunch menus are always priced lower than dinner menus. If you want to splurge on one of the better restaurants, go for lunch, or for the early-bird special. Even in moderate-priced restaurants, lunch menus are sometimes cheaper than dinner ones. Consider making noon your big meal of the day and go lighter later on, when prices go up.

At expensive restaurants, drinks are expensive, too. Think about enjoying a cocktail at a cheaper place before or after dinner (or in your hotel room) to save money. If you take the room route you also should consider the BYOB option or stopping at a local liquor mart. Prices in those in-room minibars, presuming yours has one, are usually no better than the expensive restaurants.

A Word About Taxes & Tipping

Sales taxes on restaurant meals and drinks are 6% to 7% throughout greater Orlando. (Do-it-yourselfers will find taxes don't apply to groceries.) In addition, a 15% tip is generally the standard in full-service restaurants and perhaps a 12% tip is warranted at a buffet where a server brings your drinks and cleans the table. Those who have that predinner drink in the bar should leave a small tip to reward the server. The practice of tipping the head waiter has all but disappeared, but money can talk in a crowded restaurant where you want a special table.

No Monkey Suits Required:
What to Wear to Orlando Restaurants

Even the fanciest restaurants in the theme parks have a very casual dress code for dinner, because most of their diners have been worn out by a day on the hoof. Neat and casual is the rule.

There are, however, a few exceptions. Jackets are required in some of the better spots, including Victoria and Albert's. You won't be overdressed if you wear a tie and jacket in places frequented by people here on business. The better hotel restaurants more often than not insist on your Sunday best. You'll find a dress code in the individual restaurant listings in chapter 10.

Dollars & Sense

Don't overlook Orlando's supermarkets. Goodings, Albertson's, Kash 'n' Karry, and Publix have extensive deli sections that offer a big selection of hot and cold foods for take-out. Picnic by the pool, on your balcony, or in a grassy park for little more than a meal you'd prepare at home.

If you'll be dining alfresco under the Florida sunshine, cover up those bald heads, and pasty arms and legs, at least until you get a base tan. Otherwise, you may start to look like a lobster before you get to eat one. Carry some sunscreen during the hot and sticky months, or find a table with an umbrella. Think twice about dining outside in winter months, or at least bring along a sweater. While most don't expect it, Central Florida nights can get pretty chilly. (In fact, we'd suggest taking a sweater or jacket to dinner in any season, because even in summer there's always the chance the staff thermostat czar has lowered the air-conditioner dial to subzero.)

Eek, a Mouse! Dining with Disney Characters

It's a beguiling idea. Combine a meal with a host and hostess who will leave your children wide-eyed: Pocahontas and her friends, Mickey and Minnie, Cinderella, or Aladdin. It's not the cheapest way to go, and some of you may want a break from fantasy friends, but the kids will love the added exposure. *Priority Seating is a must, and you should make the call as far in advance as possible.* Also, note that restaurants inside theme parks require park admission. Children ages 2 and under eat free. All of these restaurants take American Express, MasterCard, and Visa.

🌟 **Artist Point**
        You and your kids can feast on an all-you-can-eat breakfast buffet with Pocahontas and friends in a rustic North Woods lodge.

In Disney's Wilderness Lodge, 901 Timberline Dr. ☎ ***407/939-3463. Prices: $14.50 adults, $8.95 children 3–11. AE, MC, V. Open: Daily 5:30–11am.***

Cape May Café

Have a generous buffet breakfast or dinner with Chip 'n' Dale, Admiral Goofy, or Pluto. You never know who or what will show up, but the photo ops are sure to be good when they do.

In Disney's Beach Club Resort, 1800 Epcot Resorts Blvd. ☎ *407/939-3463.* **Prices:** *$14.95 adults, $8.50 children 3–11. AE, MC, V.* **Open:** *Daily 7–11am and 5:30–9:30pm.*

Chef Mickey's

Chef Mickey will whip up a buffet breakfast, or a prime rib dinner buffet, and still find time to schmooze with his pint-sized guests.

In Disney's Contemporary Resort, 4600 N. World Dr. ☎ *407/939-3463.* **Prices:** *$14.95 adults, $7.95 children 3–11 for breakfast; $19.95 adults, $8.95 children 3–11 for dinner. AE, MC, V.* **Open:** *Daily 7:30–11:30am and 5–9:30pm.*

Beating the Lines

All theme-park restaurants, cafeterias, and food courts are mobbed between 11:30am and 2pm, and between 6 and 9pm. Try to eat at other hours to avoid long lines here. You can ride the most popular rides with shorter lines while everyone else is chowing down!

Cinderella's Royal Table

What a nifty way to start your day in the Magic Kingdom! Eat all you want from the buffet while various Disney characters, including Cinderella, shower you with thrown kisses. Park admission is required.

In Cinderella's Castle, Magic Kingdom. ☎ *407/939-3463.* **Prices:** *$14.95 adults, $7.95 children 3–11. AE, MC, V.* **Open:** *Daily for breakfast (Mon, Thurs, Sat 7:30–10am; all other days 8–10am); daily 4pm until park closes for dinner.*

Coral Café

This is a great way to sleep in a little on Sunday, still have an early meal with your favorite characters, and then tackle one of the parks or another area attraction.

1200 Epcot Resorts Blvd. in the Walt Disney World Dolphin. ☎ *407/934-4000. Priority Seating required.* **Prices:** *$16.95 adults, $12.95 children 4–12. AE, CB, DC, DISC, MC, V.* **Open:** *Sunday brunch only, 8am–noon.*

Fulton's Crab House

Captain Mickey and his riverboat crew dish out a hearty breakfast to sea dogs 7 days a week.

1670 Buena Vista Dr. between Pleasure Island and Disney Village Marketplace. ☎ *407/934-2628. Reservations suggested.* **Prices:** *$12.95 adults, $7.95 children 3–11. AE, MC, V.* **Open:** *Daily 8:30–10am.*

Kids Garden Grill

This is one of the more entertaining character meals available because the Disney gang hosts your ride through a desert, a prairie, and the Great Plains. The restaurant revolves while you sit in a semicircular booth. The food is hearty American all the way. Park admission is required, of course.

In the Land Pavilion, Epcot. ☎ *407/939-3463.* **Prices:** *breakfast $14.95 adults, $8.25 children 3–11; lunch $16.95 adults, $9.95 children; dinner $17.50 adults, $9.95 children. AE, MC, V.* **Open:** *Daily 8:30am–8pm.*

Kids Garden Grove Café

The once-a-week breakfast shindig with Goofy and Pluto gives you a choice of à la carte or buffet breakfasts with some character favorites. If you're not in the mood to wake up with a 'toon, consider joining the dinner circuit, Monday, Wednesday, Thursday, and Friday, with Rafiki, Timon, Winnie the Pooh, and Tigger, too.

1200 Epcot Resorts Blvd. in the Walt Disney World Swan. ☎ *407/934-3000, ext. 1618. Priority Seating accepted.* **Prices:** *breakfast $12.95 adults, $7.95 children 3–12; dinner (menu prices) $17–$30. AE, CB, DC, DISC, MC, V.* **Open:** *Saturday 8–11am; daily 6–10pm.*

Kids Liberty Tree Tavern

In a stately colonial setting, a gaggle of Disney regulars stops by to make sure your kids get plenty to eat from a menu that includes roast chicken, marinated flank steak, sausage, smashed spuds, rice pilaf, vegetables, and apple crisp with ice cream. Park admission is required.

In Liberty Sq., Magic Kingdom. ☎ *407/939-3463.* **Prices:** *$19.95 adults, $9.95 children 3–11. AE, MC, V.* **Open:** *Daily 4pm–park closing.*

Dollars & Sense

Happy-hour specials are held at almost every bar in town. Some offer two-for-one drinks; others offer free buffets so generous that you won't need dinner. It pays to call ahead to a few bars to ask what's available, and when. It also pays to scout those coupon publications for leads.

Kids Minnie's Menehune & Mickey's Tropical Luau

The breakfast is Minnie's masterpiece, served family style, while Disney characters lend a hand. The children can play a Polynesian instrument in the daily parade. Later in the day, Mickey's luau is a shorter version of the Polynesian Resort's Luau Dinner Show, and it's ideal for younger tots who need to eat and go to bed early. The menu is set, serving roast chicken, vegetables, cinnamon bread, and an ice-cream sundae. You'll receive a shell lei as you leave.

In Disney's Polynesian Resort, 1600 Seven Seas Dr. ☎ *407/939-3463.* **Prices:**

*breakfast $14.95 adults, $8.95 children
3–11; luau dinner (without characters) $38
adults, $19.50 children. AE, MC, V.* **Open:**
Daily 7:30–10:30am; luau at 4:30pm.

1900 Park Fare
Mary Poppins, Winnie the Pooh,
Goofy, and Pluto are just a few of the
Disney gang that join you for breakfast or
dinner. A mammoth pipe organ makes
this one of the kingdom's most impressive
rooms. Breakfast is a lavish buffet. Mickey
and Minnie come out for a dinner of
prime rib, fresh fish, or stuffed pork.

*In Disney's Grand Floridian Beach Resort,
4401 Floridian Way.* ☎ *407/939-3463.*
Prices: *breakfast $15.95 adults, $9.95
children 3–11; dinner $19.95 adults, $9.50
children. AE, MC, V.* **Open:** *Daily
7:30–11:30am and 5:30–9pm.*

Bet You Didn't Know

A meal plan is available to
guests at Walt Disney World
resorts. It isn't widely publi-
cized, but you'll save 10% if
you're planning to buy all
your meals from Walt. (Of
course, if you buy at least
some of them outside the
parks you might save more
than 10%.) Ask about the
meal plan when you reserve
your accommodations.

Watercress Café
Disney characters cavort while you dine from the buffet or order
from the menu.

In the Buena Vista Palace, 1900 Buena Vista Dr. ☎ *407/827-2727. No reservations accepted; arrive early.* **Prices:** *buffet $12.95 adults, $6.95 children 3–11.
AE, MC, V.* **Open:** *Sun 8–10:30am.*

McFood: Drive-Thrus, Pizzerias & the Chain Gang
Like every city in America, Orlando has its share of burger barns, familiar
restaurant chains, and pizzerias (including several that deliver to your room).
All of the towns and neighborhoods in this guide, except Walt Disney World,
have a huge choice of chain- and fast-food factories for those times when
chowing down on a burger is all you want. You won't have to drive more
than a few minutes on International Drive or U.S. 192 to find a place that
satisfies the whole family. Driving north to south from Kirkman Road on
International Drive, you'll find Howard Johnson's, Wendy's, Ponderosa, Pizza
Hut, Chili's, Olive Garden, Burger King, Goodings (a chain supermarket with
great take-out), Friendly's, and Bob Evans.

Chapter 10

Restaurants A to Z

In This Chapter

➤ Easy-to-scan indexes of restaurants by location, price, and cuisine

➤ Full reviews of the best restaurants in the area

Hungry yet? Stomach growling like a cornered wildcat? Ready to eat things no sane person would eat—like those orange peanut-butter crackers, a pickled egg, or, heaven forbid, a Moon Pie?

Look no further. The cuisine cavalry is riding to the rescue (yep, that's us). We've gone through Orlando's restaurants, picked those we think are the best (why waste your time reading about places we don't love?), and reviewed them in alphabetical order. We've even thrown in handy indexes so you can scan them by location, price, and type of cuisine, too. All you have to do is decide which food mood you're in and how much you want to cough up. Then pick your restaurant *du jour* from the indexes in the front and turn to the review deeper in this chapter.

Heads Up: All sit-down restaurants in Walt Disney World are happy to accept American Express, MasterCard, and Visa, and all of them have children's menus. All WDW restaurants are smoke-free, meaning if you have to light up, you must do it on the patios and terraces. No alcohol is served anywhere in the Magic Kingdom, though it is available at some Epcot, Disney–MGM Studios, and Animal Kingdom restaurants.

Quick Picks: Orlando's Restaurants at a Glance
Restaurant Index by Location

Walt Disney World

Restaurants within all WDW theme parks require park admission, of course. Eat here on days when you want to be in the parks anyway, unless you have a World Hopper Pass that allows you to drift from park to park without paying additional admission. If you haven't already paid the $5 daily parking fee, that's another expense for the pleasure of park dining. Restaurants at Disney resorts don't require paying admission. While Pleasure Island has an admission charge, diners can slip into restaurants without buying a ticket for the complex. Since liquid muscle relaxants can be critical at the end of a day surrounded by marauding, sugar-fixed kids, don't say we didn't remind you one more time: *No booze is served in the Magic Kingdom,* and we don't recommend sneaking it in like some of you do at football games. Enough said?

Akershus (Epcot) $$

Artist Point (Fort Wilderness) $$

Au Petit Café (Epcot) $$

Bistro de Paris (Epcot) $$$$

California Grill (Contemporary Resort) $$–$$$

Cinderella's Royal Table (Magic Kingdom) $$$

Citricos (Grand Floridian) $$–$$$

Coral Reef (Epcot) $$$

Fulton's Crab House (Pleasure Island) $$$$

Hollywood Brown Derby (Disney–MGM Studios) $$$

L'Originale Alfredo di Roma Ristorante (Epcot) $$–$$$

Marrakesh (Epcot) $$$

Nine Dragons (Epcot) $$$

Planet Hollywood (Pleasure Island) $$

Plaza Restaurant (Magic Kingdom) $$

Prime Time Café (Disney–MGM Studios) $$–$$$

Rainforest Cafe (Downtown Disney Marketplace and Animal Kingdom) $$

Sci-Fi Dine-In Theater Restaurant (Disney–MGM Studios) $$–$$$

Victoria and Albert's (Disney's Grand Floridian Beach Resort) $$$$$

Yachtsman Steakhouse (Disney's Yacht Club Resort) $$–$$$

Lake Buena Vista

Arthur's 27 $$$$$

Columbia $$$

Portobello Yacht Club (Pleasure Island) $$

129

U.S. 192/Kissimmee
New Punjab $

International Drive Area
Atlantis $$$$$

Bahama Breeze $$

Bergamo's $$–$$$

Black Swan $$$$$

B-Line Diner $$–$$$

Cafe Tu Tu Tango $$

Capriccio $$$

Chatham's Place $$–$$$

Christini's Ristorante $$$

Dux $$$$$

Landry's Seafood House $$–$$$

Michelangelo $$$$

Ming Court $$$

Morton's of Chicago $$$$

New Punjab $

Race Rock $–$$

Wild Jack's $$$

Downtown
Café Europa $$$

Le Provence $$$–$$$$

Little Saigon $$

Manuel's on the 28th $$$$$

Numero Uno $$

Pebbles $–$$

Thanh Thuy $

Near North
Antonio's La Fiamma $$

Boston's Fish House $

Bubbaloo's Bodacious BBQ $–$$

Enzo's on the Lake $$$

La Scala $$–$$$

Maison et Jardin $$$$

130

Park Plaza Gardens $$–$$$

Rolando's $–$$

Straub's Boatyard $$

South Orlando

Le Coq Au Vin $$

Far South

Chalet Suzanne $$$–$$$$

Restaurant Index by Price

Our price ranges, assuming that you'll have an appetizer, a main course, a dessert, and one drink, pay the state sales tax (as if you have a choice), and leave a tip, are as follows:

$$$$$ = $60 and up

$$$$ = $40 to $60

$$$ = $25 to $40

$$ = $15 to $25

$ = $15 and under

$$$$$

Arthur's 27 (Lake Buena Vista)

Atlantis (International Drive Area)

Black Swan (International Drive Area)

Dux (International Drive Area)

Manuel's on the 28th (Downtown)

Victoria and Albert's (Disney's Grand Floridian Beach Resort)

$$$$

Bistro de Paris (Epcot)

Fulton's Crab House (Pleasure Island)

Maison et Jardin (Near North)

Michelangelo (International Drive Area)

Morton's of Chicago (International Drive Area)

$$$–$$$$

Chalet Suzanne (Far South)

Le Provence (Downtown)

$$$

Café Europa (Downtown)

Capriccio (International Drive Area)

Christini's Ristorante (International Drive Area)

Cinderella's Royal Table (Magic Kingdom)

Columbia (Lake Buena Vista)

Coral Reef (Epcot)

Enzo's on the Lake (Near North)

Hollywood Brown Derby (Disney–MGM Studios)

Le Provence (Downtown)

Marrakesh (Epcot)

131

Ming Court (International Drive Area)

Nine Dragons (Epcot)

Wild Jacks (International Drive Area)

$$-$$$

Bergamo's (International Drive Area)

B-Line Diner (International Drive Area)

California Grill (Contemporary Resort)

Chatham's Place (International Drive Area)

Citricos (Grand Floridian)

Landry's Seafood House (International Drive Area)

La Scala (Near North)

L'Originale Alfredo di Roma Ristorante (Epcot)

Park Plaza Gardens (Near North)

Prime Time Café (Disney–MGM Studios)

Sci-Fi Dine-In Theater Restaurant (Disney–MGM Studios)

Yachtsman Steakhouse (Disney's Yacht Club Resort)

$$

Akershus (Epcot)

Antonio's La Fiamma (Near North)

Artist Point (Disney's Wilderness Lodge)

Bahama Breeze (International Drive Area)

Cafe Tu Tu Tango (International Drive Area)

Le Coq Au Vin (South Orlando)

Little Saigon (Downtown)

Numero Uno (Downtown)

Planet Hollywood (Pleasure Island)

Plaza Restaurant (Magic Kingdom)

Portobello Yacht Club (Lake Buena Vista)

Rainforest Cafe (Downtown Disney Marketplace and Animal Kingdom)

Straub's Boatyard (Near North)

$-$$

Au Petit Café (Epcot)

Bubbaloo's Bodacious BBQ (Near North)

Pebbles (Downtown)

Race Rock (International Drive Area)

$

Boston's Fish House (Near North)

New Punjab (International Drive Area; also U.S. 192/Kissimmee)

Rolando's (Near North)

Thanh Thuy (Downtown)

Restaurant Index by Cuisine
American

Artist Point (Disney's Wilderness Lodge) $$

B-Line Diner (International Drive Area) $$-$$$

Bubbaloo's Bodacious BBQ (Near North) $-$$

California Grill (Disney's Contemporary Resort) $$–$$$

Chalet Suzanne (Far South) $$$–$$$$

Chatham's Place (International Drive Area) $$–$$$

Cinderella's Royal Table (Magic Kingdom) $$$

Citricos (Disney's Grand Floridian) $$–$$$

Hollywood Brown Derby (Disney–MGM Studios) $$$

Pebbles (Downtown) $–$$

Planet Hollywood (Pleasure Island) $$

Plaza Restaurant (Magic Kingdom) $$

Prime Time Café (Disney–MGM Studios) $$–$$$

Race Rock (International Drive Area) $–$$

Rainforest Cafe (Downtown Disney Marketplace and Animal Kingdom) $$

Sci-Fi Dine-In Theater Restaurant (Disney–MGM Studios) $$–$$$

Wild Jacks (International Drive Area) $$$

Asian

Little Saigon (Vietnamese; Downtown) $$

Ming Court (Chinese; International Drive Area) $$$

Nine Dragons (Chinese; Epcot) $$$

Thanh Thuy (Vietnamese; Downtown) $

Continental

Park Plaza Gardens (Near North) $$–$$$

French

Au Petit Café (Epcot) $$

Bistro de Paris (Epcot) $$$$

Le Coq Au Vin (South Orlando) $$

Le Provence (Downtown) $$$–$$$$

Maison et Jardin (Near North) $$$$

Italian

Antonio's La Fiamma (Near North) $$

Bergamo's (International Drive Area) $$–$$$

Capriccio (International Drive Area) $$$

Christini's Ristorante (International Drive Area) $$$

Enzo's on the Lake (Near North) $$$

La Scala (Near North) $$–$$$

L'Originale Alfredo di Roman Ristorante (Epcot) $$–$$$

Michelangelo (International Drive Area) $$$$

Portobello Yacht Club (Lake Buena Vista) $$

Other Ethnic

Akershus (Norwegian; Epcot) $$

Bahama Breeze (Caribbean; International Drive Area) $$

Café Europa (German and Hungarian; Downtown) $$$

133

Columbia (Cuban; Lake Buena Vista) $$$

Marrakesh (Moroccan; Epcot) $$$

New Punjab (Indian; International Drive Area and U.S. 192/Kissimmee) $

Numero Uno (Cuban; Downtown) $$

Rolando's (Cuban; Near North) $–$$

Haute Cuisine

Arthur's 27 (Lake Buena Vista) $$$$$

Atlantis (International Drive Area) $$$$$

Black Swan (Lake Buena Vista) $$$$$

Cafe Tu Tu Tango (International Drive Area) $$

Dux (International Drive Area) $$$$$

Manuel's on the 28th (Downtown) $$$$$

Victoria and Albert's (Grand Floridian Beach Resort) $$$$$

Seafood

Atlantis (International Drive Area) $$$$$

Boston's Fish House (Near North) $

Coral Reef (Epcot) $$$

Fulton's Crab House (Pleasure Island) $$$$

Landry's Seafood House (International Drive Area) $$–$$$

Straub's Boatyard (Near North) $$

Steaks

Morton's of Chicago (International Drive Area) $$$$

Straub's Boatyard (Near North) $$

Yachtsman Steakhouse (Disney's Yacht Club Resort) $$–$$$

Our Favorite Restaurants A to Z

Akershus

$$. Walt Disney World (Epcot; park admission required). NORWEGIAN.

A huge table spills over with the traditional hot and cold dishes of a Scandinavian smorgasbord: venison in cream sauce, smoked pork with honey mustard sauce, and gravlax (for the culturally impaired, this is a cured salmon whose itty-bitty bones have been yanked out with tweezers). The trimmings include yummies like red cabbage (please stay downwind of everyone after dinner), boiled potatoes, a frosty Norwegian beer, and for dessert, a classic "veiled maiden." Crisp linens, glowing woods, and gleaming crystal surround you. Ask about the child care center, where kids play while you dine.

Norway Pavilion, World Showcase Epcot. ☎ *407/939-3463. Arranging Priority Seating in advance is recommended.* **Prices:** *Lunch buffet $11.95 adults, $4.75* *children 4–9, free for children under 3. Dinner buffet $18.50 adults, $7.95 children 4–9. A nonsmorgasbord child's meal is $4. AE, MC, V.* **Open:** *Daily 11:30am–4pm; 4:15pm–park closing.*

Antonio's La Fiamma
$$. Near North. ITALIAN.
Go looking for a good time and enjoy the loud, frenetic atmosphere. The ground floor has a wood-burning oven and lighter fare. Upstairs you can order traditional Italian favorites, choose from a pretty respectable wine list, and enjoy the view of Lake Lily. Antonio's also has a full bar and a gourmet food-and-wine shop.

611 S. Orlando Ave., Maitland. ☎ *407/645-5523. Reservations recommended. Casual.* **Main courses:** *$10–$25. AE, DISC, MC, V.* **Open:** *Daily 11:30am–2:30pm; Mon–Thurs 5–10pm, Fri 11am–2:30pm, Fri–Sat 5–11pm.*

Arthur's 27
$$$$$. Lake Buena Vista. HAUTE CUISINE.
The views from this splendid 27th-floor restaurant are spectacular at sunset and when Disney fireworks light the sky. Romantic and mellow, it has the mood of a smart supper club in a 1930s movie, minus the clouds of cigarette smoke. You'll choose from selections like pan-seared breast of squab with chestnut risotto, or steamed scallops and poached oysters with black cappellini pasta. Don't skip dessert—especially good is the chocolate cake. There's an impressive wine list.

In the Wyndham Palace Resort, 1900 Lake Buena Vista Dr., just north of Hotel Plaza Blvd. ☎ *407/827-2727. Reservations required.* **Parking:** *free self-parking; validated valet parking.* **Prices:** *Main courses $20–$30; fixed-price menus $49–$60. AE, DC, DISC, MC, V.* **Open:** *Daily 6:30–10:30pm.*

Beating the Lines
If you plan to eat at a restaurant in Walt Disney World, we can't stress this enough: *Make a Priority Seating reservation before you go!*

Kids Artist Point
$$. Walt Disney World.
AMERICAN NORTHWEST.
Pack your outdoor spirit and climb aboard for a trip to the Pacific Northwest. Don't forget your appetite, too. Keeping with its theme, this restaurant's menu is bursting with game and salmon as well as steaks, chops, and other marine delicacies that are grilled over an open, hardwood fire. Options include cocktails, a health-conscious menu, and a character breakfast.

Disney's Wilderness Lodge, 901 W. Timberline Dr. ☎ *407/824-3200. Reservations recommended. Casual.* **Parking:** *valet parking.* **Main courses:** *$15–$25. AE, MC, V.* **Open:** *Sun–Sat 7:30–11:30am and 5–10:30pm.*

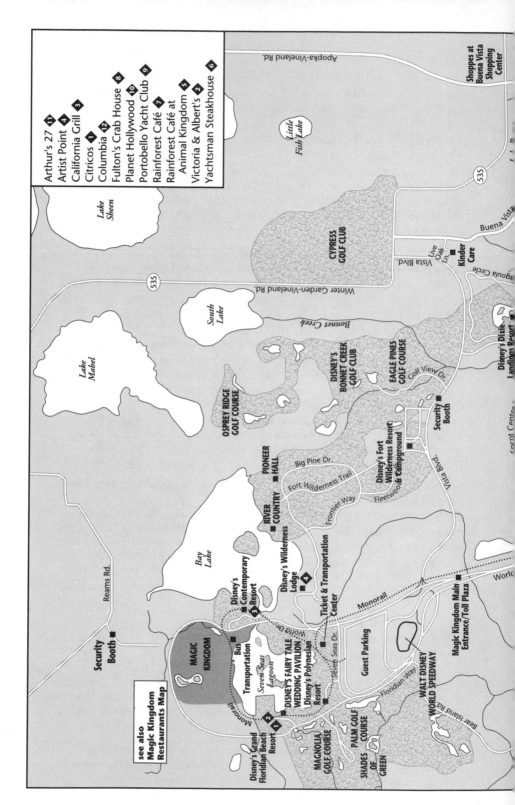

Arthur's 27 **1**
Artist Point **4**
California Grill **3**
Citricos **4**
Columbia **12**
Fulton's Crab House **8**
Planet Hollywood **10**
Portobello Yacht Club **9**
Rainforest Café **7**
Rainforest Café at Animal Kingdom **5**
Victoria & Albert's **2**
Yachtsman Steakhouse **6**

see also
Magic Kingdom
Restaurants Map

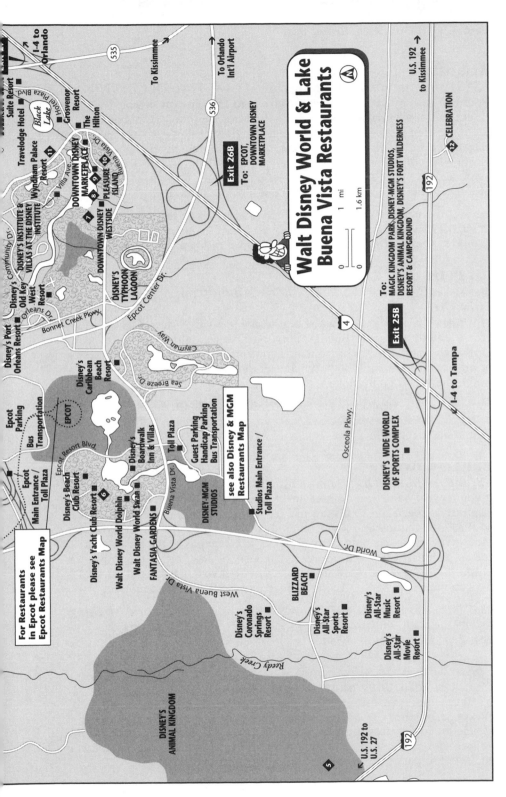

Walt Disney World & Lake Buena Vista Restaurants

To:
MAGIC KINGDOM PARK, DISNEY-MGM STUDIOS,
DISNEY'S ANIMAL KINGDOM, DISNEY'S FORT WILDERNESS
RESORT & CAMPGROUND

To: EPCOT, DOWNTOWN DISNEY MARKETPLACE

Exit 26B

Exit 25B

0   1 mi
0   1.6 km

For Restaurants in Epcot please see Epcot Restaurants Map

see also Disney & MGM Restaurants Map

I-4 to Orlando

To Kissimmee

To Orlando Int'l Airport

U.S. 192 to Kissimmee

CELEBRATION

I-4 to Tampa

U.S. 192 to U.S. 27

Hotel Plaza Blvd.

Suite Resort

Travelodge Hotel

Wyndham Palace Resort

Grosvenor Resort

The Hilton

Black Lake

Disney's Institute & Villas at the Disney Institute

DOWNTOWN DISNEY MARKETPLACE

PLEASURE ISLAND

DOWNTOWN DISNEY WESTSIDE

DISNEY'S TYPHOON LAGOON

Disney's Port Orleans Resort

Disney's Old Key West Resort

Buena Vista Dr.

Villa Ave.

Orleans Dr.

Disney's Community Dr.

Bonnet Creek Pkwy.

Epcot Center Dr.

Disney's Caribbean Beach Resort

Sea Breeze Dr.

Cayman Way

Epcot Parking

Bus Transportation

EPCOT

Epcot Main Entrance / Toll Plaza

Epcot Resort Blvd.

Disney's Beach Club Resort

Disney's Yacht Club Resort

Walt Disney World Dolphin

Walt Disney World Swan

Disney's Boardwalk Inn & Villas

FANTASIA GARDENS

Toll Plaza

Guest Parking Handicap Parking Bus Transportation

Studios Main Entrance / Toll Plaza

DISNEY-MGM STUDIOS

Buena Vista Dr.

West Buena Vista Dr.

World Dr.

Osceola Pkwy.

DISNEY'S WIDE WORLD OF SPORTS COMPLEX

Reedy Creek

DISNEY'S ANIMAL KINGDOM

BLIZZARD BEACH

Disney's Coronado Springs Resort

Disney's All-Star Sports Resort

Disney's All-Star Music Resort

Disney's All-Star Movie Resort

5

6

7

8

9

10

535

536

4

192

42

Atlantis
$$$$$. International Drive Area. SEAFOOD/HAUTE CUISINE.

In one of the city's most elegant settings, you can dine on sirloin steak, succulent scallops, or roast rack of lamb, while housed in a picture-book dining room. Beveled glass, crystal glasses, and the glow of rich woodwork create an elegant feel and look. Candlelight creates just the right sparkle on tables that gleam with china and silver. Appetizers, soups, salads, and desserts are inspired. Watch out for the after-dinner liqueur cart, though—a sip of some of the brandies can cost more than the rest of the dinner.

In the Renaissance Orlando Resort, 6677 Sea Harbor Dr., across from Sea World. ☎ ***407/351-5555.*** *Reservations strongly recommended.* **Main courses:** *$20–$28. AE, DC, DISC, MC, V.* **Open:** *Mon–Sat 6–10pm.*

Au Petit Café
$–$$. Walt Disney World (Epcot; park admission required). FRENCH.

This sidewalk cafe would not be out of place in Nice or Paris. Make sure you're seated in time for IllumiNations, and have a light supper of *salade niçoise,* croissant sandwiches, quiche Lorraine, chicken baked in puff pastry, or prawns basted with basil butter. Linger over a glass or two of wine and watch the World go by. (Sigh.)

France Pavilion, World Showcase, Epcot. ☎ ***407/939-3463.*** *Reservations not accepted.* **Main courses:** *$7.75–$15.50. AE, MC, V.* **Open:** *Daily 11am to an hour before park closing.*

Bahama Breeze
$$. International Drive Area. CARIBBEAN/CREOLE.

If you try real hard, you can imagine you're in the Bahamas as you dine on island-style specialties in a straw market setting. From the people who created the Olive Garden and Red Lobster, this is the prototype for a new chain that serves paella, coconut curry chicken, key lime pie, and a mean piña colada pudding. Choose from among 50 beers or dare one of the fruity rum drinks. If you're pressed for time, make sure to arrive before 6pm on weekdays and 5pm on weekends or you'll face a 2-hour wait for a table.

8849 International Dr. ☎ ***407/248-2499.*** *Reservations not accepted.* **Parking:** *No problem, mon.* **Main courses:** *$6.95–$14.95. AE, MC, V.* **Open:** *Sun–Thurs 4pm–1am, Fri–Sat 4pm–1:30am.*

⭐Kids Bergamo's
$$–$$$. International Drive Area. ITALIAN.

It's in the middle of Tourist Way, a.k.a. International Drive, and it's almost always packed, but the singing waiters are nearly as fun as the food. We're talking Broadway show tunes and opera mixed with roasted veal and steamed mussels among other treats from northern Italy. Even if you don't eat, this is a good spot to park your keister and enjoy the show over cocktails.

Mercado Shopping Village, 8445 International Dr. ☎ *407/352-3805. Reservations recommended. Casual.* **Main courses:** *$12–$37. AE, DC, MC, V.* **Open:** *Sun–Thurs 5–10pm, Fri–Sat 5–11pm.*

Bistro de Paris

$$$$. Walt Disney World (Epcot; park admission required). CLASSIC FRENCH.

The classic French cuisine here is hard to fault. The temptations are so compelling that diners tend to forget the wonderful mood setters, such as the candlelight and art nouveau touches, once the food starts coming. You're really a complete idiot if you don't start with renowned chef Paul Bocuse's famous duck foie gras salad with fresh greens and artichoke hearts. Main dishes include roasted red snapper in potato crust, cradled in a bed of spinach and ladled with a red-wine lobster sauce.

France Pavilion, World Showcase, Epcot. ☎ *407/939-3463. Arranging Priority Seating in advance is required.* **Main courses:** *$20.50–$26.95. AE, MC, V.* **Open:** *Daily 4pm to an hour before park closing.*

Extra! Extra!

If you're looking for kid-friendly restaurants without mice there are plenty of other good restaurants to take kids to, even if they don't have Disney characters to keep the youngsters entertained. The food may not be gourmet, but it's a little more interesting than the usual fare served in character dining rooms. It's also a heck of a lot better than the fast fooderies.

The kids will love the following:

B-Line Diner (International Drive Area; $$–$$$)
Planet Hollywood (Pleasure Island; $$)
Prime Time Café (Disney–MGM Studios; $$–$$$)
Race Rock (International Drive Area; $–$$)
Rainforest Cafe (Downtown Disney Marketplace and Animal
    Kingdom; $$)
Sci-Fi Dine-In Theater Restaurant (Disney–MGM Studios; $$–$$$)

Black Swan

$$$$$. International Drive Area. HAUTE CUISINE.

This is the perfect place for a romantic dinner accompanied by a fine vintage chosen from an extensive wine list. Try the grilled portobello mushrooms snuggled in a bed of wilted arugula with a drift of Asiago cheese, followed by the rack of lamb roasted to pink perfection or Southwestern-style chicken served with black beans, roasted corn relish, and cilantro chili fettuccine.

Save room for one of the meal cappers—perhaps an apple tart that's been drenched with caramel sauce and whipped cream, or one of the dessert wines or liqueurs.

In the Hyatt Regency Grand Cypress, 1 N. Jacaranda, off FL 535. ☎ **407/ 239-1999.** *Reservations recommended.* **Main courses:** *$25–$34. AE, CB, DC, DISC, JCB, MC, V.* **Open:** *Daily 6–10pm.*

Extra! Extra!

If you're looking for a romantic dinner, head for:

Atlantis (International Drive Area; $$$$$)
Arthur's 27 (Lake Buena Vista; $$$$$)
Bistro de Paris (Epcot; $$$$)
Black Swan (International Drive Area; $$$$$)
Café Europa (Downtown; $$$)
Chalet Suzanne (Far South/Lake Wales; $$$–$$$$)
Le Provence (Downtown; $$$–$$$$)
Maison et Jardin (Near North; $$$$)
Manuel's on the 28th (Downtown; $$$$$)
Victoria and Albert's (Disney's Grand Floridian Beach Resort; $$$$$)

 B-Line Diner
$$–$$$. International Drive Area. AMERICAN
Gleaming chrome and tile create a vision of yesterday's roadside diners in this informal, inexpensive gathering place popular with visiting celebrities. Kids have their own menu. Grown-ups can order diner classics as well as sophisticated specialties, health foods, vegetarian specials, comfort foods, and pastries to eat in or take out. Order drinks from the full bar. An added bonus: It's open 24 hours, so this is the place to go when you've just gotta have that 2am cheeseburger.

In the Peabody Orlando, 9801 International Dr. ☎ **407/345-4460.** *Reservations not accepted.* **Parking:** *free self-parking; validated valet parking.* **Main courses:** *dinner $8.95–$22. AE, CB, DC, DISC, JCB, MC, V.* **Open:** *Daily 24 hours (dinner 5–11pm).*

Boston's Fish House
$. Near North. SEAFOOD.
The fried and broiled seafood dishes here play to a packed house because the portions are so generous and the prices are so modest. This is a terrific bargain in a no-frills setting. You place your order at the counter and wait at your table until the meal is brought. If you're a light eater, the hearty

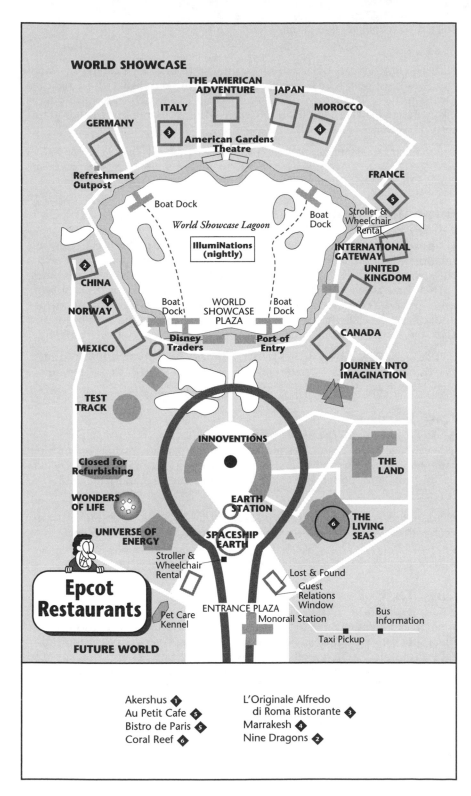

WORLD SHOWCASE

THE AMERICAN ADVENTURE

ITALY
JAPAN
MOROCCO

GERMANY

American Gardens Theatre

FRANCE

Refreshment Outpost

Boat Dock

World Showcase Lagoon

Boat Dock

Stroller & Wheelchair Rental

IllumiNations (nightly)

INTERNATIONAL GATEWAY

UNITED KINGDOM

CHINA

Boat Dock

WORLD SHOWCASE PLAZA

Boat Dock

NORWAY

CANADA

MEXICO

Disney Traders

Port of Entry

JOURNEY INTO IMAGINATION

TEST TRACK

INNOVENTIONS

THE LAND

Closed for Refurbishing

WONDERS OF LIFE

EARTH STATION

THE LIVING SEAS

UNIVERSE OF ENERGY

SPACESHIP EARTH

Epcot Restaurants

Stroller & Wheelchair Rental

Lost & Found

Guest Relations Window

Pet Care Kennel

ENTRANCE PLAZA

Monorail Station

Bus Information

FUTURE WORLD

Taxi Pickup

Akershus ❶
Au Petit Cafe ❺
Bistro de Paris ❺
Coral Reef ❻

L'Originale Alfredo di Roma Ristorante ❸
Marrakesh ❹
Nine Dragons ❷

seafood chowder can make a meal. Or choose from today's catch of ocean or freshwater seafood. For landlubbers, there are chicken dishes and burgers. Dishes arrive piled high with food and fixings like french fries, hush puppies, and coleslaw. This is a good landing zone when you aren't in the mood to return to your room and get all gussied up.

In the Aloma Square Plaza, 6860 Aloma Ave. (Rte. 426), Winter Park. ☎ *407/ 678-2107. Reservations not accepted.* **Main courses:** *$6.75–$11.95. No credit cards.* **Open:** *Fri–Sat 11am–9:30pm, Sun and Tues–Thurs 11am–8:30pm.*

Bubbaloo's Bodacious BBQ
$–$$. Near North. BARBECUE.

If smoke billowing from the chimney indicates a real pit barbecue, this one qualifies. Children love the name and informality of this place, but watch the sauces. Even the Mild is hot for young 'uns, and the Killer sauce comes with a three-alarm warning; it's meant only for those with taste buds of asbestos and a ceramic-lined tummy. The pork platter with fixin's is a deal and a half, or tackle the chicken, beef, or clams. They come with beans and slaw. Of course, it wouldn't be a barbecue without plenty of beer on hand.

5818 Conroy Rd. Take I-4 east to Lee Rd., exit 45, then left. ☎ *407/295-1212. Reservations not accepted.* **Main courses:** *$4.95–$7.95. AE, MC, V.* **Open:** *Sun–Thurs 10am–9:30pm, Fri–Sat 10am–10:30pm.*

Café Europa
$$$. Downtown. GERMAN/HUNGARIAN.

The cabbage rolls, fisherman's pie, and chicken paprika in this *gemütlich* pub are like what Mama used to make (if Mama was a hearty Bavarian). The cookies and coffee for dessert hark back to Vienna. The beer and wine choices are international.

Church Street Market, 55 W. Church St. ☎ *407/872-3388. Reservations not necessary.* **Parking:** *Use one of the downtown parking lots.* **Main courses:** *$5.95–$17.50. AE, DC, DISC, MC, V.* **Open:** *Mon–Thurs 11am–3pm and 4:30–10pm; Fri–Sat 4–10pm; Sun noon–10pm.*

Cafe Tu Tu Tango
$$. International Drive Area. TAPAS.

A smart tapas bar where every order comes in a miniature size, this is an ideal spot for grazing. Or make a meal by sharing several tapas around the table. Try Cajun-style eggrolls, tuna sashimi with noodles and spinach in soy vinaigrette, and dozens of other chi-chi appetizers. For dessert, have guava cheesecake with strawberry sauce. *Note that ordering several tapas and drinks can turn this into a $$$ restaurant.*

8625 International Dr., just west of the Mercado. ☎ *407/248-2222. Reservations recommended.* **Parking:** *free self-parking; valet parking available.* **Main courses:** *tapas $3.75–$7.95; even those with the smallest appetites will want to order at* *least 2 per person. AE, DISC, MC, V. **Open:** Sun–Thurs 11:30am–11pm, Fri–Sat 11:30am–midnight.*

Kids California Grill
$$–$$$. Walt Disney World. NEW AMERICAN.

This panoramic spread, laid out buffet-style for you high atop Disney's Contemporary Resort, may offer the best views in the Kingdom. The package includes show kitchens where folks can grill (not literally, of course) the chefs, who work their magic before your eyes. Legend has it the art-deco dining room was inspired by Spago of Los Angeles, something that wouldn't mean a thing to Floridians but might impress some outsiders, especially those who have actually gone to Spago or at least know it isn't some new health drink. By the way, the food isn't bad. Expect some California-born veggies blended with pizzas and pastas, plus, for dessert junkies, there are hall-of-famers like crème brûlée. This one comes with a grand wine list (by California standards) and a full bar.

> **Extra! Extra!**
>
> For child care while you dine, head for:
>
> Akershus (Epcot; $$)
> Atlantis (International Drive Area; $$$$$)

Disney's Contemporary Resort, 4600 World Dr. ☎ ***407/824-1576**. Reservations not necessary. Casual. **Parking:** valet parking available. **Main courses:** $13–$30. AE, MC, V. **Open:** Daily 5:30–10pm.*

Capriccio
$$$. International Drive Area. TUSCAN/NORTHERN ITALIAN.

The decor is chic and modern, with an Italian flair including a showcase kitchen with wood-fired pizza ovens. For starters, try fried calamari, then order one of the heavenly pizzas or pastas. The pan-seared tuna with braised fennel and radicchio served with lentil flan is a nice alternative. When the crusty bread lands on your table, dip it into a puddle of extra-virgin olive oil. For dessert have the *zuppa inglese*. The wine list is extensive.

In the Peabody Orlando, 9801 International Dr. ☎ ***407/352-4000**. Reservations recommended. **Parking:** free self-parking; validated valet parking. **Main courses:** $12–$22. AE, CB, DC, DISC, JCB, MC, V. **Open:** Tues–Sun 6–11pm.*

Kids Chalet Suzanne
$$$–$$$$. Far South. AMERICAN.

This one is a bit of a hoof from Orlando, about an hour's drive (40 miles) from Magicville to Lake Wales, but it's worth the time away from the frenzy. Fact is, some folks might consider it a necessary break—sort of like a trip to a sanitarium, but one with a groovy menu. The chalet is rated one of Florida's best by the critics, as well as the real judges—diners. Think about sinking your fangs into mainliners like grilled lamp chops, lobster thermidor, and shrimp curry. All meals here are prix fixe, and if you're after the package deal, there's a six-course special. The chalet has an "A" wine list and lounge.

3800 Chalet Suzanne Lane, Lake Wales. ☎ *941/676-6011. Reservations accepted. Dressy casual.* **Main courses:** *$30–$45. AE, DC, DISC, MC, V.* **Open:** *Daily 8–11am; Tues–Sun noon–5pm; Tues–Thurs and Sun 5:30–8pm, Fri–Sat 5:30–9pm.*

Chatham's Place
$$–$$$. International Drive Area. AMERICAN.
When it comes to location, some pilgrims may be discouraged by this strip-mall inhabitant. Too bad, the vittles here are worth the lack of view. If your taste dial is set on seafood, this place is a must. While some folks practice a wise rule of thumb (never, never, *never* eat under-the-sea food unless you're on the coast), Chatham's offers a strong argument for breaking the rule. After all, no place in the state is more than 35 miles from the Gulf or Atlantic. Savor a serving of the black grouper from the Cajun-and-pecan persuasion. If you insist on straying, you'll find a menu that includes beef, lamb, and venison. The servers will be happy to bring you wine or beer, but forget the hard stuff. It's not an option.

7575 Dr. Phillips Blvd., a.k.a. Sand Lake Rd. ☎ *407/345-2992. Reservations strongly recommended. Casual.* **Main courses:** *$19–$27. AE, DC, DISC, MC, V.* **Open:** *Sun–Thurs 6–9pm, Fri–Sat 6–9:30pm.*

Christini's Ristorante
$$$. International Drive Area. ITALIAN.
Some folks measure an eatery by accolades. If you're one of them, check out the awards and trophies lining the namesake's walls. If you're one of those who insist on more than "atta-boys," count on this one for great service, a gander at show-biz celebs from down the road in Universalville, pricey cuisine, and a full lounge.

7600 Dr. Phillips Blvd. ☎ *407/345-8770. Reservations recommended. Semiformal.* **Main courses:** *$20–$40. AE, CB, DC, MC, V.* **Open:** *Daily 6pm–midnight.*

Cinderella's Royal Table
$$$. Walt Disney World (Magic Kingdom; park admission required). AMERICAN/ENGLISH.
Cinderella will probably be on hand to greet you before you dine in Gothic splendor under knights' banners hanging from the vaulted ceiling. Here you'll feast on chicken, fish, or king-size cuts of prime rib or sirloin served with fresh vegetables and a hearty soup.

In Cinderella's Castle, in the Magic Kingdom. ☎ *407/939-3463. Arranging Priority Seating in advance is recommended.* **Main courses:** *dinner $17.50–$25.75; cheaper at lunch. AE, MC, V.* **Open:** *Daily 11am–park closing.*

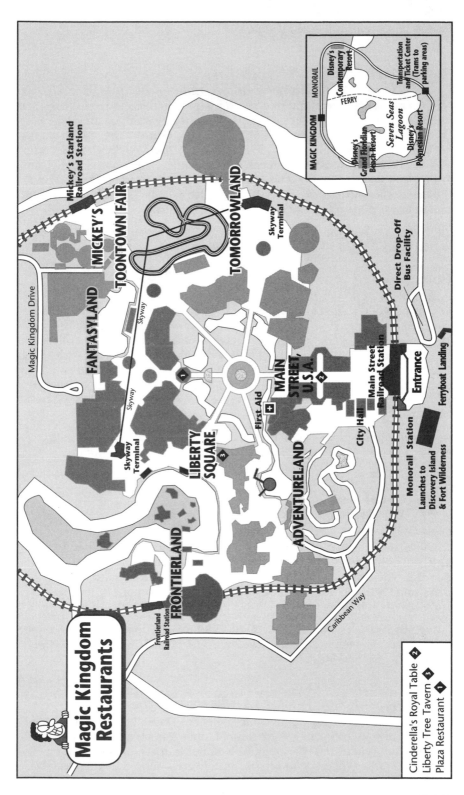

Magic Kingdom Restaurants

Mickey's Starland Railroad Station

MICKEY'S TOONTOWN FAIR

TOMORROWLAND

Skyway Terminal

FANTASYLAND

Magic Kingdom Drive

Skyway

Skyway

Skyway Terminal

LIBERTY SQUARE

MAIN STREET, U.S.A.

First Aid

ADVENTURELAND

City Hall

Main Street Railroad Station

Entrance

Ferryboat Landing

Direct Drop-Off Bus Facility

Monorail Station

Launches to Discovery Island & Fort Wilderness

FRONTIERLAND

Frontierland Railroad Station

Caribbean Way

MONORAIL

Disney's Contemporary Resort

Transportation and Ticket Center (Trams to parking areas)

FERRY

MAGIC KINGDOM

Seven Seas Lagoon

Disney's Grand Floridian Beach Resort

Disney's Polynesian Resort

Cinderella's Royal Table ❷
Liberty Tree Tavern ❸
Plaza Restaurant ❶

145

Citricos

$$–$$$. Walt Disney World (Grand Floridian). AMERICAN.
Native Florida cooking is spiced up with a Mediterranean touch in this resort restaurant bathed in Provençal colors and capped by an open-air kitchen. Dining here is a visual symphony as the chef orchestrates the meal from his kitchen stage. Your options include Florida lobster *ratatouille* with lamb loin as well as grilled fish, and a heavenly citrus soufflé. Forget butter and cream. They're not part of the mix. Oils are transfused with herbs and spices. And the desserts—chocolate ravioli with licorice ice cream—raise more than eyebrows. Citricos has a bar and well-stocked wine cellar.

4401 Floridian Way. ☎ *407/824-3000. Reservations recommended. Dressy casual.* **Main courses:** *$19–$36. AE, MC, V.* **Open:** *Daily 5–10pm.*

Columbia
$$$. Lake Buena Vista. CUBAN.
When the world's most famous rodent and one of Florida's favorite restaurants team up, it's news. The original Columbia was founded in Tampa in 1905 by the great-grandfather of its present operators. It's still a family affair. You'll dine on freshly starched linens in a bright room decorated with splashes of old Tampa and Havana: tiles, shiny woodwork, wrought iron, and bentwood chairs. The 1905 Salad, flan, paella, arroz con pollo, snapper Alicante, and Spanish bean soup are a definite cause for celebration. Cigar smokers are welcome.

649 Front St., in Celebration. ☎ *407/566-1505. Reservations recommended.* **Main courses:** *$10.95–$21.95. AE, DC, DISC, MC, V.* **Open:** *Daily 11:30am–10pm.*

Coral Reef

$$$. Walt Disney World (Epcot; park admission required). SEAFOOD.
Classical music and incredible views of the Living Seas aquarium transport diners to a romantic spot under the sea, filled with flickering lights and flitting fish. The seafood is the star here. Meals are unhurried, and the kids don't mind because they are captivated by the kaleidoscope of fish, sharks, and rays.

Living Seas Pavilion, Future World. ☎ *407/939-3463. Arranging Priority Seating in advance is recommended.* **Main courses:** *$12.15–$23.75. AE, MC, V.* **Open:** *Daily 11am–park closing.*

Dux
$$$$$. International Drive Area. HAUTE CUISINE.
The name honors a family of live ducks that splashes all day in the marble fountains of the Peabody's grandly formal lobby. This is a favorite of celebrities, who dine here after shooting (movies, not tourists, of course) at Universal Studios. There is an eclectic and diverse menu that changes with

the seasons. Possibilities include dumplings stuffed with portobello mushrooms, scallions, and goat cheese with a garnish of Asiago cheese; lamb
chops in Hunan barbecue lacquer; grilled grouper in Cajun spices; and a
hazelnut meringue napoleon topped with ice cream. Choose a wine from a
long, inspired list.

In the Peabody Hotel, 9801 International Dr. ☎ *407/345-4550. Reservations recommended.* **Parking:** *free self-parking; validated valet parking.* **Main courses:**
$19–$45. AE, CB, DC, DISC, JCB, MC, V. **Open:** *Daily 6–10:30pm.*

Enzo's on the Lake
$$$. Near North. ITALIAN.
Enzo Perlini's Mediterranean-style villa is the perfect setting for memorable
sunsets on Lake Fairy, but his cooking is generally what causes folks to come
knocking. His menu is a treasure chest of veal, chicken, beef, and seafood
caressed in a wonderful array of sauces. Regulars attest to the Great Perlini's
wizardry. Count on a dandy wine list and a full bar.

1130 S. Hwy. 17/92, Longwood. ☎ *407/834-9872. Reservations recommended.
Dressy casual.* **Main courses:** *$16–$35. AE, DC, DISC, MC, V.* **Open:** *Mon–Fri
11:30am–2:30pm; Mon–Sat 6–11pm.*

Fulton's Crab House
$$$$. Walt Disney World (Pleasure Island). SEAFOOD.
Lose yourself in this first-class world of brass, shining mahogany, and river
charts. Today's catch can be presented charcoal-grilled, broiled, fried with a
dusting of cornmeal, blackened, or
steamed. The cioppino is a feast of lobster,
clams, mussels, red potatoes, and corn. Or
have the filet mignon with whipped pota-
toes. The wine list is comprehensive;
there's a full bar. For dessert, don't miss
the milk-chocolate crème brûlée.

Aboard the Riverboat at Pleasure Island.
☎ *407/939-3463. Reservations not accept-
ed.* **Parking:** *free self-parking; valet parking
$5.* **Main courses:** *$14.95–$50. AE, MC, V.*
Open: *Daily 4pm–midnight; snacks avail-
able 11:30am–2am.*

Dollars & Sense
You don't have to buy
admission to Pleasure Island
to dine at Fulton's Crab
House, the Fireworks
Factory, Planet Hollywood,
or the Portobello Yacht
Club.

Hollywood Brown Derby
*$$$. Walt Disney World (Disney–MGM Studios; park admission
required). AMERICAN.*
The place where Hollywood's stars gathered during the 1930s and '40s is real-
istically replicated in a parklike setting. Caricatures of the stars who were regulars at the California original line the walls here. Dine on fresh grouper
served atop creamy pasta, followed by the famous grapefruit cake with
cream-cheese frosting, or the white chocolate cheesecake.

Hollywood Blvd., Disney–MGM Studios. ☎ **407/939-3463.** *Arranging Priority Seating in advance is recommended.* **Main courses:** *$16.50–$23.75; early-bird dinner $15.75. AE, MC, V.* **Open:** *Daily 11am–park closing.*

Landry's Seafood House
$$–$$$. International Drive Area. SEAFOOD.
This is the local outpost of a chain that originated in Texas. Its accent is on seafood with Cajun and Caribbean touches. The salmon with lemon butter is simple and flavorful. Or have the fresh catch of the day, which can be grouper, mahi-mahi, or snapper. For starters try the seafood-stuffed mushrooms. Key lime pie is the favorite dessert here.

8800 Vineland Ave. (FL 535), east of I-4. ☎ **407/827-6466.** *Reservations accepted for parties of 8 or more.* **Main courses:** *$11.95–$15.95. AE, DC, DISC, MC, V.* **Open:** *Mon–Fri 4–11pm, Sat–Sun 11:30am–11pm.*

Bet You Didn't Know

Okay, let's say you're a diabetic, a vegetarian, a struggling dieter, or you need to keep kosher. You probably wring your hands on every trip to a strange place. You won't have to worry about finding the right things to eat in the Disney parks. If you are bunking with Mickey, consult your hotel's Guest Services desk about special dining options. Otherwise, contact the restaurant you would like to eat at via the Disney switchboard (☎ **407/824-2222**) to make special eating arrangements. The Magic Mickey has made a concerted effort to add healthier foods to its menus even at the cafeterias and fast-food counters. One minor quibble—skim and low-fat milk are hard to come by in the Disney parks and resorts.

La Scala
$$–$$$. Near North. ITALIAN.
You better be opera friendly, or at least opera tolerant, because they're singing it while they're preparing goodies from the north of Italy. Expect good service, a lot of smiles, and a full bar.

205 Loraine Dr., Altamonte Springs. ☎ **407/862-3257.** *Reservations recommended. Dressy casual.* **Main courses:** *$12–$28. AE, DC, MC, V.* **Open:** *Mon–Thurs 11:30am–2:30pm and 5–10:30pm; Fri 11:30am–2:30pm and 5–11pm; Sat 5–10:30pm.*

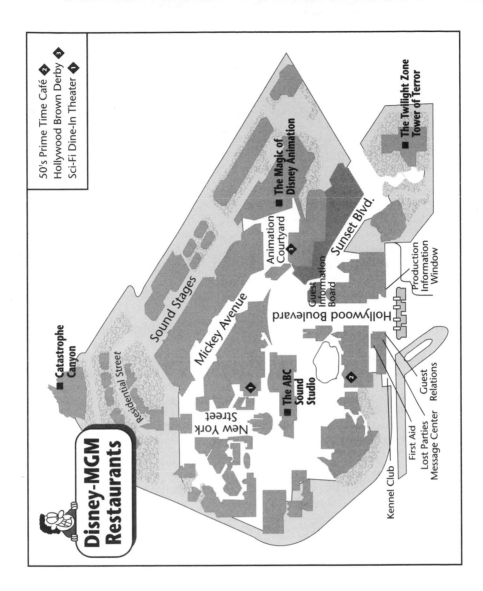

Disney-MGM Restaurants

50's Prime Time Café ②
Hollywood Brown Derby ③
Sci-Fi Dine-In Theater ①

■ Catastrophe Canyon

Residential Street

Sound Stages

Mickey Avenue

New York Street

■ The ABC Sound Studio

Hollywood Boulevard

Guest Information Board

Animation Courtyard

■ The Magic of Disney Animation

Sunset Blvd.

■ The Twilight Zone Tower of Terror

Production Information Window

Kennel Club

First Aid
Lost Parties
Message Center

Guest Relations

Le Coq Au Vin
$$. South Orlando. FRENCH.

Owner-chef Louis Perrotte loves country cooking and changes his menu seasonally. You might run into rack of lamb, braised rabbit, or grilled salmon depending on when you touch down. (If you want to eliminate the mystery, call first.) This one has a bistro atmosphere and regulars who attest to its staying power. Some insist this is Florida's best French eatery. Perrotte serves beer and wine.

4800 S. Orange Ave. ☎ ***407/851-6980.*** *Reservations required. Casual.* **Main courses: $12–$25. AE, DC, MC, V. Open:** *Mon–Fri 11:30am–2pm and 5:30–10pm; Sat 5:30–10pm; Sun 5:30–9pm.*

149

Le Provence

$$$–$$$$. Downtown. CLASSIC FRENCH.

A stately setting transports guests to the French Riviera, where fine wines are paired with sophisticated cuisine. Order à la carte: an authentic foie gras or terrine, then lobster bisque and a fish, game, meat, or vegetarian main dish. Or choose the fixed-price *menu gastronomique* or the simpler *menu du marche*. Both offer a parade of courses at reasonably fair prices. Live jazz plays in the library-style lounge.

50 E. Pine St., 1 block north of Church St., just east of Court. (Note that Orange Ave. is one-way southbound here.) ☎ *407/843-4410. Reservations strongly recommended.* **Parking:** *A parking garage is just east on Pine St., between Magnolia and Rosalind.* **Main courses:** *$19–$29.95; fixed-price menus $25.95 and $51.* **Open:** *Mon–Thurs 5:30–9:30pm, Fri–Sat 5:30–10:30pm.*

Little Saigon

$$. Downtown. VIETNAMESE.

In the heart of a tiny but vibrant Vietnamese neighborhood, this treasure is run by, and for, its regulars. Order food by number, and if you need a description of the dish, ask for the manager, whose English is better than that of many of the servers. Don't miss the summer rolls with peanut sauce. Beer and wine are available.

1106 E. Colonial Dr. From I-4, take the Colonial exit (Hwy. 50) and go east; look for the fish mural between Mills and Thornton. ☎ *407/423-8539. Reservations required.* **Main courses:** *$4.25–$7. AE, DISC, MC, V.* **Open:** *Daily 10am–9pm.*

L'Originale Alfredo di Roma Ristorante

$$–$$$. Walt Disney World (Epcot; park admission required). ITALIAN/MEDITERRANEAN.

Feast on fettuccine Alfredo the way the recipe's originator wanted it. Sample southern Italian cuisine in a "seaside" Italian palazzo lined with huge murals. Try veal scaloppine with roasted potatoes, a steaming plate of grilled vegetables, or a divine linguine pesto, then tiramisu for dessert. The three-course early-bird dinner is a bargain.

Italy Pavilion, World Showcase, Epcot. ☎ *407/939-3463. Arranging Priority Seating in advance is recommended.* **Main courses:** *$9.25–$29.75; fixed-price dinner menu served 4:30–6pm.* **Open:** *Daily 11am to an hour before park closing.*

Maison et Jardin

$$$$. Near North. CLASSIC FRENCH.

Formal and romantic, Maison et Jardin (*House and Garden* just sounds so much prettier in French, doesn't it?) is a time-honored local favorite, and a consistent award winner. The menu has just the right blend of cuisine, including the signature beef Wellington or the medaillons of elk (venison, if you will) served with raspberry sauce. The wine list is pretty doggone impressive.

430 Wymore Rd., Altamonte Springs, 10 min. north of Orlando. Take I-4 east to Maitland Blvd., east exit, then right at Lake Destiny Rd. At the next light, turn left onto Wymore Rd. ☎ *407/862-4410. Reservations recommended. **Main courses:** $18.50–$28.50. AE, DC, DISC, MC, V. **Open:** Mon–Sat 6–10pm; Sun brunch 11am–2pm and dinner 6–9pm.*

Manuel's on the 28th
$$$$. Downtown. HAUTE CUISINE.
Take the elevator to the 28th floor for a stunning after-dark view of the sparkling, sprawling metropolis that Orlando has become. At most "view" restaurants, the food can't match the scenery. This is one of the two or three in Central Florida where the cuisine may even outstrip the surroundings. Expect a friendly, professional staff. They'll help you pair the perfect wine with rack of lamb, a veal-chop-and-scampi combination plate, or a steak wreathed in fresh vegetables.

390 N. Orange Ave., in the Barnett Bank building. ☎ *407/246-6580. Reservations required. **Main courses:** $24–$32. AE, DC, DISC, MC, V. **Open:** Tues–Sat 6–10pm.*

Marrakesh
$$$. Walt Disney World (Epcot; park admission required). MOROCCAN.
Hand-laid mosaics in intricate patterns set the scene for lavish North African dining, complete with belly dancers. Try the Moroccan *diffa* (traditional feast) to sample saffron-seasoned harina soup made with lamb and lentils, beef *brewats* in a broth of spices and a cloak of pastry, roast lamb with rice pilaf, chicken with green olives, couscous with vegetables, Moroccan pastries, and mint tea.

Morocco Pavilion, World Showcase, Epcot. ☎ *407/939-3463. Arranging Priority Seating in advance is recommended. **Main courses:** $13.75–$19.95. A fixed-price diffa is served for $29.95 for 2 people at lunch, $53.90 for 2 people at dinner. AE, MC, V. **Open:** Daily 11am to an hour before park closing.*

Michelangelo
$$$$. International Drive Area. ITALIAN/MEDITERRANEAN.
The veal Michelangelo is meltingly tender, and the marinated prime rib is a feast. Homemade pastas can be ordered on the side, or as a main dish. A substantial menu offers a nice choice of appetizers, soup, main dishes, and desserts. There's a full bar and a decent wine list.

4898 Kirkman Rd., in the Kirkman Shoppes, a quarter-mile north of Universal Studios. ☎ *407/297-6666. Reservations recommended. **Main courses:** $13.95–$28.95. AE, DC, DISC, MC, V. **Open:** Daily 6–11pm.*

151

Ming Court

$$$. International Drive Area. CHINESE.

Dine in an ethereal setting, graced with lotus ponds filled with glowing goldfish, while you're entertained by—get this—zither music. You'll rub elbows with more locals than tourists here. Try the crisp chicken in a tangy tangerine sauce, spicy Szechuan beef or shrimp, or butter-tender filet mignon with crisp-tender vegetables.

9188 International Dr., between Sand Lake Rd. and the Bee Line Expressway. ☎ *407/351-9988. Reservations recommended.* **Main courses:** *$7.95–$16.95. AE, CB, DC, DISC, MC, V.* **Open:** *Daily 11am–2:30pm and 4:30pm–midnight.*

Extra! Extra!

When money is no object, make a beeline for:

Atlantis (International Drive Area; $$$$$)

Arthur's 27 (Lake Buena Vista; $$$$$)

Chalet Suzanne (Far South/Lake Wales; $$$–$$$$)

Maison et Jardin (Near North; $$$$)

Victoria and Albert's (Disney's Grand Floridian Beach Resort; $$$$$)

Morton's of Chicago

$$$$. International Drive Area. STEAK HOUSE.

Chicago knows beef, which is served here in straightforward meat-and-potatoes style. The cuts are costly, but they are butter-tender and aged to perfection. Side dishes are à la carte, which can add up to an expensive evening if you go overboard. The no-smoking section could be larger and more smoke-free. There's a full bar.

7600 Dr. Phillips Blvd., in the Marketplace at Dr. Phillips. ☎ *407/248-3485. Reservations recommended.* **Main courses:** *$16.95–$29.95. AE, DC, MC, V.* **Open:** *Mon–Sat 5:30–11pm, Sun 5–10pm.*

New Punjab

$. International Drive Area and U.S. 192/Kissimmee. INDIAN.

Whether you have a yen for vegetarian cooking, a fiery curry, or a tangy tandoori, they're all served without pretense in a comfortable, informal setting decorated with Indian motifs. Have lamb tandoori, chicken with spinach, vegetables masala, or a spicy vindaloo, followed by a fruity ice dessert to put out the fire. Beer and wine are available.

7451 International Dr. ☎ *407/352-7887. Or 3404 Vine St., Kissimmee.* ☎ *407/931-2449. Reservations not accepted.* **Main courses:** *$7.95–$14.95. AE, MC, V.* **Open:** *Tues–Sat 11:30am–11pm; Sun–Mon 5–11pm.*

Nine Dragons

$$$. Walt Disney World (Epcot; park admission required unless you're a guest at the Swan or Dolphin hotels). CHINESE.

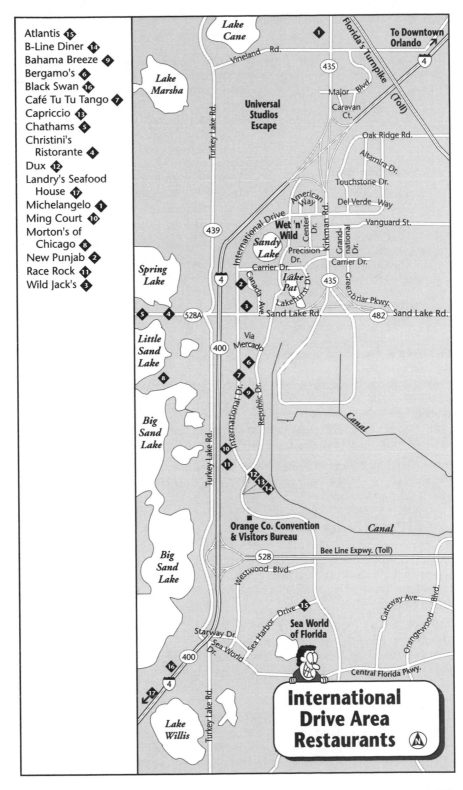

Atlantis ◆15
B-Line Diner ◆14
Bahama Breeze ◆9
Bergamo's ◆6
Black Swan ◆16
Café Tu Tu Tango ◆7
Capriccio ◆13
Chathams ◆5
Christini's
   Ristorante ◆4
Dux ◆12
Landry's Seafood
   House ◆17
Michelangelo ◆1
Ming Court ◆10
Morton's of
   Chicago ◆8
New Punjab ◆2
Race Rock ◆11
Wild Jack's ◆3

International Drive Area Restaurants

153

This is one of the loveliest of the World Showcase restaurants. It boasts intricately carved rosewood paneling and an amazing dragon-motif ceiling.

Order shredded duck with sweet peppers and Chinese pancakes, spicy Szechuan shrimp, stir-fried chicken with rafts of vegetables, or sliced sirloin stir-fried with broccoli and oyster sauce. The fresh fruit juices are delicious, with or without an alcohol kicker. For dessert, try the sweet red-bean ice cream with fried banana. Aw, c'mon, lose that frown. It's delicious.

Extra! Extra!

For a knockout view after dark, your best bets are:

Arthur's 27 (Lake Buena Vista; $$$$$)
California Grill (Contemporary Resort) $$–$$$
Manuel's on the 28th (Downtown; $$$$$)

China Pavilion, Epcot. ☎ *407/939-3463. Arranging Priority Seating in advance is recommended.* **Main courses:** *$10.50–$25.50; a dinner sampler is $21.95. AE, MC, V.* **Open:** *Daily 11am to an hour before park closing.*

Numero Uno
$$. Downtown. CUBAN.

This family-operated hole in the wall isn't fancy, but you won't notice the decor once the paella hits your table. Or have *ropa vieja* (literally "old clothes" because the beef is so tender), roast pork, or a remarkable arroz con pollo. Dishes come with plantains and refried beans. Dessert is the traditional three-milk cake. Beer and wine are served.

2499 S. Orange Ave. ☎ *407/841-3840. Reservations recommended.* **Parking:** *limited, but free.* **Main courses:** *$7.95–$18.95. AE, DC, DISC, MC, V.* **Open:** *Mon–Fri 11am–3pm; Mon–Sat 5:30–9pm.*

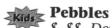 Park Plaza Gardens
$$–$$$. Near North. CONTINENTAL.

The gardenlike atmosphere (look, up in the sky, a glass roof!) is an elegant touch that goes with the cuisine, which is sophisticated and health-conscious. There's also a popular brunch on Sunday, a pampering staff, and a full bar.

319 Park Ave. S., Winter Park. ☎ *407/645-2475. Reservations recommended. Semiformal.* **Parking:** *streetside.* **Main courses:** *$18–$30. AE, CB, DC, DISC, MC, V.* **Open:** *Mon–Thurs 11am–2pm and 6–10pm; Fri–Sat 11am–2pm and 6–11pm; Sun 11am–9pm.*

Pebbles
$–$$. Downtown. AMERICAN.

This is as close as Orlando gets to a local chain. Renowned restaurateur Manny Garcia has taken a step toward affordability with the Pebbles line, offering entrees such as duck, lamb, and pasta dishes as well as tapas, burgers,

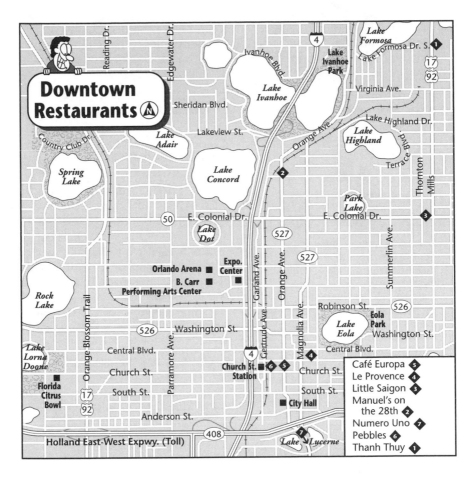

Downtown Restaurants ⓜ

Café Europa	5
Le Provence	4
Little Saigon	3
Manuel's on the 28th	2
Numero Uno	7
Pebbles	6
Thanh Thuy	1

and homemade soups. His eateries come with bars, respectable wine lists (you order by the glass), a tiki bar and patio outside, and a fun California atmosphere throughout.

17 W. Church St., Orlando; ☎ ***407/839-0892.*** *2110 W. State Rd. 434, Longwood;* ☎ ***407/774-7111.*** *12551 State Rd. 535, Lake Buena Vista;* ☎ ***407/ 827-1111.*** *Reservations accepted. Casual.* **Main courses:** *$9–$20. AE, CB, DC, DISC, MC, V.* **Open:** *Mon–Thurs 11am–11pm; Fri 11am–midnight; Sat noon– midnight; Sun noon–11pm.*

Kids **Planet Hollywood**
$$. Pleasure Island. AMERICAN.

Your kids already know about it, and they're probably clamoring to go. This place is part restaurant and part showcase for Hollywood memorabilia. Diners are surrounded by clips from some soon-to-be-released movies and more than 300 show-biz artifacts ranging from Peter O'Toole's *Lawrence of Arabia* costume to the front end of the bus from *Speed!* You might expect

155

mediocre food amidst all the hype, but it's not quite that bad. It's, well, sort of okay. You can gnaw on appetizers like hickory-smoked buffalo wings, pot stickers, or nachos, or try out the selection of burgers, sandwiches, pastas, and pizzas.

1506 E. Buena Vista Dr., Pleasure Island. ☎ ***407/827-7827.*** *Reservations not accepted.* **Main courses:** *$7.50–$18.95 (most under $13). AE, DC, MC, V.* **Open:** *Daily 11am–2am.*

Bet You Didn't Know

Once in a while, a deep, double booming noise shakes things up a little. No, it's not a roller coaster crashing—it's the sound of the space shuttle landing at Cape Canaveral. It produces a twin sonic boom when it reenters the atmosphere. The boom-boom can be heard coast-to-coast for several counties north and south.

Plaza Restaurant
$$. Walt Disney World (Magic Kingdom; park admission required). AMERICAN.

Take a breather from the hot sun and teeming crowds with a lunch break at everyone's hometown restaurant, located appropriately enough at the end of Main Street in the Magic Kingdom. The menu offers burgers plain or fancy, sandwiches hot or cold (try the Reuben or the double-decker hot roast beef), salads big and small, and milkshakes in three flavors.

Magic Kingdom, Walt Disney World. ☎ ***407/939-3463.*** *Arranging Priority Seating in advance is recommended.* **Main courses:** *$7.75–$10.75. AE, MC, V.* **Open:** *Daily 11am–park closing.*

Kids Portobello Yacht Club
$$. Lake Buena Vista/Pleasure Island. ITALIAN.

You're right. A floating trattoria with "nouveau" Old World cuisine sounds a bit bizarre, but it works in this case thanks to creative chefs and an attentive staff. Try dining on the patio overlooking the water if the weather is good. Inside or out, be prepared for crowds. A full bar, a menu for the health conscious, and a lively atmosphere are included in the package.

1650 Buena Vista Dr. ☎ ***407/934-8888.*** *Reservations recommended. Casual.* **Parking:** *valet parking available.* **Main courses:** *$15–$25. AE, MC, V.* **Open:** *Daily 11:30am–midnight.*

Prime Time Café
$$–$$$. Walt Disney World (Disney–MGM Studios; park admission required). AMERICAN.

Return to the age when TVs were black and white, and Mom made you finish your vegetables before you could have dessert. Comfort foods like meat loaf and mashed potatoes, pot roast like Grandma's, and Dad's chili are served in a 1950s kitchen, where tables are covered with the familiar boomerang-pattern Formica. Mom (your server) will scold you if you put your elbows on the table or don't clean your plate, but order the banana split anyway. While you eat, *I Love Lucy* reruns play on the flickering TVs.

Disney–MGM Studios, near the Indiana Jones Stunt Spectacular. ☎ *407/ 939-3463. Arranging Priority Seating in advance is recommended.* **Main courses:** *$11.95–$20.25 at dinner; cheaper at lunch. AE, MC, V.* **Open:** *Daily 11am–park closing.*

Race Rock
$–$$. International Drive Area. AMERICAN.
Two words: *very loud*. Between the music and racing sounds it's really hard to complete a thought, much less a sentence. But gearheads of all ages love this infield-like pit stop, where big burgers, pizza, eggrolls, soups, salads, and sandwiches are served up while heart-stopping race scenes play on a giant screen. Inside and out, Race Rock's eye candy includes some of the biggest monster trucks in the world, plus dragsters and hydroplanes. Kids have their own Quarter Midget Menu with games and coloring. Speaking of kids, it's not a bad idea to keep the sugar away from them. This place lights their little fuses without any ingested assistance.

8986 International Dr., just south of Sand Lake Rd. ☎ *407/248-9876. Reservations accepted only for groups.* **Main courses:** *Prime rib $17.95; sand-wiches $6.95–$7.95. AE, DC, DISC, MC, V.* **Open:** *Daily 11am–11pm or later if it's crowded.*

Rainforest Cafe
$$. Downtown Disney Marketplace and Animal Kingdom. AMERICAN.
This is another one the kids love! The food's pretty respectable, but it's really the decor that makes this restaurant. As its name suggests, entering the Rainforest Cafe is like walking into a rain forest—there are lifelike silk plants all over, Animatronic monkeys chattering, and occasional rain and thunder rumblings. The extensive menu features California-influenced house special-ties such as Chicken Monsoon with shrimp and linguine, and Rasta Pasta (bow-tie noodles with a variety of vegetables and a creamy garlic-pesto sauce). Another branch is located in Animal Kingdom.

In the Downtown Disney Marketplace, 1800 E. Buena Vista Dr., Lake Buena Vista. ☎ *407/827-8500. Reservations not accepted. The other restaurant is in Disney's Animal Kingdom near the entrance.* **Main courses:** *$5.50–$17.95. AE, DISC, MC, V.* **Open:** *Sun–Thurs 10:30am–11pm, Fri–Sat 10:30am–midnight.*

Rolando's
$–$$. Near North. CUBAN.
Mountainous platters of traditional Cuban food make for memorable dining in an unpretentious setting of hanging plants and Formica tables. Order tra-ditional things like pork, red snapper, tamale pie, or chicken. Try the hearty rice pudding for dessert.

157

870 E. Semoran (FL 436), between Red Bug Rd. and U.S. 17–92. Take I-4 east to the East–West Expressway, then east, then left on Semoran Blvd. (FL 436). ☎ **407/767-9677.** *Reservations not accepted.* **Main courses:** *$7.75–$17.50. AE, DISC, MC, V.* **Open:** *Tues–Sat 11am–10pm, Sun 1–8pm.*

Sci-Fi Dine-in Theater Restaurant

$$–$$$. Walt Disney World (Disney–MGM Studios; park admission required). AMERICAN.

Think of *Happy Days,* and you'll get the idea. Carhops bring burgers and malts curb service–style while you and the kiddies sit in a real sedan. Oh, yeah, horror flicks that are too hokey to be scary play on the screen while

you stuff yourself with barbecued ribs accompanied by vegetables and fries, Cajun-style grilled chicken, free popcorn, and, for dessert, The Cheesecake That Ate New York. You can enjoy a milkshake or order from the full bar. You'll probably have a good time even though the meal isn't five-star.

Extra! Extra!

For an evening of quiet conversation, try:

Arthur's 27 (Lake Buena Vista; $$$$$)

Bistro de Paris (Epcot; $$$$)

Black Swan (International Drive Area; $$$$$)

Café Europa (Downtown; $$$)

Capriccio (International Drive Area; $$$)

Maison et Jardin (Near North; $$$$)

Manuel's on the 28th (Downtown; $$$$$)

Disney–MGM Studios, near the Monster Sound Show. ☎ *407/939-3463. Arranging Priority Seating in advance is recommended.* **Main courses:** *$9.50–$22.75 at dinner; cheaper at lunch. AE, MC, V.* **Open:** *Daily 11am–park closing.*

Straub's Boatyard

$$. Near North. STEAKS/SEAFOOD.

The grill is mesquite-fired, and most of the seafood is flown in (tourist-class) from the frigid waters around New England. While those who find aesthetics important may find the decor a little lacking, the specialties from tuna and crab to T-bones and chicken are not only good but in some cases imaginative. You'll find a lounge, a health-conscious menu, and early-bird specials.

743 Lee Rd. ☎ *407/628-0067. Reservations recommended. Casual.* **Main courses:** *$12–$25. AE, DC, DISC, MC, V.* **Open:** *Mon–Thurs 11am–10pm; Fri 11am–11pm; Sat 4:30–11pm.*

Thanh Thuy

$. Downtown. VIETNAMESE.

Here's the place to find a filling family meal in an unpretentious room in Orlando's growing Vietnamese community. Start the meal with one of the fried spring rolls, then try a hot soup or one of the chicken, pork, or

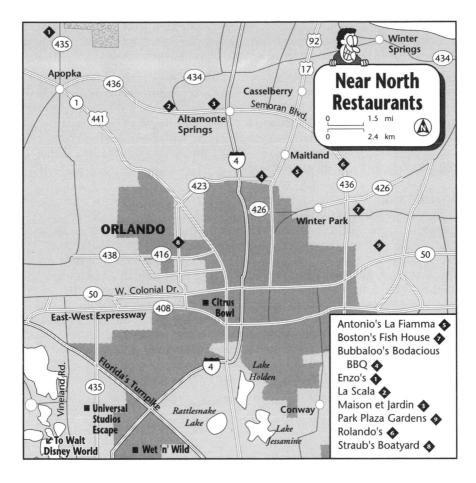

beef combinations. The flashy tableside presentation menu is great fun to watch, and to eat, as course after course comes to the table. Beer and wine are available.

1227 N. Mills Ave., about 12 blocks north of Colonial Dr. ☎ **407/898-8011.** *Reservations not accepted.* **Parking:** *limited but free.* **Main courses:** *$3.75–$7.95. AE, DC, DISC, MC, V.* **Open:** *Daily 10am–10pm.*

Victoria and Albert's
$$$$$. Walt Disney World. HAUTE CUISINE.
This is the most memorable (and memorably expensive) restaurant in Orlando. If money is no object and you're serious about food (or romance), head here. You'll be greeted by a harpist or a violinist at the entryway of this plush, intimate dining room, which has exquisitely appointed tables. The cuisine is impeccable and is presented with a flourish by the attentive and professional staff. You can also reserve weeks ahead for a private dinner, served in a special kitchen alcove, by chef Scott Hunnell and his staff. You

159

could come for a regular dinner for $80 plus $30 for a wine pairing, but here is a chance to gild the lily. The dining experience lasts 3 to 4 hours, and you will remember it for a lifetime. The menu changes each time.

In the Grand Floridian Beach Resort, 4401 Floridian Way, Walt Disney World. ☎ *407/939-3463 or 407/824-1089. Reservations required well in advance.* **Parking:** *free self-parking; validated valet parking.* **Prices:** *A meal costs $80 per person without wine and $110 with wine pairings. Dining in the kitchen costs $115 per person without wine and $160 per person with 5 wines served course by course. AE, MC, V.* **Open:** *Two dinner seatings nightly at 5:45 and 9pm. The chef's kitchen is by special reservation only.*

Wild Jacks
$$$. International Drive Area. AMERICAN.

Come loving red meat or don't come at all to this chuckwagon-style restaurant. The atmosphere includes mounted buffalo heads, long-dead jack-a-lopes, and more dying-calf-in-a-hailstorm, twitch-and-twang country-western music than an average city slicker should have to endure in one lifetime. The kitchen is bursting with steaks on an open-pit grill. In addition to the Texas-size hunks of cow served with jalapeño smashed potatoes and corn on the cob, the menu has a selection of skewered shrimp, tacos, chicken, or pasta, though it's not a good idea to order experimental stuff in a beef house. Wash the meal down with an iced longneck from the bar and, for dessert, feast on peach cobbler à la mode. Wild Jacks also has locations in Altamonte Springs and Kissimmee.

7364 International Dr., between Sand Lake Rd. and Carrier Dr. ☎ *407/ 352-4407. Reservations not accepted.* **Parking:** *Plenty, pardner, and it's free.* **Main courses:** *$6.95–$17.95. AE, CB, DC, DISC, JCB, MC, V.* **Open:** *Sun–Thurs 4:30–10pm, Fri–Sat 4–11pm.*

⭐ Kids Yachtsman Steakhouse
$$–$$$. Walt Disney World. STEAKS.

This one is regarded as a world-class steak-and-chop house where diners select their own steaks. (Bet you're glad they aren't like lobster houses where you pick dinner while it's still alive.) This is the place to come if you love red meat and are too young, or too carefree, to worry about arterial blockage. The steaks are aged, the cattle from which they came were grain-fed, and the beef is carved by a staff butcher. This one, too, is prone to crowds, but most folks say it's worth the wait. Yachtsman also has poultry and seafood dishes, a full bar, and daily specials.

1700 Epcot Resorts Blvd. ☎ *407/939-3463. Reservations recommended. Casual.* **Parking:** *valet parking available.* **Main courses:** *$22–$32. AE, DISC, MC, V.* **Open:** *Daily 6–10pm.*

Part 5

Exploring Walt Disney World & Orlando

You've decided on a hotel and you know where to eat.

Now what?

Well, hang onto your socks. You're going to Disney World!

Of course, so are the Super Bowl champions, not to mention half of their fans, gobs of Mary Kay conventioneers, and most of the Sixth Fleet—which is on a weekend pass out of Jacksonville. That means business as usual: tens of thousands of sweaty bodies—and all of them are hell-bent on riding the same rides and eating in the same restaurants that you are. That's why you'll have a lot more fun if you know up front which parks and rides are worth waiting in lines for and which are forgettable. It's also why we're going to spend the next few chapters giving you as many specifics as possible.

In this section, we'll talk about the kingdoms in the vast Mickey Metropolis and tell you how to negotiate all of them. You'll also discover there's a lot more to Orlando than Disney World. You're going to learn about the fun that's waiting at Universal Studios, Sea World, Cypress Gardens, Gatorland, and all of the other parks trying to reach into your wallet. We'll tell you which are worth your time and which will have your kids saying, "I'm bored."

We'll also help you design a personalized itinerary that will put smiles on everyone's faces and make the most of your park time.

Chapter 11

The Wonderful World of Disney

In This Chapter

➤ What and where are the Disney parks?

➤ Getting around

➤ Tickets and passes

➤ Tips on maximizing your fun and minimizing your stress

We've been to the Magic Kingdom and other Walt Disney World parks dozens of times since Mickey and Minnie made their debut in 1971. Early, it was with our kids. These days the grandchildren are the ones dragging us back. When it comes to multiple repetitions, you either love it or hate it. But you never know it—not all of it. We still feel like rookies—yes, complete idiots—every time we plan another trip. There are new roads, new parks, new rides, new hotels, new restaurants, and new razzle-dazzle shows.

About 14 million souls visit the Magic Kingdom every year. That's equivalent to Florida's population. Almost 12 million people visit Epcot and Animal Kingdom. Attendance at Disney–MGM Studios is around 10 million. Universal Studios Florida entertains another 11 million, while Sea World and Busch Gardens in Tampa cash that many tickets combined each year. Fact is, the number of annual visitors to the six parks equals about 30% of America's population.

So whether this is your first trip or your 40th (some Floridians buy annual passes and come once a week!), it's worth taking a few minutes to get your bearings and plan a little strategy.

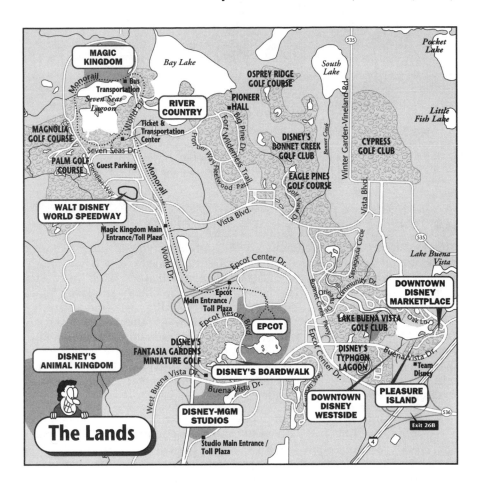

First, realize you're not the only "newbie" in town. Most of the folks sharing your air space are first-timers, too, and a lot of them don't have this book to show them around. So you're already way ahead of the game.

Also, realize that things at Disney are constantly evaluated and improved. Old gardens are replaced with new blooms. Lines are reconfigured to keep you out of the sun as much as possible, and to ease pedestrian traffic jams. A popcorn wagon moves under a shade tree to make your wait in line a tad cooler. A marching band pops up on *that* street for maximum crowd exposure. Mickey or Goofy uses *this* path because planners knew you'd take it, not the other one.

Maybe you're feeling a little pressure when you look at all this. Will it cost you a bloody fortune? Is it going to live up to your expectations? Are the kids going to think you're a hero or a goat? Well, straight off, it's going to cost nearly $45 per person just to get *into* the parks, then you're going to pay *mucho dinero* for food, drinks, souvenirs, and film. But let's break this down into manageable bites and take it a step at a time.

Bet You Didn't Know

More than 1,400 couples are married each year at WDW. Many of the ceremonies take place in the Wedding Pavilion, an elegant Victorian summerhouse on its own island near Disney's Grand Floridian Beach Resort & Spa (☎ **407/828-3400**). Walt Disney World is also the single most popular honeymoon destination in the United States.

What in the World *Is* All This?

The universe known as Walt Disney World actually consists of four major parks, several smaller ones, and an assortment of villages, resorts, and shopping areas. But even WDW veterans mistakenly say Disney World when they mean the Magic Kingdom—the flagship park where Mickey and Donald mingle with guests while they ride rides, visit Cinderella's Castle, and watch the parades roll down Main Street, U.S.A. The other major theme parks are Epcot, Disney–MGM Studios, and Animal Kingdom. A short summary of each will follow. Chapter 12 covers the Magic Kingdom and gives you strategies for maximum enjoyment. Chapter 13 is devoted exclusively to Epcot, chapter 14 tells you how to tackle Disney–MGM Studios, and chapter 15 opens the gate to Disney's newest, Animal Kingdom.

➤ The **Magic Kingdom,** symbolized by Cinderella's Castle and dating back to 1971, is the first (and still the most popular) of WDW's theme parks. Everyone should give it at least 1 full day. It has the most to offer for children, particularly younger ones, as well as their parents. It also has broad appeal to first-timers. If you fall into those categories, we recommend 2 days or more provided you have the time and budget. It's divided into seven lands—Main Street, U.S.A.; Adventureland; Frontierland; Fantasyland; Mickey's Toontown Fair; Liberty Square; and Tomorrowland. At last count the seven lands had 41 major attractions.

Bet You Didn't Know

So how come you never see Mickey kicking back with his head off, or Winnie the Pooh taking a smoke break? Because the folks inside the character costumes have to abide by a very strict code of conduct, which includes no talking or stepping out of character. The "cast" travels through under-the-park tunnels that are off-limits to most of the public. We'll tell you how to become one of the exceptions later in this chapter. Watch for behind-the-scenes tours.

➤ **Epcot,** built as an exposition of human achievement and new technology, is symbolized by Spaceship Earth, the thing that looks like a huge golf ball. In Future World you'll see exhibits dealing with innovations. Then you'll pass into the World Showcase, where pavilions of a dozen countries surround a peaceful lagoon. This is another place where it's good to allow at least 2 days for the shows, rides, specialty shops, and ethnic restaurants.

➤ **Disney–MGM Studios** is the Tinseltown of the 1930s and 1940s. It's a blend of working studio tours, animated and live shows such as the "Indiana Jones Stunt Spectacular," and rides like the chilling (sometimes-spilling) "Twilight Zone Tower of Terror." It's worth a day, but you can stretch it to two if you're a film freak.

➤ **Disney's Animal Kingdom** is the new kid on the block. It's symbolized by the 14-story Tree of Life, which is to this park what Cinderella's Castle is to the Magic Kingdom. This wildlife exhibit, zoo, and theme park is filled with captivating shows and rides such as "It's Tough to Be a Bug" and "Countdown to Extinction." You should have little trouble filling at least 1 day here.

Extra! Extra!

Those elusive, furry, adorable characters actually are short folks buried under layers of fabric. They're particularly elusive during the summer, when they can lose up to 5 pounds of water weight a day. Since they're out for shorter periods, here's our "Cliff Notes" version on how to catch the character crew. Simply stop at the following places to get up-to-the-minute information on where your favorite cartoon critters will be, and when: City Hall in the Magic Kingdom, Epcot's Guest Relations, Crossroads of the World at Disney–MGM Studios, and Camp Minnie–Mickey in Animal Kingdom.

But Wait—There's More!

In addition to the four major theme parks, there are several other types of attractions owned by the Disney empire. Here are brief bios on each. They will be covered in more detail in chapter 16.

➤ **Walt Disney Wide World of Sports™** complex has a 7,500-seat baseball stadium and facilities for more than 30 sports, including soccer, softball, basketball, and track and field. It's the spring-training home of the Atlanta Braves, and a training site for the Harlem Globetrotters.

➤ **Walt Disney World Speedway** has a stock-car racing track that hosts daily races throughout September, with additional events in

October and November. Year-round, visitors can sign up for the **Richard Petty Driving Experience,** in which you can learn to drive at 145 miles an hour. (Those of you from Talladega and Darlington probably already know how.) Call ☎ **407/939-0130** for details.

➤ **Water parks** for those of you who like to surf, glide along lazy rivers, scream down water slides, and stay cool can be found in WDW—there are three of them. They'll seem pretty appealing when it's 90° and 90% humidity, which means May to September. They are **Blizzard Beach,** surrounding the "snow"-covered Mount Gushmore; **River Country,** based on Tom Sawyer's ol' swimmin' hole; and **Typhoon Lagoon,** where you're shipwrecked on Mt. Mayday.

Several marketplaces, shopping villages, and nightlife areas round out Planet Disney. These are covered in more depth in chapters 19, 21, and 22.

Bet You Didn't Know

Chewing gum is allowed in the theme parks, but is not sold in any; cigarettes are sold in all the parks, but smoking is allowed only outdoors.

Disney's BoardWalk is a good place to stroll the waterfront, dine, dance, or linger in an eye-popping sports bar where even the rest rooms have televisions.

Downtown Disney, which opened in 1997, comprises **Pleasure Island,** which opened in 1989 as a nightclub theme park for adults, as well as **Downtown Disney Marketplace,** with dining and shopping, and **Downtown Disney West Side,** with more shopping, dining, the Cirque du Soleil, the House of Blues, and DisneyQuest.

The **Disney Institute** is a different kind of vacation. You'll sleep and dine in a luxury resort while attending working seminars, classes, and sessions on anything from animation to rock climbing, gourmet cooking, and cinema. The Institute has its own health club, radio and television studios, performance center, amphitheater, tennis courts, and demonstration kitchens— plus, it's smack dab in the middle of the **Lake Buena Vista Golf Course.** It's the only Disney property not devoted solely to entertaining the masses. (A novel concept, isn't it?) Instead, adults can pick from a long menu of hands-on experiences in five categories: animation and the story arts, culinary arts, gardening and the great outdoors, television and film, and Disney behind the scenes. You can produce and paint your own cartoon cells, learn the secrets of cooking healthy, try your hand at canoeing, scale a 26-foot rock wall, create magical miniature gardens, test your acting or camera skills at TV Studio Five, or experiment with new tastes in the Wine, Wonders and Song course. Other options include lessons on still photography, time management, personal productivity, and Disney architecture. Most are half-day courses, but many have beginning and advanced levels in case your heart's set on becoming an expert in some area. There are also art, show biz, make-up, illustration, wildlife, and other programs for youths 7 to 15. Call ☎ **800/496-6337** if you want to learn more.

In addition to the shops found in the theme parks, **Disney Village Marketplace** is a parklike mall filled with shops and restaurants. Admission is free.

Behind-the-Scenes Tours

If you'd like to get an insider's look at how Uncle Waltie's heirs make their magic, **Behind-the-Scenes Tours** are the way to go. There are so many options the Disney folks have trouble keeping up. They begin with the 4$^{1}/_{2}$-hour **Keys to the Kingdom** tour that guides guests through tunnels under the Magic Kingdom ($45, plus $42 admission). The others include **Hidden Treasures of World Showcase,** featuring the architecture and culture of Epcot pavilions; **Gardens of the World,** an Epcot garden tour; and the **Wonders of Walt Disney World,** which has several programs for kids ages 10 to 15. On the top of the price chain ($185 per person) is **Backstage Magic,** a 7-hour, self-propelled and bus tour through areas of Epcot, the Magic Kingdom, and Disney–MGM Studios that aren't seen by mainstream guests. The daily tour (except Sunday) is limited to 20 adults and you might have trouble getting a date unless you book early. Some will find this one isn't worth the price, but if you have a brain that must know how things work, or you simply want to know more than your family or friends, you might find it well worth the cost. You'll see WDW mechanics and engineers repairing and building Animatronic beings from "It's a Small World" and other attractions. You'll peek over the shoulders of cast members who watch close-circuit TVs to make sure other visitors are surviving the harrowing rides. And at the Magic Kingdom, you'll venture into tunnels used for work areas as well as corridors for the cast to get from one area to the others without fighting tourist crowds. It's not unusual for tour takers to see Snow White enjoying a Snickers bar, find Cinderella having her locks touched up at an underground salon, or view woodworkers as they restore the hard maple muscles of the carousel horses. By the way, the Disney herd debuted in 1917 in Palisades, New Jersey.

The backstage areas at Epcot and Disney–MGM are behind the parks. At MGM, you'll learn to draw Goofy, then paint animation cells of Mickey and the gang. The Epcot side of the bargain lets you watch the Body Wars ride from the outside. (*Tip of the day:* If you ride this one later, head for the front row if you're prone to motion sickness. That way, you won't have to see the bobbing heads of your fellow passengers. That, and the fact that Disney reduced the ride from 5 to 4 minutes, will significantly reduce the odds of you contaminating the floor with what the guides like to refer to as "protein spills."

Some of the more entertaining guides also help dispel some of the myths that seem to linger around the Land of Mickey. Walt Disney, for example, is

167

not cryogenically frozen in Cinderella's Castle. (Sorry, but it's time some of you grow up and face reality.)

Remember: Reservations are more than recommended for most behind-the-scenes tours. They're essential. You can make them by calling ☎ **407/ 939-8687.**

How Do I Get to All This?

If you're driving to Walt Disney World, take I-4 to exits 25, 26, or 27. From there, you'll see colorful signs directing you to the parks. Heck, you'll need to close your eyes to miss the signs.

Parking is a snap. Just do what the people in the yellow-striped shirts ask you to do. If you park in the size XXXL Magic Kingdom lot, you'll probably want to ride the tram to the front gate (the trams are a hoot—the seats are made out of petrified plastic, so if you lack posterior padding, you'll probably remember the ride for a while). At Epcot, Disney–MGM, and Animal Kingdom, it's probably faster to walk unless you have really small children, or sore feet from yesterday. Parking costs $5.

If you didn't rent a car, or if you'd prefer not to take it, you have options. If you're staying at a Disney resort, you can take the Disney transportation system to get to the parks (see below). And even if you didn't choose a Disney hotel, most accommodations in the area offer shuttles for a fee. We've noted all of these in the hotel reviews.

Time-Savers

Write down where you left the sedan: the parking lot area (Goofy, Pluto, whatever) and the row number. We can't stress this enough. After a day spent standing in lines, listening to screaming kids, and being tapped out by the cash registers, most of you will never remember where you parked. All the rental cars look alike, and the increasing number of sport utility vehicles and minivans may keep you from seeing your auto from a distance. (By the way, if you're disabled, a handicap permit is required to park in special spaces at WDW or most anywhere else in Florida. Having a Disabled Veteran license plate won't cut it.)

Getting Around the World

If you can read a subway schedule or bus timetable, you'll ace the WDW transportation system faster than you can say "monorail." Most transportation runs continuously; you *can* get anywhere you want to go, but it could involve as many as two transfers and a long wait.

Getting from your hotel to any park usually involves only one ride. Things get more complicated if you want to get from one resort to another, so consider all the possible complications before deciding to dine at a hotel far from your own. If you have your own wheels, it's often easier to drive.

The **monorail** is just part of WDW's huge transportation web, which also has buses and ferryboats. The Contemporary Resort, Polynesian Resort, Grand Floridian, Transportation and Ticket Center (TTC), and Magic Kingdom are served by the monorail. The Magic Kingdom is also served by ferryboat. A monorail runs to Epcot from the Ticket and Transportation Center.

Tourist Traps

Some restaurants in the WDW parks have started adding an "instant tip" of 10%. Check your bill before adding your tip—you don't want to pay twice!

Some pointers on using the WDW transportation system:

➤ If you're staying at a Disney hotel, keep your hotel ID handy. During crowded times, WDW guests are given preference. If you can't prove you're staying in a WDW hotel, you'll have to wait in line with the non-Disney guests.

➤ Eating and drinking aren't permitted on board, but there aren't any armed guards either. So if you break these rules, you won't be hauled to the dungeon to await execution at dawn.

➤ Strollers must be folded and out of the aisles during transport. If you don't mind the $6 charge, which includes a $1 refundable deposit, a better idea is to leave yours in your hotel room or car and use the rentals at the park entrance.

➤ All WDW transportation is wheelchair-accessible, usually via the rear entry. Everybody else should therefore board through the front doors. Don't sit in seats that are reserved for the disabled. If they're needed, you'll be asked to move.

➤ During peak periods, you may have to stand.

What in the World Does All This Cost?

If you've got an itinerary, chances are the folks at Disney have already thought of a ticket package to match it. The following table lists the most popular plans. Kids age 10 and over pay adult prices; those under age 3 are admitted free. Prices do not include sales tax and are subject to change.

Disney World Admission Prices

Ticket Package and Description	Adult	Ages 3–9
Any one park (1 day)	$42	$34
4-day Value Pass (1 day each at the Magic Kingdom, Disney–MGM Studios, and Epcot, plus another day at the park of your choice)	$149	$119
5-day Park Hopper Pass (unlimited in-and-out admission to the theme parks, including any combination on any day)	$189	$151
6-day All-in-One Hopper Pass (unlimited admission to the theme parks, in any combination, for 5 days, plus admission to the water parks and Pleasure Island for 7 days from date of first use)	$249	$199
7-day All-in-One Hopper Pass (same as above, with 1 extra day)	$274	$219
Theme Park Annual Pass (unlimited admission to the theme parks for 1 year)	$299	$254
Florida Resident Theme Park Annual Pass	$255	$217
Premium Annual Pass (unlimited admission for a year to the theme parks, water parks, and Pleasure Island)	$399	$339
River Country (1 day)	$15.95	$12.50
Water Parks (Typhoon Lagoon or Blizzard Beach) for 1 day	$26.45	$20.70
Pleasure Island (1 evening)	$18.95	N.A.
Disney's Wide World of Sports (1 day)	$8	$6.75

Dollars & Sense

Before leaving home, make sure your budget takes everything into account. The average family will spend $80 to $100 per person per day on park admissions, food, and souvenirs. That doesn't include allowances for hotels, airfares, rental cars, and parking.

WDW also sells multiday passes customized to the length of your stay. They range from a 1-night/2-day pass ($111, adults; $89, kids) to a 6-night/7-day pass ($269, adults; $215, kids). These are all-in-one park-hopper passes that are good at 10 attractions (the Magic Kingdom, Epcot, Disney–MGM Studios, Animal Kingdom, Pleasure Island, Blizzard Beach, Typhoon Lagoon, River Country, and Disney's Wide World of Sports).

Parking is $5 for a car and is good all day at all WDW parks, but make sure you keep the permit.

Getting the Most Out of the World

Face it. You can't possibly do everything. You're going to have to miss out on some of the splendor, no matter how much time you spend in each park. But you can cut a few corners that will let you get the most out of every day. We'll supply specific instructions for each park in subsequent chapters, but you'll enjoy your trip a lot more if you follow some sound advice.

Clever engineers arranged for the parks' most popular rides to be distributed evenly throughout, so massive crowds don't choke any area. The downside (for you) is that you may have to crisscross the entire park several times to get to all of the blockbuster rides. This is a conscious tactic on the part of designers. What better way to get you into a restaurant for a soda, a store for a T-shirt, or onto one of the less-crowded rides before climbing into Space Mountain a second time? A battle plan is definitely in order.

Beating the Lines

The best way we know to beat the lines is to go to the theme parks during low-traffic times of the year. On high-volume days, make it a point to allot plenty of time for each park, and budget your time sensibly. Plan to spend all morning in one section of the park and all afternoon in another. That way you won't waste time and energy running back and forth between Fantasyland and Tomorrowland. Spend 2 days if necessary. Most rides and shows have signs giving you information about waiting times. They usually read something like "The wait time from this point is approximately XXX minutes." Ask (or read) about height or health considerations before you get in line. You don't want to wait for nothing, and some rides, as you'll discover in the next few chapters, have so many warnings that it takes several minutes to read all of them.

Buy Your Tickets in Advance

Tickets to all of the parks are available in most hotels (sometimes at discounted rates) and at more places than we can name. It's a small savings in time, but your kids will be jumping out of their pants if you get that close to the main gate and then have to wait in line to buy tickets. And trust us, unless you arrive well after opening time, you *will* wait for tickets.

Get a Show Schedule As Soon As You Enter the Park

This is essential. Spend a few minutes looking over the schedule as you enter the park, noting where you need to be, and when. Many of the attractions are nonstop, but others occur only at certain times or only once a day. You'll find maps and schedules at counters on one side or the other (sometimes both) just inside the turnstiles.

Go Where the Crowds Aren't

It sounds obvious, but a lot of sheep, er, tourists follow a crowd just because it's a crowd. Head to the left when the rush is moving to the right. Make a beeline for the ride you care most about first thing in the morning, but after that, save the sexy attractions for late in the day. Eat when other people are riding rides (that is, before noon or after 2pm), and ride the rides when the others are stuffing their faces (noon to 2pm).

Avoid Rush Hour

I-4 is woefully overcrowded, especially during rush hour (7 to 9am and 4:30 to 6pm). In addition to the thousands of people heading for a day at the parks, thousands of locals are heading to work. For the most part, you want to get to the park early. But the most crowded days are the ones when people staying in WDW resorts are allowed to enter parks early (see the schedule in chapter 6). If you're not entitled to this privilege, sleep late that day.

Pace Yourself & Take Care of Yourself

You've got all day in the hot sun, and you'll be doing plenty of walking. Wear sneakers or good walking shoes, comfortable clothes, and don't forget to lather your bare skin with sunscreen. (Locals spot tourists by their bright-red "lobster tans." Take breaks for water periodically, or simply to sit under a shade tree for a few minutes. Stagger long lines with air-conditioned shows. If you're staying at a WDW hotel, go back to your room for a late-afternoon nap or a dip in the pool before returning to the park for more fun. Get your hand stamped on the way out and you'll have no trouble getting back in.

Make Dining Reservations Ahead of Time

If a sit-down dinner at a certain venue is important to you, be sure to get Priority Seating reservations as soon as you arrive. Also, a sit-down lunch is a good way to recharge your batteries.

Travel Light

Resist the temptation to take half of your belongings. You'll be cursing your heavy bag or overloaded purse by midafternoon. And don't carry large amounts of cash. The Pirates of the Caribbean aren't the only thieves in WDW. There are ATM machines in all of the parks if you run short of cash.

Words to the Wise

Everyone's looking for a shortcut and no wonder. The lines at Disney and other major theme parks can be incredibly long and irritating if you visit at the wrong time.

Twenty minutes is considered cruising when it comes to waiting for a reasonably sexy ride—30 to 45 minutes is standard for the primo rides. In peak periods—including anytime the kids are out of school—it can take an hour or longer to reach the end of the line, and in 3 or 4 minutes it's over. Restaurants can be every bit as bad.

You can opt for one of the VIP or priority services, but you're also going to pay for the privilege of cutting in line. There's another choice that costs nothing—in fact, you may save a few dollars through special discounted admissions during off-peak periods. Parks offer lower prices for some guests—Florida residents, for instance—or the second day free for all guests (Universal and Sea World do this) at certain times of the year. Hotels usually have lower rates in the same periods. Ask when making reservations, and if your vacation dates are flexible, consider targeting those dates. You'll save money.

Here are some bad times, good times, and other tips:

➤ School is out during the summer, Christmas holidays, and spring breaks. These are family times—the times that the lines will try anyone's patience.

➤ Monday, Thursday, and Saturday are the busiest days in the Magic Kingdom. Tuesday, Friday, and Saturday are the busy days at Epcot. Sunday and Wednesday are crowded at Disney–MGM Studios and Animal Kingdom.

➤ What time is the 3 o'clock parade? Don't take what seems to be a no-brainer for granted. Park schedules are constantly changing when it comes to live entertainment. Check at guest services for weekly schedules.

➤ If you stay on a Disney property, you can get into the parks 90 minutes before the swarm. The park rotation schedule is listed in chapter 6.

➤ Disney parks have tip boards that provide up-to-the-minute information on show times and ride waits. You can find the boards at Main Street, U.S.A., near Coke Corner in the Magic Kingdom, on Hollywood Boulevard near the entrance to Sunset Boulevard in Disney–MGM Studios, in the southwest quadrant of Innoventions Plaza near Epcot's Future World Fountain, and in Safari Village at Animal Kingdom.

➤ Speaking of Epcot, you can burn 1.3 miles of calories if you tackle the promenade walk around the World Showcase Lagoon.

➤ When you do dine at Disney, it's smart to make reservations early in the day to lock in the time you want to eat. If you're staying at a WDW resort, you can make reservations by calling ☎ **407/939-3463.**

➤ It's not guaranteed, but the parks tend to be less crowded during parts of April to May and October to November. Better yet, if you have the option to go in the middle of the week, do it. Also, while most would steer clear on rainy days, the parks are less crowded and you won't miss much other than parades, because most of the good stuff is indoors. Remember that adult ponchos cost $4.95 at most parks—BYOP or go bust.

➤ Pack Valium (just in case), and to prepare yourself for the lines, practice standing at home an hour at a time, half of it in the sun, shuffling 30 inches every $2^1/2$ minutes.

➤ Speaking of the lines, while you're standing in them with nothing else to do, look at the faces around you. All of a sudden it doesn't look like magic, does it?

➤ Yes, it's insanity—but you'll love it.

Trivial Pursuit & the Hidden Mickeys

If you're older than 45 or you have the rerun channel, you'll probably remember this ditty:

Extra! Extra!

Some folks are simply ga-ga over Mickey. This illness is sometimes called Disneyitis. If you have access to the Internet, you can take a little test to see if you're afflicted. You get a point for each of the symptoms you suffer. They include things like:

➤ You must buy anything you see that has a Disney logo—hats, jackets, ties, socks, toothbrushes, and, yes, underwear.

➤ Most of your framed photographs have family members standing next to Disney characters.

➤ You built a miniature Cinderella's Castle in your backyard.

➤ You watch the Disney Christmas parade on a Spanish channel because it's the only one showing it.

➤ You froze your Mickey butter from your very first visit.

➤ You know what EPCOT stands for.

These and other get-a-life symptoms are collected by Jeff Bloom. If you want to take the test or at least get maximum exposure, head to **http://users. aol.com/jbloss2/jmb_dsny.htm**.

Now it's time to say goodbye to all our family.

M-I-C—see you real soon.

K-E-Y—why? Because we like you.

M-O-U-S-E.

Well, now it's time to wade into some final appetizers before you get into the thick of the Magic Kingdom and the other theme parks.

Mickey Minutiae

The official scorers at Disney World keep track of some pretty odd stuff. Here's a sampling guaranteed to impress the lane lizards at your neighborhood bowling alley when you get back home.

➤ Mickeyopolis—The four worlds and assorted trimmings cover 47 square miles, the size of San Francisco or two Manhattan islands. Of the 30,000 acres, one-quarter is developed and another 25% is a preserve.

➤ Earffel Tower—Disney–MGM Studios' landmark water tower has its own custom set of mouse ears. They're hat size 342.

➤ Speaking of Ears—The Rat That Roared sells enough of those signature ear hats annually to cover the head of every human in Pittsburgh, and enough T-shirts to put Mickey's mug on the chest of every man, woman, and child in Chicago.

➤ Hickory Dickory—While we're counting, those gift shops sell 500,000 Mickey watches a year.

➤ Tall Order—Most folks think Spaceship Earth, that far-larger-than-life sphere at Epcot, looks like a giant golf ball. If Disney wanted to match it with a giant golfer, he or she would have to be nearly $2^1/2$ miles tall.

➤ Second Verse—Before we leave Spaceship Earth, that huge hunk of aluminum and plastic alloy tips the scales at 16 million pounds, more than the weight of three fully fueled Space Shuttles.

➤ Big Gulp—The All-Star Sports Resort loves big icons. Its symbols include a mammoth tennis-ball can that's big enough to hold 9,474,609 real tennis balls, and a Coke capable of holding 1.9 million gallons of the carbonated beverage.

➤ Hold the Mustard—WDW guests gobble enough hamburgers and hot dogs to reach from Orlando to Philadelphia if they were stretched end to end. They also eat 5 million pounds of french fries and guzzle more than 46 million soft drinks.

➤ Pick Up Your Room—An average Disney housekeeper makes 11,680 beds a year.

➤ Who's on First—160 of the Disney characters have costumes to greet park guests, but not all 'toons are created equal. Minnie owns 200 outfits from evening gowns to cheerleading skirts. Mickey has 175 in his closet. The other characters usually have only one.

➤ No Trespassing—You don't see many bugs on Disney's public properties. That's because millions of good bugs are let loose to beat up the bad bugs.

➤ Lost & Found—Sunglasses are the hottest commodity at Disney lost and founds. About 100 pairs are turned in daily at the Magic Kingdom alone. (The oddest recovery was a glass eye. Yes, it was claimed.)

➤ Disney's parks have 6 million flowers, trees, and shrubs and 3 million annuals. That's enough to keep 650 gardeners, pest control types, and irrigation specialists hopping.

Hidden Mickeys

They started decades ago as inside jokes among Disney employees, who became so consumed with the game it evolved into a time-honored tradition.

The idea is to put a not-so-obvious image of Mickey in an obvious place. He's in the stars in the sky in Epcot's Spaceship Earth, a Body Wars mural at Disney–MGM Studios, a red-brick walkway at Disney's Wedding Pavilion and scores of other rides, attractions, and decorations.

At first, the hiding places were more imaginative than the Mickeys, which usually took the shape of a head-and-ears silhouette, a large circle capped with two proportionately smaller ones. They're in the trees on guide maps of Disney parks. They take the form of lady bugs and bubbles on souvenir mugs. They decorate a large pair of cowboy boots at the All-Star Music Resort.

Then the designs got more imaginative—like the broccoli Mickey in that Body Wars mural, his clunky yellow shoes seen on the Great Movie Ride, and the stuffed Mickey dolls hidden on Disney–MGM's Tower of Terror.

There is no official list. Hidden Mickeys sometimes are in the eyes of the beholder, but purists have drafted some rules of fair play to prevent things from becoming hallucinogenic.

First, Hidden Mickeys aren't huge. If someone claims to have seen one that's a water tower or, heaven forbid, an entire park, chances are reasonably good they've been nibbling on wild mushrooms again. Second, its ears and head need to be proportioned correctly. Third, you shouldn't have to use too much imagination to see it. (If you have to squint, turn your head cockeyed, and wait for a full moon, it's probably not what you want it to be.) Finally, Disney didn't create the rest of the world. If you think you found one among the oil stains in your driveway, keep it to yourself. Your neighbors will hate it when the pilgrims start landing.

The Magic Kingdom

If you have young kids or a soft spot for Mickey, you might as well make your way to this one first since it is the headliner. The kids will probably want to come back for a second helping. It's the most popular of the Disney enterprises—attracting more than 14 million visitors each year, or an average of 40,000 people a day! If you've ever had to stand in the beer or bathroom lines at Soldier Field or the Meadowlands, you probably get the picture. Mickey's house is the most formidable in all of Disney World—heck, in any world. If you need proof of the Magic Kingdom's staying power, consider that this park has changed or added little since it opened in 1971. Even new things like ExtraTERRORestrial and Timekeeper fall short of the 3-D and virtual dynamics you'll encounter at other theme parks, but the kingdom is still the fairest of them all.

You'll park in a lot the size of Asia and spend an eternity just to get to the entry, so do get here early. As you take the tram to the gate, drivers will remind you where you're parked. Don't forget it. You'll never find your car if you do. *Write down your location and put it in your wallet or purse.* Yes, there is an echo in here, but we can't overemphasize the sick feeling of leaving the park at the end of the day, exhausted and hungry, grumpy, too, then realizing you have no idea where—in that sea of tens of thousands of cars—yours

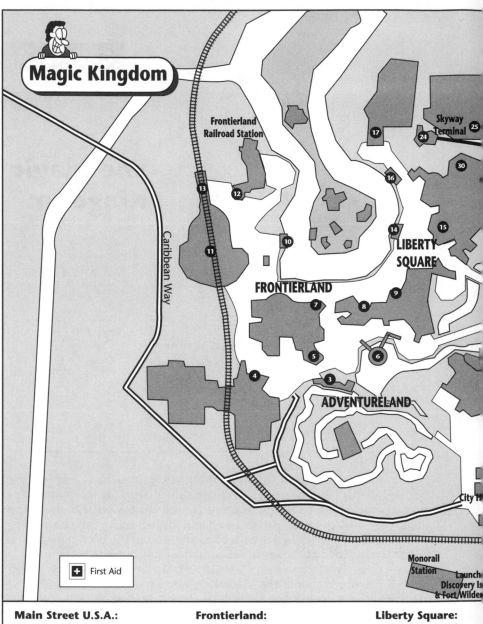

Magic Kingdom

Main Street U.S.A.:
Main Street Cinema ❷
Walt Disney World
    Railroad ❶

Adventureland:
Jungle Cruise ❸
Pirates of the
    Caribbean ❹
Swiss Family Treehouse ❻
Enchanted Tiki Room ❺

Frontierland:
Big Thunder Mountain
    Railroad ⓭
Country Bear Jamboree ❼
The Diamond Horseshoe
    Saloon Revue ❾
Frontierland Shootin'
    Arcade ❽
Splash Mountain ⓫
Tom Sawyer Island ❿
Walt Disney World
    Railroad ⓬

Liberty Square:
The Hall of Presidents
The Haunted Mansion
Liberty Belle Riverboat
Mike Fink Keelboats ⓰

Fantasyland:
Ariel's Grotto ㉖
Castle Forecourt Stage
Cinderella's Castle ⓳
Cinderella's Golden
    Carousel ⓴

178

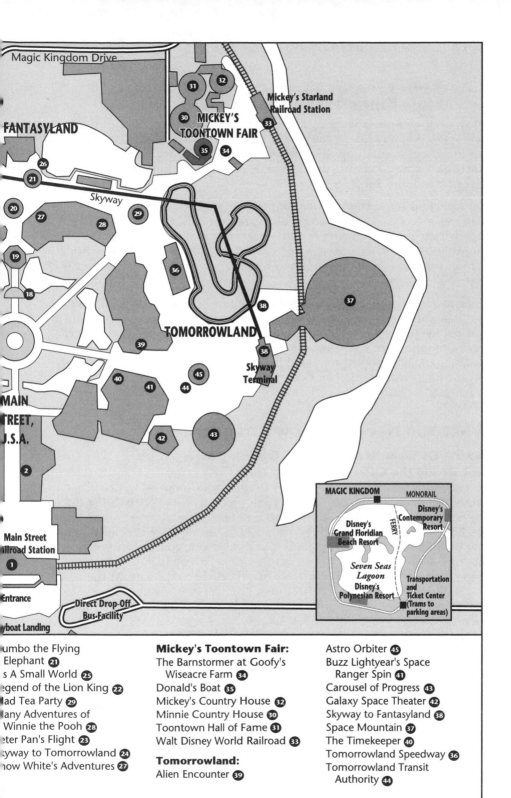

Magic Kingdom Drive

31 32

Mickey's Starland Railroad Station

30 **MICKEY'S TOONTOWN FAIR** 33

FANTASYLAND

35 34

26

21

Skyway

20 27 28 29

19

36

18

38 37

TOMORROWLAND

39

Skyway Terminal 38

45

40 41 44

MAIN STREET, U.S.A.

42 43

2

Main Street Railroad Station

1

Entrance

...yboat Landing

Direct Drop-Off Bus Facility

MAGIC KINGDOM | **MONORAIL**

Disney's **Grand Floridian Beach Resort**

FERRY

Disney's **Contemporary Resort**

Seven Seas Lagoon

Disney's **Polynesian Resort**

Transportation and Ticket Center (Trams to parking areas)

...umbo the Flying
Elephant **21**
...s A Small World **25**
...egend of the Lion King **22**
...ad Tea Party **29**
...any Adventures of
Winnie the Pooh **28**
...eter Pan's Flight **23**
...kyway to Tomorrowland **24**
...now White's Adventures **27**

Mickey's Toontown Fair:
The Barnstormer at Goofy's
Wiseacre Farm **34**
Donald's Boat **35**
Mickey's Country House **32**
Minnie Country House **30**
Toontown Hall of Fame **31**
Walt Disney World Railroad **33**

Tomorrowland:
Alien Encounter **39**

Astro Orbiter **45**
Buzz Lightyear's Space
Ranger Spin **41**
Carousel of Progress **43**
Galaxy Space Theater **42**
Skyway to Fantasyland **38**
Space Mountain **37**
The Timekeeper **40**
Tomorrowland Speedway **36**
Tomorrowland Transit
Authority **44**

179

is. Even if you ignore everything else we say, please follow this piece of advice. You'll thank us and we won't have to say: We told you so!

Okay, okay, that's it. No more planning. You're off to meet Mickey! We won't attempt to list every ride in the park (a dab of spontaneity is good, after all), but this chapter rounds up the highlights and provides your first **"Jake Ratings"**—those honest-to-goodness ride report cards from our 7-year-old expert, grandson Jake.

Our tour of the Magic Kingdom starts at the front gate and moves counterclockwise from section to section. Your own path through the park won't be nearly so orderly (see suggested itineraries a little further into this chapter), and you'll probably double back more than once, or end up taking the long way from Tomorrowland to Frontierland, but so what? The only thing that matters is that you're having fun.

Once you're through the pay windows, you have your second choice (the first was which ticket option to take): the monorail or the ferry. Either one will get you to the action. (If you figured the rides started just on the other side of the windows, you figured wrong. You still have a ways to go.) The choice is a jump ball—the monorail is quicker in terms of actual travel time, but the lines can be horrendous compared to the ferry, which carries more passengers per load. So you pick 'em.

What You Need to Know About the Park

Hours: Or When Is the Official Opening Time Not Really the Official Opening Time?

The Magic Kingdom is open every day from 9am to 7pm. That's what they *say,* but there are exceptions—and the gates almost always open earlier than the "official" opening time. Are we going to tell you to get there early? Uh-uh. But if you arrive extra early (up to an hour before the posted opening), you might be rewarded big time. (As if your kids were going to let you sleep late that day anyway!) You'll also beat the traffic, which includes Disney employees, and you may even be able to park closer to the gate. At the other end of the spectrum, closing is later than 7pm during the summer and on holidays. The Magic Kingdom may be open as late as midnight for its special events.

Services & Facilities

➤ **ATMs** are located at the main entrance, the SunTrust Bank on Main Street, and in Tomorrowland.

➤ **Baby-changing facilities** are located next to the Crystal Palace at the end of Main Street, and they include rocking chairs and toddler-size toilets. Disposable diapers, formula, baby food, and pacifiers are for sale there, too, in the Gerber Baby Center. This, of course, isn't the best place to buy them, but it will do in an emergency. You get two disposable diapers, two wipes, doses of vitamins A and B, and some itty-bitty ointments for $3.50. The changing tables are free; they're located in the center as well as in all women's rest rooms and some of the men's.

➤ The **First Aid Center,** staffed by registered nurses, is located alongside the Crystal Palace and the Gerber Baby Center. Again, we hope you heeded warnings to bring essentials with you, but if not, you can get two Advils for $1 or two Imodium capsules for $2.

➤ **Lockers** can be found in an arcade underneath the Main Street Railroad Station. The cost is $6, including a $2 refundable deposit.

➤ **Lost children.** There's no charge. If your kids get lost, somebody will most likely take them to City Hall or the Baby Care Center, where lost children logbooks are kept. It's smart to make kids under 7 wear nametags. It's easier for park staffers to read them than to drag a name from a frightened, crying young 'un.

➤ **Packages** can be sent from any store to Guest Relations in the Plaza area so you can pick them up all at once at the end of the day instead of hauling souvenirs around with you.

➤ Make **Priority Seating** arrangements when you enter the park if you care about having a sit-down meal at a special venue. See chapter 9 for more details.

➤ **Special shows.** When you enter the park, study the *Entertainment Show Schedule,* which lists all the special events of the day. You might find special concerts, otherwise unannounced visits from Disney characters, and information about fireworks and parades. Plan these events first, as they're the only ones that you won't get a second chance to see. You'll find these at counters just inside the entrance (not the ticket windows).

➤ **Strollers** can be rented at the Stroller Shop near the entrance for $6 a day, including a $1 deposit.

Extra! Extra!

Wheelchairs can be rented at the Transportation and Ticket Center or the Stroller and Wheelchair Shop just inside the main entrance. The cost is $6 for a regular wheelchair and $40 for an electric, including a $10 deposit.

➤ **Not quite necessities.** The prices of consumables are pretty much standard among Disney parks. The Magic Kingdom will nail you to the tune of $1.55 for a soda, $2.50 for bottled water, $2 for an ice-cream bar, $2.50 for a pineapple float, and $1.15 for a cup of cocoa. **Many of these are common prices,** even at Universal and Sea World, so we'll list some different items at other parks.

Meeting Characters

We know: Little Johnny has his heart set on meeting the Mickster, but you haven't the foggiest idea where to find a rodent in these crowds. Don't

181

worry—it's a piece of cake. Just ask any employee. If they don't know, they'll be able to make a quick phone call and find out for you. You're very likely to spot characters right away at City Hall on Main Street as you enter the park. Another good bet is Mickey's Toontown. You'll also see many of them in the afternoon and evening parades.

Most characters will sign autographs (they can't really carry pens in those costumes, so bring one for your kids), pose for pictures, or hug your child. Characters in heads are not allowed to talk, though, because they wouldn't get the classic voices right.

Also, don't be surprised if your kids turn a little shy or become star-struck just like you would if you ran into Julia Roberts or Brad Pitt. You'll want to stay close to your toddlers as they meet their cartoon pals.

Main Street, U.S.A.

Main Street is a place to lose yourself in pleasant nostalgia for yesteryear—although we recommend passing through quickly when you arrive. (Get thee to the popular stuff right away before the lines get too bad!) You'll have to make a return voyage on Main Street when you cry "uncle" at the end of the day. You can browse through the shops at a more leisurely pace before you exit the park.

You don't have to pay admission to the **Main Street Cinema,** where you can watch Disney cartoons—though no seating is available. There's also a lot of shopping here, for Disney gift items, old-fashioned candy, crystal animals, sports memorabilia, and more.

From here, you can take the **Walt Disney World Railroad** on a free loop around the park, or get off at stops in Frontierland or Mickey's Toontown Fair. Other vehicles departing Main Street include horse-drawn trolleys, horseless carriages, jitneys, buses, fire engines, and shoes—yours.

Time-Savers

When entering the park, agree on a family meeting spot in case you get separated, and write it down for everyone. All of these parks get so crowded you can lose the rest of your group when they're no more than a few feet away. Even older children become disoriented and can't find their way back to "that bench" or "under this tree." They must be able to explain to a park official that they need to get to City Hall, the rest rooms at the Main Entrance, or wherever else you decide. Make sure everyone understands they must not go through the turnstile and return to the car. The crush of people and cars makes this a dangerous place at closing time.

Tomorrowland

Disney completely overhauled Tomorrowland back in 1994 because its vision of the future in the 1960s, when the park was designed, was starting to look too retro. Originally, it imagined a 21st century with neither computers nor answering machines. The updated take on the future enlisted the talents of *Star Wars* director George Lucas, among others, and has now been souped up to be a whole lot more high tech (*read:* more aliens, robots, and state-of-the-art video games). The new Tomorrowland is where older kids will want to start their Magic Kingdom adventure, and where they'll be begging you to buy them cool space toys and Star Wars memorabilia in the shops. Hang a right when you get to the hub at the end of Main Street and blast off into the future.

On the ride front, **Space Mountain** is one of the most popular ones in the park. Imagine a rock 'n' roller coaster. Then imagine it in the dark. Teenagers and adrenaline junkies bolt for this one (the same goes for ExtraTERRORestrial Alien Encounter, Buzz Lightyear Space Ranger Spin, and Thunder Mountain Railroad) as soon as they clear the entrance, so lines can be long. Get here immediately if you can, or head here during any off-hours, such as lunch or when crowds are thin in the late afternoon and evening.

It's a classic roller coaster, with the added fear of being lost in space, in the dark, plunging, and spinning. Hang onto your hats, and everything else for that matter, when you blast off, or your things are likely to end up in orbit. It's for ages 10 and up. There is a bailout area for those who want to ditch at the last minute. Thrill-seekers take the first cars. You must be 44 inches tall to ride this puppy.

 Jake Rating: "Wow, that's double awesome!"

George Lucas helped design the **ExtraTERRORestrial Alien Encounter,** an extremely popular ride and another white-knuckle special. This recent kingdom addition carries a very legitimate child warning about it being dark and confining inside. The recommended age is 10 and older, and while some younger ones might love it, that's probably a pretty fair recommendation. The confinement part is a hard shoulder plate that lowers over your head to lock you into your tomb, er, seat. After you're locked and loaded, something goes terribly awry with your teletransporter's aim and it sucks in a disgusting creature from Tennessee, or some other part of outer space. Did we mention the alien is a meat-eater? The lights alternate on and off, but mainly off, and the alien gets loose. Sitting in utter darkness with a strobelike flash every once in a while, you're treated to down drafts as the creature "flies" over-head, spritzes of water (mucous if you'd prefer to think that way) on your face, and the neatest touch near the end: this little blast of hot breath on the back of your neck.

 Jake Rating: "Uh, no thanks. You guys have fun."

The **Astro Orbiter** whirls astro-orbit wannabes high into the galaxy in colorful rockets. If you have a problem with heights, or ridiculously long lines, this is one ride you can afford to pass up. It's fine for ages 6 and under. Yawn.

The **Timekeeper** is a rousing robot show that combines IMAX scenes with CircleVision and AudioAnimatronics. The Timekeeper actually is a 'tronic Robin Williams and his sidekick, 9-Eyes, who needs little description with a name like that. This 360° movie is a chuckler in which Williams's character takes you back in time to the age of dinosaurs, through the medieval years, and then he inadvertently kidnaps Jules Verne for a reluctant trip into outer space. Don't plan on resting your feet here—you have to stand for the entire performance.

Jake Rating: "That was dumb." It *was* pretty boring.

Buzz Lightyear's Space Ranger Spin takes you—hey, where else?—to infinity! Get ready to rock in an interactive space adventure while helping Buzz Lightyear defend Earth's supply of batteries from the evil Emperor Zurg. As you climb aboard an XP-37 space cruiser, you become a commissioned junior ranger armed with twin laser cannons and a joystick capable of spinning the craft very much like Linda Blair's head in *The Exorcist*. (Rangers who tend to get motion sickness should sit this one out. There's enough space debris flying around without your cookies.) While you cruise through space, you collect points by blasting anything that smells remotely like Zurg. Light, sound, and animation effects are triggered by your hits. In the end, Buzz finally shows up. Together, you trash the Zurgmeister and his evil henchmen, and the world as you know it is allowed to survive.

The **Tomorrowland Speedway** puts you behind the wheel of an Indy car knockoff. Children ages 6 through 14 could ride it all day, but adults may find the waiting time, and the steering, to be less than stellar. It's tame because you can't get above 7 miles per hour and there's a thick iron bar separating your tires, so you're pretty much kept on track. Children have to be 52 inches tall to drive alone. This is another oldie that can be boring if you and your kids are used to the quicker pace of go-karts, or those cars at Malibu Grand Prix.

The **Galaxy Space Theater** stars Mickey Mouse and his friends in a talent show. Young kids won't want to miss it.

Skyway to Fantasyland is a cable-car ride for all ages. It beats walking from one section of the Magic Kingdom to another, and it provides an exciting view from about 40 feet above the park.

The **Tomorrowland Transit Authority** is ideal for all ages. Unique linear-induction motors propel cars on an elevated people-mover. You'll wind around Tomorrowland and into Space Mountain on a lazy ride that will encourage you to nod off if it's late in the day and you have covered 4 or 5 miles on the old pedometer. Better yet, there's usually no waiting involved.

The **Carousel of Progress** is a Disney oldie that was refurbished in 1993, and its view of tomorrow is still somewhat behind the times. A revolving theater traces the technological progress made by humanity since the Gas Light era of the 1930s. In the final act, *Progressing Present,* an American family is shown using virtual reality games and voice-activated appliances (which still manage to burn the Christmas-dinner turkey). It's a nice place to relax on a hot day, but if you're pressed for time, skip it.

Beating the Lines

The slowest lines in the Magic Kingdom, alas, seem to lead to those rides that little kids want most: Dumbo, Mad Tea Party, the Carousel, and the Astro Orbiter. Since these rides have a fixed number of riders and everybody gets on and off at once, the lines move in herky-jerky fashion. Check these lines first, and promise your kids to come back later if the wait seems too long. With so many wonders to choose from, it's best to keep on the move. Signs at several rides indicate how long you'll have to wait from that point and provide a good reference point.

Mickey's Toontown Fair

If you have young kids, go here first. (If you don't want to walk, you can get here on the WDW Railroad from Main Street.) Tucked behind Tomorrow-land, this is a gentler section of the park, largely geared to the little ones, so older kids might be bored. This is a major meet-and-greet spot for **Mickey** and **Minnie Mouse, Donald Duck, Goofy,** and countless other Disney characters. Stroll through **Mickey and Minnie's Country Houses,** explore the **Toontown Hall of Fame,** or cool off on a hot day at **Donald's Boat.** The **Barnstormer** is a kiddie roller coaster located on **Goofy's Wiseacre Farm** that will be a blast for 4- through 6-year-olds. The lines to meet the characters here may have you wishing you were elsewhere, but your kids will be enthralled.

Fantasyland

The rides and attractions here are based on the Disney movies we all grew up with way back when, as well as some of the more recent additions to the Disney treasure trove of films. Young kids will want to spend lots of time here—don't worry, you will be.

The symbol of the Magic Kingdom, **Cinderella's Castle,** is at the end of Main Street, right in the center of the park. A lot of you will want to take family photos here, just for the view. If you come at the right time, Cinderella might pay you a visit. To enter Fantasyland from Main Street, just pass directly through the castle, and take a gander at the lovely murals and mosaics of the Cinderella story on the walls—yes, that's real gold and silver.

Cinderella's Golden Carousel is a gorgeous merry-go-round that will delight young children. The organ plays—what else?—Disney classics like "When You Wish Upon a Star" and "Twist and Shout"—no, wait, that was the Beatles.

Ariel's Grotto is a splashy (literally—kids get wet) area with fountains and the Little Mermaid, in person. Waits can be long, but Ariel is at the end of the line, happy to say "howdy, partner" and have her photograph taken if you promise not to eat fish sticks.

For some, **It's a Small World** is very, very cute, but it's a real gagger for teens and some adults. Nevertheless, you have to ride it at least once. Think of it as an initiation. You won't get accepted in Phi Pluto Pi until you hear that sickening theme song (in Munchkin voices) that crawls in your head and refuses to leave for months. You'll glide around the world meeting Russian dancers, Chinese acrobats, French can-can dancers, and a Venetian gondolier, and every blessed one of them sings the song from hell. For ages 2 to 5, it's a load of fun. For the rest of us, it's like "Groundhog Day," the movie. So bring garlic and a silver bullet!

Dollars & Sense

Your entertainment dollars go further if you don't try to see an entire park in a day. With a multiday pass, you can relax and not feel panicked that you have to see every attraction in a blur. Leave the park at midday, have a picnic or inexpensive lunch at your hotel, and then have a nap or a swim before returning to the park for the afternoon and evening.

Mr. Toad's Wild Ride hurtles you through dark rooms. Wait! What? It doesn't? Oh. Scratch that. Mr. Toad's Wild Ride used to hurtle you through dark rooms. Maybe you remember us talking in the last chapter about how Disney engineers always are refining things in the Land of Mickey. Well, J. Thaddeus Toad's ride got refined out of the picture in summer 1998, but not without a ruckus from his fans. Well, the fans lost and so did the frog, so please observe a moment of silence before the details. (Pause.)

Okay, then. Where Toad once drove you head-on into a locomotive and then to the gates of hell, the **Many Adventures of Winnie the Pooh** is opening in honor of this guide hitting the bookstores. There's not so much as a marble marker in Toadie's honor. Just a memory.

Before he perished, diehard toad-heads mounted a brave last stand that included peaceful protests. There even was an Internet drive (**www.savetoad.com**), toad-ins at the park, and green T-shirts that begged viewers to "Ask me why Mickey is killing Mr. Toad." It was one of the park's original rides. His appeal? Some of his biggest fans found themselves at a loss to describe it. Maybe it was that he wasn't the stereotypical, do-gooder Disney hero. He was crazy. He stole cars. He was an outlaw. He was even flatulent. But he's past tense now. R.I.P., Mr. Toad.

Pooh, meanwhile, lives. But at least he's not Barney!

Everyone's favorite chubby little honey-grubbing bear comes to life with Piglet, Eeyore, Gopher, Owl, Rabbit, Tigger, Kanga, and Roo for a magical journey into the Hundred Acre Wood.

Special effects and a hum-dinger of a musical score highlight this adventure as Hunny Pot vehicles whisk you through a Blustery Day. Along the way, you come across Owl's toppling house, bounce along with Tigger, appear in Pooh's dream of Heffalumps and Woozles, save Piglet from the rising water in a Floody Place and, finally, arrive at one honey of a party with the whole gang.

Dumbo, the Flying Elephant won't do it for adrenaline-addicted older kids, but it's a favorite for ages 2 through 5 or so. Ride Dumbo, whose big ears keep you airborne for a gentle, circular flight, with a few little dips. Most kids older than 6 would be humiliated if you even suggested they ride. But if your kids will clamor for Dumbo, break for this ride ASAP—the wait times on this one are brutal!

Legend of the Lion King is a lavish stage show starring Simba and his friends as they tell the beloved jungle story. Children under 4 may get fussy; those over 10 might find it too childish. If the wait isn't bad, it's a great place to park yourself for 30 minutes on a hot day.

The **Mad Tea Party** is a ride that can be wild or mild, depending on how much you choose to spin the teacup that is your chariot. The ride is based on *Alice in Wonderland* and is suitable for ages 4 and up. If you don't like getting dizzy, steer clear, or you'll end up as woozy as the mouse that periodically pops up from the center teapot.

Peter Pan's Flight will delight children ages 3 through 8 with its pirate galleons and a flight over London in search of Captain Hook, Tiger Lily, and the Lost Boys. This is one of the old glide rides heralding the technology available when the Magic Kingdom was born in 1971. For adults, the lovely views of nighttime London almost make the ride worth the long wait. It's a soothing, though short, flight through Neverland.

Snow White's Adventure takes you to the dwarfs' cottage and the wishing well, and ends with the prince's kiss to break the evil spell. It's less scary now than when it was introduced in 1971, when it was really dark and menacing. Still, be careful about taking kids younger than 5 inside.

Skyway to Tomorrowland is a real cable-car ride that takes you from Small World (there's that blooming song again!), high over Mickey's Toontown Fair, to Space Mountain. It's good transportation and a great ride for all ages.

Liberty Square

Sandwiched between Fantasyland and Frontierland, this re-creation of Revolutionary-era America will infuse you with Colonial spirit in no time at all. Many of the historical touches (like the 13 lanterns symbolizing the original 13 colonies) will be lost on younger visitors, but they'll delight in seeing a fife-and-drum corps marching along the cobblestone streets—and the opportunity to pose for a picture while locked in stocks.

Beating the Lines

Most rides and shows continue throughout parade times, but because thousands of people are drawn to the parade route, the lines at popular attractions such as Space Mountain, Splash Mountain, Pirates of the Caribbean, and Alien Encounter become much shorter. If you don't care much about a parade, this is your chance. Bolt for the good stuff, but check with a uniformed staffer to see what routes or transportation vehicles close during parades. Once crowds form at parade sites, you can't move through them.

The **Hall of Presidents** will appeal to adults and bright children over age 10, but the program may drag for younger children. It's a magnificent, inspiring production, based on painstaking research. Pay special attention to the roll call of presidents. The Animatronic figures are incredibly lifelike; they'll come alive, fidget and whisper, and talk to the audience.

The **Haunted Mansion** is another favorite. It's changed little over the years, but the special effects still work, and the atmosphere is grand. You may even chuckle at the corny tombstones you'll find as you wait to get in. It doesn't get much scarier than spooky music, eerie howling, things that go bump in the night, weird flying objects, and sudden, though minor, surprises. It actually takes a great deal of effort to keep the place looking bedraggled, which may explain why your haunted hosts are only a handful of Disney cast members that you'll find without smiles plastered on their faces. (Jake passed on a rating, but he jumped at the jump-up ghosts.) Don't take the wee ones, but those 5 or 6 and older should enjoy it.

Boat rides aboard the *Liberty Belle* and Mike Fink Keelboats take you through the Rivers of America. You may tangle with a few pirates or rustlers, but mostly this is a pleasant way to rest tired feet and imagine that you're on the Tennessee River in Davy Crockett's day. Kids over 6 will be beguiled.

Frontierland

Frontierland is gussied up to look like the Old West, with rustic log cabins, wooden sidewalks, swinging-door saloons, and Disney cast members dressed like cowboys and frontier women. It's tucked way back behind Adventureland and adjacent to Liberty Square.

The real highlight here is **Splash Mountain,** one of the Magic Kingdom's favorite thrill rides. While it really doesn't compete with Sea World's Journey to Atlantis (see chapter 18) in terms of size and height, this is a nifty voyage on a flume that has a substantial vertical drop (about 52 feet) with a good splash factor (around 200 megatons worth of wet). If you're lucky enough to have some real heavyweights in the front seat, look for a little extra explosion on the downhill. On a hot day, this can be a lifesaver, but on cool days, parents may want to take steps to protect kids (and themselves) from a chill. Teenagers rush here first and take the trip time after time. It hits a 6.5 on the thrill scale, reaching speeds of 40 miles per hour. Your dugout carries you through swamps, waterfalls, and a heart-thumping five-story fall. It's recommended for 8 and up. Riders must be at least 44 inches tall.

Big Thunder Mountain Railroad is also pretty intense for children under 5 or 6, but older kids (riders must be at least 40 inches tall) will love it. It's one of the kingdom's favorites, something of a low-grade roller coaster. Reverse magic works on this one. If you practice what we preach on Big Thunder Mountain Railroad (go to the sexiest, furthest rides first), you'll probably get burned. It's been around long enough that even rookies make a beeline for it. Our best advice here is to give it until 11 or 11:30am, then join the fun. Even then you're going to wait. This isn't the usual Disney line maze. It has an upper and (shorter) lower-level line. At midday on a moderately crowded day, the wait usually runs 30 to 45 minutes; double that if you go earlier, or on the high-traffic days. If the park is open late, try it at night when a parade is running—Railroad veterans swear the ride is more exciting after sunset. When you finally board, you'll jounce around an old mining track, barely escaping floods, a bridge collapse, a rockslide, and other mayhem.

Jake (who insists on riding this until everyone in the family turns green) **Rating:** "Yeeeee-haw!" Then, "That was awesome!"

Tom Sawyer Island takes you across a narrow "river" by log raft to a real island where you'll find Injun Joe's Cave, swinging bridges that threaten to throw you into a gaping chasm, and an abandoned mine. On the kid front, this one usually pleases ages 4 through 14. While you're an islander, you might consider having lunch or a snack at **Aunt Polly's,** which overlooks the "river."

Time-Savers

Attendants allow parents to split up just before entry to scary rides, so one parent can stay with any children who are too small to ride. When the other parent and older kids finish the ride, the family can unite again. The second parent is then in a position to ride without going through the line again. Rules vary, so ask the first attendant you see and keep asking as you move through the line.

The **Country Bear Jamboree** is a 15-minute Animatronic show featuring bears that sing country-and-western style. It's a park standard—a show that's been around since Disney invented dirt. This is one of the ones to see early since the crowds rush to the primo stuff first. While you wait for the show to begin, the Disney vending machines urge your kids to pay 50¢ for a flattened penny—yes, *one stinkin' Lincoln*—that the machine spits out with a Disney logo. (We warned you: These folks are geniuses about getting everything including the lint out of your pockets.) Show time begins with some talking wall mounts like Melvin the Moose. Though these are pretty old, they're still a tribute to Disney ingenuity. It's an audience participation show where there's a lot of hand-clapping, knee-slapping, foot-stomping music from stars like Liver Lips McGraw with his ballad on ugly women, the Sunshine Girls singing "All the Guys That Turn Me On Turn Me Down," and Big Al moaning "Blood in the Saddle" way off-key and out of synch with the band. There's enough noise and variety to keep most toddlers wide-eyed, but it's best for 4 and up.

 Jake Rating: "Pretty neat." (He probably was just happy to be out of the sun for a spell.)

The **Diamond Horseshoe Saloon Revue & Medicine Show** takes you back to the rootin'-tootin' West where fancy ladies, honky-tonk pianos, and gamblers entertained. This, too, is air-conditioned, which is a big plus on sweltering days. It's suitable for ages 5 and over. Seven shows play daily. Those of you who'd prefer not to be part of the production should sit in the balcony. Come for lunch and choose from a menu of popular sandwiches.

The **Frontierland Shootin' Arcade** is probably the most elaborate shooting gallery you'll ever play. Infrared bullets are shot from reproduction buffalo rifles into a world where fog creeps in, thunder claps, coyotes yowl, and the graveyard comes alive. You get 15 shots for 50¢. It's best for sharpshooters ages 8 and over.

Adventureland

Adventureland is a left turn off of the hub at the end of Main Street. *Swashbuckling* is the operative word here. Kids can envision life in the jungle or the forest, while walking through dense tropical foliage (complete with vines), or marauding through bamboo and thatch-roofed huts.

Pirates of the Caribbean has been completely keel-hauled to be more politically correct, and the pirates are now less scary, too. Even so, the 10-minute ride is still one of the most enjoyable at the Magic Kingdom. Stroll through a dungeon before boarding a ship that sails through pirate battles and rum-induced raids. Kids under 5 (and one 7-year-old in particular) may find a pirate's life a little too scary. Those children who try it on for size too early, including our own ride critic, harbor a lasting impression.

 Jake Rating: "I *don't* like that ride." We don't know what scared him back when he was 3 or so (it's pretty slow, calm, and tame), but something did and stuck with him like Poohs on fresh honey. Most 7-year-olds, though, will like it.

The **Jungle Cruise,** for most ages, is a funny-scary, 10-minute narrated sail on the Congo, the Amazon, and the Nile, where you'll see jungle "animals,"

lush foliage, a temple-of-doom-type camp, and lots of surprises. Some of the captains get their passengers pretty rowdy. The ride passes Animatronic pygmies and pythons, elephants and rhinos, gorillas, and a herd of hippos that pop threateningly out of the water and blow snot—well, it could have been snot if they weren't robots—on the tourists. This is a near-30-year-old exhibit, which means it's pretty hokey when you compare it to Animal Kingdom (coming in chapter 15).

 Jake Rating: "I guess it's okay."

Nearby, the **Swiss Family Treehouse** can captivate ages 4 through 12 for hours of swinging, exploring, crawling fun. The beloved Joann Wyss story of the Swiss Family Robinson, who made a comfortable home from things they salvaged from their ship or found on their desert island, comes alive here. It's fun but simple, void of all that high-tech stuff so popular in today's parks. Be prepared to stand on busy days in a slow-moving line. It's sort of like those processions that file past the coffin of a dead head of state. But there are no stiffs on this one.

The **Enchanted Tiki Room—Under New Management** is best for ages 2 through 8, and adults whose feet are tired. It's a corny but sweet sing-along staged by four Animatronic birds perched on an enchanted fountain, and also features appearances by Iago of *Aladdin* and Zazu of *The Lion King*. A chorus of 250 tropical-bird friends joins in the fun. Children are mesmerized by the "Tiki, tiki, tiki," song, and you'll all leave this theater humming a happy tune. Luckily, it's not a maddening ditty like the one in "It's a Small World"—well, not *as* maddening.

Time-Savers

If you have only 1 day in the Magic Kingdom, skip lengthy meals. Instead, enjoy a character breakfast or elaborate dinner on some other day, like the day you saved for sunning and swimming at your hotel.

Oohs & Aahs, Parades & Fireworks

Disney Magical Moments Parade. It's float after float of all the recent and some of the old Disney characters and movies. There's lots of singing and character interaction, as characters stop to dance and frolic with kids as they walk down the street. This parade goes off daily, depending on the weather, at 3pm. The parade route goes through Liberty Square and Frontierland, and winds up at City Hall on Main Street. Get your seat early—but don't sit on the grass or you'll be asked to move.

Spectro-Magic, the current dazzling, after-dark parade, will be replaced by the original **Main Street Electrical Parade** at some point in 1999. More than 700,000 lights will adorn the 26 floats of fantasy that travel down Main Street in the Magic Kingdom. It's a spectacular show that shouldn't be missed. Stake your claim even earlier to a curbside spot.

191

Fireworks are a nightly spectacle in the Magic Kingdom in summer and during peak holiday periods. The show starts with a flight of Peter Pan from the pinnacles of Cinderella's Castle, followed by a fortune's worth of pyrotechnics that light up the sky like it's the 4th of July. (Of course, averaging 40,000 visitors a day and at $42 a head, Disney can afford a fortune, right?) Liberty Square, Frontierland, and Mickey's Toontown Fair are good viewing spots, as are some of the Disney hotels closest to the park.

Have a Goofy Day: Some Suggested Itineraries

Whew! That's a lot to digest, much less to try to fit into 1 or 2 days. And that's without waiting on lines or stopping to eat, drink, shop, or tie the little ones' shoes.

Undoubtedly you'll have your own ideas about what you'd like to do most, but here's some advice in case you don't know which type of fun to have first. We've planned two itineraries for the Magic Kingdom. The first one will primarily interest families with younger children. The second one will have more appeal for adults and teenagers (if they can stand to be seen with their parents).

Each itinerary is for 1 day. If you spend a second day at the Magic Kingdom, even a complete idiot won't need an itinerary to remember which rides and attractions are worth repeating.

The Magic Kingdom in a Day with Kids

1. Make a Priority Seating reservation at **Cinderella's Royal Table for dinner,** located inside Cinderella's Castle.

2. If you have very young kids, go straight to the **Walt Disney World Railroad** station on Main Street and take the first train out. Get off at **Mickey's Toontown Fair,** where the tots will be wowed by the sight of Mickey, Minnie, and the gang. They can ride their own roller coaster, see where Mickey lives, and see all their dreams come true before the day even begins.

3. Walk just west of Toontown to **Fantasyland.** Ride **Dumbo the Flying Elephant** and **Peter Pan's Flight.** See the **Legend of the Lion King** and **It's a Small World.** For very young children, linger longer in Fantasyland to ride **Cinderella's Golden Carousel** and perhaps ride Dumbo again.

4. Take the **Skyway to Tomorrowland,** where preteens can do all of the thrill rides. Or, for younger children, see the 22-minute **Walt Disney's Carousel of Progress.**

5. Is it lunchtime already? Have a hot dog, deli plate, or barbecue at **Cosmic Ray's Starlight Café** and enjoy the stage show.

6. Due west of Tomorrowland is **Liberty Square** with its restful **boat ride,** patriotic theme, and the **Hall of Presidents,** which is best for ages 10 and older. If you didn't eat in Tomorrowland, have lunch in

the **Liberty Square Tavern,** which specializes in down-home American meals such as turkey and stuffing or pot roast with mashed potatoes.

7. When you finish in Liberty Square, proceed through Frontierland, resisting its temptations for now, to board the train at the **Frontierland Railroad Station.** It's a delightful, restful ride around the entire Magic Kingdom. Take it all the way around and end up back in Frontierland. Older children will now want to ride **Big Thunder Mountain Railroad** and **Splash Mountain.** Suitable for all ages are **Tom Sawyer Island,** the **Diamond Horseshoe Saloon Revue & Medicine Show** (food is available), and the **Country Bear Jamboree.**

Bet You Didn't Know

Mickey Mouse's costumes include a scuba-diving outfit and a full dress tuxedo.

8. Check the time of today's parade. Start hunting for good spots along the route about an hour beforehand. If you're not sure whether you've picked a good spot, ask a cast member (a Disney employee, preferably one in costume). You don't want to be shooed off the grass once the parade starts.

9. Head over to Adventureland and ride **Pirates of the Caribbean,** the **Jungle Cruise,** and the **Tropical Serenade.** Older kids like the **Swiss Family Treehouse.**

10. Keep an eye on your watch so you'll be back at Cinderella's Castle in time for your dinner seating. Then check the entertainment schedule for after-dark fireworks or parades.

The Magic Kingdom in a Day for Teenagers & Adults

1. Make Priority Seating reservations for dinner at the **Liberty Tree Tavern** for a feast served family-style, **Tony's Town Square** for grilled fish or steaks, the **Plaza Restaurant** for burgers and salads, or the **Crystal Palace** for meats and a sundae bar.

2. On the right-hand side of Main Street as you walk in, be at the Plaza Pavilion Restaurant when the barrier opens; go through the restaurant to Tomorrowland to ride **Space Mountain** and then the **ExtraTERRORestrial Alien Encounter** pronto. Check out the video arcades and any other of the rides or shows you want to see here.

3. Cross back through the center of the park, through Liberty Square, to Frontierland, and get in line to ride **Splash Mountain.** The line won't get any shorter all day.

4. Leaving Splash Mountain, veer left to ride **Big Thunder Mountain Railroad,** and then do the **Haunted Mansion.** Head back toward

193

Cinderella's Castle and Fantasyland, where you can see **Legend of the Lion King** in a huge theater that seats 500. Lines move quickly here.

5. Start thinking about lunch at 11 or 11:30am before the crowds get too thick, unless you have Priority Seating somewhere. While you're eating, work out plans to view the afternoon parade. People start staking out the best spots an hour in advance.

6. The **Hall of Presidents,** in Liberty Square, is a great way to beat the midday heat. You get to sit in a comfortable seat in an air-conditioned theater while watching a show that is both educational and entertaining.

7. Fantasyland is the most toddler-friendly section of the park, so visitors with older children and teens will probably want to split quickly (although **It's a Small World** has a cult following among some Disney regulars who don't mind that song haunting their brains) and take the **Skyway** to Tomorrowland and back. It's a great ride.

8. If you want to see the **parade,** stake out your spot around now (about an hour before parade time). If you're in doubt about whether the spot is a good one, ask a uniformed cast member. You don't want to be rousted at the last minute from an area that is cleared at parade time. The parade is worth the wait; even jaded teenagers will love it. However, this is also a good chance to try those rides and shows that were too crowded at other times. The parade draws some of the mobs away.

9. If you're really into Mickey and Minnie, check out **Mickey's Toontown Fair,** just east of Fantasyland. Kids of all ages (including grandparents) love it. This is a good place to catch the train that circles the entire Magic Kingdom. It's an entertaining, breezy ride that will give you a breather and good views of the various parts of the park.

10. Get off the train at the Main Street Station and head into Adventureland to ride the **Jungle Cruise** and **Pirates of the Caribbean.** Play in the **Swiss Family Treehouse** and, if you're really into animation, see the **Tropical Serenade with the Enchanted Tiki Birds.** Beware, though; like It's a Small World, this attraction gives some people the screaming meemies. Try your luck at the **Frontierland Shootin' Arcade.**

11. Have dinner and enjoy the evening parade and fireworks. After the rest of the park closes, Main Street stays open for strolling and shopping.

Chapter 13

Epcot

In This Chapter

➤ Logistics and services

➤ Exploring Future World

➤ Enjoying the World Showcase

➤ Suggested itineraries

What's an Epcot?

You may be suffering Disneyitis (see chapter 11) if you know the answer without flipping back. Epcot is half amusement park, half museum with lots of interactive, hands-on experiences. Think of it as a trip around the world without the jet lag (though some would say it's just as draining after you make the World Showcase loop with hyperactive kids). If the Magic Kingdom is every tot's shining dream brought to life, Epcot appeals to the imaginations and fantasies of older children and adults.

Walt Disney originally envisioned the Experimental Prototype Community Of Tomorrow (EPCOT) as a high-tech city with 20,000 residents. But after Walt's death, what was built instead turned out to be more theme park than community, and the name became simply Epcot, because, well, it fits on one line in the snazzy brochures they hand out.

We strongly suggest at least a 2-day visit to the park because it is so large and varied. In the **World Showcase,** you can experience exotic, far-flung lands without a passport. With the luxury of time, you can sit on a park bench in downtown London and watch the world go by (or slip into a pub and wash down some fish-and-chips with a pint of stout). You can sit in a sidewalk cafe, munching some of the best pastries this side of Paris, or climb aboard

Norway's pretty docile boat ride, **Maelstrom,** for a true sense of Viking legend.

In **Future World** you can touch, taste, hear, and ride the new millennium as you learn about the latest cutting-edge technology. Yes, there are thrill rides, but you'll actually learn something, and it'll be pretty painless. When the kids get back to school, they'll have a new mental hook on which to hang lessons about aquaculture, oceanography, nutrition, computers, transportation, and many other studies. Future World gives them the real-world context for all sorts of realities that might translate into better grades in the classroom, or even extra credit.

For some of WDW's best dining, shows, rides, and simple strolling in a pretty setting, Epcot is a standout.

Extra! Extra!

On October 1, 1999, Epcot, like other Disney and non-Disney parks, will kick off a 15-month celebration for the new millennium. The festivities will focus on the triumphs, challenges, and breakthroughs of mankind. Countries and companies from around the world will showcase their new contributions to the millennium. Epcot will also introduce a completely new nighttime spectacular, filled with lasers, fireworks, and special effects. While the fine print wasn't written in time for this edition of *The Complete Idiot's Travel Guide to Walt Disney World & Orlando,* you can bet it's going to be one of the biggest global parties ever held.

What You Need to Know About the Park

➤ **Hours.** Epcot is generally open daily from 9am to 9pm, and as late as midnight on special days in summer and on holidays. As with the Magic Kingdom, you should consider arriving about an hour before the official opening time since the gates sometimes open earlier. You'll also beat the traffic that way, and you should even be able to park closer to the gate so you won't have to hoof it as far at the end of the day, when you're as spent as a marathoner running the last mile.

➤ **ATMs** are located at the front of the park, in the Germany pavilion, and on the bridge between World Showcase and Future World.

➤ **Baby-changing facilities** are located in Future World, near the Odyssey Restaurant, and are furnished with rocking chairs and toddler-size toilets. Disposable diapers, formula, baby food, and pacifiers are for sale. There are changing tables here as well as in all women's rest rooms, and some men's rest rooms. Disposable diapers are also sold at

Guest Services. As we did in chapter 12, we're giving you a gentle reminder to bring baby things, medications, and such, so you don't have to take out a second mortgage for them in the parks.

➤ The **First Aid Center,** staffed by registered nurses, is located in Future World, near the Odyssey Restaurant.

➤ **Lockers** can be found just west of Spaceship Earth, outside the Entrance Plaza, and near the Bus Information Center near the bus parking lot. Cost is $3 plus a refundable $2 deposit.

➤ **Some nonnecessity prices.** Popcorn is $2; bottled water $2.50; chips $1.25; frozen margarita $4.25; apple or orange 85¢; soft pretzel $2; wedge of Italian cheesecake $3.95; funnel cake $3.25; ice-cream sandwich or bar $2.

➤ **Lost children.** If your kids get lost, somebody will most likely take them to Earth Center or the Baby Care Center, where lost children logbooks are kept. Children under age 7 should wear nametags, which will help the cavalry alert you if your kids are too busy crying to divulge their name.

Time-Savers

Even though strollers can be a nuisance and are not allowed on some park transportation, they are lifesavers, even for older children, who will be grateful to be able to collapse into one when their little feet are tired. The stroller deposit at most parks is only $1 or $2, so some people just abandon them rather than stand in line for a refund.

➤ **Package pickup.** If you buy something early in the day and don't want to haul it around with you, have the clerk send it to Guest Relations, which is just inside the Entrance Plaza. There are also package pickup locations at the International Gateway and at the main entrance to Lost and Found. Make sure you specify where you are going to pick up your stuff. The service takes about 3 hours, and you can pick up all of your purchases on the way out.

➤ **Strollers** can be rented at stands on the east side of the Entrance Plaza and at the World Showcase International Gateway. They cost $6 per day, including a $1 refundable deposit.

➤ **Video cameras** can be rented at the Kodak Camera Center at the Entrance Plaza, at the Lagoon's Edge World Traveler between Future World and the World Showcase, or at Cameras and Film in the Journey into Imagination pavilion. The cost is $25 per day plus a $300 deposit. You can buy disposable cameras throughout the park.

First Things First
➤ **Write down your parking space number before you enter the park!** (We lied earlier when we said we wouldn't warn you again.)

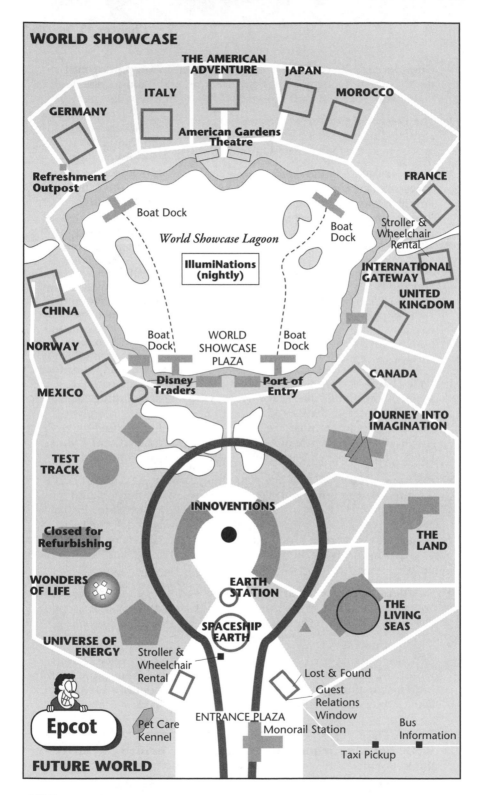

➤ **Make your Priority Seating arrangements for Epcot restaurants pronto!** Remember all the advice from the dining chapter? No? Well, Priority Seating is as close to a reservation as you can get in Walt Disney World. It's especially important at Epcot, since this park has some of Disney's best inside-the-park restaurants. You can book ahead by calling ☎ **407/WDW-DINE** (407/939-3463) up to 60 days in advance. We strongly recommend calling ahead. But if you didn't, make a beeline for the Worldkey Interactive Terminals at Guest Relations in Innoventions East or in World Showcase. You can also do this by stopping in the restaurants themselves. We think the Living Seas is a terrific and relaxing choice for lunch; and for dinner, France, Japan, and Morocco have the best food of all the "countries" in the World Showcase.

➤ **Pick up an Epcot map and entertainment schedule at the Guest Relations Lobby.** Take a minute in the morning to look over the map so you can plan what shows and entertainment you want to schedule throughout your day. That minute will save you some time and mileage later.

Future World

Future World comprises the front, or northern, section of the park (even though it will probably be at the bottom of most maps, including the one in this book). It consists of several theme pavilions surrounding the giant silver golf ball that Disney calls Spaceship Earth. Each area is sponsored by a major corporation and focuses on discoveries and scientific achievement in different fields. Following is an alphabetical list and a brief description of each pavilion; for advice on how to see and do it all (and which pavilions not to miss), check out "The Whole World in Your Hands: Some Suggested Itineraries" section later in this chapter.

Innoventions

Innoventions is located in two half-moon-shaped buildings just beyond Spaceship Earth. Here's where you'll see state-of-the-art electronics long before they arrive in stores. (HDTV and Virtual Reality are already old hat here.) Kids will flock to try out the as-yet-unreleased computer programs and Sega games. Adults looking for a lesson in computers and electronics will find exhibits sponsored by Motorola and GE among others. Generally, the pavilion is for ages 8 and over, but if you're 30, 40, or 50, don't be surprised if you get hooked on the fun, too.

Time-Savers

Agree on an exact meeting spot in case anybody in your family gets lost. (Put name tags on children under 7.) Individual pavilions are so large that you have to specify *where* you'll meet in Germany or The Land. As with any of the mega-theme parks, it's real easy to lose a child or the rest of your party—even if they're only a few feet away. Crowds can make feet seem like miles.

Journey into Imagination

This pyramid-shaped salute to creativity will play well with the kids. A track ride escorts you through the creative processes of your hosts, Dreamfinder, and his pint-sized purple dragon, Figment. Young children will probably be delighted with the fanciful settings, but their parents may be a less captivated audience.

All audiences, except the youngest of children, will want to catch the crowd-pleasing ***Honey I Shrunk the Audience*** 3-D film. Vibrating seats and other visual and tactile stimuli give the audience the feel that they are ant-size creatures being pursued by cats, mice, and even scarier things. The 3-D here isn't quite as active as the one in Animal Kingdom's "It's a Bug's Life" (chapter 15) or DisneyQuest, but the video portion certainly is crisper than the bug production.

 Jake Rating: "Neat."

After getting shrunk, you'll wander into an interactive playground at **Image Works.** Kids and adults can build ugly faces by touching the monitors, step on floor panels to play music, use a wand to color a drawing on the screen, or conduct an orchestra by waving their hands above lighted buttons. This is more like yesterday's Disney.

 Jake Rating: "Nice, I guess." He was being kind, but in fairness, it's tough to be next in line after a fun adventure like *Honey, I Shrunk the Audience.*

Note: **Journey into Imagination** will be closed until October 1999 for refurbishing. Since many things can throw off a reopening, check before you leave that everything is up and operating. ***Honey I Shrunk the Audience*** will continue to play throughout the period the pavilion is closed.

The Land

The Land is the largest Future World pavilion. Its educational rides, displays, films, and shows make agriculture, a seemingly ho-hum subject, come to life. It has something for just about everyone, although children under age 8 might get restless.

Living with the Land is an entertaining and educational boat ride that focuses on agriculture and passes through several natural settings. As part of the ride, the tour moves through greenhouses, which include hydroponic gardens that grow a variety of fruits and vegetables vertically in perlite-filled pools (floating gardens) and in other ways that do not involve soil. You can sample the vegetables grown in the greenhouses when you eat at the Garden Grill Restaurant in The Land pavilion.

The **Food Rocks** attraction does for nutrition what the old *Schoolhouse Rock* animated shorts did for grammar, multiplication, and U.S. history. You won't have to wait more than 15 minutes before the show, featuring songs like Neil

Moussaka's "Don't Take My Squash Away" and the Refrigerator Police's "Every Bite You Take," prods you to watch what you eat.

A great movie for both adults and children is *Circle of Life,* an emotion-tugging epic outlining the effects of development on the planet. Shown in the Harvest Theater on The Land's top level, the video uses real clips that are supplemented by cartoon characters from the Lion King. In the film, Pumbaa and Timon plan to build a resort as a get-rich-quick scheme, and Simba tries to get them to understand how their plans will endanger the forest. Simba shows them clips of bulldozers destroying trees and explains the disastrous effects. In the end, Pumbaa and Timon decide not to build the resort, because in the process they will lose something far more important than money. It's a nice moral played out in an entertaining format.

Tourist Traps

Innoventions is one of the most controversial areas of Future World. Those who love computer games can't be dragged away from it; to others, it's just a loud video arcade where too many kids are clamoring to use too few machines. Unless you have time to kill or are a devout computer junkie, skip it.

The Living Seas

The Living Seas is one of Florida's many aquariums, a 5.7-million-gallon tank filled with more than 4,000 sea creatures including sharks, colorful reef fish, rays, and dolphins. You'll see a brief film and then "descend" to **Seabase Alpha** for the **Caribbean Coral Reef Ride** that showcases many of the life-forms swimming in the glass tanks around you. After the short ride, you are free to explore an ocean research base of the future. Unless children are intensely interested in the sea, those under age 12 will soon lose interest. Other points of interest include two manatees that are in pretty tight quarters.

If you're a certified diver, you can sign up in advance to get into the tank by calling ☎ **407/937-8687.**

D.E.E.P., Disney's Dolphin Exploration and Education Program, is another feature at the Living Seas. In a 3-hour program, offered on weekdays, you'll get a behind-the-scenes lesson in dolphin behavior. Call ☎ **407/WDW-TOUR** for more info. (Speaking of the dolphins, they tend to get a little too playful with some of the other marine critters. They're segregated to keep them from playing sports like the sea-turtle spin and stingray Frisbee.

Spaceship Earth

Spaceship Earth is Epcot's signature attraction, a 180-foot-high geosphere. This is the one everybody calls the giant golf ball. At the park's 9am opening, it's literally packed out and around by folks who gravitate to the first ride in a place. The best time to hit this one is on your way out or not at all. It's another slow-track journey back in time (yawn) focusing on communications (its sponsor is AT&T), the arts, and language as it brings you to the present and beyond. If it's still there, try to ignore the red EXIT light that bleeds

Beating the Lines

If lines are too long at Spaceship Earth, consider taking a break at Global Neighborhood, the electronic playground at the far side, or exit area, of the sphere.

through the "heavens" curtain at the end. Jeremy Irons's narration and a new musical score give the Spaceship trip a bit more pizzazz than it used to have.

Jake Rating: "What's next?"

Test Track

Presented by General Motors and replacing the **World of Motion,** this new guaranteed-to-thrill attraction takes you behind the scenes of automobile testing, putting you through the paces of acceleration, braking, hill climbs, curvy roads, straightaways, rainstorms, and just about anything else that gets in the way of younger drivers' No. 1 craving: speed. This baby originally was scheduled to open in 1997, but glitches pushed things back to 1999. Disney folks say the computer problem wasn't a safety glitch, but one that gave a false safety reading: A computer breakdown said there were problems when there were not. As a new attraction, the wait times will be long, but once you get into the queue area, there is plenty to see before riding.

Universe of Energy

Ellen DeGeneres and Bill Nye the science guy are the video hosts of **Ellen's Energy Adventure,** a dream sequence tour that begins with her getting trashed by a snooty rival (played by Jamie Lee Curtis) on *Jeopardy!* Then Bill takes Ellen on a time travel trip to the age of dinosaurs, with energy as the theme. The ultra-wide screen trip begins with our slow-moving 96-or-so-seat barge going back 220 million years into the land of *brontosauri.* The Animatronic beasts, before we can move, clear their sinuses at us, though unlike at some of the Animal Kingdom and other Epcot attractions (see *Honey I Shrunk the Audience* a little earlier in this chapter), we don't get wet. This ride continues through the jungle and includes radio broadcasts of historical milestones, including Willard Scott's birthday greetings for the cockroach, which on today's date, 55 million B.C., is 220 million years old. The journey continues on to the present and a look at modern energy sources. Ultimately, Ellen gains enough wisdom to turn the tables in the *Jeopardy!* game.

Jake Rating: "That was really neat."

Wonders of Life

Body Wars is a virtual ride through the human body. Rick Moranis ought to be here, shrinking you, your temporary teammates, and your travel pod to the point you can be injected into a human body. But Disney imagineers do the job for him. The turbulence warning before you climb aboard is no joke. The pod jukes and jives, making sharp and sudden turns. If you have the time and budget for the **Backstage Magic Behind-the-Scenes tour** (see chapter 11), you'll get to see what makes it rattle and hum. If you don't (or take it after you test Body Wars), here's an inside tip: Engineers designed this ride from the last row of a pod. That's where to sit if you want the most bang for your buck. Otherwise, try to sit near the front. Also note that the park shaved about 45 seconds off the ride's length. That saved a lot of, uh, postlunch cleanup.

Jake Rating (upon seeing his first white blood cell): "That's disgusting." Then, near the end of the first half, "Mayday, Mayday." Finally, "That was pretty neat." He was luckier than one of our copilots. At the first juke, she giggled. At the first jive, it became a nervous laugh. At the dipsy-do, she started frantically fanning herself. By the time the exit doors opened, she was in serious danger of setting a new world record for projectile vomiting.

Cranium Command is a cute cartoon-and-Animatronic lesson on the brain and mutual cooperation. An aspiring Cranium Commando named Buzzy is assigned to pilot the brain of that most harrowing of creatures— a 12-year-old boy. A gruff-but-goodhearted drill-sergeant 'toon helps whip Buzzy and the rest of his all-star body crew into shape. In the same complex, the excellent film *The Making of Me,* starring Martin Short, gives a tasteful description of conception and birth. Unfortunately, the theater for this film is extremely small and the wait to get in to see it may feel like 9 months.

World Showcase

The pavilions surrounding a sparkling lagoon represent a spectrum of nations. Each has shops, food, and displays or a show, as well as gardens or streetscapes authentic to that country. Adding an extra touch of authenticity to the mix is the fact that most of the staff at the World Showcase are natives of the countries the pavilions represent. One of the most pleasant ways to spend time here is to find a park bench in "England" or grab a croissant in "France," and pretend you're overseas. Of course, if you're trying to do this with two or more excited kids, good luck. Those under 8 tire quickly of this part of the park; ditto for a lot of older ones unless they have a yearning for learning.

The pavilions are listed alphabetically here, but you'll probably just go clockwise or counterclockwise around the lagoon. See the suggested itinerary later in this chapter for advice on what to see and do in each "country." Keep in mind that the World Showcase usually opens later than the rest of Epcot, so plan accordingly when mapping out your schedule.

Don't forget to return here for the **IllumiNations** presentation after dark. This fireworks, light, and laser show is synchronized to the fountains in the World Showcase Lagoon. It's a must-see for everyone in the family, even jaded teenagers and tired 6-year-olds. Check your show schedule when you enter the World Showcase, and then find a seat anywhere around the lagoon about a half hour before show time.

American Adventure

Housed in a colonial-era building, the **American Adventure** is a patriotic half-hour show that speeds through a "Cliff Notes" version of U.S. history. The presentation mixes a stirring film with Animatronics (some of Disney's best) as Ben Franklin and Mark Twain recall some of America's principal historical figures and events. It's filled with joy, pride, and poignancy. The **Voices of Liberty** vocal group often performs in the pavilion's foyer, a perk that will ease you through the waiting time to get into the show. As you enter the park, check the Entertainment Schedule to see if anything is playing in the **America Gardens Theater.**

Tourist Traps

Disney hotel guests are allowed early entry to Epcot on some days. Avoid those mornings if you're staying at any other lodgings or everything will be packed by the time you get into the park. And yes, they check to make sure you're a Disney hotel guest. If you're not, just wave the white flag; there's no use trying to sneak in.

Canada

Disney's Canadian Rocky Mountains may be made of cement and chicken wire, but that gives them no less a majestic appearance. Pass by a totem pole before entering a replica of Victoria's Butchart Gardens and the Hôtel du Canada. *O Canada!* is an awesome CircleVision 360° movie that surrounds you with Royal Canadian Mounties, plunges you into Niagara Falls, takes you into the Canadian Rockies, and shows you an ocean of northern wildflowers. You also have to rough it in this wilderness and stand for the whole movie—there's no seating in the theater.

China

A divine replica of Beijing's Temple of Heaven dominates the landscape in China. Pass through the temple's Hall of Prayer for Good Harvests before entering the theater that shows the CircleVision 360° film, the **Wonders of China.** You'll climb the Great Wall, sail the Yangtze, and travel inside the Forbidden City, all without leaving the theater. Guests stand throughout the 19-minute film, which is tiring, but you'll want to keep turning around to see the entire screen. The **House of the Whispering Willows** exhibits some ancient dragon-embellished artifacts including a hand-carved lacquer throne from the Qing Dynasty, which is on loan from the Palace Museum in Beijing. You can also try your luck at finding some reasonably priced Chinese crafts along **Young Feng Shangdian,** a small shopping arcade whose name translates as the Street of Good Fortune.

France

Stroll the streets of Paris as it was during the 19th century's belle epoque (Beautiful Age) to the tune of a piped-in accordion. Only in Disney World can you shop in the Galleries des Halles market that no longer exists in the actual City of Lights. View the elegant, wide-angle film, ***Impressions de France,*** which is shown in the plush sit-down theater, the Palais du Cinema. Linger on the grounds to see the replica Eiffel Tower, flowering trees, and formal Parisian gardens. Then dine in one of the pavilion's restaurants, which are among the best in the World, if not the world. Bon Appétit!

Beating the Lines

Line up for continuous presentations (like the France movie) just after one show begins. You'll have to wait 20 minutes for the next show, but you'll be one of the first in line and you'll get the best seats. Some rides, such as the Maelstrom in Norway, can add additional seating as crowds grow, so the wait won't be as long as you think.

Germany

Germany offers a change of pace, with a rollicking beer garden, oompah bands, a cobblestone courtyard, and a Hummel store where you'll probably see an artist at work creating actual Hummel figures. In the center of the Bavarian village setup is a statue of St. George, the patron saint of soldiers, who, according to legend, slew a dragon while on crusades. If you arrive here on the hour, a glockenspiel will entertain you. There are no rides; the real show is the year-round Oktoberfest that plays in the *bierstube.*

Children and model train enthusiasts will enjoy the detailed miniature village and model train set located along the path between Germany and Italy.

Italy

Perhaps the most successful pavilion at generating a feeling of architectural authenticity, Italy is a favorite for its warm scenes straight from the old country: gondolas floating in the lagoon, a bell tower, a piazza with pretty fountain, olive trees, and street performers presenting *commedia dell'arte*. Venice's Doge's Palace and St. Mark's Square are faithfully reproduced here, and you'll find shops selling Italian crystal, leather, and, more importantly, Italian cuisine.

Japan

Japan presents traditional music, dance, magic, and other arts. Check your show schedule as you enter the park. The central pagoda was modeled on Nara's Horyuji Temple. The building to its right was modeled on Kyoto's Imperial Palace and houses several restaurants and a branch of Mitsukoshi's Department Store. The food here is tasty, and the gardens are some of the most restful respites in the Showcase. Take time to study the red Gate of

Honor *(Torii)* on the lagoon, the pebbled footpaths, and other traditional touches, all masterfully done. Gardeners especially will find a good deal to study and enjoy. The Story of Carvings of Old Japan showcases a wonderful miniature art form and is housed in the **Bijutsu-Kan Gallery.**

Mexico

Mexico does a fine job of presenting snippets of its varied cultures. The pavilion's attractions are based inside a Mayan pyramid that is draped in lush vegetation. Once inside, you can take a boat ride, *El Rio de Tiempo: The River of Time,* and get a glimpse of the volcano Popocatapetl, see traditional dances, and end your voyage on the River of Time at a fiesta. You can also visit **Plaza de Los Amigos,** the re-creation of a small-town market that sells local crafts and jewelry. **Reign of Glory** is an exhibit of some 70 pre-Colombian pieces including artifacts from the National Museum of Natural History, Smithsonian Institution.

Morocco

Morocco is one of the most beautiful and exotic "countries" in the World Showcase. A replica of the Koutoubia Minaret, a famous prayer tower in Marrakesh, overlooks the old city, which you enter through the pointed arches of the Bab Boujouloud gate. The gate is a mosaic tile masterpiece, but not a perfect one—Muslims believe that only Allah is perfect, so you'll find an imperfection in every tile. Diners at **Restaurant Marrakesh** are entertained by a belly dancer. Don't miss the garden, with its olive trees and date palms. The **Gallery of Arts and History** showcases jewels, household objects, and musical instruments of yesterday.

Time-Savers

Because much of the IllumiNations show takes place in the air, you won't miss much by failing to stake out a prime spot long before the show. Spend your time seeing and doing things right up until show time, then, within a reasonable proximity of ground zero, just look up.

Norway

You can stroll down the cobblestone streets of Scandinavia here. A 13th-century church sits beside the village square, and a small replica of Castle Akershus is also present. Norway offers a voyage with the Vikings, called the **Maelstrom,** a very tame flume ride through the country's history. You'll sail in Viking longships through troll-populated forests before conquering the North Sea and arriving in a small coastal village. There's a charming 70mm film on the history of Norway. It's a neat historical and cultural lesson. There's also an exhibit of one of the few remaining stave churches in the world.

United Kingdom

The U.K. pavilion is authentic right down to the pub, thatched cottage, flagstone pathways, and blooming rosebushes galore. You'll even find a pair of

206

those once ubiquitous English red phone booths. Check your show schedule so that you don't miss a performance of the street players; they're a hoot, and if you're lucky, you may be recruited to join in the fun. Shops take up most of the room at the United Kingdom, and there are no rides here; soak up the atmosphere at the Rose and Crown Pub, where you can down a pint with a Merry Band of Englishmen.

The Whole World in Your Hands: Some Suggested Itineraries

To see Epcot really requires 2 or more days. Lots of people try to do it in a single day, giving rise to the joke that EPCOT really stands for "Every Person Comes Out Tired." Do yourself a favor and budget 2 days for this park, and don't go crazy trying to do everything. You'll be happier spending parts of each day here and saving some energy for swimming, sleeping late, or just hanging out by your hotel pool.

We've written both a 2-day itinerary and a 1-day schedule for people whose time is extremely limited. Be forewarned, though, that the 1-day itinerary may feel rushed and exhausting. You'll see as much of the park as is physically possible in 1 day, but you're going to miss some things and you might derive more pleasure out of a more leisurely pace.

It's a Small World After All: Epcot in 2 Days

It's tempting to skip around the park for variety's sake, and sometimes it's essential to leapfrog pavilions and then backtrack to avoid long lines. Still, we prefer taking Future World in a clockwise or counterclockwise direction on the first day, and then looping the World Showcases on the other day. Epcot is a very large park compared to the other Disney parks. Long distances between pavilions must be considered if your budget for time or energy is limited.

On Day 1

1. At the base of the big sphere in **Earth Station,** go to Guest Relations to get a park map and show schedule, and to book Priority Seating for lunch and dinner if you haven't already. Ask if any rides or attractions are closed, and find out the park's official opening time for tomorrow.

2. Remember how Disney knows most people go right, 'cause their right-handed? Well, break left once inside the park, head to *Honey I Shrunk the Audience* at **Journey into Imagination.** There's a short movie before the 3-D viewing and it's in a word—*inspiring*. The colorful slide show really makes you think about using your imagination.

3. From Journey into Imagination, head over to **The Land** and board the **Living with the Land.** Afterward, see the *Circle of Life* movie and take in **Food Rocks.**

4. If you like watching marine animals including cuddly manatees, **The Living Seas** is a must do. If you're hungry, you can grab a bite to eat while you watch fish swim by at the **Coral Reef Restaurant.**

5. After the Living Seas, check the lines at **Spaceship Earth.** If the line is too long proceed to **Innoventions Plaza** where you can turn the kids lose on the Sega Machines at Global Neighborhood.

6. Cross over to the **Universe of Energy** and ride along with Bill Nye and Ellen as they go back to the age of dinosaurs.

7. Exit the dino ride and head over to **Wonders Of Life.** There's lots of hands-on things here for children, and touch is encouraged. The whole family will love **Cranium Command,** an adorable show that stars an Animatronics puppet. Inside the pavilion, you'll also find the **Making of Me** movie, plus the fast and furious **Body Wars.**

8. After being piloted around inside the human body, check out the lines at **Test Track;** if they're not too long, get in line and wait it out. Since it's Epcot's newest state-of-the-art $60 million lollapalooza, you have to expect you'll be standing around a bit.

9. If you haven't waited in line for it yet, now is the time to head for the 16-minute **Spaceship Earth,** one of Epcot's signature rides for all ages, from preschoolers to grandparents.

10. After Spaceship Earth, head over to the World Showcase Lagoon and watch **IllumiNations** before leaving Epcot.

On Day 2

1. If you arrive when the park opens, go to any **Future World** rides or shows that you missed or want to repeat. Or sleep a little later and arrive in time to take up your position at the Port of Entry to the **World Showcase.**

2. Start in **Canada.** The movie is uplifting and entertaining. Don't miss it before moving on to the **United Kingdom** for shopping, street shows, people-watching, and a stop at the very authentic pub.

3. Proceed to **France** and see a lovely lyrical movie that will captivate all but the very young. Check out the restaurants here if you'll be returning for lunch or dinner, and then proceed to **Morocco** to find a colorful casbah with merchants, fabulous Moorish tile and arts, and little passageways that put you in Bogartville. (For some, this is better than the real Casablanca, which tends to be dirty and littered with beggars.) There's no show here, but **Restaurant Marrakesh** with its belly dancers is one of Epcot's best-kept secrets.

4. Check the schedule for programs at the **American Gardens Theater,** and then stop at **Japan** if you have time. Its store is packed with enticements, but don't miss the overall grandeur of the architecture and grounds.

5. The **American Adventure,** which anchors this section of Epcot, is a stately, patriotic triumph of audio-animated characters. The theater is huge, so waits are rarely long. Proceed to **Italy** for shopping and a snack. You'll find yourself in St. Mark's Square in **Venice,** complete

with a 105-foot bell tower. Photo opportunities are superb, but there's no show except for singing servers in the restaurant and the occasional street performer.

6. **Germany** is a good place for lunch or supper because it's a nonstop Oktoberfest with oompah band, yodelers, beer, and wursts. Don't miss the model railway and the Bavarian-looking shops.

7. Next you'll come to **China,** with its good food, bargain buys, gardens and ponds, and a CircleVision 360° movie. Position yourself to be one of the first to exit, and then rush to the **Norway** pavilion and get in line for the *Maelstrom* ahead of the throngs who will have the same idea. This much-too-short boat ride is one of Epcot's few rides.

8. At **Mexico,** you'll have completed the circle. Take time to look at the ancient artifacts around the pavilion, and then take the easygoing boat ride through a clichéd version of Mexico's history.

9. Have dinner, and then, if you missed it on day 1, grab a spot for **IllumiNations,** which will take place not long after dark.

It's a Mad, Mad, Mad, Mad World: Epcot in (Shudder) 1 Day

Put your jogging shoes on and pack your Filofax, because to do Epcot in 1 day, you'll have to be organized and move quickly.

1. Book a Priority Seating lunch at **Living Seas,** and dinner at one of the ethnic restaurants in the World Showcase, in advance. Make sure you arrive 1 hour before the "official" opening time. Grab a park map and show schedule at **Guest Relations,** just left of the big sphere. Ask a cast member if anything is closed so you don't waste any time.

2. World Showcase opens 2 hours later than the front of the park, so spend your early morning in **Future World.** Skip **Spaceship Earth** for now. It will be much too crowded and time-consuming; come back later in the day, preferably when most people are eating lunch or after 5pm. Go straight to **Test Track,** the newest thrill ride.

3. Proceed to **Journey into Imagination,** where adults and kids of all ages will delight in the *Honey, I Shrunk the Audience* movie.

4. **The Land** is located next to Journey into Imagination. Take the *Living with the Land* boat tour. It's educational and a respite from the noise and crowds outside.

> **Time-Savers**
>
> Buy park admission tickets and make Priority Seating arrangements ahead of time so you don't waste precious time and energy standing in two additional lines.

5. If you like thrill rides, cross through the center of Future World to the **Wonders of Life Pavilion** and get in line for **Body Wars,** the journey through the human bloodstream. The ride is jerky and loud, so it might not be everyone's cup of tea.

6. Cross back to **Living Seas,** where you can watch the huge aquarium forever. But don't. You picked the 1-day option and don't have time. Relax (but not for long) at **lunch.** The food is excellent and the mood mellow—the perfect retreat after the heat and bright sun. Now is also a good time to backtrack to **Spaceship Earth.**

7. Unless you're eager to see (or repeat) something else in Future World, proceed to the **World Showcase,** which is, in our view, the best part of Epcot. Pavilions surround a big lagoon, which you can cross by boat (if you are in a hurry), or walk around the lagoon.

8. Start at the **Norway Pavilion** and ride the *Maelstrom.* It's charming and only a little scary. **China** has a fabulous 360° movie. In **Germany** or **Italy,** enjoy the architecture and shops. If you're thirsty, the **Biergarten** in Germany, with its oompah music, is a good place to take a break. **But, be ready** for the WDW dinner prices in any restaurant. A 16-oz. Beck's will set you back $4.75.

9. Something is always going on at the **American Adventure.** See the 30-minute show or catch the outdoor concert at the America Gardens Theater. The **Japan** and **Morocco** pavilions are both notable for their design and architecture; Japan also boasts a **show of traditional music and dance** that is one of Epcot's best. Check your show schedule regularly so you don't miss it.

10. In the **France** pavilion, be sure to see the movie *Impressions de France.* This is a good place for dinner or a snack at the *boulangerie* (bakery). If you haven't yet made dinner reservations, make them now.

11. Proceed to the **United Kingdom** and try to catch a performance of the street theater. The shopping is good for Scottish, English, Welsh, and Irish goods, and the pub pulls an authentic, but overpriced, pint. The London-like park in the back of the pavilion is a quiet place to rest, except during **IllumiNations,** when it fills up quickly with waiting spectators. The film at the **Canada** pavilion is a beaut. If you've got any energy left, make sure to catch it.

12. Head back to Future World to fill in any time that remains between now and your dinner seating. With luck, you'll have a lagoon-front table where you can also watch **IllumiNations,** but the jockeying for views can get vicious no matter where you are. People start settling in as much as 2 hours before.

13. After the show, your choice is either to join the suffocating press of people trying to get to the parking lot or shuttles, or join the suffocating press of people who are staying in the shops until they close. Everyone is pretty good-natured, so be prepared for long waits and keep your sense of humor.

14. Whew! You did it. Epcot in 1 day! But now you need to spend tomorrow recovering. Maybe you should've planned a 2-day visit after all.

Disney–MGM Studios

Anyone who loves movies or the golden age of Hollywood will enjoy wandering the realistic streets, shops, sets, and backlots of this combination theme park and working studio. A lot of films are shot here throughout the year, so you never know whether you're seeing shtick or an actual taping. That's part of the fun of exploring this 110-acre attraction.

On any given day, Louella Parsons might beg for an interview as you enter the grounds and stroll down Hollywood Boulevard. On another day, a script girl may give you a good scolding for showing up late for your cameo appearance, or you may find yourself in the middle of a "fight" between a Checker cabbie and a Keystone cop.

If nothing else, they keep you entertained.

But is this town big enough for two studios?

Movie Wars: Disney–MGM vs. Universal

Pity the visitor who has to choose between these two stellar theme parks. Both are absolute "musts" for movie buffs. For older adults who remember

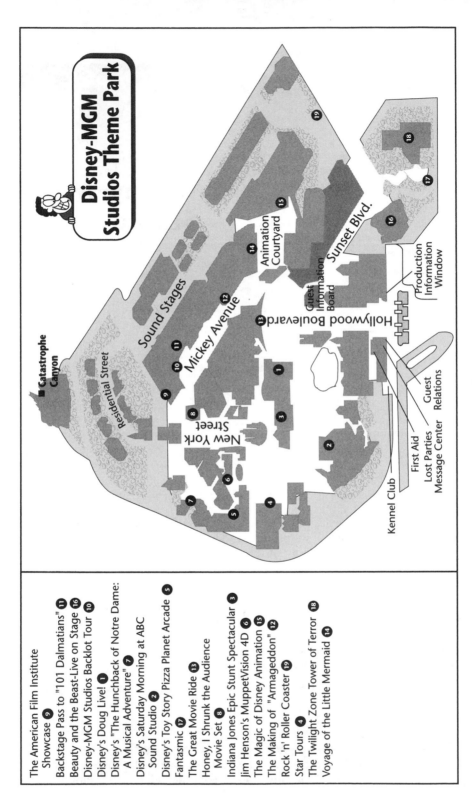

Disney-MGM Studios Theme Park

Catastrophe Canyon

Residential Street

Sound Stages

Animation Courtyard

Mickey Avenue

New York Street

Guest Information Board

Sunset Blvd.

Hollywood Boulevard

Production Information Window

Kennel Club

First Aid
Lost Parties
Message Center

Guest Relations

The American Film Institute Showcase ❾

Backstage Pass to "101 Dalmatians" ⓫

Beauty and the Beast-Live on Stage ⓰

Disney-MGM Studios Backlot Tour ❿

Disney's Doug Live! ❶

Disney's "The Hunchback of Notre Dame: A Musical Adventure" ❼

Disney's Saturday Morning at ABC Sound Studio ❷

Disney's Toy Story Pizza Planet Arcade ❺

Fantasmic ⓱

The Great Movie Ride ⓭

Honey, I Shrunk the Audience Movie Set ❽

Indiana Jones Epic Stunt Spectacular ❸

Jim Henson's MuppetVision 4D ❻

The Magic of Disney Animation ⓯

The Making of "Armageddon" ⓲

Rock 'n' Roller Coaster ⓳

Star Tours ❹

The Twilight Zone Tower of Terror ⓲

Voyage of the Little Mermaid ⓮

212

the golden age of Hollywood, Disney–MGM Studios gets the nod for nostalgia appeal. For visitors with little children, we'd give an edge to Universal Studios (see chapter 17) for its Nickelodeon, Terminator, Earthquake, Back to the Future, Fievel, and Hanna–Barbera attractions. Both parks have unavoidably long lines at the most spine-jarring thrill rides. Universal has the most exciting ones, though, including Kongfrontation, Jaws, and Twister. Universal is physically larger, which means you'll wear out more shoe leather, but it's not as congested. It's also a solid 2- or even 3-day park, whereas Disney–MGM can be done in a day, although a second day provides a nice comfort zone.

Collectors will find mountains of merchandise at both parks. MGM has the best selection of pricey movie memorabilia, including items actually owned or autographed by stars. Universal's shops will appeal to collectors of souvenirs themed to today's hits. As for dining, Universal has today's Hard Rock Café, while Disney–MGM counters with yesterday's Brown Derby. Admission is the same, but one park could have an advantage over the other depending on what multiday passes you buy.

Our overall evaluation is that MGM Studios has some neat areas, mainly Indiana Jones, Star Tours, the Muppet 3-D Adventure, and the backlot tour, but it's really not on par with Disney's other theme parks. It's also second on the movie-park circuit behind Universal, which opened its second theme park—Islands of Adventure—in 1999. Is Disney–MGM worth the sticker price ($42 not including 6% tax for adults, $34 for kids 3 to 9) that the other big dogs get? Each of you will come away with an opinion. Ours is that it belongs on a different, lower-priced tier.

What You Need to Know About the Park

➤ **Hours.** Disney–MGM is generally open daily from 9am to 7pm, and as late as midnight on special days in summer and on holidays. Get there about an hour beforehand if you can, because as with the other Disney parks, the gates sometimes open earlier than the "official" opening time. You'll also beat the traffic, and you may even be able to park closer to the gate.

➤ **ATMs** are located at the park's main entrance.

➤ **Baby-changing facilities** are located at the Baby Care Center, which also sells diapers, formula, baby food, and pacifiers for more than market price because—well, where's the competition? There are changing tables here as well as in all women's rest rooms and some men's rest rooms. Disposable diapers are also sold at Guest Services.

➤ The **First Aid Center,** staffed by registered nurses, is located in the Entrance Plaza next to Guest Services.

➤ **Lockers** can be found to the right of the Entrance Plaza, next to Oscar's Classic Car Souvenirs. The cost is $3 to $5, depending on the size.

➤ **Lost children.** If your kids get lost, somebody will most likely take them to Guest Services, where lost children logbooks are kept. If you don't believe in Velcro for children under 7, at least make them wear nametags.

Time-Savers

Make a note of where you park at Disney–MGM Studios. The parking here is more convenient to the entry than at the other parks, but the lot isn't as well marked and it's every bit as easy to forget where you left your wheels. Trams are available, but unless you are carrying two handfuls of kids, walking is a faster option. As soon as you enter, get a show schedule and work out a plan of action.

➤ **Package pickup.** If you buy something early in the day and don't want to carry it around with you all day, have the clerk send it to Guest Services, which is just inside the Entrance Plaza. The service takes about 3 hours. Don't forget to pick up your package on the way out.

➤ **Strollers** can be rented at Oscar's Super Service, just inside the main entrance. The cost is $6 per day.

➤ **Video cameras** can be rented at Hollywood Boulevard for $30 per day plus a $450 deposit. You can buy disposable cameras throughout the park.

G-Rated Attractions & Rides

Children under 10 will be frightened by some of the attractions at this park and bored by others, but they will be thrilled by the movies and productions geared specifically for them. Children over 10 will think the kiddy rides are too babyish for them, but will marvel at the more adult attractions. Divvy up your day here with a keen eye on what's appropriate for your kids.

Backstage Pass to *101 Dalmatians* shows some of the secrets behind the making of the live-action version of this movie. A furry flurry of real Dalmatians is part of the show. You'll walk through various soundstages and sets from the movie as you learn how some of the special effects were generated. Kids and adults of all ages will love it.

Located at Muppet World Headquarters, **Jim Henson's *Muppet Vision 4D*** is a delight for all ages. It's an in-your-face, 25-minute spectacle that allows the humor of the late Henson to live on through Miss Piggy, Kermit, and the gang. This production is a chuckler that mixes some pretty good 3-D effects and sensory gags with familiar puppets and a live-action character or two.

214

Disney's Saturday Morning at ABC Sound Studio is an inside look at how those loud and weird sound effects make it into your TV set. You or your kids may be chosen to try to replicate some sound effects for use in a real cartoon. Then, you get to compare your version to the way it would sound when done by a professional. Yes, a *professional*. Some folks make a living as noisemakers. Remarkable, isn't it?

Don't miss out on the interactive **Soundworks** exhibit area that you will exit into after leaving the show. This gem is often overlooked, but your kids will love the opportunity to produce special sound effects or dub their voices over Mickey Mouse's and Roger Rabbit's. Adults and kids alike will love the 3-D **Soundstations** where an audio meeting with The Mouse turns into a hair-raising experience.

Disney's Doug Live replaced **Superstar Television** in the spring of 1999. The Nickelodeon cartoon star, Doug, comes to life on stage and explains how "It's tough to be 12." If you're very lucky, you may be picked to play a small part during the performance.

Time-Savers

Before you go, buy tickets to minimize standing in line. Check on the shuttle schedule from your hotel, and call Disney at ☎ **407/ 824-4321** or check with Guest Services at your WDW hotel to see what time you can enter the park. Remember: Hotel guests get early admission to a rotating schedule of parks. Also, before you arrive in the park, call ☎ **407/ WDW-DINE** to book Priority Seating for lunch (and dinner if the park will be open late).

PG-Rated Attractions & Rides

These productions aren't designed to appeal to the littlest tots, but will have an interest range of mild to intense for kids ages 7 to 8 and older.

American Film Institute Showcase offers a walk through Hollywood history and memorabilia. It gives visitors an appreciation of all the people who pitch in to turn an idea into a feature-length motion picture.

MGM Studios Backlot Tour is a very cool special-effects tour that starts on foot. Two folks out of the audience are outfitted in two-piece rain gear with hoods. Why? Well, the suspense doesn't last long. They're quickly sent to the lagoon, where one climbs aboard a tugboat suitably named Miss Fortune to endure a rainy, rocky, windy ride, capped by a huge wave that rolls over the pilot house. Then, all that footage is blended with remote effects on screen to make it look just like the movies. In real life, the studio audience member gets wet but is saved from drowning by the rain gear. The second victim, uh, volunteer gets into a fake submarine where underwater air cannons make it look like depth charges are blowing and machine gun bullets are riddling across the surface. After that demonstration, you board a tram for a 25-minute ride through Disney's costume department (the world's

215

largest), sets from popular (and not-so-popular) TV shows and movies, the real L-1011 that was used to film *Passenger 57,* and the domain of the special-effects wizards. The highlight is **Catastrophe Canyon,** where an "earthquake" causes a tanker truck to explode, rocking the tram, and then a very large, *very wet* wave throws 70,000 gallons of water your way. The rides run every $3^{1}/2$ minutes, which is how long it takes the wave to recycle.

Beating the Lines

The best time to find shorter lines at the most popular rides, such as Star Tours and the Twilight Zone Tower of Terror, is during the Indiana Jones Stunt Spectacular or the parade.

Jake Rating: *"Wow!"*

Go behind the scenes at the **Magic of Disney Animation,** but keep in mind that most of the new animation studio is restricted. You'll meet animation artists and view some classic Disney animated films such as *Snow White and the Seven Dwarfs.* A short preshow film, *Back to Neverland,* starring the famous comedy team of Robin Williams and Walter Cronkite (yes, you read that correctly), explains how an animated film is produced. Animation buffs willing to shell out an extra $49 can take a special tour and witness firsthand the creations of resident artists by looking through the glass walls that surround the animation studio. After walking through the studios, a Disney artist puts on a live presentation featuring clips from Disney classic films. The tour is for ages 16 and older only.

The **Great Movie Ride** is a slow journey down MGM's memory lane. It starts in the 1930s using robotics of Cagney, Wayne, and Eastwood to re-create some of their most memorable scenes. Then, some live bandits show up and blow up the bank. One of the bad guys will kidnap you and your mates, but—revenge is so sweet, isn't it?—he goes the wrong way, into Alienville, which has an uncanny resemblance to one of the *Raiders of the Lost Ark* sets. The alien from *Alien* is waiting in the ceiling, then the right wall, and pretty soon your bank-robbing buddy gets incinerated when he tries to steal the sphinx's jewel. Then you're off to Bogie's Casablanca, and Oz, where a remarkable robotic likeness of the witch warns, "I'll get you my pretty, ahahahaha!"

Jake Rating: Sorry folks—his eyes glazed early and he napped through the ride, but we loved it.

The **Indiana Jones Stunt Spectacular** is a 30-minute rock'em-sock'em extravaganza guaran-double-teed to keep you entertained and on the edge of your seat. It's held in a big open-air pavilion with lots of audience (all adult) volunteers. "Indy" begins by rappelling down from the rafters and the nifty special effects soon have him dodging spikes, falling into a pit of molten something-or-other, surviving two ax-swinging gargoyles, grabbing a priceless amulet, then outrunning fire, steam, and a large, round boulder that nearly flattens him—all before the first commercial break. The actors, special-effects folks, and director use the breaks to explain what you just saw or are about to see—including stunt secrets. Later setups have Indy battling the evil Nazis in a Cairo marketplace and at an airport-munitions dump. True to the film, good triumphs over evil, a big Nazi gets chopped up by an airplane propeller, and the ammunition dump does its Fourth of July number, all to the delight of a cheering audience.

 Jake Rating (pumping his fist): "Yeah!"

Star Tours. This Star Wars thrill ride begins with a winding walk (read—a line) through a bunch of 'droids. There's also a preride warning about high turbulence, sharp drops, and sudden turns. By now,

Time-Savers

Blocks of shops in the theme parks are connected even though they look like separate shops from the outside. When streets are crowded, you can often make better time getting from Point A to Point B inside the shops.

though, you're going to be a seasoned warrior of such things and laugh mockingly for the benefit of theme-park newbies. If you're not 40 inches tall, you can't ride. Once you get through the waiting zone, there's roughly a 4-minute final wait at the loading dock while the group in front of you finishes the ride. This is another one of those virtual rides where you go nowhere, but it feels like you do. It starts kind of slow, but it finishes fast in a good-guy fighter with R2-D2 and C3PO helping you make passes through the canals of Lord Vaders's mother ship. The special effects include hitting warp speed (you feel like you're going up with a very small G-force) and falling. This could have had more animation. It was certainly more sensory than visual. Still,

 Jake Rating: "I love that!"

Time-Savers

When entering the theme parks you'll be dazzled, but don't rush to the first thing you see. By studying the map, making a plan, and noting which attractions are closed, you'll save time and shoe leather.

Rock 'n' Roller Coaster. Get ready to *rock!* This new state-of-the-art scream-and-thrill machine is sandwiched between Indiana Jones and the Twilight Zone Tower of Terror. Its multiple high-speed inversions, twists, and turns make this a no-go for the faint of heart. The attraction's twists and turns are bad enough without sound effects, but just in case you think motion alone is for sissies, an amplified, synchronized rock soundtrack resonates from speakers mounted about 3 inches from your ears.

The **Twilight Zone Tower of Terror** has been torqued to new thrills since its introduction in 1994, and Rod Serling would be proud. It's scarier than ever. You enter the abandoned Hollywood Tower Hotel during a thunderstorm and ride through a lot of spooky stuff and nonsense before your elevator plunges 13 stories. This may be the best thrill ride in the whole park. You must be 44 inches tall to ride. Some folks swear you must be a few other things too—like nuts.

Extra! Extra!

It may not be a twisting roller coaster, but the drop at the Twilight Zone of Terror is extreme enough to cause lightweight objects, such as camera bags and purses, to float if you aren't hanging onto them.

Oohs & Aahs: Parades, Shows & Fireworks

A giant **Mulan** towers above mere mortals during a 3pm parade. This draws about 70% of the park's guests, so if you're planning to watch, get a good spot on the parade route early. If you're not going, it's a good time to try those rides and shows that get the biggest crowds.

The Hunchback of Notre Dame: A Musical Adventure is a 32-minute live musical performance designed for all ages. Dozens of singers and dancers help tell the story of Quasimodo, who was orphaned and given to a church where, because of his looks, he was sent to live in the bell tower. The human cast, aided by puppets, follows the Disney animated score and story line that has Quasi ultimately losing more than his beloved Esmerelda. The production is held at the **Theater of the Stars,** an open-air arena. There are only three performances a day, so if you want to attend, pay attention to the schedule (it's on the park's map) and arrive early for a good seat.

Jake Rating: "I liked that."

Honey, I Shrunk the Kids **Movie Set Adventure** is an enormous playground with something for toddlers to 10-year-olds. More than a playground, it's entertainment where inanimate objects seemingly come to life, complete with sound effects, and filled with Disney's magic touches.

Voyage of the Little Mermaid re-creates the underwater world of the movie, with live performances, movie clips, puppetry, and special effects. You'll get to hear Sebastian sing "Under the Sea," and see Ariel's live performance of "Part of Your World." The Voyage has some scary scenes, but just like the movie (which every kid has most likely seen) it has a happy ending.

The audience actually gets misted during the performance, making this an especially good experience during hot days.

Fantasmic! is a visual feast and a nighttime spectacular where the Magic Mickey comes to life (without any help from Godzilla's creators) at the Hollywood Amphitheater. Laser light shows, shooting comets, balls of fire, and animated fountains are among the special effects that really charge up the audience during this 25-minute dream sequence. The cast includes 50 performers, a giant dragon, a king cobra, and 1 million gallons of water—most of it orchestrated by a sorcerer mouse that looks more than remotely familiar. You'll probably recognize other characters as well as scenes and musical scores from Disney movie classics like *Fantasia, Pinocchio, Snow White and the Seven Dwarfs, The Little Mermaid,* and *The Lion King.* You'll also shudder at the villainy of Jafar, Cruella de Vil, and Maleficent, in the battle of good vs. evil that replaces the park's stale fireworks show, Sorcerer in the Sky. Fantasmic! duplicates its enormously successful sister show, which made its debut at California's Disneyland in 1992. The Florida version is a once-a-night show (at 7:30pm), but it's planned for three times a night during summer. The amphitheater accommodates just short of 10,000 souls (only 6,500 of them get to sit), so be prepared to wait in line a while, or come late and try your luck at a last-minute entry.

So Many Rides, So Little Time: A Suggested Itinerary

Unlike Epcot and the Magic Kingdom, Disney–MGM is a park you can manage in a single day. If you're a real movie buff, spend 1 day here and 1 day at Universal Studios Florida, and then return to the park you liked best if you have a third day.

1. If you're an early bird, arrive an hour before the posted opening. Make a note of where you parked and walk to the entrance. Trams are available, but the walk is short compared to other parks. Put a nametag on all children age 7 and under. Agree on a meeting spot in case you're separated, and write it down. If you haven't made Priority Seating arrangements for sit-down dining, do so at the kiosk at Hollywood and Vine.

2. Rush directly to the **Twilight Zone Tower of Terror** or the **Rock 'n' Roller Coaster.** Both are high-voltage rides that are fun for everyone except young children and big folks who are claustrophobic, have a fear of falling, or have one of those standard don't-get-on-it medical conditions (such as a heart condition, pregnancy, or a tendency to get motion sickness). If you get there early, you might avoid the long lines that form fast. After riding it, go back toward the entrance and Guest Relations for a map of the park and show schedule. Ask a cast member if any rides or shows are closed.

3. The park is small, so backtracking isn't the concern here that it is at other parks. Consider passing up attractions that have long lines and

coming back at a better time. After the Tower of Terror, head over and unwind a bit at ***Doug Live,*** a new stage show at ABC Studios. The new stage adventure follows 12-year-old Doug Funnie and his adventures with his friends and dog, Porkchop.

4. Waits can be long at the **Great Movie Ride,** which lasts a half hour, and **Star Tours,** which takes about 15 to 20 minutes after you board. Both are absolute musts. So is the **Indiana Jones Stunt Spectacular,** which allows people to enter up to 5 minutes after the show begins. Unless the theater is filled to capacity, you can dash in after everyone else is inside and avoid a long wait in line. If you have a choice, sit at the far right of the stage and you'll exit sooner. Almost every seat has a good view.

Time-Savers

If you're not a guest at a WDW hotel, avoid going to theme parks on days when WDW guests are allowed early entry. By the time you get in, long lines will have already formed at every ride. Don't try to fake it. They check for proof that you're a WDW guest.

5. **Voyage of the Little Mermaid** is a must for little ones. After the first show, it plays continuously. Ask a cast member or note the sign indicating the waiting time. If it's a half hour or less, that's probably the best you're going to do all day. See **Jim Henson's *Muppet Vision 4D*** or, if you're not a Muppets fan, spend time in the shops or pick a park bench on one of the street sets and enjoy the scenery. It's deliciously realistic.

6. With luck, you've made it through all of the above before lunch at the **Prime Time Café,** which we recommend for a noisy, good-times atmosphere with comfort foods, or the **Brown Derby** for a quieter setting and California cuisine.

7. Enjoy **The Magic of Disney Animation,** and then take the **Backlot Tour.** These attractions take about an hour and have appeal for the whole family.

8. Check the schedule for afternoon shows and parades. This park themes its entertainment heavily toward Disney films with an emphasis on the current hits, so shows change often. The **ABC Sound Studio** is always good entertainment, and you can also see what's going on at the **Theater of the Stars** and the **Backlot Theater.**

9. *New!* If you want to see the spectacular new night-time show **Fantasmic!** grab a bite to eat in one of the restaurants and unwind before heading over. It's gonna be packed. The new state-of-the-art laser light and film show will wow you as it is projected onto three huge water screens. Mickey, posing as the Sorcerer's Apprentice, makes the stars come to life. On your way out, shop along Hollywood Boulevard, have your picture taken, and price the movie memorabilia.

Chapter 15

The Mouse That Roars: Disney's Animal Kingdom

> **In This Chapter**
>
> ➤ Logistics and services
>
> ➤ Rides, shows, and attractions
>
> ➤ Dining tips at the Animal Kingdom

As recently as 1997, this was a far different kind of kingdom. The nearest things to "relief" were the frequent cow patties and fire-ant mounds. But the pasture has given way to a forest with rivers, ravines, hills, and savannas. And, for a single installment of $42 plus 6% sales tax—$34 for kids ages 3 to 9—Animal Kingdom is yours for the day.

Is it a front-line park, or is it riding on Disney's coattails? Oh, what a debate the new park caused. Shortly after tons of reporters got their first look, travel stories and columns debated the issue ad nauseum. Many said Animal Kingdom was overrated. They chastised Disney because 18 animals died at, or in transit to, Central Florida, and they said the park was second fiddle to Tampa's Busch Gardens. The counterrevolution said "phooey." Animal Kingdom was not only a tribute to Disney imagineers but also to its real-animal handlers, who made conservation and wildlife welfare their top priority. And, if the other reporters weren't so all-fired eager for thrill rides, they might see this was well worth the money.

Which side was right?

Well, both arguments have merit. Journalists aren't the only ones hell-bent on finding the rides. And at first blush, asking $42 and $34 for adults and kids, respectively, is a shade steep. But this is a different kind of park. Rides take a backseat to the animals, and that can make it worth the price of admission *if* you take the time to enjoy its living attractions. Maybe the best reason to visit here is that you might not feel quite as rushed as you do in some other parks, and you can still spend 2 days enjoying this kingdom.

It takes that long just to see most of the animal species. You'll run into some familiar ones—African lions, towering giraffes, a cheetah here, an elephant over there, white rhinos, black rhinos, lowland gorillas, and 7,000-pound hippos. You'll also bump into a few that might be new to you, like bongos (the antelopes, not the drums) and naked mole rats (these cuties are pink, near hairless, buck-toothed, and they love building subterranean toilets.)

This state-of-the-art wildlife theme park is built on a sometimes subtle, sometimes urgent, conservation message. Frontier outposts, ingeniously disguised rides, and animal-friendly habitats are part of the mix. So are the kingdom's six major lands: Safari Village, Africa, Asia, DinoLand U.S.A., the Oasis, and Camp Minnie–Mickey. But nothing is as much this 500-acre park's heart and soul as its 145-foot **Tree of Life** and its carved-animal honor roll.

We'll tell you a lot more about it and other marvels in a little while. But first, let's get your landing gear down.

Logistics & Services

➤ **Directions.** Animal Kingdom is in the southwest corner of WDW, near Blizzard Beach and the All-Star resorts. Take I-4 to exit 25B, the main WDW entrance, then follow the signs.

➤ **Hours and admission.** Animal Kingdom is open daily from 8am to 5pm. We've already told you standard 1-day admission is $42 for adults, $34 for children 3 to 9. See the chart in chapter 11 for a run-down of prices for multipark passes.

➤ **Parking** is always a problem. The lots are always crowded, forcing many to park in a different dimension. Get here **early.**

➤ **ATMs** are at the main entrance and Safari Village.

➤ **Baby-changing facilities** are located in Safari Village. Many shops have disposable diapers behind the counters. Just ask and be prepared to pay a premium.

➤ The **First Aid Center,** staffed by registered nurses, is in Safari Village.

➤ **Lockers** are just inside the entrance. They cost $3, plus a refundable $2 deposit.

➤ **Lost children.** If your kids get lost, somebody will most likely take them to Guest Services. Children under 7 should wear nametags.

➤ **Package pickup.** If you buy something early in the day and don't want to carry it around with you, have the clerk send it to Garden Gate Gifts, which is just inside the Entrance Plaza. It takes about 3 hours. Don't forget to pick up your package on the way out!

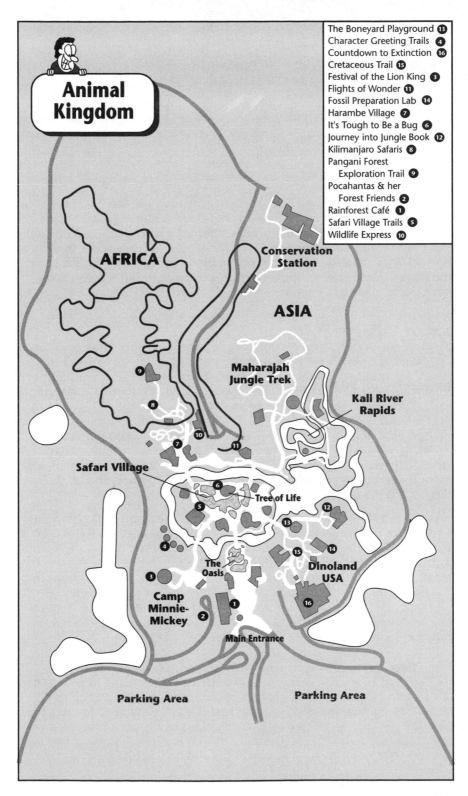

Animal Kingdom

AFRICA

Conservation
Station

ASIA

Maharajah
Jungle Trek

Kali River
Rapids

Safari Village

Tree of Life

The
Oasis

Dinoland
USA

Camp
Minnie-
Mickey

Main Entrance

Parking Area

Parking Area

➤ **Strollers** can be rented just inside the main entrance to the right. The cost is $5 plus a refundable $1 deposit.

➤ **Not so necessities.** You'll find the standard theme-park prices at concession stands and other eateries: popcorn $1.88; a waffle cone $2.85; coffee $1.35; lemonade $2.25; bottled water $2.50; soda $2; one half of a rotisserie chicken $7.95.

The Oasis

This is the first area you come to after entering the park. Like Main Street in the Magic Kingdom, there are no rides, but there are lots of plants, pools, and waterfalls. The vegetation provides a home for miniature deer, brilliant macaws, anteaters, iguanas, sloths, tree kangaroos, and otters, but the foliage is so thick that sometimes you tend to overlook the critters, which is part of the charm. When they want to get away from us, they can. Their habitats have lots of nooks and crannies.

Safari Village

This centrally located island is linked to Animal Kingdom's other five "lands" by bridges, the same way spokes link the hub to the outside of a wagon wheel. Safari Village is home to the **Tree of Life,** which serves as the park's focal point—like Cinderella's Castle is for the Magic Kingdom, or Spaceship Earth is for Epcot. The tree is clearly an oxymoron, a wonderful symbol of life that's made of steel, concrete, and stucco, but it's hard to tell until you're right in front of it. Artists gave it about 8,000 limbs, 103,000 fluttering leaves, and a 160-foot crown. They carved 325 mammals, reptiles, bugs, amphibians, birds, dinosaurs, and hidden Mickeys into its trunk, limbs, and roots. (But those are real wood ducks, flamingos, kangaroos, and small-clawed otters living around it.)

Take the path through the tree's 50-foot base, grab a pair of 3-D glasses, and settle into a comfy theater seat for the delightful multimedia adventure, *It's Tough to Be a Bug,* which is based on the Disney–Pixar film, *A Bug's Life.* By now you're probably used to warnings. This film may not be suitable for kids 2 to 4, mainly because it's loud, and if you're not a bug fan, creepy, but *it is fun,* as ants, beetles, spiders, and others spin a funny, sometimes poignant yarn from a smaller perspective. While the video isn't as high caliber as *Honey, I Shrunk the Audience* at Epcot (chapter 13), it has some wonderful moments.

Jake Rating: Well, he hates bugs and wanted no part of the show. He fretted a lot while we stood in line. He even threatened to go AWOL until we explained that our publisher would fire us if he didn't bail us out. He did, reluctantly, and eventually decided it was "pretty fun." We did, too. The show includes some spritzes of water, blasts of air, and a foul smell when the stinkbug gets its revenge. The seat "crawls" under your fanny when the bugs on screen run amok, causing screams and howls of laughter.

Before you leave Safari Village in favor of one of the spokes, you can shop for souvenirs—at Beastly Bazaar, Creature Comforts, and Disney Outfitters—or grab a snack at Pizzafari or the Flame Tree Barbecue.

Camp Minnie–Mickey

Your kids will love this place. It's a favorite hangout for several Disney characters from the forest and jungle, such as Simba from *Lion King* and Baloo from *The Jungle Book.* There also are appearances by Mickey, Minnie, Goofy, Pluto, Donald, Daisy, and a variety of other headliners that appear from time to time around this woody retreat that bears a strong resemblance to an Adirondack summer camp. If you hang around until 10am, you can see the **Festival of the Lion King** at the Lion King Theater. This is an exciting and thrilling 28-minute performance that is arguably the best show in Animal Kingdom. The eight-times-a-day extravaganza celebrates nature's diversity with a talented, not to mention colorfully attired, cast of singers and dancers. While it's not quite up to Lion King caliber, **Colors of the Wind, Friends of the Animal Forest,** a show at **Grandmother Willow's Grove,** features Pocahontas, Grandmother, and a bevy of live animals.

After Camp Minnie–Mickey, head back to Safari Village, grab an early lunch at Pizzafari for the kids, and then catch the **Radio Disney River Cruise** to "Africa." The boats provide a water-level view of the other lands with a few surprises along the way, like a 30-foot iguanodon and steaming geysers.

Africa

This area is called *Harambe,* which means "coming together."

That's just what happens, in line, and on the **Kilimanjaro Safaris** ride. You'll have a ton of fun and gain a lot of knowledge, but during the summer months remember to plan to be here first thing in the morning or late in the afternoon. Florida's heat, much like Africa's, drives most of the animals to shady shelter during the middle of the day and that can mean missing some of them. Lines are usually long, with 40 to 45 minutes being normal, but the waiting area is covered, and there are overhead fans to keep you cool. There's a heavy conservation theme here, imploring you to look with your eyes and treasure with your heart. Your vehicle is a safari-like deuce-and-a-half. The critters include black rhi-

Tourist Traps

Tourists never bring enough film for these wondrous theme parks, where gift shops sell it for up to twice what you'd pay at K-Mart. Bring more film than you think you'll use and an extra battery for each camera or camcorder. One-hour film processing is offered at competitive prices in dozens of stores and in kiosks around town.

nos, hippos, antelopes, Nile crocodiles, gazelles, wildebeests, zebras, and a male lion that, if your timing is good, might offer a half-hearted roar toward some gazelle as you pass. There's even a little drama as you and your mates help the game wardens catch a dastardly bunch of poachers.

Jake Rating: "Man, I can't wait till the next time we do that!"

The ride ends at the entrance to the **Pangani Forest Exploration Trail,** a self-guided adventure that winds through the habitats of hippos, those scandalous naked mole rats, dozens of tropical bird species, and some lowland gorillas. The pools along the trail contain many rare and exotic fish.

The other major attraction in Africa is the **Wildlife Express** train ride through the belly of the park to **Conservation Station,** where you'll find interactive videos, live displays (the cast includes aardvarks, chinchillas, porcupines, and more), and demonstrations of fascinating animal habits by park staffers. You may even get to see veterinarians working in the operating room, or a baby bird put in an appearance at the nursery. Conservation Station also includes the **Affection Station,** a petting zoo where you and the kids come face-to-face with young animals including pygmy goats, rabbits, and a miniature donkey.

Bet You Didn't Know

If you forget film for your camera it will be sold in the first place you see on the right as you enter any Disney park. Disney knows most people are right-handed and tend to go to the right. Also, if you've forgotten to pick up that keepsake for your Aunt Emma, as you exit any Disney park all of the gift shops are on the right. We still haven't figured out what Disney does for the left-handed folks.

Asia

The first attraction in Asia is the **Flights of Wonder** show on the Caravan Stage. If you've been to a Florida attraction bird show, you know the plot even if the characters and actors are different. This one isn't very unique. You get close encounters and a journey through what seems like ancient Asia, but the show loses focus fast. The birds, predictably, are trained hams as are the human actors, who are at least personable.

Kali River Rapids is a thrilling white-water rafting adventure that puts you and five other foolish souls on a white-knuckle ride down a raging river, through rapids and waterfalls. If you dare open your eyes for a few moments, you'll find Asia's contribution to the environmental message—a fire-scarred forest and land so barren it looks like a moonscape. While you dry off, check out the **Maharajah Jungle Trek,** a fascinating hike through ancient villages and dense jungles where you'll see Bengal tigers, ferocious-looking Komodo dragons, playful gibbons, giant fruit bats, and other Asian animals.

DinoLand U.S.A.

Located to the right of Safari Village, DinoLand U.S.A. is Disney's attempt to capitalize on the dinosaur craze inspired by *Jurassic Park* and (ugh) *Barney*. The **Boneyard** is the first place most kids want to release some energy. They get to slide and climb over a simulated paleontological site. They can squeeze through the fossils and skeletons of a triceratops and a brontosaurus while you stand slack-jawed in front of the reconstruction of a *Tyrannosaurus rex* unearthed in South Dakota in 1990. But a warning is needed here: It's hard to keep track of your kids in the Boneyard. It's a large area, and though it's monitored by Disney staff at both ends, kids play in a multilevel arena where tube slides can take them from one level to the next in a heartbeat. After finding and losing our junior ride critic three times we gave up, nabbed him, and ushered him out.

Jake Rating (after pouting for 5 minutes): "How come I can't go back and play with the other kids?"

Once the kids are tamed by near exhaustion, you can wander the **Cretaceous Trail** to find real survivors of the age of dinosaurs, like soft-shelled turtles and Chinese crocodiles. You can shop for quirky treasures at Chester and Hester's Dinosaur Treasures, grab lunch at Restaurantosaurus, or watch Mowgli, Col. Hathi, and the rest of the cast ham it up in *Journey into Jungle Book,* which is staged in the 1,500-seat **Theater in the Wild.**

We've saved DinoLand's best for last. **Countdown to Extinction** is one of those rides to race to when the park opens. We arrived 35 minutes after opening on a Sunday and there was no line; an hour later there was a long one. Evolution, nature's fragility, and potential catastrophe are the punch lines in this lip-biting, armrest-clenching ride against time, and some very large lizards (like a 33-foot carnotaurus, named for its favorite food— meat—and its bulldog-like mug). This herky-jerky trip through the land of the dinosaurs has lots of rock 'n' roll as you and about 20 or so other time travelers try to save the last dinosaur worth saving, meaning it won't eat you. This, too, has standard warnings: Don't get on if you're pregnant, prone to dizziness or motion sickness, have heart problems, or are afraid of scaly creatures.

Extra! Extra!

Disney's Animal Kingdom Lodge is scheduled to open in 2001. This 1,300–room resort will have views over-looking the African savanna, allowing guests to see zebras, giraffes, antelopes, and more.

Jake Rating: "I think I'm gonna puke (sometime before halftime)"; then after the ride, "That's the one I like best [in Animal Kingdom]." Riders must be 46 inches tall to ride.

ᴀse Feed the People:
Food at Disney's Animal Kingdom

Animal Kingdom has surprisingly few restaurants so far. Instead, most feeding sites (for people) are of the counter-service and fast-food variety.

Try **Restaurantosaurus** in DinoLand U.S.A. for burgers and fries or **Pizzafari** in Safari Village. **Tusker House Restaurant** in Africa offers a mixture of traditional fast food, salads, and sandwiches.

The **Rainforest Café** is the only full-service restaurant in Animal Kingdom. Follow the signs and don't trust your eyes alone because a 65-foot waterfall disguises it. Like the Hard Rock Café at Universal Studios, you can get to it from inside and outside the park, which means you can dine without paying park admission. Try to steer clear of the peak lunch period (noon to 2pm). Though it has room for 575, the seats can fill pretty fast.

Suggested Itinerary

It is extremely important that you arrive at Animal Kingdom at, or before, the official opening time if you want a good chance at seeing all of the animals. This is especially true during the summer; once it gets hot, the animals head for the shade and won't emerge until late afternoon. You should also keep in mind that this is the only WDW park that does not have an early opening for WDW resort guests, so they have no advantage over those staying off the premises.

Parents with small children can eat breakfast in the Rainforest Café. Afterward, head over to the **Tree of Life** in Safari Village for *It's Tough to Be a Bug.* (Older children will want to start at **Countdown to Extinction,** which is a good choice as long as you can get there early enough to avoid long lines.) From there go to **Camp Minnie–Mickey,** meet a few characters, then see **Colors of the Wind, Friends from the Animal Forest,** and **Festival of the Lion King.** If your time allows only one, Lion King is the best choice.

Cross back over to Safari Village. If you're hungry, go for a quick lunch at **Pizzafari** or continue on to **Africa** where you can dine at the **Tusker House Restaurant.** Take the **Kilimanjaro Safaris** ride. Unless you must have a bird-show fix, skip **Flights of Wonder** in Asia, but don't miss the **Kali River Rapids.** Next, head to **DinoLand U.S.A.** and let the kids burn off some steam in the **Boneyard** while you try to take a break, and then enjoy Animal Kingdom's *must* ride, **Countdown to Extinction,** before heading for the gate. If you need some refueling before leaving, the **Flame House Barbecue** offers picnic packs and kids meals, featuring chicken, beef, ribs, and salads along with hot sandwiches.

Chapter 16

The Never-Ending World of Disney

In This Chapter

➤ DisneyQuest

➤ Happy holidays

➤ Disney's Wide World of Sports™

➤ Hitting the links

➤ Getting wet at WDW

➤ Cruising with the Disney *Magic*

You've met the A-Team—the major parks—in chapters 11 through 15, but Walt Disney World contains several smaller ones. In other cities, many of them would be big-league attractions, but here in the fun capital of the world, they can get lost in the crowd. Our job is to make sure they don't, so you have a complete picture. That's right, *there's more!*

DisneyQuest

Meet the world's most interactive video arcade.

DisneyQuest is chock-full of thrills, chills, spills, and a heaping helping of virtual reality. This one gets a 21-gun salute from the 9 out of 10 people who pass through the doors and allow themselves to be launched in the Cyberlator, the world's most enchanting elevator ride. The voice of Robin Williams's genie (the good guy in Disney's *Aladdin* and *Return of Jafar*) combines with the fireworks-style flickering lights and a 'toon video to make this ascent everything but conventional. It's a short trip from the outside world to the inside action, but the two seem light-years apart.

This isn't your mother's video arcade. It's five—count 'em, five—floors and 100,000 square feet. Most of its games are life-size, or at least larger than traditional ones. Virtual experiences like Invasion: An Extraterrestrial Alien Encounter, Ride the Comix, and Hercules in the Underworld top the food chain. There also are low-tech games like the ones you would find at the county fair.

Are your seatbelts buckled?

The Explore Zone

You can play your way through several Disney animated adventures in this land of make believe. The **Virtual Jungle Cruise,** for example, is a raft trip through prehistoric jungles to the present day. You start by parking your keister in a rubber raft in front of a large video screen. Once the rapids get roaring, you have to use paddles to steer while the video races by, and the equally rubber "water" beneath you toils and boils thanks to hydraulics. The raft responds to what's on screen (rapids, waterfalls, etc.) as well as any mistakes you make, like taking the short course instead of the slow and easy. The further you get, the better you've done, but the cataclysmic comet is coming, so hurry.

You straddle the saddle of a motorcycle-like seat and fly **Aladdin's Magic Carpet** by using a control panel to steer left, right, up, and down (in most cases the flying is pretty erratic, but after a while you begin to get the hang of things). Your virtual reality head gear provides good 3-D and sound effects while you fly through beautiful downtown Agrabach, then head off to the Cave of Wonders, where with luck you run into the genie. Along the way, you pick up diamonds and other worldly doodads to help you get inside restricted areas, or to buy your way out of trouble.

Jake Rating: "Did that ride make you nervous?"

Hercules in the Underworld is one of the best virtual experiences in Orlando. This adventure for up to four players lets you decide whether to be Herc, Pegasus, Mel, or Phil, that cute little round thing that seems to be of the same blood stock as Pan. If you pick Pegasus, you drive the team chariot when the 3-D story reaches that point. Before that, you and your mates run around the underworld and grab lightning bolts, while dodging all sorts of obstacles, including monsters, whirlpools, and boulders. The more lightning bolts you have, the better chance you have of blowing Hades to the ever-after. If you succeed, you rule. Fail, and all living things as you know them turn to crispy critters.

Jake Rating: "Awesome!"

To expand on that just a tad, the special effects and 3-D were spectacular. Bravo.

The floor beneath **Treasures of the Ancient Incas** is a maze where remote-control vehicles scurry about. Game players drive them by using

230

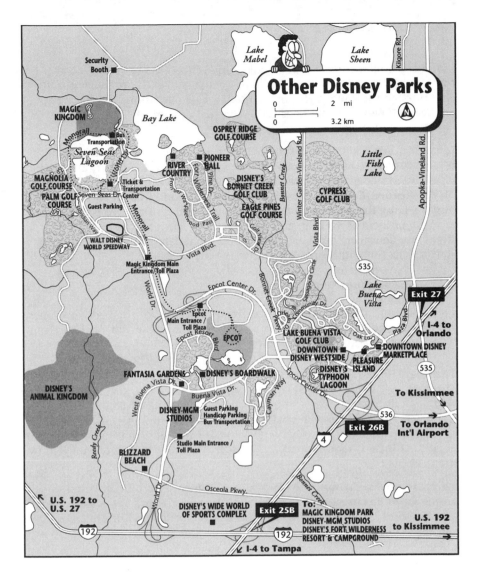

steering wheels and video monitors that reveal images from minicams mounted on the vehicles. If you find the treasure (aw, even if you don't) you get tickets you can trade for inexpensive trinkets at the Intergalactic Trading Post.

The Score Zone

As soon as you exit the Cyberlator, you run into the **Mighty Ducks Pinball Slam,** an interactive life-size pinball game where players climb aboard platforms and use body English to score points. All of the action is displayed on a big screen that's one-third the size of a drive-in movie screen.

In **Ride the Comix,** you reenter the world of virtual reality with head gear and what amounts to a light saber. You ride a hover seat while fighting cartoon scoundrels in a futuristic comic-book world. This is as neat to watch as it is fun to play. Jake drew quite a crowd as he lustily hacked and whacked his way through the enemy. He got so intent on two occasions—hollering "hee-ya, hee-ya, hee-ya!"—that he sliced his virtual nose off. (He finished to cheers from his fans.)

Invasion: An Extraterrestrial Alien Encounter ranks almost as high on our virtual list as Hercules. The 360° adventure sends up to four players on an intergalactic mission to save colonists from a mess of alien uglies. One player flies the module while the others fire cannons and missiles, simultaneously helping the pilot to rescue 22 fleeing colonists. The idea is to pick up as many of them as you can and hurtle back to Earth before the bug-eyes shoot you down, or the planet explodes. Despite Jake's marksmanship, our starship crashed and burned. That lowered the

Jake Rating: "Pretty neat."

The score zone also includes life-size video games, shoot-the-bad-guy games, snowboard and MX races where you ride a stationary but flexible board or bike, and other adrenaline-thumping games.

The Replay Zone
The headliner is **Buzz Lightyear's AstroBlaster,** a two-seat bubble-top car that has a distinct similarity to a bumper car. Players do the bump while using cannons to shoot foam balls. Direct hits send opponents spinning out of control. This is one of only two rides in DisneyQuest that has a minimum height (51 inches) requirement. Kids under that aren't properly snuggled by the seatbelts.

Midway on the Moon, the other area in this zone, is a Disney-theme arcade where the games include Dumbo's Water Race and Whack an Alien. It also has some traditional video games like Centipede and Dig Dug where you can earn tickets for cheap prizes.

The Create Zone
If your mind can imagine it, you can create it in this imagineering masterpiece. **Cyberspace Mountain** is an excursion where Bill Nye the Science Guy helps you build the ultimate roller coaster with loops, corkscrews, spirals, and jumps. You get up to 10,000 feet of track. Your ride is rated on a 1-to-10 scale—with 10 earning you a trip to the cardiac ward. If you have bladder control, the next step is entering a virtual-reality simulator where you ride your monster.

Animation Academy is a minicourse in Disney animation, and **Sid's Create-a-Toy** gives you a chance to do the obvious using a video monitor and a warehouse of 60 odd parts. When you're done you can buy the toy for $10.

Refueling Stops

FoodQuest offers a quick gourmet fix of sandwiches, salads, pizza, and various other fun food ($2.50 to $18.95). The **Wired Wonderland Café** has sinful desserts and beverages like lattes, cappuccinos, and micro-brewed teas ($1.65 to $5.25). While you're enjoying your treat, you can slip into a booth and send funny e-mail to a friend, or just surf the Internet.

The Cost

Initially, DisneyQuest was a pay-for-play facility, but there is now a single admission price for the attraction. A 1-day admission to DisneyQuest costs $25 plus tax for adults, and $20 plus tax for children 3 to 9. This will allow you to ride or play all of the arcade games inside.

 Overall Jake Rating: "That was killer cool!" Translation: Wow!

Coming Soon

Does Disney think there's a future in this virtual-reality concept?

As sure as dead presidents buy groceries.

DisneyQuest is branching out. Chicago has No. 2 locked in. But don't fret if the windy city is a bit too far for you to roam. The folks behind the Mouse That Roared are planning as many as 30 others in major domestic and international markets. So batten down the kids—and think about a second mortgage to buy passes.

Quest for Quest

DisneyQuest is located in Downtown Disney, part of a complex that includes Pleasure Island (1000 to 1500 E. Buena Vista Dr., Lake Buena Vista). It's open 10:30am to midnight. Call ☎ **407/828-4600** or visit **www.disneyquest. com** on the Internet.

Happy Holidays

Few commercial ventures put folks in the spirit like Disney does.

Mickey's Very Merry Christmas Party, held on Thursday and Friday for 3 weeks in December, mixes holiday music with machine-made snow flurries (with apologies to purists, but this *is* Central Florida). While flakes fall on Main Street, U.S.A., parades, fireworks, and shows ring in the year's most celebrated holiday. Advance tickets for the 8pm to 1am party are $29 for adults and $19 for kids 3 to 9. (At the gate they're $5 more.) Call ☎ **407/934-7639**.

Over at Epcot, **Holidays Around the World** has become Disney's main holiday event. From late November to late December, it celebrates the holiday traditions of all the World Showcase countries. The **Candlelight Processional at the America Gardens Theatre** features the story of Christmas narrated three times nightly by celebrity guests. A mass choir (500 or so voices) and a 50-piece orchestra support this stirring event. This seasonal pilot-light starter isn't what it was 15 years ago, when it had a single celeb and a wonderful Magic Kingdom backdrop, but it's still a bit south of commercial. And the **Holiday IllumiNations** blowout over the World Showcase lagoon makes it even better with fireworks and laser lights. You can add dinner at an Epcot restaurant for $39.95 ($10.95 for ages 3 to 9). The cost includes preferred seating for the processional, a 15% merchandise discount, and free parking, but not park admission.

Epcot's **Lights of Winter** adds a canopy of sparkling lights across the bridge from Future World to the World Showcase. The nightly tree-lighting ceremony includes carolers, trumpeters, and storytellers. At 9:30pm, there's a seasonal version of the park's laser, light, and fireworks show, Holiday IllumiNations.

The **Osborne Family Spectacle of Lights** is held from late November to early January at Disney–MGM Studios. The display includes more than 4 million lights, enough to turn night to day on Residential Street, the Washington Square backlot, and New York Street. At the same time, Downtown Disney gets into the spirit with entertainment and a nightly tree lighting. Pleasure Island has musical guests, plus a New Year's Eve street party.

The Disney Institute's **Holiday Magic from the Garden** gets an early jump—usually the first two weekends in November—on its guests' holiday "to-do" lists. The programs center on creating unique gifts and decorations. The $469 package includes 3 days of programs and 2 nights of lodging. Call ☎ **800/496-6337** for more information.

Disney's Wide World of Sports™

This 200-acre complex includes a 7,500-seat baseball stadium where the Atlanta Braves work the kinks out during spring training. It's also a training site of the Harlem Globetrotters, and hosts the ERA Clay Court Tennis Championships. It's equipped for 30 additional sports, including soccer, softball, and track and field. Spectators can find some kind of championship event almost any time. Guests who want more than a sideline seat can sharpen passing and punting skills in the NFL Experience, or drive the test track at 120 mph in the Richard Petty Driving Experience. Golf, tennis, softball, and bass fishing are some of the other sporting pastimes you can tackle here. Call ☎ **407/363-6600**. The general admission is $8 for adults, $6.75 for kids 3 to 9. Prices for special events vary. Tickets are through Ticketmaster (☎ **407/ 839-3900**).

Putting A Round

Ninety-nine putts are left on the course, 99 putts on the course, one more down and putting around, 98 putts left on the course.

Walt Disney World offers 99 holes of golf. (Its most famous hazard is a sand trap on the Magnolia Course's 6th hole; it's shaped like Mickey Mouse.) All Disney golf courses are open to the public and offer driving ranges, pro shops, locker rooms, snack bars or restaurants, and PGA-staffed teaching and training programs. Golf packages are available and reservations can be made in advance by calling ☎ **407/939-4653.** For group events, call the Golf Events Sales Office (☎ **407/824-3001**). For tee times and information, call ☎ **407/824-2270** up to 7 days in advance. (Disney resort guests can reserve up to 30 days in advance.) Call ☎ **407/W-DISNEY** for information about golf packages.

Here's a rundown of some of Disney's best courses:

The Palm Course—18 Holes
The Palm is rated one of America's Top 75 Resort Courses and is Disney's toughest to play. Set among natural Florida woodlands, the elevated greens, water, and sand traps offer more hazards than I-4. Good luck with the 18th hole; it's rated the fourth toughest hole on the PGA Tour.

The Magnolia Course—18 Holes
This is the longest course on Disney property and is designed in the classic PGA style. Wide fairways are deceiving; you've got to hunker down and whack the ball here, but be careful too, because there are 11 holes with water hazards and 97 bunkers on the course. The 6th hole has a special Mickster surprise.

The Lake Buena Vista Course—18 Holes
It's classic country club. Lots of pine forest, and located in the Disney Resort's residential area. Well bunkered, it's a challenge that demands accuracy. This course is one of a few that have hosted a PGA, LPGA, and USGA event.

Green fees for the Palm, Magnolia, and Lake Buena Vista courses: January to April 25, 1999: resort guests $115; day guests $120. Twilight special (late afternoon) $65. April 26 to October 2, 1999: resort guests $85; day guests $90. Twilight special $50; Price Slice Special $45.

The Eagle Pines Course—18 Holes
Expansive sand beds and sloping fairways follow the natural lay of the land. Rough pine straw and sand replace grass rough on this course, along with 16 holes with water hazards.

The Osprey Ridge Course—18 Holes
Tropical wilderness surrounds Osprey Ridge. This Fazio-designed course combines rolling fairways cut through forests of scrub oaks, pine, palmetto, cypress, and bay trees. The Osprey course is ranked as one of the best public and resort places to play golf in the United States.

Greens fees for Eagle Pines and Osprey Ridge courses: January to April 25, 1999: resort guests $135; day guests $140. Twilight special (late afternoon) $75. April 26 to October 2, 1999: resort guests $95; day guests $100. Twilight special $55; Price Slice Special $50.

The Oak Trail Course—9 Holes

If you can't go a day without getting in a few holes, but don't have time for the 18-hole courses, this is the place to spank the ball. This 9-hole walking course is designed for families, or for a quick golf fix.

Greens fees year-round are $32.

Tiny But Tough: Miniature Golfing at WDW

Disney's miniature golf courses are every bit as classy, and in some cases, difficult, as their full-size counterparts. They're a charming way to while away an afternoon (if it's cool), and make a nice evening outing for the whole family. There are two miniature golf parks on WDW. The first, **Disney's Fantasia Gardens,** is located across the street from the Swan Hotel, off Epcot Resorts Boulevard. It features a choice of two courses, and one round will set you back around $10 per adult, $8 per child. It is usually open from 10am to midnight, but may close because of bad weather. For more information, call ☎ **407/560-8760.**

The **Fantasia Gardens** course clearly takes its lead from the Disney classic, *Fantasia.* Hippos, ostriches, and gators dot the course, and the Sorcerer's Apprentice himself presides over the final hole. It's a good bet for beginners and kids. Seasoned minigolfers will probably prefer **Fantasia Fairways,** which is a scaled-down golf course complete with sand traps, water hazards, and tricky putting greens.

Disney's newest miniature golf Mecca is **Winter Summerland.** Located next door to Disney's Blizzard Beach, it has two pint-size 18-hole courses for the younger set. The first is for elves who like winter; the second is for elves who want to keep warm. Both courses have interactive elements: On the "snow" course, Squirty the Snowman sprays water on the putters; on the "sand" course, you putt over a sleeping Santa who is buried in the sand. Both courses collide on the 18th hole, where you'll find model trains, a Christmas tree, and a special greeting from Santa.

Blizzard Beach

This is one of three water parks in the Disney stable, and like the others there's something for everyone, from ankle-deep water for toddlers, to the most shivery thrill rides for teens. Of all of the parks, this one has the most thrills, so it fills up. (When the beach is full, the gate is closed.)

Cross Country Creek is this park's lazy river—floating you on an inner tube around the park. The relaxing route takes 30 minutes or so. **Mount Gushmore** is laced with speed slides and flumes, including the **Slush Gusher,** and **Summit Plummet,** billed as the fastest water slide in the world. By the way, unless you want to put on a show for the viewing stands below, one-piece bathing suits are a must for women who brave the speed slides. On the **Toboggan River,** guests race headfirst down an eight-lane water slide. **Run-Off Rapids** lets you run down four flumes in an inner tube. The **Ski-Patrol Training Camp** is aimed at preteens who can swing on a rope, take the T-bar to drop into the water, and pick their way through the ice.

Buses to Blizzard Beach are available throughout WDW. It's opposite from Disney–MGM Studios and is bounded by Osceola Parkway, World Drive, and the extension of Buena Vista Drive.

It's open daily from 10am to 5pm, later in summer. Ticket prices are $26.45 for adults and $20.70 for ages 3 to 9. Towels and lockers are extra.

River Country

This nostalgic low-key attraction is fashioned after Tom Sawyer's favorite place to get wet. There's an **Ol' Wadin' Hole** for younger folks, a nature walk, and a playground.

Light meals are available at Pop's Place. Towels and lockers are for rent. You can take your own lunch and use the picnic tables.

Slippery Slide Falls are two 16-foot slides that send you crashing into the **Up Stream Plunge. Whoop 'n Holler Hollow** has two water slides where humans, rather than logs, speed down the flume to the mill. **White Water Rapids** treats you to a dunking aboard rubber tubes that shoot the rapids and splash into the swimming hole.

You can reach River Country by WDW bus, the boats near the gates of the Magic Kingdom, or your personal sedan.

Hours are daily from 10am to 7pm most of the year, later in peak summer days. Admission for adults is $17.95; for children 3 to 9, it's $14.50. Call ☎ **407/824-4321** for more details.

Typhoon Lagoon

Thrill-seekers may find it hard to choose between Typhoon Lagoon and Blizzard Beach. There's plenty here for the whole family, from heart-pumping speed slides to little rides for the little squirts. The park also has one of the world's largest wave pools.

This is another one where the gates close when capacity is reached, so get here as early as 9am on peak (read: hot) days. You can't bring your own flotation devices, but you can bring food and relax at the picnic tables. Light meals are also available at two restaurants and the beach bar sells beer and soda.

Castaway Creek is a cool and captivating float along a 2,100-foot river. **Ketchakiddee Creek** is for children under 4 feet tall. It's filled with waterfalls and wonderment designed for fun and happy squeals. You can literally swim with the sharks at **Shark Reef,** a 15-minute snorkel trip among real fish. Snorkeling gear is provided and you'll get instructions on how to use it. **Typhoon Lagoon** is a giant lagoon with *big* waves for surfing and smaller waves for bobbing. **Mt. Mayday** towers over the park and is the site of the park's big guns. White-water rides come in three types: **Keelhaul Falls** is winding and spinning; **Humunga Kowabunga** is steep and scary. Families can ride **Gangplank Falls** together on large tubes. Less intimidating, but not by much, are a trio of **Storm Slides** that are aptly named **Rudder Buster, Jib Jammer,** and **Stern Burner.** Modest maidens will want to wear a one-piece if they plan on tackling Typhoon's thrill rides.

There's direct transportation from some WDW resorts. From all other points, go to the Transportation and Ticket Center.

Route 536 and Buena Vista Drive bound the park.

Hours are daily from 10am to 5pm, later in summer. Admission for adults is $27.50; for children 3 to 9, it's $21.75. Call ☎ **407/824-4321** if you must know more.

Disney *Magic*

Okay, it took them a while to catch on, something that's unusual for Disney. But they finally discovered another place to expand the empire—the high seas. Of course, their baptism wasn't a walk in the park. The Disney *Magic's* inaugural voyage was delayed, thanks to a backlog at the shipyard. There were the usual first-time-out kinks, too. But overall Disney made the kind of splash that only Disney can make.

The *Magic's* maiden voyage was in the spring of 1998. Its 3- and 4-day itineraries from Port Canaveral stop at Nassau and Castaway Cay, Disney's private island. Week-long packages add 3 or 4 additional days at one of the Disney resorts. By the end of its first year, the kinks were gone and the line was preparing to launch a sister ship, the 2,600-passenger Disney *Wonder.* It will follow the same itinerary.

Back on the *Magic,* here's a breakdown of some of the fun.

Dining

The Disney Line offers a unique dine-around feature that allows you to eat in a different restaurant every night while keeping the same servers and (here's hoping you get along) the same table mates. The chefs are different, so there's less chance of enduring the entire cruise with a cook you'd like to divorce but can't.

There's one exception to that same-same rule. **Palo,** which happens to be what you call the colorful poles lining the canals of Venice, is an adults-only, reservations-required restaurant. It features northern Italian cuisine, an exhibition kitchen, and a 270° view of the ocean. While you're there, your children can eat with friends at the Topsider Buffet, which is kids-only at night.

Back on the movable-feast front, **Lumiere's** adds a French flair to continental cuisine. It's Disney's version of the grand dining rooms of yesterday's liners—complete with sparking chandeliers, high-brow dining, and breaking the mood a little, a sweeping mural from *Beauty and the Beast.* **Parrot Cay** is casual and colorful, a swirl of pastel tones blended with a Caribbean meal of fresh fish, meat, fruit, and vegetables. **Animator's Palate** literally opens your evening in black and white, like a sketch, then turns it to color with Disney characters as your meal progresses. On the creative side, you help create what you eat.

A few words of warning, though: Be prepared to wait. Lines are as much a fact of life here as anywhere in Disneyville, land or sea, but lines usually are a part of any cruise. If you don't want to wait, there's always **Pinocchio's Pizzeria.**

Entertainment

The Walt Disney Theatre is a 975-seat palace that's three decks high. Broadway-style shows vary by trip. The menu includes *Hercules, A Muse-ical Comedy, Disney Dreams,* and *Island Magic,* performed by a troupe of singers and dancers. The Buena Vista Theatre is a 275-seat theater showing new Disney movies and the classics. Cabaret acts and game shows are part of the fun at Studio Sea and Beat Street, the adult district, which offers clubs where you can enjoy old-time rock 'n' roll, country-western, jazz jams, improv comedy, or, if you don't care about losing friends, karaoke. The Oceaneer Club, Oceaneer Lab, and Common Grounds are night-time hot spots for the younger set, while the ESPN Skybox is a favorite of those who can't take a vacation from the sports world.

For the Young & Restless

Disney ads claim the *Magic* has 10 times more kids' activities and space than any ship afloat. That's probably not stretching things in the least. Virtually an entire deck is devoted to youngsters.

The Oceaneer Club, for 3- to 8-year-olds, flies Capt. Hook's flag and has three dozen things to do, such as music jams and flights to Never Land. Programs for 3- to 5-year-olds have one counselor for every 15 kids. Activities have them creating "moo juice" shakes and, on Castaway Cay, hunting musical instruments so that they can participate in Sebastian's "Little Mermaid" band. The ratio for 6- to 8-year-olds is one counselor for every 25 members. They get to help Buzz Lightyear complete his journey to "Infinity and Beyond" and look for shark's teeth and stingray bones on the island.

The Oceaneer Lab, for 9- to 12-year-olds, is a bit more high-tech. Nine- and 10-year-olds join Goofy's Gumshoe Investigators on their way to earning forensics certificates, then they bake solar pizzas in homemade ovens on the Cay. The 11- and 12-year-olds learn about marine biology in a game show, create messages on digital postcards, and use land-side clues to find an island treasure. Both groups participate in computer games (there are several stations) and play electronic games on giant video walls.

Kids' activities run from 9am to 1am. Right after passengers board, counselors meet with parents to discuss itineraries. All kids get "parent pagers" so adults can enjoy themselves with a reasonable certainty that the kids can reach them for important things, like getting more money for the arcade.

The teen programs are centered on Common Grounds, a trendy coffee house for their use only. It's not only a hangout, but a place for them to prepare for their comedy hour (the improv pros teach them funny-stuff basics). They can also dance or play games inside. But, ask yourself an honest question before paying their freight: Have your teenagers outgrown Disney?

At the other end of the spectrum, there are structured activities for children under 3, like bubble fun and story time, and in-room baby-sitting is offered. But there are a limited number of baby-sitters, so make your reservations right after boarding.

Recreation, Fitness & Leisure
The *Magic* has three pools; basketball, paddleball, and volleyball courts; a quarter-mile walking and jogging track; a state-of-the-art fitness center; and a spa.

Cabins & Suites
Economy class begins with inside staterooms that sleep two to four, then the options progress up the price scale. Seventy-three percent of the cabins are outside (ocean-view), and 44% of those have private verandas. The family suites have beds for five, as do most of the one-bedroom, two-bedroom, and Royal suites.

The Itinerary
Both 3- and 4-day Bahamas itineraries make port in Nassau and Castaway Cay, Disney's private out island. The 18-hour stop in Nassau gives you a day and an evening to go sightseeing, shopping, or casino hopping. Shore excursions range from an inexpensive harbor cruise ($20 for adults, $14.50 for kids) to a half-day deep-sea fishing excursion, which at $770 a head makes some people reach for the smelling salts.

Castaway Cay is another day-long stop. The 1,000-acre island has an activity for everyone, from beach chairs for those who want to catch some extra ZZZZs, to a mile-long secluded beach for hikers, to a 15-acre lagoon for snorkelers. You can also rent sailboats and motorboats.

The Sticker Price
If you're traveling on a thin budget, or simply like to shop for the cheapest deal around, the bottom-class inside stateroom sleeps two and goes for $799 to $929 for a 3-day cruise depending on your choice of departure dates. That's per person, double occupancy, as are all rates in this section. The same room is $909 to $1,039 for a 4-day cruise. (Bottom-rate cabins have room for two, *period*.) The cheapest rates for ocean-view cabins are $1,149 to $1,279 for 3-day cruises, and $1,259 to $1,389 for 4 days. At the top end of the scale, Royal Suites are $2,659 to $2,789 (3 days), and $2,869 to $2,999 (4 days).

The rates include round-trip airfare from 150 cities in the United States and Canada, ground transfers, meals, and entertainment. As is the case with most cruises, things like shore excursions, tips, liquor, soft drinks, and bottled water are not included. The fare for kids 2 and under sharing a stateroom with their parents is $275 for 3- or 4-day cruises. Children 3 to 17 traveling as third, fourth, or fifth guests in a stateroom are $679 (3 days) and $779 (4 days). Those are flat rates, regardless of category.

Surf-and-turf packages match lodging categories on land and sea. A 7-day vacation at a moderately priced Walt Disney World resort (Dixie Landings or Port Orleans) with an inside cabin on the *Magic* costs $1,295 to $1,935 per person, depending on dates. The rates for a deluxe resort (Beach Club, BoardWalk Inn and Villas, the Contemporary or Polynesian resorts, Walt Disney World Swan, or Walt Disney World Dolphin) with an outside state-room range from $1,865 to $2,835. A flagship resort (the Grand Floridian Resort & Spa) combined with an onboard suite is $3,185 to $4,225.

BLUE-LIGHT SPECIAL Don't be shy. Always ask the magic question: Is that the best rate available? On a show-off voyage for journalists, one Disney executive said 3-day, cruise-only rates might go as low as $379 if you don't need "free" air and are able to get the lowest-class cabin onboard. Hey, we're not talking about "oar class" on a Viking ship. Class on modern cruise ships often is a state of mind.

Call ☎ **800/939-2784,** 407/566-7000, or catch a wave to the line's Internet site at **www.disneycruise.com** for more information.

Universal Studios Escape

Is Orlando the town that Disney owns? Not anymore. Universal moved in a few years ago and stole a little of Mickey's thunder. Now the new kid is pressing the action, though the franchise player has a comfortable lead, and probably always will.

As Disney plans a fifth major park (under the usual veil of secrecy), Universal is opening its second—Islands of Adventure. Universal is also raising its bet with CityWalk, the shopping, dining, and nightlife area that began opening in stages in 1998 (see chapter 21 for more details), and it is also building theme hotels such as the Portofino Bay.

Most people don't follow the movie business enough anymore to know which studio produces what, but in Orlando you soon get the big picture, literally and figuratively. Both Universal and Disney–MGM Studios spend a lot of their dollars, and your time, plugging their movies and characters. At Universal that means *Earthquake, Hercules* (the live-action show, not the animated feature), *Terminator, Back to the Future,* Barney, Yogi Bear, *Jaws, E.T.,*

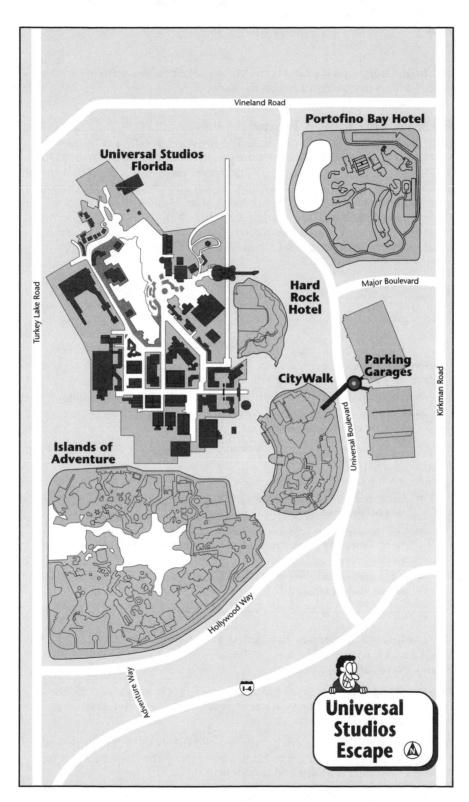

243

and many more. And it's not just a theme park; it's also a working studio where visitors might see a film being made.

Before You Leave Home

Start planning early so you can make the most of your days at Universal. Call the **Universal City Travel Company** (☎ **800/224-3838** or 407/ 363-8000) and ask for a theme park and travel package. Packages that include an auto rental, airfare, airport transfers, beach add-ons, and tickets to some other attractions are available at savings. Extras include such perks as a Nickelodeon Kids Travel Tote, early park admission, or complimentary transportation from your hotel to Universal. The mailing address is Universal Studios Florida, 1000 Universal Studio Plaza, Orlando, FL 32819.

Time-Savers

Here's what you can do in advance so you don't waste as much of your park time standing in line or dealing with arrangements:

➤ Check on the shuttle schedule from your hotel to Universal Studios.

➤ Call Universal at ☎ **407/363-8000** the day before you go to ask for tomorrow's official opening time.

➤ If you have small kids, make reservations for a character breakfast by calling ☎ **407/224-6339.**

➤ When you arrive at the park, *make a note of your parking area and number.*

➤ Get in the right line (entrance, tickets, or voucher redemptions) 45 minutes before opening.

➤ Get the day's show schedule and a park map. Note what, if anything, is being filmed at Nickelodeon, and what attractions are closed on the day you visit.

➤ Put a nametag on each child under age 7. Agree on a family meeting spot in case you get separated.

You can **book a character breakfast** ahead of time at ☎ 407/224-6339. You'll eat in the International Food Bazaar with stars such as the Flintstones, Barney, Fievel, and Yogi Bear.

For current news on special events at the park, ticket prices, and vacation packages, check Universal's Web site at **www.usf.com/tickets/ index_cap.html.**

If you belong to AAA, you can get discounted tickets to Universal through your local office. Don't forget to bring your card to the theme park; it's also good for discounts at shops and restaurants.

What Does It Cost?

Like the Disney folks, the people at Universal Studios give you a dizzying array of ticket options from which to choose, hoping that discounted prices will encourage you to spend more than 1 day.

If you like diversity, a good choice is the **Orlando FlexTicket,** which comes in 7- and 10-day varieties and gives you a taste of multiple parks. During certain months, everyone gets a second day free or Florida residents get a discount (proof of residency is required). For studio passes or Flex-Tickets ahead of time, call ☎ **800/224-3838;** for annual passes, call ☎ **800/ 889-7275.**

The following table lists the most popular ticket plans. Kids under age 3 are admitted free. Multiday passes include admission to both Universal Studios Florida and Islands of Adventure. Check to see if your hotel offers discounted admission packages. Prices include sales tax and are subject to change.

Universal Studios Florida Admissions Prices

Ticket Package and Description	Admission Price	
	Adult	Ages 3–9
1-day ticket	$44	$36
2-day pass	$84	$68
Annual Celebrity Pass	$190	$164
If your plans include Wet 'n' Wild and Sea World, your best bet is the Orlando 7-Day FlexTicket (unlimited admission for up to 7 days to Universal Studios Florida, Islands of Adventure, Sea World of Florida, and Wet 'n' Wild)	$170	$135
Orlando 10-Day FlexTicket (unlimited admission for up to 10 days to Universal Studios Florida, Islands of Adventure, Sea World of Florida, Wet 'n' Wild, and Busch Gardens)	$208	$168

What You Need to Know About the Park

➤ **Directions.** Take I-4 to exit 30B, which is Kirkman Road, off Florida Route 435. Get into the far right lane and follow the signs.

➤ **Parking.** Universal is the only theme park in Florida that offers covered parking, which is a boon in the blistering sun. *Be sure to make a note of where you leave the car so you can find it later.* Parking is $6 for cars, $7 for RVs, and $12 for valet parking.

➤ **Park hours.** The park is open every day from 9am to 7pm, except during Halloween Horror Nights when it closes at 5pm and reopens from 7pm to midnight. It's open later for special events such as Mardi Gras and New Year's Eve. Call ahead for a schedule.

➤ **ATMs** are found just inside and outside the entrance.

➤ **Baby-changing facilities** are in all men's and women's rest rooms. There's also a nursing area at Guest Relations.

➤ The **First Aid Center** is located between New York and San Francisco, next to Louie's Restaurant.

➤ **Lockers** are across from Guest Relations. The rental fee is $3 a day.

➤ **Lost children** will most likely be delivered to Guest Relations near the entrance or to Security (behind Louie's Restaurant, between New York and San Francisco). Children under age 7 should wear nametags.

➤ **Strollers** may be rented in Amity and at Guest Relations. The cost is $6 for a single stroller, $12 for a double-wide.

➤ **Sample prices:** Ponchos $4.95 for adults, $4.25 for kids; 4-ounce sunscreen $6.95 to $8.95; large draft beer $4.50; turkey sandwich $6.29; hot dog $3.25; cappuccino $2.30; popcorn $2; a small bunch of grapes $1.75.

It's a Ride. No, It's a Movie. Actually, It's Both!— Universal's Top Attractions

The rides and shows at Universal are located in five different zones: Production Central, New York, San Francisco/Amity, Expo Center, and Hollywood. Guests enter the park through the Front Lot. Most of the attractions here use cutting-edge technology such as giant IMAX screens and other special effects. While you wait in line, you'll be entertained by preshows that are better than the ones down the road at Disney.

Attractions are listed here alphabetically. Check "Exploring the Universe: Some Suggested Itineraries" later in this chapter for advice on which attractions are worth the long waits.

Back to the Future: The Ride

This has more warnings than a centipede has legs. Topping the list: If you have a problem with motion sickness, don't get on. If you don't have a problem with motion sickness, but have a problem with other people getting motion sick on you, you might want to invest $4.95 in one of those ponchos. (No sense ruining your new Mickey shirt, right?) There also are warnings for would-be riders who are pregnant or become dizzy, as well as those who are claustrophobic or have neck, heart, or back problems. This is time travel in a simulator made to look like a DeLorean. Six to eight of you are packed into a "car" after a video briefing from Christopher Lloyd, a.k.a. Dr. Emmett Brown. Biff has stolen another DeLorean and you have to catch him.

The fate of the universe is in your hands. The huge screen makes this one very intense, but if you didn't heed the warnings and begin to feel some of the symptoms, just stick your neck out. You can see the other cars, lending the real perspective that you're really only in a theater. Kids must be 40 inches to climb aboard.

 Jake Rating: "Wow! Can we ride it again?"

Beetlejuice's Graveyard Revue
Horrible creatures including Dracula and Wolfman show up to scare you silly. It's too loud and scary for very small children (say, under 6), but teenagers love the rock music and pyrotechnics. Let your kids go on this one by themselves; most adults find it pretty stupid.

Curious George Goes to Town
This is the largest area in the kid zone and begins with a mock zoo where Curious George has set the animals free. Kids can play in cages, swing on tires, and slide into the polar bear den. A town behind the zoo has another play area with water guns and water games.

Time-Savers

Universal's VIP Package provides a 5-hour guided tour with priority entrance to rides and special seating in theaters. Prices start at $359, including 3 hotel nights, park admission, and one dinner.

Dynamite Nights Stuntacular
Boats roar around the lagoon, which is alight with flames and fireworks. This show is well worth staying in the park for to the end of the day, even though it means joining the crowds that flock to the parking lot.

 Jake Rating: "Too cool!"

Earthquake: The Big One
This is a loud one with sparks flying. It begins with a lesson in how the movie was made, including a look at part of the $2.4-million set model. Then you shuffle off to a soundstage for a filming with seven audience members who do silly things before your eyes, but thanks to cameras, a backdrop, and video monitors, the replay looks like they're really riding an escalator in a mall when "The Big One" hits. The ride part of this adventure is underground. You climb onto a BART train in San Francisco and things start pretty slowly, then there's an exploding gas tanker, an unoccupied tram is derailed, the street buckles, and a flood comes. Yes, it's your typical day in San Francisco. Kids must be 40 inches tall.

 Jake Rating: "I liked that a lot!"

Universal Studios Florida

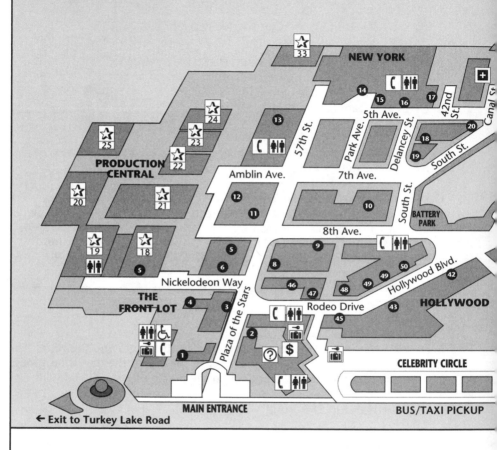

NEW YORK

5th Ave.

PRODUCTION
CENTRAL

Amblin Ave.

7th Ave.

8th Ave.

57th St.

Park Ave.

Delancey St.

42nd St.

Canal St.

South St.

BATTERY PARK

Nickelodeon Way

THE
FRONT LOT

Plaza of the Stars

Rodeo Drive

Hollywood Blvd.

HOLLYWOOD

CELEBRITY CIRCLE

MAIN ENTRANCE

BUS/TAXI PICKUP

← Exit to Turkey Lake Road

The Front Lot:
Nickelodeon Kiosk ❹
On Location ❷
Studio Gifts ❶
Universal Studios Store ❸

Production Central:
Alfred Hitchcock: The
Making of Movies ❽
The Bates Motel Gift Shop ❾
The Bone Yard ⓬
The Futuristic World of
Hanna-Barbera ❻
Hanna-Barbera Store ❼

Hercules & Xena: Wizards
of the Screen ❿
Jurassic Park Kiosk ⓫
Nickelodeon Studios ❺

New York:
Arcade ⓰⓴
Bull's Gym ⓳
Doc's Candy ⓲
Kongfrontation ⓮
Safari Outfitters Ltd. ⓯
Second Hand Rose ⓱
Twister ⓭

San Francisco/Amity:
Beetlejuice's Graveyard Revue
Dynamite Night Stuntacular ㉑
Earthquake-The Big One ㉒
Jaws! ㉖
Quint's Nautical Treasures ㉕
Salty's Sketches ㉔
Shaiken's Souvenirs ㉓
Wild West Stunt Show ㉗

Expo Center:
Animal Actors Stage ㊲
Back to the Future Gifts ㉚

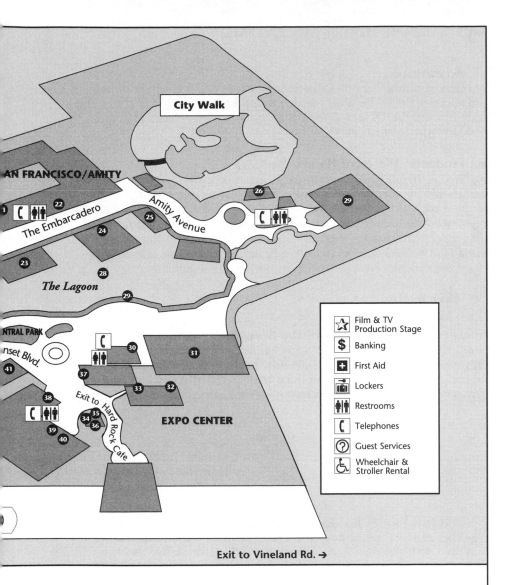

City Walk

AN FRANCISCO/AMITY

The Embarcadero

Amity Avenue

The Lagoon

NTRAL PARK

nset Blvd.

EXPO CENTER

Exit to Hard Rock Cafe

	Film & TV Production Stage
$	Banking
✚	First Aid
🔒	Lockers
🚺🚹	Restrooms
☎	Telephones
?	Guest Services
♿	Wheelchair & Stroller Rental

Exit to Vineland Rd. →

E.T. Adventure

For many families, this now-classic adventure is worth the price of park admission by itself. The wait is made more pleasant by a glade of cool trees. You'll fly with E.T. by bicycle on a mission to save his planet while being serenaded by the familiar movie music.

The Funtastic World of Hanna–Barbera

Yogi Bear is the pilot on your simulated spaceship. Your virtual-reality mission, should you decide to accept it: Save Elroy from Dick Dastardly. There's plenty of rock 'n' roll, turns, dives, and air blasts when things blow up. Yogi negotiates you through Bedrock, Scoobie's Haunted Castle, and finally Jetsonville. Drat, Dick loses again! After the ride there's an interactive theater with a Flintstones house and a cartoon machine that makes those *boing, splat, gulp,* and *patter* noises. Kids must be 40 inches tall.

Jake Rating: "It's awesome."

Hercules & Xena: Wizards of the Screen

It's not the animated Hercules. This is the live-action Hercules, of TV program syndication fame. The interactive show dazzles audiences by mixing live performers, eye-popping costumes, and special effects, as well as a sword fight between good and evil. It's recommended for ages 8 and up.

Dollars & Sense

FlexTickets are a good buy compared to single-park admission. You can leave, go back to your hotel for lunch and a nap, spend the hot afternoon at Wet 'n' Wild, and then come back to Universal for the Dynamite Nights Stuntacular. A parking fee is paid at the first park you visit and it's good for all qualifying parks, all day.

Jaws

It's a boat ride aboard Capt. Jake's (no kidding) Amity Boat Tours, and though you never leave the wharf area, Jaws comes after you. Your captain won't be able to hit the broad side of a barn or dock with his grenade launcher as Jaws terrorizes you and the village, ramming the boat, causing propane tanks to explode, and generally creating consternation and constipation until he fries himself by biting a power line. That gets your boat sprayed with steam and water droplets, but it probably won't dampen your spirit unless it's a cold day.

Jake Rating: This ride gave him a stiff neck the first time he rode it, 3 months earlier. But this time he was a trooper. He kept hollering, "Gimme the gun. I'll shoot the shark!"

Kongfrontation

The line winds through a dark, scary New York subway station where you hear periodic and worsening newscasts about what the big ape is up to. Once on the ride, count on going out of control. Big flames erupt around you while Kong pounds on your elevated car, causing it to bounce around like a toy. Then he picks you up and drops you. This is a pretty short ride. Kids must be 40 inches to ride.

Jake Rating: "That ape was pretty stupid."

Nickelodeon Studios Tour

See a beloved television show come alive (someone will even get slimed!) as you learn how things happen behind the scenes. You'll tour sets, sound-stages, and video production areas. Allow plenty of time to try the newest Sega video games.

Terminator 2: 3-D Battle Across Time

After seeing all the 3-D rides, virtual and otherwise, this is the best, bar none, at any theme park we visited. It's *a must.* Live actors and six giant Cyborgs interact with the Schwarzenegger movie dude on three big 70mm screens. There's plenty of motorcycle action and gunfire. It's intense, typically Arnold (including his humor), and the crowd goes wild. There also are sensory effects from the chair: When liquid mercury falls from the screen, cold water lands on your legs.

> **Bet You Didn't Know**
>
> TV shows, including ***America's Health, World Wrestling Champion-ships,*** and many Nickelodeon programs, are taped at Universal Studios, and admission is free to park guests. Watch for signs, or ask at Guest Services as you enter, to see if you can be part of a studio audience.

Jake Rating: "That's my favorite."

Twister

The curtain goes up in the movie town of Wakita. Outside there are monitors with video of real tornadoes, which are pretty humbling. You stand on a set where you're treated to fire, wind, rain, and lightning. The sensory elements are pretty incredible. Power lines spark and fall, an oak splits amid more sparks from lightning, there's a flying cow that sounds like it doesn't want to fly, the roof blows up and nearly off, and at the climax the floor starts to buckle under you. It may be too intense for very young children.

Jake (who is wide-eyed at the end) **Rating:** "That was pretty scary, but I liked it."

Wild, Wild, Wild West Show

How do the stunt people fall off horses and clobber each other with saloon chairs without getting killed? You'll learn their secrets at this live-wire show. As you enter, note the Splash Zone and don't sit near it unless you want a shower.

Woody Woodpecker's Kid Zone

This 8-acre area is for the younger set and includes several theme areas. The **Woody Woodpecker Nuthouse coaster,** a kid-size roller coaster, is the strongest magnet for most of them. It has a slightly scary 30-foot drop, the speed is conservative, and it's a wild-and-wacky contraption that looks as if Woody put it together with an assortment of bolts, gears, and other gadgets. If your kids are Barney fans, they'll love **A Day in the Park with Barney,** though you may need some Thorazine if you possess the same sentiments we have for the little purple dinosaur. Young fans have probably insisted on Barney pajamas, the plush stuffed animal, countless videos, and that song that weasels into your head. What other Barney paraphernalia could there be? How about an environmental message from the purple dinosaur, complete with singing and dancing by Barney, Baby Bop, and BJ? Anyone pint-sized will be enchanted.

 Jake Rating: In his best adult impersonation, he suggested we euthanize the entire Barney clan.

The Parallel Universe: Other Attractions

The attractions listed above are our favorites, but there are tons of others to see and do here—not to mention shopping and eating.

Fievel's Playland is a delightful playground themed to the Wild West and packed with things for kids to try. It's a great place to go after lunch so toddlers can nap in their strollers while big brother and sister run their batteries down a little.

The **Gory, Gruesome & Grotesque Horror Makeup Show** lets you behind the scenes to see how monster and ghoul makeup is done. *Small Soldiers* is a neat behind-the-scenes look at the movie with props, models, and some of the characters. *I Love Lucy,* **a Tribute,** is a must for Lucy buffs.

In **Alfred Hitchcock: The Art of Making Movies** you'll be led by Tony Perkins through some memorable scenes from popular Hitchcock films such as *Psycho* and *Rear Window.* The **Bone Yard** will please movie buffs. It's a storage space for old props. In the **Animal Actors Show** you'll meet Benji, Mr. Ed, and Lassie lookalikes that do pet tricks for you.

Shopping

The shops at Universal Studios are a Mecca for movie buffs who collect merchandise. The menu includes *Back to the Future,* the Bates Motel, *E.T., Jurassic*

Park, and Hanna–Barbera shops. Others sell all kinds of serious and frivolous gifts, souvenirs, and collectibles. If you run out of time, go to the airport well before your flight and shop the Universal Studios store there.

Time-Savers

Don't have lunch in the Hard Rock Café on days when you're paying to be in the park. Park admission isn't required to dine here, so the waits are longer than at other park restaurants. Go on a day when you're not trying to see and do all of the Universal things. If you must eat here on a park day, do it at the end when you're pooped and don't mind parking your kazoo for a long time.

Dining at Universal Studios

Universal has a lot of restaurants, as well as plenty of places to grab a snack.

Classic Monsters Café (formerly Studio Stars Café) is frightfully fun. Diners order vittles cafeteria-style, then find a table in one of the four theme rooms: Outer Space, Egyptian, Sea Creature, and Gothic Haunted House. In addition to the expected special effects, chefs in the exhibition kitchen scare up salads and pasta dishes such as linguine primavera. Rotisserie chickens constantly turn over a flame, and the cafe features a full dessert menu (the butterscotch/chocolate parfait looks absolutely decadent). A pizza will run you around $6.50 and a chicken Caesar salad costs $7.95.

Finnegan's Bar & Grill is a great place to sit, relax, and have a drink. It's one of three places in Universal that, unlike those within the Magic Kingdom, offer spirits. A casual atmosphere blends with traditional Irish-American grub and entertainment. There's a happy hour, and be sure to check out the specials. A meal here will set you back approximately $10.

The menu at **Lombard's Landing** includes steaks and pastas, but think seafood. Universal did a nice job re-creating a slice of San Francisco's Fisherman's Wharf in a restaurant that has a casual, inviting setting. It's one of the nicest places to eat in the park, and one of the few that won't allow you to leave hungry. Prices can be a tad steep (sometimes more than a tad) at all attraction feeding troughs, but this one gives you your money's worth. It takes a special effort to leave room for dessert, but try to, because there's an excellent pastry shop next door. Sandwiches will run you around $10, and entrees average $12 to $17. There is also a children's menu.

Hard Rock Café. If you've seen one, it doesn't take much to imagine the others. An overdose of rock memorabilia is served amid American cuisine: burgers, fries, chicken, salads, and more. As always, the Hard Rock is wherever it is, if only because of the groupies. But the Orlando restaurant *is* one of the largest on the planet.

Other eateries include **Louie's Italian Restaurant,** pizza and pasta; **Richter's Burger Co.,** chicken, burgers, and a fixings bar; **Chez Alcatraz,** hot dogs, shrimp cocktail, clam chowder, cold sandwiches, and an interesting selection of draft beer; **Midway Grill,** hoagies, Philly cheesesteak sandwiches, and beer; **Boardwalk Snacks,** corn dogs, cotton candy, sodas, and ice cream; **Animal Crackers,** hot dogs, chicken fingers, and smoked-sausage hoagies; **Cafe La Bamba,** chicken and barbecue sandwiches, burgers, ribs, and a bar; **Mel's Drive-In,** burgers, fries, shakes, and malts; **Schwab's Pharmacy,** ham and turkey sandwiches, cold drinks, and soda-foundation delights; and **Beverly Hills Boulangerie,** gourmet sandwiches, coffee, cappuccino, and French pastries.

Can't figure out what to eat? The **International Food Bazaar** has an interesting assortment, including pizza, hamburgers, and Cantonese and Mexican specialties. It's a large indoor dining area loaded with televisions showing clips of people eating. It's also open for breakfast.

Exploring the Universe: Some Suggested Itineraries

Universal Studios can provide hours of pleasure day after day. There are movie sets all over the park and a scaled skyline that looks like a distant metropolis until a crow lands at the top. In addition, some of the rides and shows are worth seeing more than once, and the streets are alive with entertainers and celebrity lookalikes. There are more than two dozen shops, 18 places to dine or snack, and three dozen street sets where you can imagine you are filming at an industrial park, Coney Island, or the World's Fair. Bring your camera and loads of film because you can spend an entire day doing nothing but taking pictures.

We've provided two itineraries here: one for young children and one for adults and older kids. If you plan to spend 2 days, you'll have plenty of experiences you'll want to repeat, and assuredly, some you weren't able to get to on the first day.

Universal Studios in a Day with Kids

1. If you haven't already eaten, the **Beverly Hills Boulangerie** just inside the entrance is a good place to have a sweet roll and a drink.

2. Walk down Plaza of the Stars, turn right onto Rodeo Drive, and follow it into **Hollywood.** Head straight for the **Gory, Gruesome & Grotesque Horror Makeup Show** (though it may not be appropriate for children under age 7).

3. Continue along Exposition Boulevard to **Expo Center** and get in line for the **Back to the Future** ride. It's not for preschoolers, but kids 8 or older won't want to leave without doing it at least once. Very young kids will delight in **A Day in the Park with Barney,** just past the entrance to Hard Rock Café. Just about everybody in the family will love the **E.T. Adventure,** which is well worth what may be a long wait. Shops in the area sell items having to do with E.T., Fievel, and other favorites.

4. Take the kids to **Fievel's Playland** and rest your feet while they roar around the playground. Then catch a show at the **Animal Actors Stage.** You'll meet Benji, Lassie, Mr. Ed, and other stars. If you're hungry, double back to Hollywood and have lunch at the **Cafe La Bamba** or **Mel's Drive-In.**

5. Proceed around the lagoon to **Amity,** which quickly leads to **San Francisco** and then **New York.** Pose for a family picture with your heads in Jaws, and enjoy the comely scenery around the lagoon and the New England village. If you haven't eaten yet, have lunch in **Richter's Burger Co.** in San Francisco. This is a busy, popular part of the park because of the **Earthquake, Jaws,** and **Kongfrontation** attractions. Kids over 8 will want to spend all afternoon here, but if your kids are younger, you can minimize your time in this area. Young kids will want to stop at **Beetlejuice's Graveyard Revue** before leaving this area, however.

6. Turn left onto 57th Street and walk back toward the main gate. At the corner of Nickelodeon Way, don't miss the **Funtastic World of Hanna–Barbera,** a space ride with Yogi Bear. Children must be at least 40 inches tall, but any child tall enough to get in will love it. **Twister** is just up 57th Street, but this is another attraction that isn't a good choice for young kids.

7. Continue along Nickelodeon Way to **Nickelodeon Studios,** where you'll see pilot shows, play games, and learn how slime is cooked in the Universal Studios kitchen.

8. You're probably exhausted, but if you want to eat dinner before you fight traffic back to your hotel, **Classic Monsters Café** is not far from the main entrance/exit. If dinner (or a nap in the stroller) rejuvenates you and your kids, stick around for the **Dynamite Nights Stuntacular.**

Universal Studios in a Day for Teenagers & Adults

1. Have breakfast in your hotel or on the way; you can have lunch at the park. If you arrive at the park hungry, have a sandwich or pastry at the **Beverly Hills Boulangerie** near the entry.

2. Head straight to **Expo Center** and get in line for the **Back to the Future** ride. Lines tend to build up quickly, but you still may want to ride it a second time. Then walk back toward **Hollywood** and try the **E.T. Adventure** ride.

3. Head back toward Back to the Future and cross the bridge to the New England village of **Amity.** Get in the **Jaws** line. When you leave, you'll be headed for San Francisco, but skip Earthquake for now and head for **New York** to ride **Kongfrontation** and **Twister.** Then go back to **San Francisco** to ride **Earthquake.**

4. If your stomach has stopped churning, check out possibilities for lunch. The biggest selection for families with different appetites is at

the **International Food Bazaar,** near the Back to the Future ride. For quieter sit-down dining, try **Classic Monsters Café** on 57th Street, or splurge on a meal at **Lombard's Landing** across from Earthquake. While eating, check out the shows scheduled for the afternoon. If something special is going on, you'll have to tailor your itinerary to fit it in.

5. Head back down Hollywood Boulevard to Rodeo Drive, where you'll find **Terminator 2** on your left. Then continue along Rodeo Drive toward the park entrance, but instead of turning left to the main gate, turn right onto Plaza of the Stars/57th Street and check out the **Alfred Hitchcock** attraction.

6. If you have any energy left, you can try a return trip to some of the most popular rides. Or take a stroll back toward Amity and check out the **Wild West Stunt Show.**

7. If you want to stay on for the evening spectacular, have dinner at the **Hard Rock Café** and have your hand stamped for reentry to the park. Lines here can be longer than those for the rides, but for hard-core rock fans it's an icon that must be visited. Lines at the gift shop aren't as long. If you don't dine here, you can at least grab a T-shirt to add to your collection.

The Expanding Universe: Islands of Adventure
Round two and the challenger comes out swinging.

Universal Studios is going after the Magic Mickey's championship belt. For years, Disney was the only show in town. Even when the competitors got a grip, it was by their bloody fingertips. Now, though, the No. 2 player in town is no longer satisfied with its one-dimensional fight with No. 3 (read: SeaWorld) or a stagnant share of the tourist pie. That's why Universal is breaking out of its funk with Universal Studios Escape—which more than doubles the stakes by adding a second theme park, Islands of Adventure, theme hotels such as the Portofino Bay, and a dining, shopping, and nightclub venue called **CityWalk.** Universal also plans four more hotels and two golf courses by 2005. There's also pretty serious talk of two more theme parks.

Islands of Adventure will be open about the time this guide hits bookstores. Some things will change, but you can take most of the information on these pages to the bank—based on Universal's preliminary permit proposal, blueprints, and actual construction. The park has five islands dotting a large lagoon. Some, like **Seuss Landing,** will appeal to a younger audience (à la the Magic Kingdom at Disney). **Jurassic Park, the Lost Continent, Marvel Super Hero Island,** and **Toon Lagoon** should have broader appeal in terms of the action, if not individual themes. They're also pretty nonstop. You're hunted by T-Rex on one island, and a few minutes later on another, you're fighting a dragon over the enchanted forest.

If those sound tempting, sit back and enjoy a little more of this drawing-board guide.

Port of Entry

Think of the port as GO in Monopoly. The entire game is before you, but the creators of Islands of Adventure want to juice you slowly. The aesthetics are along the lines of a faraway marketplace that you'd find in Indiana Jones—oops, that's *another* movie company. Sorry. Anyway, this is the garden-variety "now-that-we-have-you-what-can-we-sell-you" gate area where they hawk stuff like junk food, souvenirs, and other completely unnecessary things while you're still stunned by the ticket price. The Port of Entry also has a first-aid station, lost and found, camera store, lockers, guest services, stroller-wheelchair rental desk, and ATM.

From here, you can walk to the five other islands dotting the lagoon or, if you want a shortcut, catch one of the boats that chug to the opposite side of the park. We're going to make you get a little exercise and walk you around in a counterclockwise route.

Seuss Landing

Expect an adventure that's as fun, frivolous, and fractured as one of the late Theodore Geisel's books. The 10-acre Dr. Seuss island is a blend of bright pastels, wavy buildings, three rides, and **If I Ran the Zoo,** an interactive play area with 19 stations, including the wet and funny flying water snakes, and "toe tickle" stations where kids make Seussian animals chuckle.

All aboard! **The Cat in the Hat** shuttles 1,800 guests per hour on six-passenger couches. The 18 landing zones showcase 30 Animatronic characters like The Cat, Thing 1, and Thing 2, as well as a revolving 24-foot tunnel in which your perception goes far south. Passengers on **One Fish, Two Fish, Red Fish, Blue Fish** better pay attention, or be willing to get soaked. The idea is to fly a fish up or down while navigating counterclockwise through waterspouts. Three 18-foot squirt posts blast those who don't listen closely and follow the special rhyme. The **Caro-Seuss-El** is a 54-mount carousel in which traditional wood horses give way to animal characters like Cowfish, Dog-a-Lopes, Elephant Birds, and Mulligatawnies. It also has a system that loads wheelchairs onto a platform for a rocking chariot ride.

Lost Continent

Goodbye wackiness. Hello mythology, dark forests, fire-breathing dragons, and more. **Dueling Dragons** is one of three attractions on this island. And what an attraction it is! Universal's most deviant minds dreamed up—are you ready for this?—dual, dueling roller coasters. The timer on this puppy is only set for $2^1/2$ minutes but has several health warnings, and a scream factor of 11 on the 10-scale. Top speed is 60 mph, and there are three places where the coasters come within a foot of each other before taking automatic evasive action in the form of a camel-back, double helix, and compact inversion. Getting rid of the technospeak, you hang upside down and your feet dangle.

257

Some might wonder whether that kind of evasive action is any better than a head-on. Ride greeters ought to pass out Depends and a 20cc syringe of epinephrine. In addition to motion, pregnancy, and other warnings, you must be 52 inches tall to ride them.

Of a more sensible nature, **Escape from the Lost City** begins with a walk through a cavernous entrance where The Keeper tells his story about the city that disappeared under the sea. Of course, that's too tame for any thrill ride—passengers actually are prisoners and pass into a 42-foot vortex boiling with 17,500 gallons of water, then they survive a water-and-pyrotechnic show where Zeus and Poseidon hurl entire oceans and 25-foot fireballs at each other. You are, of course, in the line of fire.

The third adventure, the **Eighth Voyage of Sinbad,** is a spectator sport, a stunt show that has a half-dozen water explosions and 50 fiery special effects.

Jurassic Park

This partly interactive adventure offers face-to-face encounters with Dinobots—a variety of prehistoric critters, many of which are designed to bat their eyes, flinch when they're touched or, in the case of Spitters, launch a spitball at guests who get too close. (Isn't it amazing what amuses people?)

Jurassic Park River Adventure throws passengers into a world of stormy skies and five-story dinosaurs, including T-Rex, the most unrelenting, fearsome bully to walk the planet. And this ride is set up to give you a feel of his breath as he sends your launch on an 85-foot plunge the Universal folks are sure is the "longest, fastest, steepest water descent" around. The minimum height on this is 44 inches.

Sure it's make believe (the techno word is Animatronics), but **Triceratops Encounter** will make you wish it was real. Here's a chance to pet a 24-foot-long, 10-foot-high three-horned dinosaur that's a wonder of hydraulic physics and space-age robotics. While staffers lecture about its family history and guests stroke its body, the triceratops responds with realistic blinks and flinches.

The **Discovery Center** is a learning venue that's reminiscent of the visitors' center in *Jurassic Park*. Chemists in white lab coats study specimens under microscopes while a raptor hatches from its egg. The exhibit also has the skeletal remains of a tyrannosaurus.

Maybe you remember the childhood rhyme that went, "Birdie, birdie, in the sky, why'd you do that in my eye?" Well, **Pteranodon Flyers** will make you wonder if our cave-dwelling ancestors had to worry about things with 10-foot wing spans dropping a rather large load on their craniums. Fortunately, you're on, not under, the bird in this one, flying a dinosaur for a bird's-eye view of Jurassic Park and the surrounding area.

Last but not least, **Camp Jurassic** is an interactive jungle set in an active volcano. You can search deep lava pits for dinosaur bones, but watch out for the Spitters that lurk in the rain forest.

Toon Lagoon

Finally, a chance to step into the funnies.

While this island is pretty Popeye happy, **Dudley Do-Right's Ripsaw Falls** has an alternative view. It's your job to help the Gump-like Mountie save Nell from Snidely Whiplash. The wet-and-wild rescue attempt circles the 400,000-gallon lagoon and ends with you and the other prisoners-of-flume falling 50 feet through the roof of a dynamite shack, and into an exploding dive that sends you 15 feet below the surface. There is a small amount of smoke and mirrors in this one. Thanks to that, you survive. Kids have to be at least 42 inches to help Dudley.

Popeye & Bluto's Bilge-Rat Barges is another journey on water, this one a churning, turning, twisting, listing, white-water raft ride that reaches a top speed of 16 feet per second. *You will get wet.* Even if you survive the white water, you won't survive the water cannons manned by other guests who have a clean shot at you. Kids under 42 inches can't ride, but they can fire those cannons.

You can join your kids at **Popeye's Boat** and get some revenge on the next group of raft riders before touring **Comic Strip Lane,** which features 80 life-size characters including Betty Boop, Krazy Kat, Hagar the Horrible, and Beetle Bailey.

Marvel Super Hero Island

Universal figures most theme-park pilgrims enter, then head to the right, because they're right-handed. So they set up the main kids' attraction as the first stop on the right. There also is a theory that rebellious teens go against the grain, or left, so this zone (which Universal's preopening pollsters feel will appeal to teens) is the first island encounter for those going clockwise.

Adventures of Spider-Man is expected to be the best-of-the-best because it combines moving vehicles, filmed 3-D action, and special effects in one ride. The script: The boys in black hats have used an antigravity gun to filch the Statue of Liberty. Your mission is to help Spidey return it to New York. Near the end of this rapid ride through a $1^1/2$-acre set, Dr. Octopus zaps you with the Doomsday gun, sending you on a sensory 400-foot drop. Oh, yeah. The lights are out. If your tag-alongs are under 40 inches, they can't go.

If the Dueling Dragon coasters sound like sissy rides, then the **Incredible Hulk Coaster** is for you. It's sure to knot your shorts and your stomach—a green flash that literally goes from 0 to 40 in 2 seconds. Universal's ad writers swear it has the same thrust as an F-16 fighter. Oh, boy! "Entering Dr. Bruce Banner's lab, guests climb inside their vehicle and realize something has gone terribly wrong." That will ring especially true for those who fail to read the ride warnings. Right after blastoff, your hair will stay behind as you're treated to a complete inversion 100 feet from the ground and, get this, you go weightless. Of course, this would be a poor time to lose the contents of your stomach, because they also would be weightless, and pretty much hang around your space. Fortunately, the ride only has seven rollovers and lasts 135 seconds. At night the track glows green. Minimum height: 52 inches.

259

Dr. Doom's Fearfall. If that sounds a lot like free-fall, you're on the right page. And if the name doesn't scare you off, then, well, you deserve what you get. Those twin 200-foot towers you can see from two counties away on your way into the park are the doc's towers. This is another 52-inch minimum ride in which you and three other victims, er, guests are hoisted in a car, with your feet dangling, only to be dropped at an unthinkable speed. This is for those devil-may-care souls whose tent flaps aren't nailed down.

Dining at Islands of Adventure

After all that action and angst, you must be hungry. Well, the **Green Eggs and Ham Café** has its namesakes for breakfast, and more conventional burgers and grilled chicken sandwiches are served later in the day. The park's signature restaurant, **Mythos** in the Lost Continent, is fancier and pricier. It uses wood-burning ovens and rotisseries to create delicacies like pepper-painted salmon with lemon couscous and pan-fried crab cakes. On the other side of the island, the **Enchanted Oak Restaurant** features turkey drumsticks and beef ribs barbecued on an oak-fired grill, and its **Alchemy Bar** serves Dragon Scale Ale. Toon Lagoon eateries include **Blondie's Deli** (Dagwood sandwiches) and **Wimpy's** (American-style burgers). **Thunder Falls Terrace** in Jurassic Park serves tropical fare (char-broiled chicken with fruit-base sauces, kabobs, and conch fritters) cafeteria-style.

If you're looking for something lighter, you can grab a cold one or a snack at several stops among the islands including **Backwater Bar** and **Croissant Moon Bakery** (Port of Entry), **Moose Juice Goose Juice** (frozen treats, Seuss Landing), the **Watering Hole** (Jurassic Park), and **Freeze** (snow cones, Marvel Super Hero Island).

Admission

Islands of Adventure will have the same price structure as Universal Studios Florida. That means a **1-day ticket** will cost $44 for ages 10 and over, $36 for children 3 to 9. A 2-day pass is $84 for adults, $68 for children 3 to 9. An annual pass is $190 for adults, $164 for children 3 to 9. All prices above include sales tax. See Universal Studios Florida (above) for more pass options and service prices.

All multi-day passes allow you to move between Universal Studios Florida and Islands of Adventure during the course of a single day. Since the parks are within walking distance of each other, you won't lose too much time in transit. It is a long walk however, so parents with small kids should consider strollers, and people with disabilities, wheelchairs.

Chapter 18

But Wait, There's More

In This Chapter

➤ SeaWorld

➤ Still more theme parks

➤ Science centers and other attractions kids will like

➤ Out-of-this-world attractions

For most visitors to Central Florida, a theme-park vacation begins and ends with Disney, and a trip to Universal Studios is thrown in somewhere along the line. But for those who can't get enough of the theme-park experience, the Orlando area has more than enough attractions to satisfy their cravings.

SeaWorld

It's tough being No. 3, because for most Central Florida visitors, a theme-park vacation begins and ends at Disney, with a trip to Universal Studios thrown in somewhere around halftime.

But for the millions who can't get enough, the area has even more attractions to whet your appetite. The most prominent is SeaWorld, home of (drum roll, please) Shamu the killer whale.

This modern marine park focuses more on natural discovery than on thrill rides, though it offers its share of excitement with **Journey to Atlantis.** SeaWorld's more than 200 acres of wet, educational fun beckon the family to learn about the sea and its creatures. Shamu, as well as Klondike and Snow, the polar bears in the Wild Arctic section, are huge crowd pleasers. So are the many wading and feeding pools where visitors can get close to the animals.

Logistics

➤ **Directions.** SeaWorld is located at 7007 SeaWorld Dr. Take I-4 to the Bee Line Expressway west (also known as State Road 528). Then follow the signs. The route is well marked.

➤ **Hours.** The park is open daily from 9am to 7pm, later in summer and on holidays, when nightly firework extravaganzas light the sky. Allow a full day to see the shows and exhibits; a 2-day pass is an excellent value, and you won't run out of things to do.

➤ **Admission.** Park admission, including sales tax, is $44 for everyone over age 10, and $36 for children 3 to 9. Other options include the 4-park Flex Pass good for admission to Sea World, Universal Studios Florida, Islands of Adventure, and Wet 'n' Wild, for $170 and $135. A 10-day Flex Pass adds admission to Tampa's Busch Gardens, for $208 and $168. Before paying your hard-earned cash for the latter, however, note that Busch Gardens is 3 or 4 hours round-trip by car from Orlando, and it's a park that deserves a full day of your time.

➤ **Parking** is $5 for cars, $7 for RVs. Take a tram to the entrance, or walk. *It's time for that incessant echo: Make a note of the section where you left the car.*

➤ **Food.** Restaurants and food kiosks are found throughout the park. With reservations, you can see the **Aloha Polynesian Luau Dinner and Show** (☎ **407/351-3600** or 800/227-8048) at 6:15pm. It's $29.95 for anyone over 12, $19.95 for ages 8 to 12, and $9.95 for those 3 to 7.

➤ You can get **additional information** by calling the park (☎ **407/ 351-3600**), or visiting its Web site at **www.seaworld.com**.

Top Rides, Shows & Attractions

Everything in SeaWorld is suitable for children and adults of all ages except where indicated below. Here are our favorites.

Everyone comes to SeaWorld to see the big guy at **Shamu Stadium.** The featured event is a well-choreographed show, planned and carried out by very good trainers, and very smart Orcas. The whales really dive into their work. The fun builds until the video monitor flashes an urgent Weather Watch, and one of the trainers utters the fateful warning: "Uh-oh!" Hurricane Shamu is ready to make landfall. At this point, a lot of folks remember the warnings posted throughout the grandstand: *If you want to stay dry, don't sit in the first 14 rows.* Those who didn't pay attention get one last chance to flee. Then the Orcas race around the edge of the pool, creating huge waves of icy water that profoundly soak everything in range.

 Jake Rating: *"I'm fr-fr-fr-freezing!"*

Intensity Games is one of the many water-ski shows at the Atlantis Bayside Stadium. While themes frequently change, the enthusiasm is constant as daredevil skiers go from one high-energy demonstration to the next.

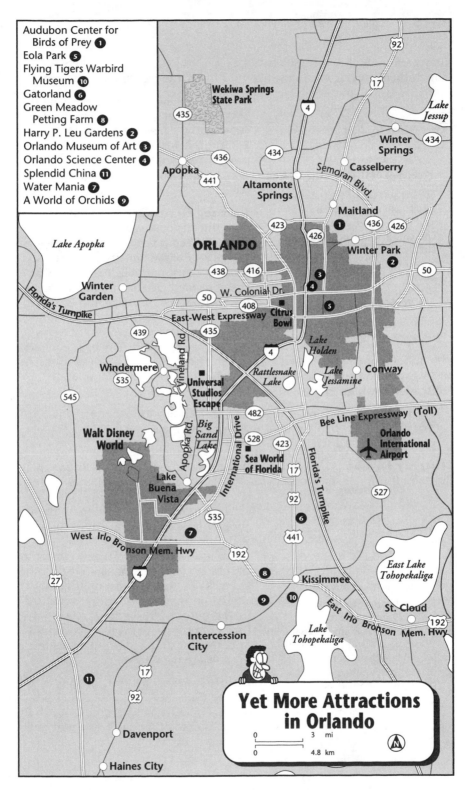

Audubon Center for
  Birds of Prey **1**
Eola Park **5**
Flying Tigers Warbird
  Museum **10**
Gatorland **6**
Green Meadow
  Petting Farm **8**
Harry P. Leu Gardens **2**
Orlando Museum of Art **3**
Orlando Science Center **4**
Splendid China **11**
Water Mania **7**
A World of Orchids **9**

Wekiwa Springs
State Park

92

17

Lake
Jessup

435

Winter
Springs

434

436

434

Casselberry

Semoran Blvd.

Apopka

441

Altamonte
Springs

Maitland

423

426

436

426

1

ORLANDO

Winter Park

2

50

438

416

3

W. Colonial Dr.

4

50

408

5

Lake Apopka

Florida's Turnpike

Winter
Garden

East-West Expressway

Citrus
Bowl

Lake
Holden

439

435

4

Rattlesnake
Lake

Lake
Jessamine

Conway

Windermere

535

Vineland Rd.

Universal
Studios
Escape

545

Apopka Rd.

Big
Sand
Lake

International Drive

482

Bee Line Expressway (Toll)

**Walt Disney
World**

528

423

Orlando
International
Airport

Sea World
of Florida

17

Lake
Buena
Vista

92

535

441

527

Florida's Turnpike

West Irlo Bronson Mem. Hwy

7

192

East Lake
Tohopekaliga

27

4

8

Kissimmee

9

10

St. Cloud

East Irlo Bronson Mem. Hwy

192

11

17

Intercession
City

Lake
Tohopekaliga

92

**Yet More Attractions
in Orlando**

Davenport

0   3   mi

0   4.8 km

N

Haines City

They perform high-speed aqua-batics, race across the surface barefoot, and launch themselves from ramps that send them 120 feet through the air.

Bet You Didn't Know

For an additional $125 each, adults can don a wet suit and get into a tank with the cast in the **Dolphin Interaction Program.** This is an extremely popular activity with very limited space. If you're interested, call ☎ **407/363-2380** early.

The famous duo of Clyde and Seamore, SeaWorld's star seals, have a brand new show called ***Clyde and Seamore Take Pirate Island.*** Located in the **Sea Lion and Otter Stadium,** it's a zany production about a quest for treasure and fresh fish.

Journey to Atlantis is a flume ride with the customary surgeon general's warnings about heart problems, pregnancy, neck or back ailments, seizures, dizziness, or claustrophobia. (Until the seat cushions were padded, there was something about hemorrhoids, too. It shows what happens when lawyers get involved.) The first time you ride this puppy, the *big plunge* may be the longest $4^1/2$ minutes of your life. There's a shorter, "fun" dip later, followed by a fast and tight spiral that has a lot more zing than Big Thunder Mountain Railroad at the Magic Kingdom.

 Jake Rating: "I'm gonna puke." He actually looked green around the gills for a few minutes. But he also wanted to ride it again.

Key West at SeaWorld blends shops with bottle-nosed dolphins. **Stingray Lagoon** is a feeding and petting area. You get a half-dozen sardine-size fish for $3, or two trays for $5. This is a neat trick, especially when

Dollars & Sense

The **Orlando FlexTicket** is a $94.95 pass good for 7 consecutive days at Universal Studios, SeaWorld, and Wet 'n' Wild. If these attractions figure heavily into your plans, this is a smart buy.

it comes to small cast members, like stingrays. Guests feed them more than enough to keep them fat and sassy so SeaWorld doesn't need to. But a word about moderation: This is a fun thing to do, but it's used in other areas with other animals. You can spend half of your admission on sardines before you know it. The point is driven home a few moments later when you reach the dolphin feeding area and counters, where the fish are the same price.

Dolphin Fest is the usual Florida marine park show, but with high standards. The stars include Cindy and Dolly, a pair of Atlantic bottlenose dolphins that do back flips and twists that build to the dolphin world's version of the Olympic high jump.

Manatees: The Last Generation is a nice tribute to the endangered mammals. While it's not the same as seeing them in the wild, it's as close as most folks get to these gentle giants.

The **Penguin Encounter** has a moving sidewalk that leads the way through Tennessee Tuxedoville. The stars are behind a Plexiglas shield in an environment that's 22°F. They preen, socialize, and on occasion, swim under the surface at bulletlike speed. You'll also see puffins and murres in a similar chamber.

When you walk around **Pacific Point Preserve** you'll encounter seals and sea lions screaming in heart-wrenching fashion. Know what they're after? That's right: those $3 fish snacks that will leave your wallet in heart-wrenching condition.

Terrors of the Deep is what used to be called Shark Encounter. The new, improved version has other species, too. Pools out front have small sharks and rays, but no feeding is allowed. (Even SeaWorld knows when to stop pushing its luck.) The interior aquariums have big eels, beautiful but poisonous; lionfish; hauntingly still barracudas; and fat, ugly, and bug-eyed pufferfish. Yes, the same pufferfish that are considered a delicacy in Japan. They also pack the world's deadliest poison in their liver, kidneys, skin, ovaries, and eyes. Pufferfish have, on more than one occasion, turned careless chefs into killers.

Extra! Extra!

Discovery Cove, Sea World's second Orlando park, will open in the summer of 2000. About 1,000 guests will be admitted daily to this unique attraction—for a whopping $150 per person. The gate price will include an arrival tour, all activities, gear, towels, and a meal. Guests will swim with, snorkel with, and feed dolphins and other aquatic life. You can get more information by calling ☎ **800/423-8368** or 877/434-7268, or visit its Web site at **www.discoverycove.com**.

And Still More Theme Parks

There seems to be no end to the number of companies trying to capitalize on King Mickey's residuals, and all of them are betting their money on you. Disney is great. Universal is, too. Even SeaWorld gets its share of the action. But most tourists want an off-speed pitch at some point in their journey— something that isn't a mega-park and doesn't require $200 to get a family of four through the gates.

Consider these contenders.

Gatorland

Gatorland is a survivor. It helps that its founder, the late Owen Godwin Sr., had a 22-year head start on Disney. But that's not what really makes it click. It gives guests a break from the high-price, all-day-and-longer attractions common to the region, *and* it's a page out of yesterday's Florida. This old-school park treats you to shows like **Jumparoo,** a crowd-pleaser where a toothy 12-footer half jumps, half lunges two-thirds of a body length out of the agua to snag a Tyson chicken reject. You can see some of the park's namesakes in various stages of development in the incubation center, and take a walk through a still growing crocodile exhibit out back. And what throwback park would be complete without the time-honored gator wrestlin' show? (Except, in these environmentally sensitive times, it's more of a lesson in alligatorology.)

This is a casual 3- or 4-hour attraction, and comparatively speaking, the prices are right: $17.95 for adults, $10.55 for children 10 to 12, $7.95 for kids 3 to 9. (Kids who come with a paying adult get in free). By the way, if you want to know what gator tastes like, this is a good place to find out. The park runs a farm for hides and meat. You can sample barbecued ribs ($5.25) or fried nuggets ($5.75) at Miss Pearl's Smokehouse, then hunt for a souvenir in the gift shop. Gatorland gets its mail at 14501 South Orange Blossom Trail, Orlando. It's open 9am to dusk. Call ☎ **800/393-5297** or 407/855-5496.

Water Mania

This is a smaller, quieter park than Wet 'n' Wild (see below) and a decent place to spend a day beating the heat. While younger adults may prefer wilder parks, this one offers plenty for everyone in the family—including your tadpoles.

Extra! Extra!

If you're in the market for a romantic stroll, Eola Park surrounds a lovely little lake where people jog, picnic on the grass, attend concerts in the band shell, and watch the illuminated fountain at night. It's located between Rosalind and Robinson streets. Call ☎ **407/246-2287** for more information.

Light meals are available here, or you can bring a picnic to eat on the tables in a shady grove. Float the lazy river, dare the speeding flumes, or take a white-water adventure. Ride a continuous wave on **Wipe Out,** the only surfing simulator in town. **The Abyss** sends you plummeting and spiraling through the darkness into the cold, wet deep. There's also miniature golf, a video arcade, and a rain-forest-theme playground for little ones.

Water Mania is located at 6073 W. Irlo Bronson Memorial Hwy. (U.S. 192), just east of I-4 in Kissimmee (☎ **407/ 396-2626**). It's open January to February daily 11am to 5pm; other times it's open daily 9:30am to 7pm, with extended hours on some weekends during spring break.

Admission is $23.95 for adults, $17.95 for kids 3 to 9. Parking is $4.

Wet 'n' Wild

This is one of the best water parks you'll find anywhere. There's endless fun for everyone, but study the brochure for ride ratings so you don't jump in over your head. Plan to spend a full day. (If you've followed our advice so far, your vacation is up to 35 days. But don't worry—your boss probably has already given away your job.) This is a great place to spend a warm summer evening. Light meals are available in the park, and picnic tables are provided if you bring your own food. Glass containers are prohibited, even baby food jars; bag checks are made as you enter the park.

The fun includes **Hydra Fighters** in which guests sit in swings that are equipped with water cannons that control how high and how fast you go. **Fuji Flyer** is a pulse-pounding water toboggan, while **Der Stuka** is for daredevils. The **Wild One** is another highlight: Two of you are towed around the lake in big tubes.

The park is located at 6200 International Dr. (☎ **407/351-1800**; www.wetnwild. com). It's open daily. Hours vary widely from season to season, so call ahead. Admission is $25.95 for children 10 and older, $20.95 for ages 3 to 9, $13 for seniors. Parking is $4.

Wonder Works

You're lost on an "uncharted island in the Bermuda Triangle" where scientists study weird science in an upside-down warehouse topped by a mysterious mansion. It's educational and fun, if you don't come expecting things to be as glitzy as they are in some of the major parks. You'll find hands-on experiments, illusions, and more. But if you're not a good shot, steer clear of the laser tag game: it costs $6 above the cover price and can make for a frustrating few minutes.

Extra! Extra!

The Rock on Ice! Ice Skating Arena is the coolest place in town. Skate to music played by a deejay, then rest while you snack in the restaurant or play the video arcade. It's at 7500 Canada Ave. in Orlando (☎ **407/352-9878**) and open daily, though hours vary seasonally. Admission is $6; skate rental is $2.

 Jake Rating: "Unfair." It's best for Kids 10 and older.

It's located in Pointe Orlando, on International Drive (☎ **407/352-0411**; www.Wonderworks@totcon.com). It's open daily from 10am to 11pm; hours may be extended during peak periods. Admission for ages 13 to 54 is $12.95; seniors 55 and older and children 4 to 12 are charged $9.95. Parking is free.

Science Centers & Other Attractions Kids Will Like

You can't stomach (or afford) another mega-park. But the kids won't be still, so you have to do something. Here are some ideas.

Florida Audubon Society's Center for Birds of Prey

In addition to being a rehabilitation center—one of the biggest and most successful in the Southeast—this is a great place to get to know the rehabilitated winged wonders that roost here and earn their keep by entertaining the few visitors who come. You can get a close look at hams like Elvis, the blue-suede-shoe-wearing American kestrel; Daisy, the polka dancing barn owl; and Trouble, a bald eagle born with a misaligned beak. Additionally, staffers give you a quick but lasting lesson about the dangers awaiting some of America's most beautiful raptors. The center is open Tuesday through Sunday 10am to 5pm. Admission is $2. It's located at 1101 Audubon Way, Maitland. Call ☎ **407/644-0190.**

Extra! Extra!

If you love gardens, don't miss **A World of Orchids** at 2501 Old Lake Wilson Rd. (County Road 545) off U.S. 192 (☎ **407/396-1887**). Orchids bloom everywhere in this lavish attraction: under waterfalls, alongside ponds filled with flashing goldfish, in rare ferns, and among rustling bamboo. Horticulturists give guided tours at 11am and 3pm. Hours are 9:30am to 5:30pm daily except New Year's Day, Fourth of July, Thanksgiving, and Christmas. Admission is $8.95 for those over age 15; seniors $7.95; ages 15 and under enter free. Parking is free.

Flying Tigers Warbird Museum

Tom Reilly displays and restores vintage flying machines from the World War II era through Vietnam. He's assisted by guides, who lead tours through a museum stuffed with hands-on exhibits, and a working shop where aircraft restorers perform their magic before your eyes. The outdoor showroom includes a B-25 Mitchell, a P-51 Mustang, a B-17, TBM Avengers, P-38 Lightnings, and three dozen other fully restored birds. Tours are $6 for adults; $5 for children 6 to 12 and seniors 60 and over. The museum is located at 231 N. Hoagland Blvd., Kissimmee. To check on the operating schedule or to get more information, call ☎ **407/933-1942.**

Green Meadows Petting Farm

Pack a picnic and make a day of it at a 40-acre farm, where a pony ride, miniature train, and hayride are included in the admission. You can pet baby animals, feed friendly lambs and chickens, and see some 200 critters including llamas, turkeys, goats, pigs, donkeys, and other barnyard friends. Everyone gets a chance to milk a cow. (This is a real hoot if you're there at the same time as someone from New York. It may not be a hoot if *you* are from New York.)

It's located at 1368 S. Poinciana Blvd. (just off U.S. 192 between Polynesian Boulevard and FL 535; ☎ **407/846-0770**). It's open daily from 9:30am to 4pm. Admission is $13 for everyone over age 2. Parking is free.

Harry P. Leu Gardens

This 50-acre spread on Lake Rowena features magnificent azaleas in spring, breathtaking camellias in winter, and orchids and century-old live oaks throughout the year. Relax in the gazebo, walk the paths, and tour the restored Leu home. Allow at least 2 hours, less if you don't take the house tour, and more if you are a flower fancier or photographer.

The gardens are located at 1920 N. Forest Ave., between Nebraska Street and Corrine Drive (☎ 407/246-2620). They're open daily 9am to 5pm, except Christmas. Admission is $4 for adults, $1 for kids 6 to 16. Parking is free.

Orlando Museum of Art

The Orlando Museum of Art has improved a lot in recent years with an expansion that allows it to host traveling exhibits such as the blockbuster Imperial Tombs of China. Permanent collections include American, pre-Colombian, and African art. **Art Encounter** is a hands-on and fun educational experience for children. Give it at least 2 hours.

The museum is at 2416 N. Mills Ave., in Loch Haven Park, off U.S. 17–92 (☎ 407/896-4231). Hours are Tuesday to Saturday 9am to 5pm and Sunday noon to 5pm, except major holidays. Admission is $4 for adults, $2 for children 4 to 11. Special exhibits may cost more and require advance ticketing. Parking is free.

Orlando Science Center

Local parents buy season passes to this museum because you can't drag the kids away from the 10 permanent exhibit areas, the planetarium, the ever-changing special exhibits, and the interactive displays for all ages. Let your kids build a bridge, fire a laser, touch an alligator, play math games, dig for dinosaur bones, single-handedly lift a Volkswagen, and star in a movie. Afterward, you can have lunch in the pleasant cafe overlooking Loch Haven Park.

The Science Center is located north of downtown at 777 E. Princeton St. (☎ 888/OSC4FUN or 407/514-2000; www.osc.org). The Culture Quest shuttle (☎ 407/855-6434) serves the museum and other cultural attractions from five hubs in the tourist corridor. Hours are Monday to Thursday 9am to 5pm, Friday and Saturday 9am to 9pm, and Sunday noon to 5pm. Admission for adults is $8, seniors $7, children $6.50 for ages 3 to 11. If you want to catch a CineDome film, the charge for adults is $6, seniors $5.50, children $4.50. Parking in the garage across the street is $3.50. Outdoor parking is free.

Splendid China

Stroll through 5,000 years of Chinese history and culture along a 10,000-mile journey. See many of China's most famous landmarks in miniature: the Great Wall, the Imperial Palace, the Tombs of Sun Yat-sen and Genghis Khan, and the Buddha of a Thousand Arms and a Thousand Eyes. Everyone loves the "The Magical Snow Tiger Adventure," which plays daily except Wednesday at

Dollars & Sense

It sounds obvious, but consider allowing a day to enjoy your hotel's pool, water slide, playground, and other features. It's a great way to recover from the high-energy theme parks. Remember, you've paid for all those facilities, so be sure you give yourself the chance to enjoy them!

11:45am and 2:15pm. "The Mysterious Kingdom of the Orient," an acrobat spectacular that's the largest show of its kind outside China, plays daily at 6pm except Monday.

It's located at 3000 Splendid China Blvd., off U.S. 192, 2 miles west of WDW's main entrance and 3 miles west of I-4 exit 25B (☎ **800/244-6226** or 407/397-8800). It opens daily at 9:30am; closings vary seasonally. Admission is $27 for ages 13 and older, $17 for children 5 to 12; ages 4 and under enter free.

Admission to "The Mysterious Kingdom of the Orient" only, Tuesday to Sunday evenings, is $16 for adults and $10.65 for kids. For dinner in the Golden Peacock Theater plus the show, the price is $34.95 per adult and $19.95 per child.

Out-of-This-World Attractions

After a few days in Orlando, you may start to think this area has just about anything you could want to see and do. So if an attraction is going to convince somebody to drive 1 or 2 hours outside Orlando, it has to have something that Orlando doesn't. As the number of Worlds in the world continues to grow, that seems ever less likely. Still, there are a few places that might merit a special trip, even though they require some portion of your day driving to and from them.

Busch Gardens, Tampa

Even though it's 90 minutes west of the Orlando attractions area, Busch Gardens is a big part of the theme-park bombast that makes up a Central Florida vacation—especially with the FlexTickets being offered in conjunction with Universal, SeaWorld, and Wet 'n' Wild. Whether Animal Kingdom's emergence erases its popularity among Orlando visitors remains to be seen.

Busch Gardens is a living zoo where the animals appear to run free. Africa is its theme: the Serengeti Plain with its herds of animals; Nairobi with its apes; the Congo with its rare white Bengal tigers; Timbuktu with its sandstorm ride and crafters; Stanleyville with its crashing rides; Egypt with the world's tallest inverted roller coaster; and Land of the Dragons with a fairytale setting, and rides just for tots.

Tanganyika Tidal Wave and **Stanley Falls** are splashy fun for the whole family—vigorous, but not terrifying. For pure terror, ride **Montu,** the inverted roller coaster. For a calming ride and a good view of the animals, ride the **monorail, sky ride,** or **Trans-Veldt Railway.**

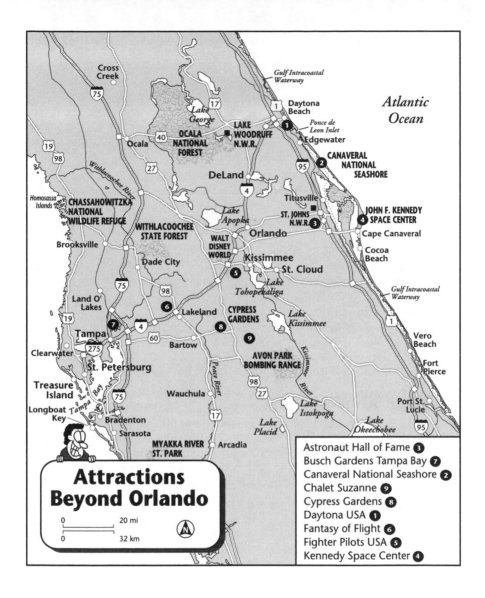

Attractions Beyond Orlando

0   20 mi
0   32 km

Astronaut Hall of Fame **3**
Busch Gardens Tampa Bay **7**
Canaveral National Seashore **2**
Chalet Suzanne **9**
Cypress Gardens **8**
Daytona USA **1**
Fantasy of Flight **6**
Fighter Pilots USA **5**
Kennedy Space Center **4**

Plan at least 1 full day for the rides, gardens, animal watching, dining, and shopping. Dress for hot weather, and expect to get soaked on some of the rides.

Busch Gardens is located at 3000 E. Busch Blvd. at McKinley Drive/North 40th Street, in Tampa (☎ **813/987-5283**). From Orlando, take I-4 west to the U.S. 41 exit, and then go right (north) on FL 583. The route to Busch Gardens is well marked. It's open daily from 9:30am to 6pm, later in peak periods and special events. Admission is $43.70 for adults, $37.70 for children 3 to 9. Parking is $5.

Extra! Extra!

If you want real adventure in the real Florida, but you'd rather leave the details up to someone else, **Adventures in Florida** will tailor a day, an overnighter, or a week in the outdoors: cookouts, camping, horseback rides, canoe trips, fishing, snorkeling, airboating, historic tours, you name it. Call ☎ **407/331-0991** or visit them on-line at **www.discover-florida.com**. The office is open daily 8:30am to 5:30pm. Prices vary according to the trip, but the average price is $75.

Cypress Gardens

FDR was still in his first term when this foundation tourist park opened in 1936. Unlike other old guard survivors, Cypress Gardens wants to do more than stay quaint or try to fill a half-day niche. Water-ski shows and flowers are still its bread and butter, but a lot of things have changed.

Wings of Wonder is a conservatory with more than 1,000 brilliant butterflies in free flight. The stars include eye-catching owl butterflies, iridescent blue morphos, lumbering giant tree nymphs, and 50 other species. The 5,500-square-foot conservatory looks like a rain forest of lush tropical foliage, waterfalls, iguanas, and exotic birds. This is the only glass-enclosed butterfly exhibit in Florida. It also has hatching display cases where you can see the insects in various stages of their metamorphosis.

Raptors and Reptiles has an entertaining show featuring anacondas, diamondback rattlesnakes, Gila monsters, rhinoceros iguanas, juvenile alligators, and crocodiles. The star is a 15-foot albino python named Banana Boy because of his yellow spots. This exhibit also showcases several birds of prey, including owls, hawks, and falcons. The raptors and reptiles are featured in a several-times-daily interactive show that focuses on anatomy, behavior, and need for preservation.

Out on the water, **Cypress Gardens's celebrated skiers** keep a legendary tradition going with standards like ramp jumping, the aqua-maid ballet line, the human pyramid, the flag line, and slapstick comedy. Today's shows have some second-generation ski champs who work the audience, give their shows a personality, and incorporate contemporary music into the act. Should anyone have the nerve to question the show's staying power, the skiers roll their eyes. Cypress Gardens's pros in 1998 passed the 1-million-mile mark. That's a lot of show time.

Cypress Gardens is about 40 miles southwest of Walt Disney World on FL 540 at Cypress Gardens Boulevard in Winter Haven. Take I-4 west to U.S. 27 and go south to FL 540, then go west. If you don't have a car, ask at your hotel about an excursion to Cypress Gardens. The hours vary seasonally, though it opens at 9:30am. It's best to call in advance for closing times. Admission is $33.90 for adults, $15.85 for children 6 to 17, and $26.30 for seniors 55 and over. Kids under 5 get in free. Call ☎ **800/282-2123** or 941/324-2111.

Daytona USA

Adjacent to the Daytona International Speedway, this state-of-the-art, inter-active blockbuster is a must for race fans. You'll see winning cars, compete in a pit-stop contest, view a spectacular IMAX film, and tour the speedway track, which is banked so steeply you'll be astounded. It's open daily except Christmas from 9am to 7pm (later during special events). Admission is $12 for adults, $10 for seniors, $6 for children 6 to 12, and free for kids under 6. Parking is free.

Daytona is about 50 miles east of Orlando, so plan on an all-day outing, per-haps with a couple of hours on the famous hard-packed sands of **Daytona Beach.** To get there, take I-4 east to Daytona, and then east on U.S. 92 to the Speedway. For information on this and other Daytona attractions, call ☎ **904/255-0415** or check them on-line at **www.travelfile.com/ get?dbacvb**.

Fantasy of Flight

This unique aviation attraction transports you back to the days when earth-lings, in this case pilots, went skydiving because they had no other choice. The fun includes flying a Corsair fighter simulator outfitted with the sights, sounds, and (hang onto your lunch) motion of a World War II combat plane. Immersion experiences give you the feeling of flying through the clouds, or gutting it out in battlefield trenches. And the exhibits include historic air-craft like the last airworthy Short Sunderland (the giant four-engine flying boat) and the Ford Tri-Motor used in two *Indiana Jones* movies. Admission is $10.95 for adults, $7.95 for children 5 to 12, and $9.95 for seniors 55 and older. It's open daily 9am to 5pm and is located at 1400 Broadway Blvd., Polk City (at exit 21 on I-4, halfway between Orlando and Tampa; from the exit, turn north and go half a mile on FL 559). Call ☎ **941/984-3500.**

Fighter Pilots USA

Pop a Dramamine, chase it with a couple of Valium, and buckle in for the ultimate adventure—flying an SF260 Marchetti, the same machine used to train F-16 fighter pilots. Notice how we're not saying anything about this being a simulator. That's because *it's not.* Whoa, Nellie! This is the Real McCoy. And for the tidy sum of $895, 7% state and local sales tax *not* included, you and your private pilot can enjoy a series—yes, more than one—of one-on-one dogfights with another customer who is equally as psy-ched. This baby flies out of Kissimmee, but you can't just show up. It takes some planning and you have to do it in advance. Visit the Web site at **www. fighterpilotsusa.com,** or call ☎ **800/568-6748.**

Kennedy Space Center & Canaveral National Seashore

The Kennedy Space Center is about an hour's drive east of Orlando, near Cocoa Beach. There's always something going on here and it's always world news, as fresh and relevant as tomorrow's headlines.

Once you get here, take the motor coach tour and the guided walking tour so you don't miss a thing. Then wander on your own. Catch the films in the back-to-back twin IMAX theaters and explore the new Launch Complex 39 Observation Gantry, a 45-foot-high observation deck overlooking the VAB, Launch Control, and Crawlerway on which shuttles are transported.

To get here, take the Beeline Expressway east to FL 207, and then left and turn right on FL 405. The entire route is well marked. Just follow the signs to the Space Center. For more information, call ☎ **407/452-2121.** For information on upcoming launches, call ☎ **407/449-4343.** Admission to the Space Center is free, but the highly recommended bus tour costs $14 for adults and $10 for children ages 3 through 11. IMAX movies are $7.50 for adults and $5.50 for children. Launches can be viewed free from the surrounding area; tickets to the viewing area in the center are $10 to $15 and must be picked up 2 days or more before the launch.

For further information on sightseeing and accommodations in the area, get in touch with the **Cocoa Beach Chamber of Commerce,** 400 Fortenberry Rd., Merritt Island, FL 32952 (☎ **407/633-2100;** www.kscvisitor.com). They'll be happy to answer your questions daily from 9am to dusk (except on Christmas and some launch days).

Canaveral National Seashore (☎ **407/267-1110**) is a great place to catch a couple of hours of sun after touring the Space Center. This 24-mile strand of beach is right next door and offers spectacular bird watching in addition to the sun and sand. The entrance is 7 miles east of Titusville, about 1 hour from Orlando. Admission is $5 per carload, with discounts for seniors over age 62.

The **U.S. Astronaut Hall of Fame,** 6225 Vectorspace Blvd., Titusville (☎ **407/269-6100**), has simulators that give you the feel of space flight and aerobatics while you view displays that honor the first 20 American astronauts. In one ride, you can pull 4 Gs. Sit in a full-size space shuttle to see a movie. The hall of fame is educational, as well as one of the best thrill-ride kicks in Florida. It's open daily 9am to 5pm. Admission is $13.95 for adults and $9.95 for children.

Charge It! A Shopper's Guide to Orlando

Hey, it's your first trip to Orlando and, with all of the options, who has time for shopping? Trust us, you'll have plenty of chances to wear the numbers off your credit cards.

Your kids probably will want T-shirts from all of the theme parks they visit, not to mention Planet Hollywood and the Hard Rock Café. That means you have to dig out the slide rule and figure how many mouse ears, baseball hats, pennants, and stickers you can possibly stuff into your suitcase—and how much they're going to cost.

Much of what's for sale in the Disney theme parks is available at Disney stores in your hometown, and a lot of it can be purchased at the airport if you decide at the last minute that you just have to have those Donald Duck boxers. In other words, don't buy it the minute you spy it. Chances are, you'll see something just like it again later (and probably cheaper).

Old Stuff: Antiques & Flea Markets

The greatest concentration of antique shops is downtown along **Orange Avenue,** between Princeton Street and New Hampshire Avenue. The 19th-century village of **Mount Dora,** with its authentic Main Street and rolling hills, is an artists' colony, a haven for retirees, and an antique hound's paradise. Take I-4 to U.S. 441 west. Follow it to Route 44B into town. Take the signs that direct you to the Business District.

Dollars & Sense

Orange County's sales tax is 6%; in Seminole County, tax is 7%. Don't forget to factor in sales tax when you're calculating your budget.

For unusual boutiques, restaurants, and art galleries, spend a day in **Winter Park,** just north of downtown Orlando. Its best concentration of shops is along Fifth Avenue.

Malls, Outlet Centers & Other Shopping Areas

In addition to nationally known chains like **FAO Schwarz** (Pointe Orlando), **Saks Fifth Avenue** (Florida Mall), and the **Virgin Megastore** (Disney West Side), the Orlando area has some regional department stores, like **Burdine's, Gayfer's,** and **Dillard's. Bealls** is a midprice department-store chain that carries family clothing and household accessories. There are **Target, K-Mart,** and **Wal-Mart** stores throughout greater Orlando in case you forgot to bring one of the basics.

Disney Village Marketplace

This big shopping center on the Buena Vista Lagoon is a colorful place to browse, people-watch, and have lunch. Shops include **Art of Disney,** a year-round **Christmas Chalet, Gourmet Pantry, Team Mickey's Athletic Club** (athletic clothes with Disney logos), **2Rs Reading and Riding** (books), **World of Disney** (collectibles), and several clothing stores selling upscale resort and beach wear. One of the hottest spots to eat at the Marketplace is the **Rainforest Café.** Stop in and give your name, then go off and shop. Waits can be as long as 2 hours—but the safari theme and AudioAnimatronic creatures make it worth waiting. You'll also find **Fulton's Crab House** and a **McDonald's.** Stores are open 9:30am to 11pm, and until midnight during peak periods. Call ☎ **407/824-4321.**

Downtown Disney Marketplace & Downtown Disney Westside

Disney Westside has uniquely tempting stores like Ghirardelli's Soda Fountain and Chocolate Shop, Guitar Gallery, Sosa Family Cigars, House of Blues, and a Virgin Megastore with more than 300 CD listening stations. A huge LEGO Imagination Center here offers a delightful (and free) play area for kids.

Florida Mall

This is the kind of mall you probably have at home, with 200 specialty shops, six department stores (including a **Saks Fifth Avenue**), and a food

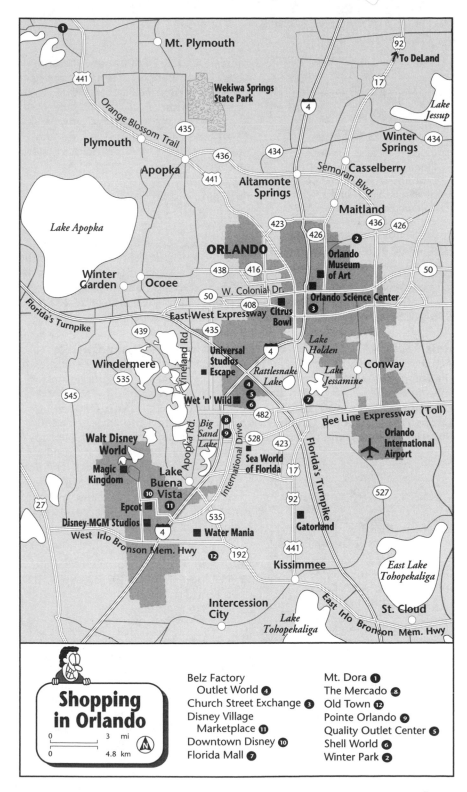

Shopping in Orlando

0 ——— 3 mi
0 ——— 4.8 km

Belz Factory
  Outlet World **4**
Church Street Exchange **3**
Disney Village
  Marketplace **11**
Downtown Disney **10**
Florida Mall **7**

Mt. Dora **1**
The Mercado **8**
Old Town **12**
Pointe Orlando **9**
Quality Outlet Center **5**
Shell World **6**
Winter Park **2**

277

Dollars & Sense

If you're headed for the Florida Mall, check the brochure racks for one of its handouts. You'll find a coupon that can be exchanged at Guest Services in the mall for a booklet of discounts and freebies.

court. It also has a 500-room Sheraton hotel. Come here for serious shopping at everyday mall prices. It's at 8001 S. Orange Blossom Trail at Sand Lake Road, 4 miles east of International Drive. Call ☎ **407/851-6255.** Hours are Monday to Saturday 10am to 9:30pm, Sunday 11am to 6pm.

Old Town

This mall re-creates Main Street of the 1950s. You can still get a bottle of cold Pepsi for a quarter, and kids can ride an old-style Ferris wheel while you shop the 75 stores. Every Saturday night, 300 classic cars cruise through the old brick streets. Admission and parking are free. It's located at 5770 W. Irlo Bronson Memorial Hwy., Kissimmee (☎ **407/ 396-4888**). Hours are daily 10am to 11pm; rides are open later.

Belz Factory Outlet World & International Designer Outlets

Actually a succession of malls and shopping areas, this enormous complex in the International Drive area has more than 160 stores, including dozens of shoe stores (**Capezio, Bally, Bass**), household goods outlets (**Fieldcrest–Cannon, Mikasa, Corning, Oneida**), clothing stores (**Van Heusen, Leslie Fay, Jordache, Calvin Klein**), as well as bookstores, jewelry shops, lingerie boutiques, and toy stores. Factory closeouts, seconds, and overruns

Dollars & Sense

When you start your shopping spree at the Mercado, head for the mall's Guest Services booth and ask for a free Privilege Card, which gives you discounts at most of the stores.

are featured, but selections are good and quality is high. Two drawbacks: The mall is so spread out that you have to drive from one end to the other and, as often is the case with outlets, everything isn't a bargain. *Caveat emptor!*

It's at 5401 W. Oak Ridge Rd., at the north end of International Drive. Call ☎ **407/354-0126** or 407/352-9600. It's open Monday to Saturday 10am to 9pm, Sunday 10am to 6pm.

The Mercado

Here's the place to go for a change of pace from the usual assortment of T-shirt shops and souvenir stands. It looks like a Mediterranean village, an attractive ramble of buildings and courtyards where you can drift from shop to shop to restaurant. Most evenings, there's live entertainment, giving the entire market a street festival ambiance. Stop at the official Orlando/Orange County Visitor Information Center for discount tickets, reservations, maps, and any other Orlando information.

The Mercado is located at 8445 International Dr., just south of Sand Lake Road (☎ **407/851-6255**). Hours vary seasonally, but are usually 10am to 10pm.

Pointe Orlando

This is the newest of Orlando's hybrid "shop'ntainment" centers. It has 70 venues and an IMAX 3-D theater. Restaurants include **Greg Norman's Down Under Grill**, the **NFL Players Grill**, a **Starbucks Coffee, Dan Marino's Town Tavern**, and the **Modern Art Café.** Stores include **Abercrombie & Fitch, Banana Republic, Foot Locker, Image Leather, Victoria's Secret, Everything But Water, Gap Kids,** bookstores, and a travel agency. Don't miss out on **Cinnabon** for sinfully tasty (and huge) cinnamon buns.

The center's most colorful and dazzling store is the **FAO Schwarz** toy store that's marked by a 32-foot-high Raggedy Ann. Parents get a special warning here: Be prepared. Consider a second mortgage, front-end load, with some tranquilizers thrown in before you crash the gate, and have a cattle prod handy (set on low power, of course) so you can drag your kid from this mega–toy store without causing a mega-scene. FAO has a separate doll room that will make you consider Barbicide. Let your imagination run wild. No, never mind; the toy maker has done it for you. There are Side-Saddle Barbies, Hula Hair Barbies, and Promenade in the Dark Barbies. (Hey, New Yorkers, can you see the muggers waiting in line?) There are Moon Goddess Barbies, Pilgrim Barbies, and Romeos and Barbiettes. There's a Pink Splendor Barbie for $900, a Reversible Leather Jacket Barbie for $1,000, and a Bob Mackie–clothed Barbie that's sure to cause sticker shock.

Looking for something with a little more action? No problem. Try out a tornado lamp for $48; a Jonathan Harris–signed, limited-edition laser pistol (remember the first *Lost in Space?*) that jingles the register to the tune of $525; and a 7-foot Darth Vader that can go home with you for $7,000.

Pointe Orlando is located at 9101 International Dr. at Republic Drive (☎ **407/ 248-2838**). It's open daily 10am to 10pm with later openings at the clubs and restaurants.

Quality Outlet Center

The directory lists 20 factory outlets including **American Tourister** luggage, **Arrow** shirts and blouses, **Laura Ashley, Le Creuset** cookware, **Great Western Boots, Florsheim** shoes, **Corning** glassware and **Revere** cookware, linens, and much more. It's located on International

Extra! Extra!

Remember that if you're making a local call in the Orlando area after December 1, 1999, you have to dial 10 digits—407 + the seven-digit local number. You don't need a "1" before the area code unless you are making a long-distance call from *outside* the zone.

Drive, a block east of Kirkman Road (☎ **407/423-5885**). Stores are open Monday to Saturday 10am to 10pm, Sunday 11am to 6pm.

Shell World

Orlando institutions for a quarter of a century, these family-run stores display more than 50,000 seashells and shell novelties from all over the world. Buy unique ornaments in the Christmas in the Caribbean section, or pick your own pearl fresh from the oyster.

There's a branch at 5684 International Dr. on the corner of Kirkman Road, in the Shoppes of International Plaza (☎ **407/370-3344**). Another location is at 4727 W. Irlo Bronson Memorial Hwy. (U.S. 192) at Marker 13, in Kissimmee (☎ **407/396-9000**). Hours are Monday to Saturday 10am to 9pm, Sunday 11am to 5pm.

Church Street Exchange Shopping Emporium & Church Street Market

Here's a place downtown that keeps your kids entertained while you shop (and there's no admission charge). You can look through more than 50 fascinating stores in the Exchange for lingerie, stones and gems, snacks and treats, and many other goodies and gifts while the children enjoy **Commander Ragtime's Midway of Fun.**

The Market, which is across the street, has another 30 shops selling confections, unusual clothing, and more gifts. It also has a **Brookstone** and a **Sharper Image.** The many eateries include **Pizzeria Uno** and **Olive Garden.**

To get there, take I-4 to downtown Orlando and exit at Anderson Street. Turn left on Boone Avenue, left on South Street, and then right on Garland Avenue, where you'll find a city parking lot. Most shops are open Monday to Saturday 10am to 10pm, Sunday noon to 6pm. Restaurants stay open later.

Chapter 20

Designing Your Own Itinerary

In This Chapter

➤ Budgeting your time

➤ Some helpful hints

➤ A handy worksheet to make tough choices easier

If you've been religiously following our advice on how to plan this trip, you're probably starting to worry. How are you going to do all of the fun stuff with the pathetic amount of vacation the boss gives you? The work-sheets and hints that follow will help you figure things out.

How to Budget Your Time

You have to start by facing the music: You simply can't do it all. So it's time to go back through the attractions and shopping centers. Choose the ones you can't leave Orlando without seeing. Write them in the chart below. Have other members of your family do the same. When you're done, total the time you want to devote to each and compare that to the time you plan to stay. If you have planned too much (here's the hard part), start whittling the list. If you have too few—well, never mind. No one ever plans too few activities.

We Can't Leave Orlando Before We . . .

Use this chart to enter the attractions you would most like to visit. That will help you see how they'll fit into your schedule. Then use the date book at the end of this chapter to plan your itinerary.

Your Must-See Attractions

Enter the attractions you most would like to visit to see how they'll fit into your schedule. Then use the date book to plan your itinerary.

Attraction and location	Amount of time you expect to spend there	Best day and time to go

Some Helpful Hints

Now, before you start deciding which day you're going to schedule for each activity, here are some pointers.

➤ Only an idiot would venture onto I-4 at rush hour (between 7 and 9am or 5 and 6pm). The traffic on this road is pretty insane at all times.

Come to think of it, traffic is pretty heavy on *all* of the roads. It always takes longer than you think to get almost everywhere. WDW transportation is superb, but during peak times, and at park closings, two or three packed transports may pull out before you reach the head of the line. When you have appointments, a tee time, or reservations, plan ahead and don't schedule activities too close together.

➤ Don't go to a theme park the first day, no matter how early you arrive. Unpack at a leisurely pace, take a nap by the pool, and read about all of the things there are to see and do before you plunk down $40 per person on a park that will wipe you out. And don't try to breeze through the parks. Lines can be long, especially on that ride you want to test a second and third time.

➤ Plan meals ahead of time so that you don't pay through the nose for sub-par lunches, dinners, and snacks. You'd be surprised how much money you save by doing a little planning.

➤ Orlando's heat and humidity take a greater toll on the body than most northerners expect. If you can reserve 2 or 3 midday hours for a nap or swim, your energy will get a boost. This is especially easy to do if you're staying at WDW, or are nearby and have a car.

➤ Cut yourself some slack. Don't try to fill in every line on the worksheet. If you want to extend your half-day at the Orlando Science Center into a full day, or if the Magic Kingdom isn't your idea of fun, give yourself permission to change plans, bail out, or linger.

➤ Consider your travel mates. Thanks to shuttles and other public transportation, everyone doesn't have to go everywhere in lock-step together. Plan mother-daughter, father-son, sister-brother, and mom-and-dad activities. Or consider a grandfather-grandson canoe trip, shopping just for the girls, a romantic romp to the beach just for him and her. Then everyone can get back together for dinner with lots to talk about.

➤ We're travelers, just like you. But we like different things than some of you. We have no idea how long you need to see an art museum or how many times you'll stand in line to ride Space Mountain. We've given average times, but if you know your 4-year-old is going to want to spend 4 hours at Mickey's Toontown Fair, by all means budget the entire morning there. Tailor your schedule to *your* interests.

➤ This is your vacation, for heaven's sake! You don't have to keep a schedule, put on a tie, or check your voice mail. Break habits. Dare to wear yourself out, sleep until noon, buy a watermelon along the roadside and eat nothing else for lunch, or hop on a city bus and ride to the end of the line just to see what's there.

283

Worksheet: If This Is Tuesday, We Must Be at Epcot

Now you can start matching attractions with vacation days. Enter the most complicated and lengthiest attractions first (for example, an all-day excursion to Epcot on Sunday), and then fit shorter, easier activities (such as lunch at the Coral Reef) around them.

DAY 1
Morning:
Lunch:
Afternoon:
Dinner:
Evening:

DAY 2

Morning:

Lunch:

Afternoon:

Dinner:

Evening:

DAY 3

Morning:

Lunch:

Afternoon:

Dinner:

Evening:

DAY 4

Morning:

Lunch:

Afternoon:

Dinner:

Evening:

DAY 5

Morning:

Lunch:

Afternoon:

Dinner:

Evening:

Part 6

On the Town:
Nightlife & Entertainment

Orlando may be all mouse ears by day, but at night the sidewalks stream with street parties and fun-seekers hurrying from one club to the next. If you have the energy for a night on the town after a day in the parks, Orlando and Walt Disney World won't disappoint you. The same people responsible for daylight entertainment haven't forgotten night owls.

Orlando's nightlife was planned wisely and is very much geared toward visitors. That means the most fashionable clubs, lounges, bars, and nightspots are usually pretty close to the major clusters of hotels—maybe even in your hotel. And if you have to drive somewhere, parking is almost always abundant.

Chapter 21

Hitting the Bars & Clubs

In This Chapter

➤ Entertainment complexes for club- and bar-hopping

➤ What's hip at the hotels

➤ Live it up Downtown

➤ Nightlife at Universal's CityWalk

➤ The gay and lesbian scene

Orlando's reputation is so dominated by its theme parks that many visitors never discover the city also has a variety of hip nightspots offering everything from folk music to jazz, country to grunge. The dress code depends on the place, but jeans are permitted in most, and enjoy even more widespread acceptance when dressed up with a jacket. Chic resort wear is seen everywhere; the only people who wear ties are young businesspeople who stop in for a drink after work, or suited professionals out for a working dinner meeting. You'll need a jacket or sweater in winter for the cool evenings outdoors, and in summer for overeager air-conditioning indoors. **The drinking age is 21** and it's rigidly enforced in bars and package stores.

If you want to escape the tourists and mingle with the locals, try heading downtown, or to Winter Park. Both are very *in* right now, and have fewer "tourist" places to go for an evening out.

The "Calendar" section of the Friday *Orlando Sentinel* provides the most current listings of which groups are playing where. Look under Nightspots, where clubs are divided into Comedy, Country Music, Dancing/Live Music, and Disco, with a special sidebar on current gigs. You can also check out the *Sentinel* online at **www.orlandosentinel.com**.

Extra! Extra!

For a sparkling view after dark, try Top of the Palace in the Wyndham Palace Resort, 1900 Buena Vista Dr., or **Topper's** in the Travelodge Hotel, 2000 Hotel Plaza Blvd., between Buena Vista Drive and FL 535 in Lake Buena Vista. Both have entertaining vistas. You can see Epcot's IllumiNations (☎ **407/828–2424** for information) from either spot.

The *Orlando Weekly* is a free magazine that often has better listings for alternative and offbeat nightlife. Look for boxes anywhere throughout the area and pick up a copy.

What's Going On in the Parks After Dark?

Of course, the theme parks are a source of nighttime entertainment, either with or without the kids, especially when something special is going on. The fireworks that go on nightly are eye-popping and should not be missed. Holidays such as Halloween, New Year's Eve, Christmas (tree lighting, carol-ing, and much more), and the Fourth of July call for extra hours and extrava-ganzas. Keep in mind, however, that only the hardiest of souls can hack a theme park all day *and* all night. If you're on a 1-day visit, take a break for lunch, a swim, and a nap before returning for the evening. Or watch local papers for news of reduced admissions after 4pm during special evening events. Those of you on a multiple-day visit might consider a split shift, doing daytime things one day and the night circuit the next.

Disney's BoardWalk

One of the newest complexes at Walt Disney World is this "seaside" village built to resemble 1930s Atlantic City, complete with boardwalk, cotton-candy vendors, clubs, restaurants, and shops. Some of the rooms and suites of Disney's BoardWalk hotel almost hang over the boardwalk, which ends at the shores of Lake Crescent. This is a grand place to spend an evening simply strolling the boardwalk while enjoying the night sounds and water views. But if you want more excitement, you can choose from a variety of nightspots here, too.

The **ESPN Club** is a razzle-dazzle sports bar with big-screen TVs in the bar and smaller TVs in the bathrooms so you don't miss a moment of the big game. Play video games, snack on buffalo wings and juicy burgers, and enjoy the sports memorabilia, decor, and trivia games.

The **Big River Grille and Brewing Works** is a restaurant and microbrew-ery offering dozens of "boutique" beers and ales.

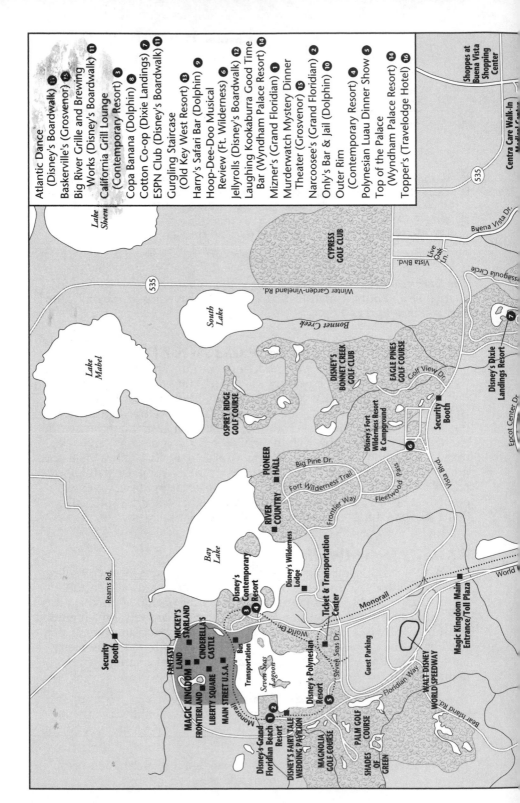

Atlantic Dance (Disney's Boardwalk) ⑪
Baskerville's (Grosvenor) ⑮
Big River Grille and Brewing Works (Disney's Boardwalk) ⑪
California Grill Lounge (Contemporary Resort) ③
Copa Banana (Dolphin) ⑧
Cotton Co-op (Dixie Landings) ⑦
ESPN Club (Disney's Boardwalk) ⑪
Gurgling Staircase (Old Key West Resort) ③
Harry's Safari Bar (Dolphin) ⑨
Hoop-Dee-Doo Musical Review (Ft. Wilderness) ⑥
Jellyrolls (Disney's Boardwalk) ⑫
Laughing Kookaburra Good Time Bar (Wyndham Palace Resort) ⑭
Mizner's (Grand Floridian) ①
Murderwatch Mystery Dinner Theater (Grosvenor) ⑮
Narcoosee's (Grand Floridian) ②
Only's Bar & Jail (Dolphin) ⑩
Outer Rim (Contemporary Resort) ④
Polynesian Luau Dinner Show ⑤
Top of the Palace (Wyndham Palace Resort) ⑭
Topper's (Travelodge Hotel) ⑯

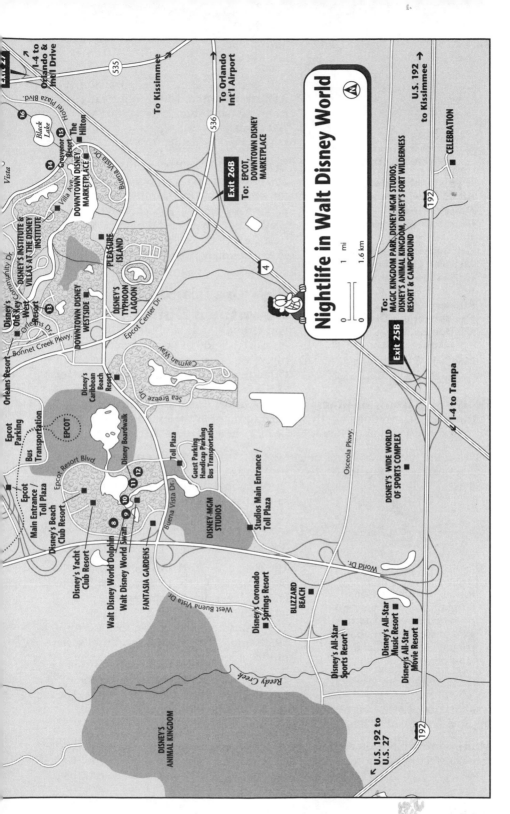

Nightlife in Walt Disney World

To: EPCOT, DOWNTOWN DISNEY MARKETPLACE

Exit 26B

Exit 25B

To: MAGIC KINGDOM PARK, DISNEY-MGM STUDIOS, DISNEY'S ANIMAL KINGDOM, DISNEY'S FORT WILDERNESS RESORT & CAMPGROUND

0 ___ 1 mi
0 ___ 1.6 km

To Orlando & Int'l Drive

I-4 to Orlando & Int'l Drive

To KissImmee

To Orlando Int'l Airport

To KissImmee

U.S. 192 → to KissImmee

CELEBRATION

I-4 to Tampa

U.S. 192 to U.S. 27

Hotel Plaza Blvd.

Black Lake

The Hilton

Grosvenor Resort

DOWNTOWN DISNEY MARKETPLACE

Buena Vista Dr.

Villa Ave.

DISNEY'S INSTITUTE & VILLAS AT THE DISNEY INSTITUTE

Old Key Community Dr.

Disney's Old Key West Resort

Orleans Dr.

PLEASURE ISLAND

DISNEY'S TYPHOON LAGOON

DOWNTOWN DISNEY WESTSIDE

Bonnet Creek Pkwy.

Orleans Resort

Vista

Epcot Center Dr.

Cayman Way

Sea Breeze Dr.

Disney's Caribbean Beach Resort

EPCOT

Epcot Parking

Bus Transportation

Epcot Main Entrance / Toll Plaza

Epcot Resort Blvd

Disney Boardwalk

Disney's Beach Club Resort

Disney's Yacht Club Resort

Walt Disney World Dolphin

Walt Disney World Swan

FANTASIA GARDENS

Buena Vista Dr.

DISNEY-MGM STUDIOS

Studios Main Entrance / Toll Plaza

Toll Plaza

Guest Parking Handicap Parking Bus Transportation

West Buena Vista Dr.

Disney's Coronado Springs Resort

BLIZZARD BEACH

World Dr.

Osceola Pkwy.

DISNEY'S WIDE WORLD OF SPORTS COMPLEX

Disney's All-Star Sports Resort

Disney's All-Star Music Resort

Disney's All-Star Movie Resort

Reedy Creek

DISNEY'S ANIMAL KINGDOM

535

536

4

192

535

8 9 10 11 12 13 14 15 16

293

Extra! Extra!

If you want to dance the night away, **Atlantic Dance** in Disney's BoardWalk, **Backstage** in the Clarion Plaza, **Cricketeers Arms** in the Mercado, **Laughing Kookaburra** in the Wyndham Palace Resort, **Mizners** in Disney's Grand Floridian, or the **Orchid Garden Ballroom** in Church Street Station are all good choices.

A 10-piece orchestra is the attraction at **Atlantic Dance,** where music ranges from big-band sounds to top 40. At **Jellyrolls,** you can sing along or just listen to the dueling pianos.

Disney's BoardWalk is located at 2101 N. Epcot Resorts Blvd., off Buena Vista Drive (☎ **407/939-5100**). Admission and parking are free. After 5pm, valet parking is available. If you're staying at WDW, ride the free transportation system. Hours are daily from 7am to 2am.

Pleasure Island & Downtown Disney

Formerly a simple shopping village, Pleasure Island has been transformed into a vast complex housing some of Orlando's most sizzling nightspots. Many of the restaurants here, including **Planet Hollywood, House of Blues, Bongos Cuban Café,** and **Wildhorse Saloon,** are an evening's worth of entertainment in themselves. But there's also no shortage of places better known for their nightlife than their food.

Have a drink or two before dinner at the safari-themed **Adventurer's Club,** which opens at 7pm, with comfy seating, no smoking, and tall tales told by a "professional hunter." The club features interactive entertainment of the wacky sort as a group of actors mingle amongst the guests, and Animatronic wall hangings occasionally come to life.

Time-Savers

Parking at Pleasure Island is tight. Take WDW transportation or a taxi and you won't have to worry about parking or driving home after drinking.

The **Rock 'n' Roll Beach Club** has bars on three levels, a dance floor on the ground level, and air hockey and pool tables on the second and third floors. The bands here play classic rock from the 1960s and 1970s, including a lot of surfer music.

The first of four nightly shows in the **Comedy Warehouse** is at 7:30pm. The resident troupe takes suggestions from the audience and does some great improv. Arrive early (there will be a line) if you want a front-row seat.

Mannequins has been at Pleasure Island since the complex opened. It's the most energetic, the most packed, and the hardest dance club to get into. Get there early if you don't want to wait in line, especially on the weekends. Its

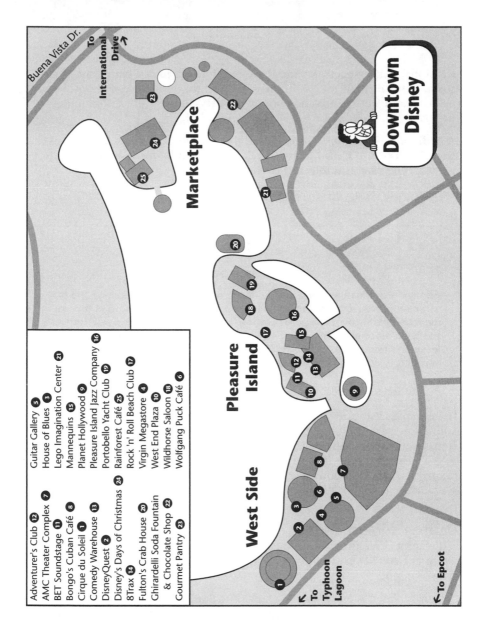

To Buena Vista Dr.
To International Drive

Downtown Disney

Marketplace

Pleasure Island

West Side

To Typhoon Lagoon

To Epcot

Adventurer's Club ⓬
AMC Theater Complex ❼
BET Soundstage ⓫
Bongo's Cuban Café ❽
Cirque du Soleil ❶
Comedy Warehouse ⓭
DisneyQuest ❷
Disney's Days of Christmas ㉔
8Trax ⓮
Fulton's Crab House ⓴
Ghirardelli Soda Fountain & Chocolate Shop ㉒
Gourmet Pantry ㉓

Guitar Gallery ❺
House of Blues ❸
Lego Imagination Center ㉑
Mannequins ⓯
Planet Hollywood ❾
Pleasure Island Jazz Company ⓰
Portobello Yacht Club ⓳
Rainforest Café ㉕
Rock 'n' Roll Beach Club ⓱
Virgin Megastore ❹
West End Plaza ❿
Wildhorse Saloon ⓲
Wolfgang Puck Café ❻

attractions include a revolving dance floor with all kinds of special lighting, other technical effects, and speakers that could wake the dead. You must be 21 to get in.

Hip hop into **BET** (Black Entertainment Television) **SoundStage Club,** a 5,000-square-foot waterfront club pouring out tunes of jazz, rhythm and blues, soul, and hip-hop with both live performances and programmed play from the SoundStage Network.

8TRAX remembers the 1970s disco style, while *Laverne & Shirley* plays continuously on televisions mounted on the ceiling. For jazz, including occasional national acts, try the **Pleasure Island Jazz Company. Wild-horse Saloon** offers a 27,000-square-foot dance floor for your boot-scootin' pleasure, and features up-and-coming country-and-western entertainers nightly.

In addition to the clubs, music groups play outdoors, usually at the **West End Plaza** or the **Hub Stage.** Check your schedule for show times or just listen for the beat and follow it to the music.

Dollars & Sense

Admission to Pleasure Island and Church Street Station is free during the day, when shops and some restaurants are open, but when there is no entertainment. Beat the cover charge by arriving in the late afternoon. If you stay in the same place all evening, you can' save the admission fee, but once you leave one restaurant or club, you'll have to pay the full freight to get into another.

The complex is located at Walt Disney World Village (☎ **407/934-7781**). Admission is free before 7pm and to holders of the World Hopper Pass. After 7pm, admission is $18.95 except for the restaurants and movies. Admission buys a plastic bracelet that pays your way into all of the clubs. Shops open at 11am, clubs at 7pm; both stay open to 2am. Self-parking is free; valet parking is available.

Disney's West Side

Just a short drive from Pleasure Island, Downtown Disney's West Side is the site of the World's latest hot spot, **Cirque du Soleil.** Lions, tigers, and bears? Oh no!

Cirque du Soleil is French for Circus of the Sun, and pronounced Sairk doo so-Lay. It's an eclectic mix of a three-ring circus and high-voltage street performers. You won't find any animals here, but what you will find will wow and amaze you.

Cirque was the brainchild of a one-time street performer, Guy Laliberté, who envisioned a show with ultra-wild, colorful costumes, high-energy acts incorporated with special lighting effects, one-of-a-kind sets, and original music. The performers execute incredible feats of athletic grace and timing on the trampolines, while mimes do comedy routines all around the stage. It's hard to watch all 64 performers racing round, but it is stimulating. A single clown walks among the acts, which include tight-wire walkers, a gymnast, a nine-person trapeze troupe, and four Chinese girls who do incredible tricks with a version of a yo-yo.

The stage they perform on has five hydraulic lifts and floor-level trampolines. The largest section of the stage lifts up a shell of a building, intricate in detail, that's three stories tall. Two trampolines are set into the sides of the set, and 20 performers bounce around (as you wonder how they manage not to collide) while some run up the sides of the building, and a few fly up through the highest windows backward—Gasp!

This show is called La Nouba, which means, "to party, to live it up," and is shown twice daily, 5 days a week.

Regular performances run Wednesday through Saturday only. Shows start at 2:30 and 8:30pm. Sunday matinees are held only at 2:30 and 5:30pm. Admission prices are $56.50 plus tax for adults; $42.50 plus tax for children 3 to 9. For reservations ☎ **407/939-7600.** You can get more information online at **www.cirquedusoleil.com**.

Lounges Without the Lizards: The Best Hotel Nightlife

Some of Orlando's best nightlife is located right in the city's hotels—perhaps one you're staying in. Even the locals head out to the resort areas for fun after dark. If you're staying at one of the places listed here, you can do an evening on the town without ever getting behind the wheel.

In WDW hotels, **Cotton Co-Op** at Dixie Landings has music and Cajun food until midnight. **Mizner's** in the Grand Floridian has orchestra music until 1am and an elegant library look. **Narcoossee's** offers Victorian decor and beer by the yard or half-yard. **Outer Rim** in the Contemporary Resort is trendy and close to the monorail. **Harry's Safari Bar** in the Dolphin has an African jungle theme, generous appetizers, draft beers, and cocktails with or without alcohol. **Copa Banana,** also at the Dolphin, features a deejay, dancing, and karaoke (they're your ears) in a festive Caribbean atmosphere.

> **Dollars & Sense**
>
> If you're staying at any WDW resort, you can attend the free campfire program and sing-along at Fort Wilderness.

The **Comedy Zone** in the Holiday Inn, 6515 International Dr. (☎ **407/934-7781**), is among the area's better hotel nightspots. There are five shows nightly starting at 7:30pm.

Backstage, in the Clarion Plaza Hotel, 9700 International Dr. (☎ **407/354-1719**), features live music and jam nights.

The **Laughing Kookaburra Good Time Bar** in the Wyndham Palace Resort, Lake Buena Vista (☎ **407/827-3722**), is open until 2am with great music, yarns, dining, people-watching, and a waterfall.

Jazz plays at **Baskerville's Restaurant** in the Grosvenor Resort Hotel, 1850 Hotel Plaza Blvd., Lake Buena Vista (☎ **407/827-6500**).

The **Lobby Bar** at the Peabody Orlando, 9801 International Dr. (☎ 407/ 352-4000), is a popular gathering spot with good piano music, drinks, and conversation.

Extra! Extra!

For easy listening and quiet conversation, the **Lobby Bar** in the Orlando Peabody is quite the scene these days. **Only's Bar & Jail** in Disney's Dolphin closes at 11:30pm; open later are the tiny **Gurgling Staircase** in Disney's Old Key West, and the **California Grill Lounge** in Disney's Contemporary Resort.

The Mercado

By day, this is a mild-mannered shopping complex; by night, it's the scene of frequent free entertainment in the **Center Court,** and contains a host of restaurants and other nightspots.

Blazing Pianos, with its three grand pianos all painted candy apple red, is one of our favorites. Admission is $5 and no one under 21 is admitted on weekend nights. It's open earlier for great burgers, sandwiches, and light meals, but the fun begins around 9pm when three piano players start pounding the ivories with lively rock 'n' roll. Smoke rises from the stage when they get to "Great Balls of Fire." The scene includes requests, audience participation, and mayhem so intense that four players are needed to rotate among the three pianos. If you enjoy live-wire fun, this one's a must. And don't miss the piano-shaped chocolate dessert.

In **Bergamo's,** servers burst into operatic arias or Broadway classics while waiting on tables. You can also dance to live music after 9:30pm nightly at **Cricketeers Arms.**

The Mercado is located at 8445 International Dr., just south of Sand Lake Road (☎ 407/345-9337). Parking and admission are free. It's open daily from 8am; restaurants and clubs are hopping until as late as 2am.

Church Street Station

This block of mammoth warehouses along the railroad tracks downtown was transformed into a glittering nighttime fun station where you can wander from club to club to enjoy easy listening, ragtime, comedy, Dixieland, and country-and-western music. **Rosie O'Grady's Good Time Emporium** is dressed up to look like a gay-nineties gambling hall/saloon and has honky-tonk piano and a Dixieland band to go along with the decor. **Apple Annie's Courtyard,** with the appearance of a New Orleans garden, plays folk and bluegrass while listeners sip fruit drinks.

Nightlife in Downtown Orlando

Apple Annie's Courtyard
(Church Street Station) **5**
Best Western Orlando West **1**
Bonkers Comedy Club **11**
Cheyenne Saloon and
Opera House (Church
Street Station) **5**
Cracker's Oyster Bar
(Church Street Station) **5**
Eight Seconds **2**

Go Lounge **12**
Harold & Maude's Espresso Bar **12**
Lili Marlene's Aviator's Pub and
Restaurant (Church Street Station) **5**
Monaco Cocktail Lounge **13**
Mulvaney's Irish Pub **7**
Orchid Garden Ballroom
(Church Street Station) **5**
Phineas Phogg's Balloon Works
(Church Street Station) **5**

Raddison Plaza Hotel **14**
Rosie O'Grady's
Good Time Emporium
(Church Street Station) **5**
Sak Comedy Lab **10**
Sapphire Supper Club **4**
Scruffy Murphy's **3**
Sloppy Joe's **6**
Terror on Church Street **9**
Upstairs Lounge **8**

For more formal dining, try **Lili Marlene's Aviator's Pub and Restaurant.** The decor is an eclectic mix: 1850s Paris with a splash of Victorian England, and a large dollop of loud and lovely Irish fun. The menu features steaks, veal, tuna, and other seafood in the moderately expensive range ($15 to $23 à la carte; the appetizers and salads run $5 or $6 extra). The food is tasty, though it's not spectacular. Pickin' and stompin' reign at the **Cheyenne Saloon and Opera House.** Order some barbecue and watch the clogging, strumming, and singing. The **Orchid Garden Ballroom** offers a regal setting for dancing to tunes ranging from big band to rock, bop, and boogie. **Phineas Phogg's Balloon Works** has dancing nightly, and on Wednesday from 6:30 to 7:30pm, beer for a nickel. You must be 21 to get in. **Crackers Oyster Bar,** mellow and woody, offers oysters and other seafood, and serves up more than 50 imported beer brands. In addition to its venues, Church Street Station ropes off entire blocks for its special events. Street parties, held during the Lynx Jazz Festival, Halloween, New Year's Eve, and Mardi Gras, are some of the best in the city.

Church Street Station is located downtown at 129 W. Church St., between Garland and Orange avenues. Take the Anderson Street exit off I-4 and follow the signs. Parking lots and garages have sprung up in the area; watch for signs. **Tip of the day:** The city-run lots are one to two blocks away and charge $5 for all day. Smart money says to take the valet route. For $6, you can leave your car at the corner of Church and Garland, save the added walk, and pick it up again at the same point.

Extra! Extra!

If you want to hear some cool jazz, try **House of Blues** and the **Pleasure Island Jazz Company** (both at Pleasure Island), or **Baskerville's Restaurant,** in the Grosvenor Resort Hotel, Lake Buena Vista. For Dixieland, **Rosie O'Grady's** downtown at Church Street Station is your best bet.

Better still, take the shuttles that operate between major hotels and downtown and you'll have a designated driver. The round-trip shuttle service runs 4 nights a week between eight International Drive hotels and downtown. Prices and times vary; call ☎ **407/422-2434** for info. You also can find them on the Internet at **www.ChurchStreetStation.com**.

The hours vary, but most shops and many restaurants are open at 11am. Shops close at 11pm; restaurants and bars stay open as late as 2am.

There's no admission charge before 5pm. After 5pm, $17.95 for adults and $11.95 for kids 4 to 12, buys admission to clubs and entertainment, though you're on your own for food and drinks. Admission to **Church Street Exchange** is always free. Its shops and arcades are fun for browsing and people-watching.

Call ☎ **407/422-2434** for more information.

Extra! Extra!

If you like to get scared silly, Terror on Church Street, 100 S. Orange Ave., downtown (☎ **407/649-3327**), is a permanent haunted house filled with ghouls, spine-chilling noises, near-misses, and blood-curdling shocks. It's not for young children or the faint-hearted. It's open Sunday to Thursday 7pm to midnight, Friday and Saturday 7pm to 1am. Admission is $12 for adults and $10 for ages 17 and under.

Too Hip for the Mall: Other Downtown Nightspots

Eight Seconds, 100 W. Livingston St. (☎ 407/839-4800), is named for the length of time you have to stay atop a bucking bull to score in nightly contests. This is a down-and-dirty club with live music, free line-dancing lessons, monster truck wars, mud runs, country dancing, beer, and snacks.

Sloppy Joe's, 41 W. Church St. (☎ 407/843-5825), has dancing to live groups nightly. It's touristy but fun and remotely patterned after the Key West bar where Ernest Hemingway did his drinking.

Go Lounge, in Wall Street Plaza, off Orange Avenue (☎ 407/422-3322), may have jazz, an open-mike night, readings, or a deejay.

Also in Wall Street Plaza is **Harold & Maude's Espresso Bar** with easy listening music nightly for ages 21 and over (☎ 407/422-3322). **Kit Kat Club** offers a pool hall, martinis, and cigars (☎ 407/422-6990). Another hot spot for jazz is the **Sapphire Supper Club,** 54 N. Orange Ave. (☎ 407/246-1419). For a bit of alternative music, **Barbarella** offers live tunes on an outdoor patio (☎ 407/839-0457). **Upstairs Lounge,** 23 W. Church St. (☎ 407/426-9100), is open for drinks and easy-listening music nightly, except Sunday. **Monaco Cocktail Lounge** in Le Provence, 50 E. Pine St. (☎ 407/843-4410), features French singers every night except Thursday, which is jazz night, and offers an intimate atmosphere.

Extra! Extra!

If you want to catch the big game, the best sports bar in town is the **ESPN Club** at Disney's BoardWalk. **Toppers,** in the Travelodge Hotel, 2000 Hotel Plaza Blvd., between Buena Vista Drive and FL 535 in Lake Buena Vista, has a great sports bar, too (☎ 407/ 828-2424).

Everyone loves **Mulvaney's Irish Pub,** at 27 W. Church St. (☎ 407/ 872-3296), for Irish folk music and pub grub.

Scruffy Murphy's, 9 W. Washington St. (☎ 407/648-5460), is less scruffy than it sounds. People come for the wide selection of Irish beer, good conversation, and easy-listening music. There is never a cover charge.

Also look for the new kid on the block, **Club LaVela,** which was still in the planning stages when this guide was being printed. It's going to be a 40,000-square-foot club with a 2,500-seat concert hall. This company has upscale nightclubs and restaurants in Miami, New Orleans, San Francisco, and Milan, Italy. The same group promises that **Goldfinger Martinis and Cigar** will open soon in Orlando.

Funny Stuff can be found at **Bonkers Comedy Club,** Sunset Strip, 25 S. Orange Ave. (☎ 407/649-8829), which features stand-up comics. **Sak Comedy Lab** at 45 E. Church St. (☎ 407/648-0001) has improvisational gigs two and three times nightly. Admission for both is usually $6 to $13.

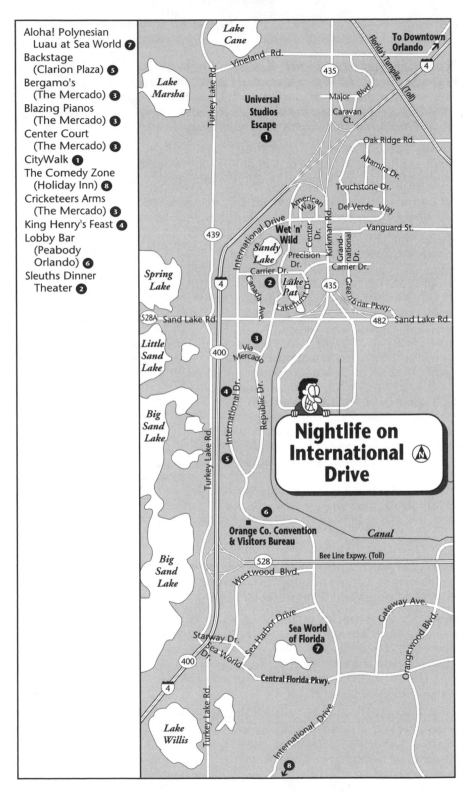

Lake
Cane

To Downtown
Orlando

Vineland Rd.

435

Lake
Marsha

Turkey Lake Rd.

Major   Blvd.

Universal
Studios
Escape
1

Caravan
Ct.

Oak Ridge Rd.

Touchstone Dr.

Altamira Dr.

International Drive

American Way

Del Verde Way

Vanguard St.

Wet 'n'
Wild

Center Dr.

Kirkman Rd.

439

Sandy
Lake

Precision
Dr.

Grand-national Dr.

Carrier Dr.

Spring
Lake

4

Canada Ave.

Carrier Dr.

2

Lake
Pat

Greenbriar Pkwy.

435

Lakehurst Dr.

482

Sand Lake Rd.

528A   Sand Lake Rd.

Via
Mercado

3

Little
Sand
Lake

400

Big
Sand
Lake

International Dr.

Republic Dr.

4

5

Nightlife on International Drive

6

■ Orange Co. Convention
& Visitors Bureau

Canal

528

Bee Line Expwy. (Toll)

Westwood Blvd.

Big
Sand
Lake

Gateway Ave.

Sea Harbor Drive

Starway Dr.

Sea World Dr.

Sea World
of Florida
7

Orangewood Blvd.

400

4

Turkey Lake Rd.

Central Florida Pkwy.

Lake
Willis

International Drive

8

Nightlife at Universal's CityWalk

Universal Studios gave the Magic Mouse a huge head start when it comes to nightlife and shopping (Downtown Disney incorporates Pleasure Island, West Side, and the Marketplace under a 120-acre umbrella). But Universal answered in late 1998 with **CityWalk.** At 30 acres, it's a fraction of Downtown Disney, but it has a reasonably broad range of eating and entertainment venues—certainly enough to make it a solid No. 2.

Hard Rock Live is that chain's first dedicated live concert venue, while **Jimmy Buffett's Margaritaville** blends canned island music with cheeseburgers from paradise. Staying on the consumable front for a moment, **NASCAR Café** has multimedia games and memorabilia surrounding its menu, **Motown Café** features music with its food, and an **NBA** restaurant (starting to see a pattern?) does it with hoop hoopla. CityWalk also has two New Orleans connections. The James Beard Foundation's Emeril Lagasse brings Creole-based cuisine, and his personality, to life at **Emeril's Restaurant,** and **Pat O'Brien's** is a clone of the famous watering hole.

E! Entertainment Television lets you look at live TV in the making at the network's only affiliated studio, while **Universal Cineplex** tempts moviegoers with 20 screens. **Bob Marley's Tribute to Freedom** honors the man and his music in a re-creation of his Jamaican home and garden, while **the groove** is a high-tech dance club.

The last two stops are among the best. **City Jazz** is a center that combines the Down Beat Jazz Hall of Fame, the Thelonious Monk Institute of Jazz, and live performances. The **Latin Quarter** is food and fun—the salsa rhythms of Latin culture blended with its delicious foods. The 20,000-square-foot quarter includes two open-air kitchens where visiting chefs give demonstrations and, if you don't know the steps, instructors in the dance studio will teach you how.

Don't worry about finding it. CityWalk's skyline is made of 10-story towers, icons, and free-form sculptures. They're pretty hard to miss.

Gay & Lesbian Nightlife

Favorite local restaurants for gay men include the **Dug Out Diner** at the **Parliament House Motor Inn,** 410 N. Orange Blossom Trail (☎ 407/ 425-7571), and the **Thornton Park Café** at 900 E. Washington St. (☎ 407/425-0033), which specializes in seafood and Italian dishes, and is in the heart of the city's most prominent gay residential neighborhood.

For nightlife, try **Uncle Walt's** at 5454 International Dr. (☎ 407/351-4866). There's also **The Complex,** 3400 S. Orange Blossom Trail (☎ 407/629-4779).

Lesbians like to dance at **Southern Nights** at 375 S. Bumby Ave. (☎ 407/ 898-0424), and drink at **Faces,** 4910 Edgewater Dr. (☎ 407/291-7571). Southern Nights is also an in-spot for gay men; on Friday night, female impersonators are featured. Theme nights are aimed especially at women on Saturday and are for men on Sunday.

Chapter 22

Dinner Shows & Orlando's Cultural Scene

In This Chapter

➤ Dinner shows for the whole family

➤ The performing arts

➤ How to find out what's going on and get tickets

Orlando has raised the dinner show to something of an art form—well, at least by Florida standards. Focused primarily on entertaining kids, these shows are a little like dining in front of the television, only the entertainment is live, sometimes misty, and in many cases you're asked—even required—to participate.

There's even a cultural side to nights out. You may find spending a night at the opera akin to going to England for its fine wines, but there is first-rate culture here. The city's Shakespeare Company is outstanding (and outdoors, often under a starlit midsummer night's sky). Orlando also has a sizable number of professional actors whose costumes include neither a giant animal head nor a long tail.

Dinner & a Show, at the Same Time

At Orlando's dinner shows there is usually a choice of two or three mediocre main dishes, all the beer, wine, or soda you want, and the diversion of a raucous performance. It's hard to say which is more pedestrian, the dinner or the theater, but kids love it, and it's sure to be an evening of fun for the whole family.

Prices of the shows listed here include food and pedestrian drinks (cheap beer and cheaper wine), but they don't include tax or tips.

Aloha! Polynesian Luau at SeaWorld

Not to be confused with Disney's Polynesian Luau Dinner Show (or maybe it is!), SeaWorld's version serves barbecue food accompanied by torch lights, lilting South Seas dances, and music. It makes for a memorable evening with a good deal of audience participation, and plenty to eat.

7007 SeaWorld Dr. (☎ 800/227-8048 or 407/351-3600 for information). Admission $29.95 adults, $19.95 children 8–12, $9.95 children 3–7. Free parking if you have a confirmed reservation, and we do recommend reservations. Nightly seatings 6:30pm.

Extra! Extra!

Dinner shows that offer a senior discount include Arabian Nights, Capone's, King Henry's Feast, Medieval Times, Pirate's Dinner Adventure, Sleuths Mystery Dinner Theater, Wild Bill's Wild West Dinner Extravaganza, and Mark Two Dinner Theater. Age limits and rules vary. Call and ask—you can save big time!

American Gladiators Orlando Live!

If you've seen American Gladiators on TV, you have an idea of how this goes. *Bash, Bam, Crunch, then, Repeat the Chorus!* Dinner shows include a full chicken dinner (so does the Colonel); snacks are served at other shows. While you eat, the gladiators battle the props, and each other.

Shows held at 5515 W. Irlo Bronson Memorial Hwy. (U.S. 192) between I-4 and FL 535. ☎ 800/BATTLE-4 or 407/390-0000. Snack and show $19.95 adults, $14.95 children 3–12. Dinner shows $39.95 adults, $21.50 children 3–12. Hours vary seasonally. Reservations strongly recommended. Free parking.

Arabian Nights

Horses are the stars of this show, which features virtually every breed on the planet, from chiseled Arabians to muscular quarter horses to Royal Lipizzaner stallions, and herds of other steeds that perform, race, preen, and prance. This is rated the No. 1 dinner show in Orlando, and if you like horses, you may think it's better than that. Most nights it opens with a ground trainer working one-on-one with a black stallion. It then proceeds to Arabian costumed riders, two old-school Wild West trick riders, a dual dressage performance, a cowgirl thrill show, Native American riding treats, horse skiing, horse soccer, chariot races, and several other demonstrations while you enjoy a prime rib dinner with all the trimmings, including all of the wine and beer you can guzzle in 2 hours. The prime rib is pretty much cut from something short on fat and tenderizer, but the show makes you forget you are losing the fillings in your teeth.

6225 W. Irlo Bronson Memorial Hwy. (U.S. 192), just east of exit 25A off I-4.
☎ *800/553-6116 or 407/239-9223. Admission $36.95 adults, $23.95 children 3–11. Nightly shows 7:30pm. Reservations recommended. Free parking.*

Hoop-Dee-Doo Musical Revue

Feast on down-home barbecue and all the fixin's while you sing, stomp, and laugh at jokes you haven't heard since second grade, and hope you won't again until you have to take a remedial course. The show is well animated and has good sound. Book the 7:15pm show and then stay for the Electric Water Pageant, which can be viewed at 9:45pm from the Fort Wilderness Beach. The menu includes unlimited soft drinks, beer, or sangría.

Disney's Fort Wilderness Resort and Campground, 3520 N. Fort Wilderness Trail.
☎ *407/WDW-DINE. Admission $37 adults, $19.50 children 3–11. Reservations required. Free parking. Shows begin at 5, 7:15, and 9:30pm nightly.*

Dollars & Sense

Look through the free magazines and newspapers distributed at all Orlando hotels and most shopping areas. Many of them include discount coupons that can be used at dinner shows. The food, of course, is the same. Too bad.

King Henry's Feast Banquet & Show

King Henry himself presides over a banquet hall where royal entertainers duel, tumble, joust, and jest. It has more jesters and fewer horses than Medieval Times (see below), but both of these Middle Ages restaurants have plenty of hijinks, audience interaction, swaggering knaves, and swooning ladies. Both are rated PG and are fun for the entire family.

8984 International Dr. ☎ *800/883-8181 or 407/351-5151. Admission $36.95 adults, $22.95 children 3–11. Shows nightly at 7pm, sometimes at 9:30pm. Free parking.*

Medieval Times

This is the Orlando branch of the restaurant Jim Carrey went to in *The Cable Guy.* Here you'll pig out on soup, barbecued ribs, or a whole chicken with all the trimmings, while knights pound around the arena on horses, jousting and clanging to please their fair ladies. Trust us: Jim ordered out. But he might have had fun otherwise. Arrive early for free admission to Medieval Village, which is patterned after a Middle Ages settlement.

4510 W. Irlo Bronson Hwy. (U.S. 192), 11 miles east of the main entrance to WDW; look for the Super Wal-Mart. ☎ *800/229-8300 or 407/239-0214;*

www.medievaltimes.com. Admission $37.95 adults, $22.95 children 3–12.
Reservations highly recommended. Shows daily at 8pm; come earlier for cocktails
and milling around the great baronial hall. Free parking.

Time-Savers

If you absolutely, positively, have to be at an evening event on time, call
ahead and get detailed directions from your hotel. You may even want to
check out the route by daylight. Signs throughout the area, including those
inside WDW, leave much to be desired; the sign makers must be either dyslexic
or from another planet. At the very least, leave yourself plenty of time to get
lost so you can find your way before the show starts.

Murderwatch Mystery Dinner Theater

The Baskerville Restaurant hosts this Saturday night staple of interactive theater, where actors intermingle with guests to set the stage for a zany criminal
caper. You can solve the mystery while feasting on a buffet of prime rib,
chicken, fish, stuffed shells, wild rice, potatoes, mixed veggies, soups, salads,
fruits, and desserts. Unlike the Sleuth's Dinner Theater, this one attracts primarily adults, though kids are welcome.

Grosvenor Resort, 1850 Hotel Plaza Blvd. ☎ ***800/624-4109.*** *Reservations*
required. Dinner and show $34.95 adults including tax, tip, and nonalcoholic
drinks. Sat 6pm; during peak season, a 9pm show is added.

Kids Pirates Dinner Adventure

Feast on a three-course meal and all the beer, wine, and soft drinks
you like, while the fun and special effects (including a full-size ship in a
300,000-gallon lagoon) keep you on the edge of your seat.

6400 Carrier Dr. ☎ ***800/866-2469*** *or 407/248-0590. Dinner $36.95 adults,*
$21.15 children 3–9. Shows start nightly 7:45pm, but get here at 6:30pm for the
preshow. Free parking.

Kids Polynesian Luau Dinner Show

Authentic South Seas dances are a delight to watch, and kids don't
get restless during the 2-hour extravaganza because they get to participate.
Most other dinner shows are air-conditioned. This one is outdoors, so it can
be chilly or steamy—you decide if you don't mind the weather. The tropical
menu features fruit, barbecued chicken, and cinnamon monkey bread (don't
worry—it's meat-free). The same venue serves up Mickey's Tropical Luau at
4:30pm daily.

Disney's Polynesian Resort, 1600 Seven Seas Dr. ☎ ***407/WDW-DINE.***
Reservations required. Dinner and show $37 adults, $19.50 children 3–11. Shows
nightly 6:45 and 9:30pm; arrive early for preshow fun. Free parking.

Extra! Extra!

Almost all dinner theaters offer a vegetarian alternative. Just ask when you
make your reservation. If you don't enjoy meat, this will save you from a
prime-rib platter. Based on some of the prime served at these theaters, the
vegetarian alternative is a safe bet, even if you're a carnivore.

Sleuths Dinner Theater

The gimmick here is a crime the audience must solve together. It makes for a
different experience each night, depending on how many budding Sherlock
Holmeses are present.

7508 Republic Dr., off International Dr. in Republic Sq., a quarter-mile behind Wet
'n' Wild. ☎ ***800/393-1985*** *or 407/363-1985; www.he.net/sleuths. Reservations*
required. Admission $35.95 adults; $22.95 children 3–11. Prime rib $3 extra.
Show times vary. Free parking.

Wild Bill's Wild West Dinner Extravaganza

Fort Liberty is a 22-acre ranch where the chuck wagon serves barbecued ribs, fried chicken, biscuits, beans, baked potatoes, corn on the cob, and
a slab of hot apple pie with all the beer, wine, or Coca-Cola you want. The
show is pretty hokey, but most everyone from old grumps to young kids love
it. There's 10 gallons of audience participation, so be prepared to make a fool
of yourself.

5260 U.S. 192, just east of I-4. ☎ ***800/883-8181*** *or 407/351-5151. Reservations*
recommended. Admission $36.95 adults, $22.50 children 3–11. Dinner 7pm nightly,
with additional 9:30pm shows some nights. Free parking.

The Arts

It ain't Broadway or the London Symphony, but Orlando's performing arts
are nothing to sneer at, either. Here's a sampling of some of the more popular venues, performers, and events.

The **Bob Carr Performing Arts Centre,** 401 W. Livingston St., Orlando
(☎ **407/849-2577**), plays host to touring Broadway shows, symphony,
opera, and more. Its box office only sells tickets to its own events, and only
in the 3 hours before show times. At other times, tickets for Bob Carr events

are available at the Orlando Arena at 600 W. Amelia St. Phone purchases must be made through Ticketmaster.

Festival of Orchestras productions, featuring internationally known conductors, play in the Performing Arts Theater in the **Orange County Convention Center** (located across the street from the Peabody Hotel on I-Drive at 9800 International Dr., Orlando, FL, 32819), and in the Bob Carr Performing Arts Centre. For schedules and ticket information, call ☎ **407/896-2451.**

The **Orlando Broadway Series** brings in international stars and shows for week-long runs at the Bob Carr Performing Arts Centre. For information, call ☎ **800/ 448-6322** from within Florida, or 407/ 423-9999.

The **Orlando Opera Company** presents several major operas each year at the Bob Carr Performing Arts Centre. For information on presentations and tickets, call ☎ **800/336-7372** or 407/426-1700.

Time-Savers

The Orlando Peabody, a major player in the local arts scene, offers packages that include accommodations and admissions to many of the city's hottest, hard-to-get tickets. Call ☎ **800/ PEABODY** or 407/352-4000 for details.

The **Orlando Philharmonic Orchestra** performs classics and light classics throughout the year at various venues. For ticket information, call ☎ **407/647-8525.**

The **Orlando–UCF (University of Central Florida) Shakespeare Festival** performs at various times and places, both indoors and under the stars. Call ☎ **407/245-0985** for details.

The **Southern Ballet Theater** usually performs at the Bob Carr Performing Arts Centre. Tickets are available from Ticketmaster or through the SBT box office at ☎ **407/426-1728.**

What's Going On & How to Get In

If you're already in town, your hotel's concierge will have the latest theater listings and ticket information. Or check the ***Orlando Sentinel,*** especially the Friday edition with its extensive Calendar section.

If you want to get tickets before you arrive, check the *Sentinel's* Web site at **www.orlandosentinel.com**.

Many of the tourist bureaus and information centers listed in chapter 1 will also have information about performances held during the week you plan to come to Orlando. Give them a call, too. National acts and other popular cultural events often sell out long in advance. If you're planning to see something for which you'll need advance tickets, check the section on "Making Reservations & Getting Tickets Ahead of Time" in chapter 4.

Ticketmaster (☎ **407/839-3900**) is the best source of tickets for almost all performances, including the blockbuster stars that fill the city's largest stadiums. American Express, MasterCard, and Visa are accepted, and you can call Monday to Friday 9am to 9pm and Saturday and Sunday 9am to 7pm. Tickets can also be purchased online at **www.ticketmaster.com,** or you may be able to call a local Ticketmaster number where you live (to avoid the long-distance charges). Ticketmaster outlets are also found at **Blockbuster Music,** 4900 E. Colonial Dr. in Orlando, and 303 E. Altamonte Dr. in Altamonte Springs.

Orlando A to Z:
Facts at Your Fingertips

AAA   For emergency road service, call ☎ **800/222-4357;** for other services, call ☎ **800/926-4222.**

American Express   There's an office providing travel services in the Sun Bank Center, downtown at 2 Church St. (☎ 407/843-0004; www. americanexpress.com/travel). If you lose American Express traveler's checks, call ☎ 800/221-7282. (If you lose cash, well, uh-oh!)

Baby-sitters   Check with your hotel or **American Childcare Services** (☎ 407/354-0082), **Anny's Nannys** (☎ 407/370-4577), **Kid's Konvention** (☎ 407/351-1100), or **KinderCare** (☎ 407/827-5444). The going rate is $9 per hour for the first child, $10 per hour for two children, $11 for three, and $14 hourly for four. Usually a minimum of 4 hours, including the sitter's travel time, is required. Advance notice of at least 24 hours is recommended. For baby equipment rental, try **All About Kids** (☎ 407/812-9300).

Camera Repair   Try **Colonial Photo & Hobby,** 634 N. Mills Ave. (☎ 407/841-1485), or **Leonard Chapman Studio Equipment,** 9460 Delegates Dr. (☎ 407/856-8252).

Doctors   For nonemergencies, try **Orlando Regional Walk-In Medical Care** (☎ 407/841-5111), **Housemed/Mediclinic** (☎ 407/396-1195), **Mainstreet Physicians** (☎ 407/238-1009), or **Buena Vista Walk-In Center–Centra Care** (☎ 407/239-7777). Your hotel may also have a list of recommended local doctors on call.

Emergencies   Dial ☎ **911** for police, fire, and medical emergencies.

Information   See chapter 1 for numbers and addresses to contact when making plans and reservations from home. Once you're in Orlando, get visitor information from the **Orlando/Orange County Convention & Visitor Bureau** (☎ 407/363-5871), the **Walt Disney World Company**

(☎ 407/934-7639), or the **Kissimmee–St. Cloud Convention & Visitors Bureau** (☎ 407/847-5000).

Liquor Laws The drinking age in Florida is 21, and if you look even remotely under 30, you'll be carded everywhere, including supermarkets. (If you're over 40, you will bow and kiss the ring of anyone who cards you.) Liquor laws vary slightly among counties and the city of Orlando. No alcohol is served in the Magic Kingdom, but drinks are available in most restaurants in Epcot and Disney–MGM Studios. Liquor can be served until 2 or 3am, although some clubs stay open later. It's illegal to consume alcohol on the street or in a vehicle. Alcohol is generally available from room service until 3am.

Newspapers The *Orlando Sentinel* is published every day and is found throughout the city in coin-operated machines and at hotel newsstands. It's available on-line at **www.orlandosentinel.com**. Its Calendar section, published Friday, is the visitor's best guide to restaurants, attractions, and events. Also, grab free publications, guides, and coupon books found at hotel desks, fuel stations, and supermarkets. Titles include *See, TV & Visitor's Guide,* and *On the Go.*

Rest Rooms Clean, safe public toilets are found in all the theme parks, supermarkets, large stand-alone stores (Target, Kmart), and shopping malls. Along the interstates, rest areas clearly identify whether they have rest rooms and security. Most have nighttime security—if they don't, hold it. Each interstate and turnpike exit has signs pointing to fuel and food stops, which have rest rooms.

Safety Orlando visitors, surrounded by good times and magic, too often let down their guard. Maintain all the same precautions you would in any large city. Lock your hotel room door, even if you'll be gone only a minute to get ice. Check the peephole before opening the door. Use the security lock. Don't invite strangers to your room or admit people you met at the pool or playground. Keep the key handy at your bedside in case you have to leave the room for a fire alarm. If you're driven back by the fire, your room may be your only safe haven. Park in safe, lighted areas and check the back seat and under the car before getting in. Keep car doors locked. A cell phone is always a safety plus when you're on the road. Keep track of where you are in case you need to summon help.

Taxes Sales taxes of 6% to 7%, depending on the county, apply to all purchases except food and prescriptions. They're also charged on restaurant meals. Hotel rooms are taxed at 11% to 12% in most counties.

Taxis Cabs are readily available at the airports, train stations, bus stations, and major hotels, but cannot be hailed on the street. Call **Yellow Cab** at ☎ **407/699-9999** or **Luxury Cab** at ☎ **407/855-1111.** Cab fare is $2.75 for the first mile and $1.50 for each additional mile.

Telephone Info   Most of the areas in Orlando have grown too crowded for seven-digit dialing. As of December 1, 1999, callers in Orlando, Kissimmee St. Cloud, and other parts of Orlando, Osceola and Seminole counties, will have to dial 10 digits—407 + the seven-digit local number. You don't need a "1" before the area code unless you are making a long-distance call from *outside* this zone.

Transit Info   To arrange a trip to outlying attractions including Kennedy Space Center, Cypress Gardens, or Busch Gardens Tampa, call **Mears Transportation Group** at ☎ **407/423-5566.** For local bus information, call **Lynx** at ☎ **407/841-2279.**

Video Camera Rental   Camcorders can be rented by the day at Epcot and Disney–MGM Studios. Or try **Videotourist** at ☎ **407/363-7062.**

Wheelchair and Scooter Rentals   These are available from Care Medical Equipment (☎ **800/741-2282** or 407/856-2273).

Handy, Dandy, You-Can't-Live-Without, Toll-Free Numbers for the Airlines, Car-Rental Agencies & Hotel Chains Worth Knowing About

Airlines

Air Canada
☎ 800/776-3000
www.aircanada.ca

Alaska Airlines
☎ 800/426-0333
www.alaskaair.com

America West Airlines
☎ 800/235-9292
www.americawest.com

American Airlines
☎ 800/433-7300
www.americanair.com

British Airways
☎ 800/247-9297
☎ 0345/222-111 in Britain
www.british-airways.com

Canadian Airlines International
☎ 800/426-7000
www.cdair.ca

Continental Airlines
☎ 800/525-0280
www.flycontinental.com

Delta Air Lines
☎ 800/221-1212
www.delta-air.com

Kiwi International Air Lines
☎ 800/538-5494
www.jetkiwi.com

Martinair Holland
☎ 800/627-8462
or 407/977-0408

Northwest Airlines
☎ 800/225-2525
www.nwa.com

Southwest Airlines
☎ 800/435-9792
www.iflyswa.com

Tower Air
☎ 800/34-TOWER (800/348-6937) outside New York, or
☎ 718/553-8500 in New York
www.towerair.com

Trans World Airlines (TWA)
☎ 800/221-2000
www2.twa.com

United Airlines
☎ 800/241-6522
www.ual.com

US Airways
☎ 800/428-4322
www.usairways.com

Virgin Atlantic Airways
☎ 800/862-8621 in the
Continental U.S.
☎ 0293/747-747 in Britain
www.fly.virgin.com

Car-Van-Truck–Rental Agencies
Advantage
☎ 800/777-5500
www.arac.com

Alamo
☎ 800/327-9633
www.goalamo.com

Avis
☎ 800/331-1212 in the
Continental U.S.
☎ 800/TRY-AVIS in Canada
www.avis.com

Budget
☎ 800/527-0700
www.budgetrentacar.com

Dollar
☎ 800/800-4000

Enterprise
☎ 800/325-8007

Hertz
☎ 800/654-3131
www.hertz.com

National
☎ 800/CAR-RENT
www.nationalcar.com

Payless
☎ 800/PAYLESS
www.paylesscar.com

Rent-A-Wreck
☎ 800/535-1391
rent-a-wreck.com

Thrifty
☎ 800/367-2277
www.thrifty.com

Value
☎ 800/327-2501
www.go-value.com

Major Hotel & Motel Chains Begging for Your Business
Best Western International
☎ 800/528-1234
www.bestwestern.com

Clarion Hotels
☎ 800/CLARION
www.hotelchoice.com/cgi-bin/res/webres?clarion.html

Comfort Inns
☎ 800/228-5150
www.hotelchoice.com/cgi-bin/res/webres?comfort.html

Courtyard by Marriott
☎ 800/321-2211
www.courtyard.com

Days Inn
☎ 800/325-2525
www.daysinn.com

Doubletree Hotels
☎ 800/222-TREE
www.doubletreehotels.com

Econo Lodges
☎ 800/55-ECONO
www.hotelchoice.com/cgi-bin/res/webres?econo.html

Fairfield Inn by Marriott
☎ 800/228-2800
www.fairfieldinn.com

315

Hampton Inn
☎ 800/HAMPTON
www.hampton-inn.com

Hilton Hotels
☎ 800/HILTONS
www.hilton.com

Holiday Inn
☎ 800/HOLIDAY
www.holiday-inn.com

Howard Johnson
☎ 800/654-2000
www.hojo.com/hojo.html

Hyatt Hotels & Resorts
☎ 800/228-9000
www.hyatt.com

ITT Sheraton
☎ 800/325-3535
www.sheraton.com

Marriott Hotels
☎ 800/228-9290
www.marriott.com

Motel 6
☎ 800/4-MOTEL6 (800/466-8536)

Quality Inns
☎ 800/228-5151
www.hotelchoice.com/cgi-
bin/res/webres?quality.html

Radisson Hotels International
☎ 800/333-3333
www.radisson.com

Ramada Inns
☎ 800/2-RAMADA
www.ramada.com

Red Roof Inns
☎ 800/843-7663
www.redroof.com

Residence Inn by Marriott
☎ 800/331-3131
www.residenceinn.com

Rodeway Inns
☎ 800/228-2000
www.hotelchoice.com/cgi-
bin/res/webres?rodeway.html

Super 8 Motels
☎ 800/800-8000
www.super8motels.com

Travelodge
☎ 800/255-3050

Index

Page numbers in *italics* refer to maps.

319

325

331

333

334